Magnetic
Disk Drive
Technology

Also of interest from IEEE Press . . .

Ferromagnetism
Richard Bozorth (1896–1981)
1994   Hardcover   986 pp   IEEE Order No. PC3814   ISBN 0-7803-1032-2

Magnetic Recording Technology, Second Edition
C. Denis Mee and Eric D. Daniel, Editors
Copublished with McGraw-Hill
1996   Hardcover   840 pp   IEEE Order No. PC5659   ISBN 0-07-041276-6

Magnetic Storage Handbook, Second Edition
C. Denis Mee and Eric D. Daniel, Editors
Copublished with McGraw-Hill
1997   Hardcover   752 pp   IEEE Order No. PC5688   ISBN 0-07-041275-8

Tribology and Mechanics of Magnetic Storage Devices, Second Edition
Bharat Bhushan
Copublished with Springer-Verlag New York, Inc.
1996   Hardcover   1152 pp   IEEE Order No. PC5676   ISBN 0-7803-3406-X

Magnetic Disk Drive Technology

Heads, Media,
Channel,
Interfaces,
and Integration

Kanu G. Ashar

With contributions by
Roger F. Hoyt
Kenneth E. Johnson
James C. Suits

IEEE
PRESS

IEEE Magnetics Society, *Sponsor*

The Institute of Electrical and Electronics Engineers, Inc., New York

This book may be purchased at a discount from the
publisher when ordered in bulk quantities. Contact:

IEEE PRESS Marketing
Attn: Special Sales
445 Hoes Lane, P.O. Box 1331
Piscataway, NJ 08855-1331
Fax: (732) 981-9334

For more information about IEEE Press products,
visit the IEEE Home Page: http://www.ieee.org/

Printed in the United States of America

10 9 8 7 6 5 4

ISBN 0-7803-1083-7

IEEE Order Number: PC4374

TK 7887.8
,D37
A83
1997
0 34410561

Library of Congress Cataloging-in-Publication Data

Ashar, Kanu G. (date)
    Magnetic disk drive technology : heads, media, channel, interfaces,
    and integration / Kanu G. Ashar.
        p. cm.
    Includes bibliographical references and index.
    ISBN 0-7803-1083-7
    1. Data disk drives. I. Title
TK7887.8.D37A83 1996
621.39'76–dc20   96-14428
                              CIP

Contents

Preface

The data processing systems of the 1960s and 1970s have been transformed into the information processing industry. With the alliance of information processing and network communication, we are now entering a new phase of development filled with exciting new possibilities, new products, and many challenges. Information storage, a subset of information processing, has a critical role to play in this progression. Of a half-trillion-dollar information processing industry, disk storage is over 10% of its economic value. The information storage industry consists of semiconductor memories, magnetic disk drives, digital tape recorders, and optical disk drives. Differences in costs, data accessing capabilities, and capacities of these devices provide a system of hierarchy for computing and information systems. The storage industry is huge, yet the information stored in these devices constitutes less than 1% of the world's total recorded information. About 4% of the information is stored on photographic microfiche and the remaining 95% is on paper. The demand for more and more on-line information from thousands of workstations and personal computers on nets has accelerated the need for larger storage capacities and a variety of functions from storage devices. Magnetic disk drives have been developed as gap fillers between semiconductor memories and tape recorders. They provide faster access to data than tape recorders and at a considerably lower cost than semiconductor memory. As information processing evolved, disk drive technology progressed at a rapid rate and became a major component of computing systems. Disk drives provide on-line storage, backup filing systems, and operational memory. Applications of disk drives range from their use in subnotebook computers to large commercial and industrial systems incorporating terabytes of storage. As these applications become expanded, there is an almost insatiable demand for disk drives with ever-increasing capacities and lower costs along with higher reliabilities and availabilities.

Increasing capacity and decreasing cost in disk drives are achieved by increasing bit areal densities, expressed in bits per square inch. The progress in technology is measured by the rate of improvement in this parameter. Areal density is a function of bit density on a track and track density on a disk surface. Progress in bit density depends on making the distance between the writing/reading head and disk as short as possible. The head-medium distance is known as the *flying height* of the head. Currently, the flying height and bit lengths in manufactured disk drives are fractions of a micrometer. Improving the track density relies on progress in the development of servomechanisms, which control the head on a track. A large number of engineers and scientists of a wide range of disciplines are engaged in the development of these technologies.

The subject of disk drive design and the dynamics of its progress are complex, involve numerous compromises, and encompass many fields, including physics, material science, electrical engineering, aerodynamics, tribology (surface science), mechanical engineering, and information theory. Despite the importance of this technology and the need for information, available pedagogical material for practitioners and students is limited. This book is an attempt to fill this gap, and it differs from other books on magnetic recording. It is dedicated to magnetic rigid disk drive recording, its components, and the electrical integration of a disk drive system. It is intended to serve as an introduction to the technology as well as a source of reference for practicing engineers, and it could serve as a text for university-level lecture courses. It is written in a tutorial mode to make learning as easy as possible with minimum prerequisites. The book covers topics of current interest such as magnetoresistance (MR) heads, biasing techniques, peak detection versus partial-response maximum likelihood (PRML) channel, contact recording, introduction to GMR (giant magnetoresistance), arrays, future trends and techniques of density increases, and so on. Much of the material in this book is from publications, patents, and presentations of the last decade and from a few classical papers published during earlier years. Over 230 figures are provided to illustrate and clarify the text material. Several examples are given with solutions and graphical plots to explain concepts. The reader interested in head/media design and modeling would find some new, unpublished information here. A concise list of references is provided at the end of each chapter to serve as a convenient source of reference material for the reader.

Kanu G. Ashar
San Jose, California

Acknowledgments

My special acknowledgment goes to Dr. Denis Mee, who encouraged me to write this book and made numerous recommendations during various phases of its progress. I greatly appreciate the external reviewers who provided valuable suggestions. My thanks to Dr. Robert Jones, Dr. Arvind Patel, Mr. Karl Elser, and several other colleagues at IBM who reviewed specific chapters of their expertise. I am grateful to Dr. James Suits and Dr. Ronald MacDonald for critically reviewing various chapters and making many helpful recommendations.

List of Symbols,
Abbreviations,
and Formulas

SYMBOLS

a	arctangent medium transition parameter
A_c	head core cross-section area
A_g	head gap cross-section area
B	magnetic induction or flux density; byte (8 bits)
B_s	saturation induction or flux density
b	bit
C	electrical capacitance; capacity; disk surface capacity
C_{max}	maximum disk surface capacity
D	time delay
d	head to medium spacing; minimum number of zeros between two ones in RLL code
d_{eff}	effective head to medium spacing
d_i	disk inner diameter
d_o	disk outer diameter
D_{50}	linear density at which signal is reduced to 50% of the maximum value
E_n	rms value of thermal-noise voltage
E_{nh}	rms head noise voltage
E_{nm}	rms medium noise voltage
E_{np}	rms head preamplifier noise voltage
E_{pp}	peak-to-peak signal voltage
f	frequency in hertz
f_c	flux changes
f_l	lowest frequency of a coded data
f_h	highest frequency of a coded data

g	head gap length
H	magnetic field
H_c	coercive field or coercivity
H_d	demagnetizing field
H_g	head gap field
H_k	magnetocrystalline uniaxial anisotropic field
H_x	head field in x direction in Karlqvist equation and MR geometry
H_y	head field in y direction in Karlqvist equation and MR geometry
h	head flying height over medium, magnetoresistive sensor stripe height
i	electric current
J	current density
K	magnetic anisotropy constant
k	Boltzmann constant; maximum number of zeros allowed between two ones in RLL code; wave number of a sinusoidal waveform $k = 2\pi/\lambda$
L	inductance of head coil
l_c	head core length
l_m	length of a magnetic circuit
M	magnetization; mutual inductance
m	magnetic pole strength
M_r	remanent magnetization (remanence)
M_s	saturation magnetization
N	demagnetization factor
n	number of coil turns in a head; refractive index
P_{50}	pulse width at which signal amplitude reduces to 50% of the peak value
PW_{50}	same as P_{50}
R	electrical resistance; reluctance; reflectivity; resolution
r_i	disk inner radius
r_o	disk outer radius
s	spacing between two magnetic medium transitions
T	temperature
T_r	read track-width
T_w	time window; write track-width
t	time; thickness of a magnetoresistive sensor
V	signal voltage
v	head to medium velocity
w	track-width in signal voltage equations
x/y	code rate for run length limited codes, x user bits converted into y coded bits
δ	magnetic medium thickness; angle between optical paths
η	head efficiency
θ	angle between current and magnetization direction (in MR sensor); angle subtended by head gap at point (Karlqvist equation)

λ sinusoidal wave length; characteristic length in transmission line; magnetostriction coefficient

μ magnetic material permeability $\mu_0\mu_r$

μ_0 permeability of free space

μ_r relative permeability of magnetic material

ρ resistivity

ρ_0 minimum resistivity of magnetoresistive stripe

σ standard deviation of a statistical distribution

ω angular frequency $(2\pi f)$

ABBREVIATIONS

AAB	advanced air-bearing (slider)
AE	acoustic emission (procedure)
AEM	arm electronics module
AFM	atomic force microscopy
AGC	automatic gain control
AMR	anisotropic magnetoresistance
b/mm	bits per mm (linear density)
BN	Barkhausen noise
B-S	bit-shift (also called PS for peak-shift)
B/sec	bytes per sec; data rate
bpi	bits per inch (b/in.), linear density
CGR	compound growth rate
cgs	centimeter-gram-second
CSS	contact start-stop testing
DASD	direct access storage device (disk drive)
DSP	digital signal processing
ECC	error correction coding
EPRML	extended partial response maximum likelihood channel
ESCA	electron spectroscopy for chemical analysis
FFT	fast Fourier transform
FM	frequency modulation
FTIR	Fourier transform infrared
GHT	glide height test
GMR	giant magnetoresistance
hcp	hexagonally close packed
HDA	head-disk assembly
HDI	head-disk interface
HIP	hot isostatically pressed
I.D.	inner diameter of a disk
ISI	intersymbol interference
MBE	molecular beam epitaxy

MFM	modified frequency modulation
MIG	metal-in-gap (head)
MIPs	millions of instructions per second
mks	meter-kilogram-second
mmf	magnetomotive force
MR	magnetoresistance or magnetoresistive
MTF	machine tapered flat
MTF	mean time to failure
MTBF	mean time between failures
NRZ	nonreturn to zero
NRZI	modified nonreturn to zero
O.D.	outer diameter of disk
PERM	pre-embossed rigid magnetic (disk)
PES	position error signal
PLL	phase locked loop
PLO	phase locked oscillator (same as PLL)
PPPE	perfluoropolyether
PR-IV	"class IV, partial response filter," coding and detection procedure
PRML	partial response maximum likelihood (coding; channel)
PTS	precision test stand
PZT	piezo-crystal; piezoelectric
RAIDs	redundant array of inexpensive or independent drives
RAMAC	random access method of accounting and control
RF	radio frequency
RLL	run length-limited (code)
ROM	read-only (semiconductor) memory
RPM	revolutions per minute
SAL	soft adjacent layer (biasing of MR sensor)
SCSI	small computer standard interface
SDT	single-disk test
SEM	scanning electron microscopy
SER	soft error rate
SNR	signal-to-noise ratio
STM	scanning tunneling microscope
TMR	track misregistration
TOV	take-off velocity
TPC	transverse pressure contour
TPI	tracks per inch (tpi), track density
t/mm	tracks per mm (track density)
VCM	voice coil motor
VFO	variable frequency oscillator
XRF	X-ray fluorescence

UNIT CONVERSIONS

Table 2.3 in the text describes the conversion procedure from cgs to SI units and SI to cgs units for magnetic and electrical parameters. Examples in Chapter 3, Section 3.10 and Chapter 6, Section 6.18 describe conversions from commonly used magnetic recording parameters to SI units.

Formulas

Some commonly used formulas for channel, integration, and testing are as follows:

$$\text{The ratio } CR \text{ (code rate)} = \frac{x}{y}; \text{ i.e., for } (1, 7) \text{ code, it is } \frac{2}{3}$$

$$\text{The ratio } \frac{b/mm}{fc/mm} = CR(d + 1); \text{ i.e., for } (1, 7) \text{ code, it is } \frac{4}{3}$$

$$\text{The ratio } \frac{f_h}{f_l} = \frac{k + 1}{d + 1}; \text{ i.e., for } (1, 7) \text{ code, it is } 4$$

$$\text{The high frequency } f_h = \frac{1}{2}\left(\frac{fc}{mm}\right)(v)(velocity \text{ as } mm/s)$$

$$v \text{ } mm/s = \left(\frac{RPM}{60}\right)(\pi d_i), \text{ } d_i = inner \text{ disk diameter } (mm)$$

1

Introduction

1.1 DISK DRIVE INDUSTRY

The progress in magnetic recording technology, particularly that for rigid disk drives, from the mid-1950s to the mid-1990s has been as dramatic as that in semiconductors. Semiconductor memory and rigid disk drives are part of the storage hierarchy of a computer system as shown in Figure 1.1 [1]. Within the high-performance memory system, a hierarchy of performance and cost ranges from bipolar cache memory at the one end to dynamic memory solid-state devices at the other, as shown in the figure. A second sector of the system hierarchy is evolving as stand-alone high-performance drives and libraries of disk drive arrays. If solid-state devices had sufficiently low cost and could be organized as reliable nonvolatile storage, there would be no need for the disk drives. With decreasing semiconductor costs, there is a temptation to consider replacement of disk drives with solid-state memories. For this reason, it is interesting to compare the evolution of the two most dynamic technologies of this era.

Cost per bit is a predominant criterion in these technologies. The cost per bit in each of the technologies is driven by the areal density or area per bit. Much has been written in the technical and popular press about semiconductors, but disk technology has received little attention. Table 1.1 shows a density progression in both semiconductor memory (DRAM) chips and disk drives for the period 1980 to 2000. It is remarkable that the bit area of the disk drives had tracked the bit (cell) area of the semiconductor memories closely throughout the period of 1980 to 1990. The ratio of semiconductor bit price to that of disk drive bit has remained approximately 100 during this period. From 1990 through 2000, the density of disk drives is increasing at a faster pace than that of the semiconductors. With these trends, it is highly improbable that the semiconductor memory bit cost could catch up with the disk drive

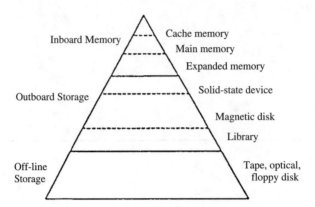

Figure 1.1 Computer storage hierarchy [1].

bit cost within the foreseeable future. In the case of semiconductors, memory cell density increases are usually attributed to improvements in photolithography. In disk drive technology, major advances are taking place due to innovations in magnetic head, media, and channel electronics.

TABLE 1.1 Density of Information Stored in Disk Drives and Semiconductor Devices (Values in parentheses are extrapolations from data between 1987 through 1994.)

	Disk drives		Semiconductors	
	Areal Density (Mb/in^2)	Bit Area (μm^2)	Chip Capacity (Mb)	Bit Area (μm^2)
1980	1.25	52	0.256	50
1987	36	18	1	20
1990	100	7	4	10
1994	500	1.29	64	2.5
1997	(1000)	(0.65)	(256)	(1.0)
2000	(6000)	(0.110)	(1000)	(0.5)

Worldwide disk drive sales volume in 1995 was estimated as 70 million drives with revenues of about $25 billion [2]. Comparatively, global semiconductor memory revenues in 1995 were $44.5 billion. The demand for disk drive storage has been steadily increasing due to the following factors:

1. Increasing demand of desktop computers and workstations.
2. Introduction of a variety of notebook, subnotebook, and laptop computers.
3. Replacement of large mainframe computer drives by arrays of small disk drives.
4. Growth of storage-hungry graphics and multimedia applications.
5. Use of removable small drives in noncomputer consumer applications.
6. Massive and yet unforeseen increases in computer storage requirements of network data bases.

Conversion of information from paper to the more accessible computer media has just begun, yet computer storage is still only a small fraction of the total amount of information stored. So, unless unforeseen conditions intervene, the expansion of the disk drive industry will continue at a high rate in the future.

1.2 DISK DRIVE TECHNOLOGY DEVELOPMENT

Introduced in 1957, the IBM Model 350, or random access method of accounting and control (RAMAC), was the first disk drive [3,4]. This drive, invented at the IBM research laboratory in San Jose, California, consisted of 50 rotating disks mounted on a vertical shaft (See Figure 1.2), each 24 inches in diameter and each having a magnetic medium coating to store data. Access to this data was by a pair of air-bearing supported heads mounted on an access arm that could be moved under servo control to 1 of the 50 disks. The heads were also able to move in and out across the radius of a disk. The storage capacity of the system was 5 MB, and users paid a rental of $130 a month for the system. The disks rotated at 1200 RPM (revolutions per minute), and the data rate of the information was 12.5 kB/s.

The inductive head and magnetic disk material for this drive originated in earlier work on tape recorders and magnetic drums. (Magnetic drums consisted of a rotating drum with a magnetic coating and a series of fixed heads mounted one head per track.) The advantage realized with the new rotating disk technology was the combination of nonvolatile storage of data with very fast access to this data and, at

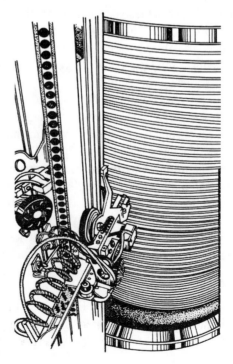

Figure 1.2 IBM RAMAC (1957) [3].

the same time, low cost due to fewer heads. These characteristics filled the technology gap of the data processing industry between inexpensive tape recorders and expensive magnetic cores used at the time for computer memory. One persistent drawback of many of the early magnetic read/write schemes was the requirement of close proximity between the magnetic medium and the read/write head. In tape recorders, for example, the tape is in contact with the tape head; if the tape were to run continuously at a high rate, the tape would soon wear out and possibly the head as well. The key development that led to disk drive technology was the invention of a low-mass, air-bearing slider carrying a magnetic head *floating* at a precise spacing between the head and the magnetic medium. Data or information is written magnetically along circular tracks on a disk. A *bit* is the smallest unit of data or information and consists of a "0" or a "1." The *linear bit density* is the number of bits written along a distance of 1 inch on one of these tracks. The *track density* is the number of tracks per inch along a radius of the disk. The *areal density* is the product of linear bit density and track density. For example, the Travelstar drive announced in 1995 by IBM, which uses magnetoresistive heads, has a linear bit density of 127.2 Kb/in. (50 Kb/cm) and a track density of 7257 T/in. (2857 T/cm), giving an areal density of 923 Mb/in.^{2} (143 Mb/cm^2). Increasing linear bit density over time has depended on the scaling down of three factors:

1. Reduction of the head to disk spacing commonly known as *flying height*.
2. Reduction of the gap size of the head.
3. Reduction of the thickness of the disk magnetic media.

Table 1.2 shows these trends in IBM disk drive characteristics from RAMAC (System 350) in 1957 to 3390 in 1989. Apparently, these three parameters have been reduced in values by about two orders of magnitude over the 32-year period. Table 1.2 spans a total period of 38 years. The linear density has improved by a factor of 1300 during this period. This is the result of progress in inductive head designs and improvements in both ferrite medium prior to 1987 and thin film medium after 1987, and also implementation of magnetoresistive heads since 1990.

Increasing track density over time has depended on improvements in the technology of accurate head positioning. These improvements include reduction in track misregistration, innovations in servo techniques, higher-sensitivity heads, and advances in track width control. Table 1.2 shows that the accompanying improvement in track density over this period is a factor of 355. Some detail on the head and slider technology are also shown in the table.

Many of the developments in heads, disks, interface controls, channel electronics, and packaging have been due to the gradual increase in understanding of the technology and development of tools. However, there are several highlights in the technology that must be pointed out.

The earliest recording heads were made of laminated Mu-metal (NiFeMoCu) with gaps formed by copper shims. A major improvement in the mid-1960s was the replacement of Mu-metal by ferrite. The high resistivity of ferrite meant that

TABLE 1.2 Thirty-Eight Years of Progress in Disk Drive Technology

Year	Model	Bit Density Kb/in	Track Density T/in	Areal Density Mb/in^2.	Flying Height nm	Gap nm	Media thickness nm	Head	Slider
1957	350	0.1	20	.002	20000	25000	30000	Mu-metal	Aluminum
1962	1301	0.52	50	.026	6250	12500	13575	Laminated Mu-metal	Stainless steel
1966	2314	2.2	100	.220	2125	2625	2125	Epoxy bonded ferrite	Alumina
1971	3330	4.04	192	.776	1250	2500	1250	Glass bonded ferrite	Barium titanate
1973	3340	5.64	300	1.69	450	1500	1025	Integrated ferrite	Taper flat ferrite
1980	3380	15.2	800	7.68	320	600	550	8 turn thin film	Ceramic
1984	3380E	16.1	1386	22.3	254	600	500	18 turn thin film	Ferrite
1987	3380K	15.2	2088	32.8	216	550	432	31 turn thin film	Ceramic
1989	3390	27.5	2241	61.6	160	550	230	31 turn thin film	Ceramic
1992	0663-E12	59	2685	158	—	—	Thin film	Magneto-resistive	Ceramic
1995	Travelstar 2LP	127.2	7257	923	—	—	Thin film	Magneto-resistive	Ceramic

head lamination was not required. In addition, ferrites are easy to shape and grind. Ferrite surfaces are wear resistant and do not corrode. Many subsequent improvements in ferrites have continued to make them competitive as an alternative head technology. One such advancement is the metal-in-gap (MIG) head. Placement of high-magnetization metal (Sendust) in the gap of ferrite heads made the use of continuous-metal, thin film medium disks possible. Thin film disks resulted in a path to higher linear densities. Continuous progress in film disks through reduction in defects, lowering of medium noise, and control of corrosion have continued to boost areal densities. An important step in head technology came in 1979 with IBM's introduction of thin film heads. This technology allowed heads to be fabricated by the same photolithographic techniques used in the semiconductor industry. This approach led to still higher linear densities and track densities.

The most recent leap in technology came in 1991 with IBM's announcement of the production of the magnetoresistive head. Magnetoresistive (MR) heads are combined with new low-noise, thin-film disk media to provide a new range of capabilities for disk drives. The MR head provides 5 to 10 times higher sensitivity compared to ferrite or thin film heads. Increases in track density are achieved by making dual element heads in which the *write* element of the head is the usual thin film inductive head and the *read* element the head is an MR sensor. Another attribute of the MR head is that its sensitivity does not vary with disk rotational velocity; hence, it is possible to provide high bit densities for small disk drives used in laptop computers.

Table 1.2 describes IBM disk file evolution and fairly well portrays the industry progress. However, it should be noted that significant progress was pioneered by several other manufacturers as well. Noteworthy among them:

1. Fujitsu's F 6525 Eagle II file, announced in 1982, had 24.4 Kb/in. linear density and 22.2 Mb/in.^{2} areal density, achieved with sputtered medium on a 10.8 in. disk, ferrite head, and head-disk spacing of about 150 nm.
2. Maxtor's XT-8760E, announced in 1987, had 31.5 kb/in. linear density and 43.5 Mb/in.^{2} areal density.
3. In 1993, Seagate shipped a 7200 RPM, 95 mm (3.5 in.) disk drive that has 4.17 ms average rotational delay, and an asynchronous data rate of 20 MB/s.
4. Areal technology in 1993 produced a 65 mm (2.5 in.) disk drive with glass substrate disk to reduce head-disk spacing. The linear density of 80 Kb/in. and areal density of 220 Mb/in.^{2} were achieved in the drive with an inductive thin film head.

Additional comparative study of disk files from several manufacturers can be found in [5].

1.3 DISK DRIVE HEAD TECHNOLOGIES

Most dramatic changes in disk drive technology have happened in head development and manufacturing. This is the reason why three chapters in this book are dedicated to heads. Table 1.3 presents a qualitative comparison of four head technologies. A plus (+) refers to a favorable property while a minus (−) refers to a less desirable attribute. The ranking of heads is based on state of the art in the early 1990s and is subject to change depending on future developments.

TABLE 1.3 Relative Merits of Various Heads

Parameter	Ferrite	MIG	Thin Film	MR
Linear Density	− −	−	+	+ +
Track Density	− −	−	+	+ +
Data Rate	−	−	+	+ +
User Experience	+ +	+	+	−
Cost/Complexity	+ +	+	−	− −

The linear density of ferrite heads is low because the low magnetization of the ferrite material creates low writing fields. MIG heads have higher magnetization, and thin film heads and MR heads provide still higher write magnetization fields.

The track density limitations of ferrite and MIG heads are due to head material and processing constraints. Some progress is likely in this field with single-crystal ferrites and incorporation of thin film technology. Track definition for thin film and MR heads is controlled by lithographic processes. The higher sensitivity of the MR head allows narrow tracks with acceptable signal levels.

The data rate for ferrites and MIG heads is limited by high coil inductance. Thin film heads have considerably lower inductance compared to ferrite heads because of miniaturized geometry. However, as the number of turns for thin film heads increases, the inductance and capacitance of the head circuit result in self-resonance, which eventually limits reading at high data rates. The MR head read sensor is effectively a single-turn read element and therefore does not suffer from these high-frequency reading problems.

Table 1.3 further indicates that over the years a great deal of experience has been built up from earlier technologies like the ferrite head. The MR head, in contrast, is relatively new and has several manufacturing and application challenges that require extra care and often add to the product cost.

Figure 1.3 [6] shows the progress and density constraints of these head technologies. One-sided and two-sided MIG heads are making progress in increasing densities. However, with progress in thin film and MR heads, importance of MIG

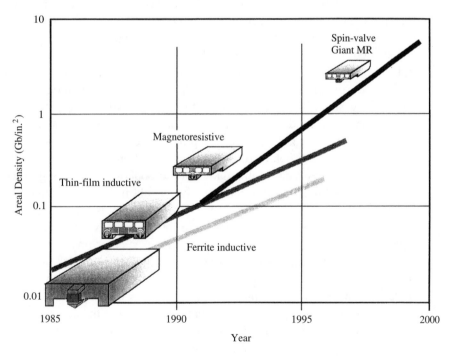

Figure 1.3 Magnetic head perspective (1994) [6].

heads for disk drives is declining. Thin-film head densities are increasing beyond prior expectations, through innovations in slider technology and reduction in inductance factor (discussed in Section 5.8). The MR head characteristics are ideal for disk drives of all sizes. The areal density limit is over several gigabits per in^2. For multigigabit per in^2 areal densities, newer approaches such as GMR (giant magnetoresistance) heads may be required. Ferrite, thin film, and MR heads are discussed in Chapters 4, 5 and 6, respectively, while GMR is described in Chapter 11. Many factors influence these limits. Improvements and innovations in any of these technologies cannot be ruled out. We shall discuss some of the reasons for these limits and point out exploratory efforts under way to extend these limits in these chapters.

1.4 SCOPE OF THE BOOK

There are several books on the subject of magnetic recording. They generally cover a wide range of magnetic recording applications, including tape recording, audio recording, and sometimes magneto-optical recording. To discuss the subject in adequate detail, this book is confined to magnetic recording on rigid disks. We describe the essential elements of rigid disk recording heads, disk media, electronic channels, and the integration of components into a disk drive. There is a long history of developments in these fields, and more innovations are taking place all the time. We offer the reader an up-to-date perspective on the technology, including relevant theory, modeling, current component design practices, design limitations, and potential innovations. Material from publications and patents up to early 1996 is included to keep the book current and useful to professionals engaged in the industry. This book is written primarily for practitioners in the disk drive industry or graduates interested in entering this field. Graduate students of science or engineering should be able to follow the content with little or no difficulty. An attempt has been made to keep the material simple and explanatory rather than detailed or exhaustive. References are provided for those who wish to explore specific topics in greater detail. Illustrations are used profusely to clarify the text and the geometries involved. Mathematics in the book are kept at a graduate student level. Examples and their solutions are given to clarify concepts and to provide help in handling magnetic unit conversions. Every attempt is made to report the latest developments in the field by emphasizing significant, new ideas and concepts. The disk drive technology involves many disciplines such as physics, chemistry, electrical, and mechanical engineering and material sciences. Also, the technology is divided into sectors such as heads, media, electronics, processing, manufacturing, development, research, and marketing. Individuals working in one area often have difficulty understanding the requirements and jargon of the other areas. One of the book's motives in providing this self-study information is to promote understanding and communication among complementing sectors. Here, managers may find helpful technical and general information to broaden their perspective about the technology and the industry.

1.5 OUTLINE OF TOPICS COVERED

A short introductory comment on each chapter is given here. This first chapter explains the importance of rigid disk drives in computers and data processing industry. Historical progress of disk drive technology is examined to get a perspective on future developments in the field. Major components of the technology responsible for dramatic enhancements in the field are briefly reviewed.

Chapter 2 explains topics of magnetism that are useful in understanding the material covered later in this book. The topics on basic magnetism cover: the origin of magnetism, magnetic fields, dipole moment, demagnetization, magnetic circuits, and magnetic and electrical units. Fundamental laws of magnetism include Ampere's law and Faraday's law. Magnetic testing of materials include properties of hard and soft materials and B-H loop (magnetic flux density B as a function of applied magnetic field H) measurements. Also, the following properties of materials are explained: anisotropy, exchange, magnetostriction, magnetoresistance, and magnetic domains. These topics are important in understanding the magnetoresistive sensor and its future evolution.

Chapter 3 covers the principles of magnetic recording. It begins with a qualitative discussion of reading and writing data with a ring head. Next, the field from a ring head is illustrated and described quantitatively. An example of head field calculation is given to clarify the importance of this parameter and to emphasize how it relates to the development of new head materials. Magnetic circuits are used to develop formulas for head efficiency and deep gap field. The general output "read signal" for a ring head is obtained using the principle of reciprocity. The signal is discussed for three types of magnetic transitions. Voltage equations and pulse-width equations are described with examples of their uses in the design and modeling of head-disk systems. The writing process is discussed with graphical illustrations. Side writing, reading, and erasing due to fringing fields are explained.

Chapter 4 begins with a description of the generic ferrite head structure in a typical slider. After a short history of the development of ferrite head materials and a listing of properties for a "good" recording head, the concept and motivation for metal-in-gap heads are discussed. A variety of MIG head structures is illustrated along with the processes used in the construction of both monolithic and composite heads. After considering the limitations of conventional MIG heads, the progress made in the construction and performance of new heads made in the last five years is described. The last part of the chapter points out possible materials and structures under development to extend the usefulness of ferrites and MIGs.

Chapter 5 starts out with a historical perspective and motivating factors for the development of the thin film head. After the discussion of three-dimensional structure of a typical film head, a (simplified) process to fabricate these heads is described. Characteristics of thin and thick film heads are addressed next. The film head writing process and an equivalent circuit of inductive and MR heads for reading is described. Simple equations for thin film head efficiency and inductance are discussed. The signal output of a thin film head is described with simplified equations, while a more exact form is provided in an appendix. Limitations on thin film head bit density are reviewed using analytical and experimental results. Developmental activities on high-moment pole materials, horizontal heads, and other innovative structures for advancing thin film head performance are summarized. Instability in thin-film voltage waveform is discussed in the last section.

Chapter 6 discusses magnetoresistive heads. Historical development and relative advantages of an MR head are discussed. MR head structure and processing are described as are MR sensor theory and its characterization curve, and the necessity for transverse biasing of an MR sensor. Permanent magnet, shunt, soft adjacent layer (SAL), barber pole, and dual stripe biasing methods are reviewed. Because narrow track disk drive sensors suffer from Barkhausen noise, with resultant instability in its signal, the methods of controlling this noise with longitudinal biasing are described. Electromigration and other reliability issues are addressed next. Yoke-type and other novel MR head structures are described. Analytical modeling of shielded-biased sensors is described and resultant equations are used to express MR signal characteristics in terms of head geometry, flying height, and media parameters. MR sensor design issues are illustrated through several graphical plots. Asymmetric track reading of the MR sensor is addressed last.

Chapter 7 summarizes historical transition of disk media from particulate to thin film type. Thin film disk structure and functions of different layers (substrate, underlayer, thin magnetic film, and overcoat) are explained. Manufacturing processing and equipment are discussed and illustrated in some detail. Macro- and micromagnetics of thin film material are described emphasizing the factors for improving signals and reducing noise. Disk tribology including surface preparations, overcoats, and lubrication procedures are discussed next. The characterization and testing methods for materials, surface topography, and finished disk testing during manufacturing and material development are summarized. Instrumentation and procedures are simply explained for nonspecialists. Disk technology future directions for substrate, magnetic film, and head-medium interactions are described.

Chapter 8 covers topics on the recording channel, coding of data, signal-to-noise considerations, and practical measurement techniques used in the development of a drive. Principles of peak detection and partial response maximum likelihood (PRML) coding for channels are explained in a simple step-by-step procedure, and differences between the two are clarified. Issues related to equalization and filtering are simplified through illustrations. On-track intersymbol interference and noise contributions by head, medium, and electronics are discussed, and procedure for measurements and analysis of signal-to-noise ratio are described.

Chapter 9 considers drive integration from an electrical point of view. The development of a disk drive requires many engineering compromises. The components go through several design iterations and testing cycles. Error rate is a critical parameter in designing bit, track, and areal densities of a disk drive. The process of drive integration is to design the head, disk, channel electronics, and servo so that the drive operates with low error rates. Essentials of practical servo control techniques are described with applications of dedicated and sector servo principles. Terms such as off-track performance, window margin, bath tub curve, 747 curve, and track misregistration (TMR) are explained.

Chapter 10 on head-disk interface begins with the historical development of air-bearing sliders and reviews self-acting air-bearing, taper flat, and self-loading sliders. Gas lubrication for air-bearing theory is abstracted with one- and two-dimensional Reynolds equation and illustrations of pressure profiles of well-known slider types. Methods of characterizing head-disk interface and measuring flying height are described next. Capacitive, optical, and piezoelectric methods used for these measurements are outlined. The terminology and processes used in mechanical integration of head-disk interface are reviewed. Contents of numerous papers related to issues of friction, stiction, contact start-stop (CSS), take-off velocity, and so on, are condensed here. Description of new slider designs developed within the last five years and reported in technical literature is summarized in Section 10.7: Advanced Slider Designs. Approaches to contact recording summarize the state of the art on this subject.

Chapter 11, the last chapter, examines the future trends in disk drive technology. Historical progress in linear, track, and areal densities and flying heights are described to project densities up to the end of the 1990s. Next, 1, 2, and 3 Gb/in^2 experiments are analyzed as an exercise in the scaling of components for 6 Gb/in^2 density in year 2000. A section describes principles of giant magnetoresistance, spin valve, and spin-valve head. Optical servos for magnetic recording and application of discrete track recording are reviewed from published papers. The perpendicular recording and special advantage of combining it with contact recording are summarized. Two disk drive applications that might steer the technology significantly are (1) arrays of small drives to simulate functions of reliable large storage systems, and (2) small drives for notebook and subnotebooks. These applications are described in two sections. Ongoing research in components and electronics for disk drives are summarized and, finally, highly advanced and speculative concepts for the next decade and beyond are explained.

REFERENCES

[1] C. Wood and P. Hodges, "DASD trends: cost, performance and form factor," *IEEE Trans. Magn.* MAG-81 (1993), p. 573.
[2] Presentation by Jim Porter at IEEE meeting in San Jose, CA, June 27, 1995. Latest information may be available from Disk Trend, Inc., 1925 Landings Drive, Mountain View, CA.

[3] L. D. Stevens, "The evolution of magnetic storage," *IBM J. of Res. and Devel.*, vol. 25 (1981), p. 663.

[4] J. M. Harker, D. W. Brede, R. E. Pattison, G. R. Santana, and L. G. Taft, "A quarter century of disk file innovation," *IBM J. of Res. and Devel.*, vol. 25 (1981), p. 677.

[5] C. Denis Mee and Eric D. Daniel, *Magnetic Recording Handbook,* New York: McGraw-Hill, p. 657, 1990.

[6] R. A. Scranton, "The era of magnetoresistive heads," paper presented at IDEMA symposium, San Jose, CA, February 1994. (Figure 1.3 courtesy of E. Growchoski.)

2

The Fundamentals of Magnetism

James C. Suits

2.1 MAGNETS AND POLES

This chapter reviews some of the principles of magnetism that are important in the understanding of magnetic recording heads and their interaction with magnetic recording materials. Our approach begins with the concept of magnetic poles, and then we discuss the ideas of magnetic fields, dipoles, and magnetization. Faraday's law is key to understanding recording write heads. Hysteresis loops, anisotropy, exchange, and domains are important in understanding magnetic materials. The concept of magnetoresistance is, of course, the dominant idea in the magnetoresistive read head. Confusing aspects of magnetism are unit and conversions, which are discussed in some detail in this chapter. The beginnings of magnetism go back to very early times. Naturally occurring magnets were discovered many hundreds of years ago. The material was called *lodestone,* and it was found that one piece of lodestone would attract or repel another piece of lodestone. It was also found that when lodestone was suspended by a thread, the material would always line up in a certain direction with respect to the earth; this property was used in the early days for ship navigation. When a magnetized body such as lodestone or iron is dipped into iron filings, the filings cling to it, especially in certain places called *poles,* which are located near the ends of the magnet.

Poles were defined more specifically as early as the year 1300. It was discovered that when an iron needle was suspended by a thread at different places above the surface of a lodestone, and lines were drawn everywhere parallel to the needle, the lines converged at two points on opposite ends of the stone. These lines may also be seen by placing iron filings on a piece of paper over a magnet as shown in

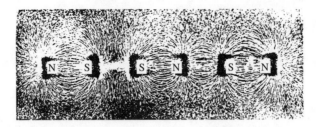

Figure 2.1 Iron filings on a piece of paper above three bar magnets showing convergence of lines on north and south poles [1].

Figure 2.1. These points were defined in this way as *magnetic poles.* In the year 1600, Gilbert discovered what every schoolboy knows today—that there are two kinds of poles: north (or positive) poles and south (or negative) poles. The north poles were defined as poles that move toward the north pole of the earth; for example, the north pole of a compass needle points toward the earth's north pole. As in the analogous case of electric charges, like poles repel and unlike poles attract.

However, there are several important differences between electric poles, or charges, and magnetic poles. First, there is no substance through which a magnetic current can flow. This is in contrast to the well-known case of an electric current in which electric charges (i.e., electrons) can move in a metal under the influence of an electric field. Second, every magnet is found to have equal quantities of positive and negative poles: for example, if you cut a magnet in two, it is found that each of the two pieces has its own pair of north and south poles. Figure 2.1 shows an example of a bar magnet that was cut into three pieces.

Although one cannot separate magnetic poles completely, one can separate them widely. Even though the earth has both a north and a south pole, they are certainly well separated. Separation of poles allows one to measure the strength of an individual pole. One experimental method is to use long, thin needle magnets. Figure 2.2 shows one needle (or bar) that is suspended by a stiff fiber at its center and is free to turn against the torsion of the fiber. A second long magnet may then be brought up near the first needle, causing it to rotate. By calibrating the system so that a certain rotation corresponds to a certain force, the force of repulsion and attraction between like and unlike poles may be measured.

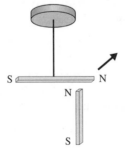

Figure 2.2 Apparatus to measure pole strength.

Even though free magnetic monopoles do not exist, pairs of magnetic poles (dipoles) do exist. As will be discussed later, these dipoles are created by nonuniformity in magnetization, and are a very useful concept for calculation of magnetic fields in many different situations, such as demagnetization fields and fields from a recording head.

2.2 FORCES BETWEEN POLES

Before talking about fields, we need to be quantitative about forces between magnetic poles. As we do this, we deal with the difficult subject of units. We will use SI units (Système International d'Unités) in this book as the primary system of units. These units are essentially what formerly was called the *meter-kilogram-second* (mks) system of units. Our equations will be derived in these units. The second system of units we will be using is the *centimeter-gram-second* (cgs) system of units. This system of units is used in magnetism more often than the former system for the description of magnetic materials. In some cases, quantities are given in both systems of units—first the quantity in SI units and then the quantity in cgs units in parentheses. A third system of units is the English system which uses inches, pounds, and seconds. We have already used the English system in Chapter 1 when discussing bits per inch, tracks per inch, and bits per square inch.

Suppose we have two magnetic poles, with pole strengths m_1 and m_2, and suppose they are separated by a distance r as shown in Figure 2.3.

In SI units, the magnitude of the force, **F**, that each pole exerts on the other is given by Coulomb's law as

$$F = \mu_0 \left(\frac{m_1 m_2}{4 \pi r^2} \right) \tag{2.1}$$

The constant μ_0 is called the *permeability of free space* and its magnitude is $4\pi \times 10^{-7}$. The unit of μ_0 is volt-second per ampere-meter (V-s/A-m). This unit is also sometimes called *henry per meter* (H/m). The unit of distance r is the meter (m), and the unit of force is the newton (N). Force **F** is a vector acting

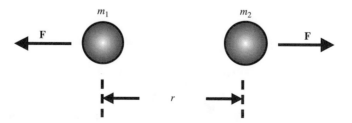

Figure 2.3 Forces acting on two like magnetic poles.

along the line joining the two poles. Vectors are printed in boldface type. Magnitudes of vectors are printed in bold type. Since we know how to measure forces and distances, and the units of force and distance are well defined, the unit of pole strength is defined by this equation. The unit of pole strength is the ampere-meter (A-m). As expected, we see from equation (2.1), that the force gets larger with increasing pole strength, and the force gets smaller as the poles get farther apart.

2.3 MAGNETIC FIELDS

Now that we can measure and predict forces between poles, we can discuss magnetic fields. The magnetic field **H** is a mathematical construction that makes it easy to describe the action-at-a-distance forces between magnetic entities such as poles. Suppose that we have a magnetic field at some point in free space. (There is always some field present, even if it is only that due to the earth.) Imagine also that we have a test pole at this particular location in space with a pole strength of m_{test}. Then, the magnetic field **H** at that location is defined to be the force on that pole divided by the strength of the test pole (and for SI units, also divided by μ_0):

$$\mathbf{H} = \frac{1}{\mu_0}\left(\frac{\mathbf{F}}{m_{test}}\right) \tag{2.2}$$

The unit of magnetic field is amperes per meter (A/m). One caveat here is that this test pole must be inserted into space in such a way that it does not disturb the field **H** which we want to measure. For example, if we are interested in the field around a particular pole, we do not want to move that particular pole by inserting our unit test pole nearby. We may now calculate the **H** field created by a single pole m_1. If we let our test pole m_{test} be located at distance r from m_1, equation (2.1) will give us the force **F** on that test pole (with $m_2 = m_{test}$). Substituting that force into equation (2.2), we find the magnitude of the field to be

$$H = \frac{m_1}{4\pi r^2} \tag{2.3}$$

and the direction of the field around a single positive pole may be shown as in Figure 2.4. At each point in space an arrow is drawn whose direction represents the

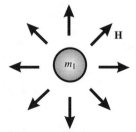

Figure 2.4 The magnetic field around a single pole.

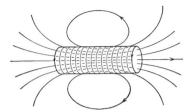

Figure 2.5 Magnetic field around a long solenoid.

direction of the magnetic field. The length of the arrow represents the magnitude of the field. We have drawn only a few arrows. All arrows will be symmetrical about the pole, and they will decrease in magnitude as we get farther from the pole. The direction of the field by definition is away from a north pole and toward a south pole.

In addition to poles, electric currents will create a magnetic field. We may consider the magnetic field around a long coil of current-carrying wire called a *solenoid*. This is shown in Figure 2.5. Long solenoids are often used in practice as the source for a uniform magnetic field in their center.

We characterize the solenoid as having n_l turns of wire per unit length of solenoid. The wire carries a current of magnitude i. The magnitude of the field at the center of the solenoid is given by

$$H = n_l i \qquad (2.4)$$

The current is in amperes (A), and n_l is in turns per meter. In this case, it is easy to see why the unit of field is amperes per meter.

2.4 DIPOLES, MAGNETIC MATERIALS, AND MAGNETIZATION

The next step in understanding magnetism is to discuss the magnetic dipole. A *dipole* is simply a pair of magnetic poles of opposite sign separated by some constant distance r. The **H** field due to a dipole is the superposition of the fields of the two individual poles. The field lines—lines parallel to the field direction—are shown in Figure 2.6. The field direction is positive going from north pole to south pole.

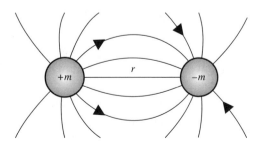

Figure 2.6 **H** field of a magnetic dipole.

We talked earlier about the strength of a single pole. The strength of a dipole, called the *dipole moment,* is given by the product of the strength of one pole in ampere-meters and the distance r in meters between the two poles; that is, the dipole strength is $p = mr$. The SI unit of the dipole moment is the ampere-meter^2(A-m^2).

A dipole **p** may be represented as a vector that points from the south pole to the north pole with a length proportional to the strength of the dipole. When a magnetic dipole is placed in a uniform magnetic field **H** as shown in Figure 2.7, the dipole will experience forces. In this figure, the north pole will experience an upward force, and the south pole will experience a downward force. These two forces cancel along the horizontal and vertical directions, and so the dipole feels no net force trying to translate it. However, since the two forces do not act along the same vertical line, these forces exert a torque, or twisting force, that attempts to rotate the dipole in a counterclockwise direction; that is, the dipole tries to line up in the direction of the applied field.

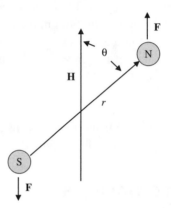

Figure 2.7 Forces on a dipole.

The energy of the dipole in field **H** may be written as

$$-pB \cos \theta \qquad\qquad (2.5)$$

where (in free space), $B = \mu_0 H$. This equation shows that the energy of the dipole is lowest when the dipole is pointing in the direction of **H** ($\theta = 0$).

Magnetic materials may be considered to be an assembly of magnetic dipoles residing on the magnetic atoms of the material. Atoms have electrons that rotate about the atomic nucleus. These rotating electrons act like tiny circular currents. These currents create a dipole moment on each magnetic atom. Another contribution to the atomic dipole moment is from electrons that rotate about their own axis. In iron, for example, it is this latter contribution that is dominant. The dipole moment of the entire magnetic material is the sum of all the dipole moments on all the magnetic atoms.

The *magnetization* of a material is the dipole moment per unit volume of material. It is the sum of all the atomic dipole moments within a particular unit volume. The SI unit of magnetization is A-m^2/m^3 = A/m. This is usually expressed in units of kiloamperes per meter (kA/m). If we replace p in equation (2.5) by the magnetization M, the energy per unit volume of a magnetic material with uniform M may be written

$$E = -MB\cos\theta \tag{2.6}$$

where (in free space), $B = \mu_0 H$. The *saturation magnetization, M_s,* is the magnetization when all atomic dipoles are lined up in the same direction. In the case of uniform dipole alignment, the magnetization may also be considered as a vector M. The direction of the vector is in the direction of the dipoles, from south to north. We will discuss one reason why all the atoms might line up their dipole moments in a later section on exchange.

The saturation magnetization of the ferromagnetic elements (at room temperature) is given in Table 2.1. The unit of magnetization often used in practice is the cgs unit of magnetization, emu/cm^3. However, it turns out that when the magnetization in SI units is expressed in kA/m, the numerical value of M is identical to its value in emu/cm^3. For example, the saturation magnetization of iron is 1710 kA/m, and it is also 1710 emu/cm^3.

TABLE 2.1 Saturation Magnetization of the Ferromagnetic Elements at Room Temperature

Material	M_s(kA/m, emu/cm^3)
Iron	1710
Nickel	485
Cobalt	1431
Gadolinium	1090

2.5 MAGNETIC FLUX DENSITY OR MAGNETIC INDUCTION

In the previous section, we described the magnetization of a magnet as being caused by the magnetic dipoles located on each atom in the material. (Here we imply only *magnetic* atoms, since many atoms such as oxygen have essentially no magnetic moment.) In Figure 2.8 on the left, we show a schematic of a bar magnet with a uniform magnetization (within the magnet) pointing upward. This would be the case if each atomic dipole were pointing upward. If each atomic dipole has the same strength, we can imagine that the north pole of one dipole will almost cancel out the south pole of the dipole above it. However, at the top surface of the bar magnet, there will be north poles on that surface that are not canceled out since there are no dipoles above it. Similarly, on the bottom surface of the magnet, there will be uncanceled south poles. We note that poles are not created on surfaces that are

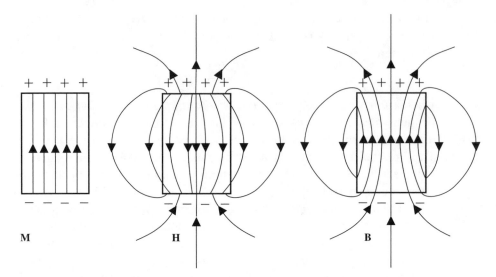

Figure 2.8 The relation among magnetization **M**, magnetic field **H**, and flux density **B** for a bar magnet.

parallel to **M**. In this way, magnetic poles are created on the surfaces of the magnet by the abrupt change in magnetization at the top and bottom surfaces of the magnet. (More generally speaking, in any region where there is a nonzero divergence of **M**, poles will be created. The density of poles will be equal to the negative of the divergence of **M**, $-\nabla \cdot \mathbf{M}$).

Since the magnetization has a value and a direction everywhere in space, we can think of **M** as a vector field also. It is plotted at the left of Figure 2.8 for the bar magnet. Since there are no atomic dipoles outside the bar magnet, the vector field **M** is zero everywhere except inside the magnet. We have assumed a "saturated" magnetization where the magnetization is uniform throughout the bar.

The uncompensated poles on the top and bottom surfaces of the bar magnet, which have been created by the magnetization, will produce the magnetic field shown in the center of Figure 2.8. This field is called a *demagnetizing field* and is discussed in more detail in the next section. It exists both inside and outside the magnet.

There is another related quantity of interest which is called the *magnetic induction* or *flux density* **B**. Its magnitude is defined (in SI units) by

$$\mathbf{B} = \mu_0(\mathbf{H} + \mathbf{M}) \tag{2.7}$$

where **B** is measured in webers per square meter (W/m²), which is the same unit as the tesla (T). On the right-hand side of Figure 2.8, we have plotted the sum of the **H** field and the **M** field (times μ_0). In contrast to the other two fields, we note that the **B** field is continuous. It is something like an electrical current in a circuit; that is, it is continuous and does not suddenly appear or disappear. Many formulas in magnetism use **B** rather than **H** in their formulation. Given a surface area A, the magnetic flux ϕ through that area is given by

$$\phi = \int \mathbf{B} \cdot dA \qquad (2.8)$$

The flux in webers is given by the flux density in W/m^2 times the area in m^2. For a uniform $\mathbf{B}$, the magnitude of flux through an area A perpendicular to B is BA. For some magnetic materials, the magnetization in zero applied field is zero, and as the applied field increases, the magnetization also linearly increases. For these materials one can define a *magnetic susceptibility* X by

$$\mathbf{M} = X\mathbf{H} \qquad (2.9)$$

One can also define a *magnetic permeability* μ by

$$\mathbf{B} = \mu\mathbf{H} \qquad (2.10)$$

For the case of free space where $M = 0$, equation (2.7) shows that $B = \mu_0 H$. Therefore, we see that the quantity μ_0, which was rather arbitrarily defined in equation (2.1) as the permeability of free space, is indeed just that. The permeability μ is usually expressed as

$$\mu = \mu_r\mu_0 \qquad (2.11)$$

where μ_r is called the *relative permeability*. For free space, $\mu_r = 1$.

We note that the $\mathbf{H}$ field outside the solenoid of Figure 2.5 looks similar to the $\mathbf{H}$ (or $\mathbf{B}$) field *outside* the bar magnet of Figure 2.8. In fact, if one looks at either the field of the solenoid or the field of the bar magnet from a distance which is large compared to the dimensions of either, one finds that the two fields are identical. We will use this fact in the discussion of reading data from a disk by a head.

2.6 DEMAGNETIZING FIELD

The direction of the $\mathbf{H}$ field within the bar magnet in Figure 2.8 is from north to south, and so this demagnetizing field is pointing opposite to the direction of magnetization. As we noted in Figure 2.7, magnetic dipoles try to line up with the applied field. Since the magnetization is upward in Figure 2.8, the atomic dipoles are pointing upward and would like to rotate in the $\mathbf{H}$ field to the downward direction. This demagnetizing field tries to *demagnetize* the magnet, and hence its name. We note that the demagnetizing field shown in Figure 2.8 is not particularly uniform within the magnet. Often in practice, one would like to have a uniform demagnetizing field. It turns out that when the magnet has an ellipsoidal shape, the demagnetizing field is uniform. Furthermore, this is the *only* shape that produces a uniform demagnetizing field. This sounds like a severe restriction. However, many of the geometries that occur in practice are close to ellipsoidal in shape: spheres, long rods, and flat plates are all special cases of an ellipsoidal shape.

For the case of a uniform demagnetizing field $\mathbf{H}_d$, the field is proportional to, and oppositely directed to, the magnetization

$$\mathbf{H}_d = -N\,\mathbf{M} \qquad (2.12)$$

In this equation, the constant of proportionality N is called the *demagnetizing factor.*

For a given ellipsoidal shape, the demagnetizing field depends upon the direction of magnetization. If we let the magnetization along the x, y, and z principal axes in an ellipsoid be M_x, M_y, and M_z, then there will be corresponding demagnetizing factors N_x, N_y, and N_z along these directions as shown in Figure 2.9. For example, the demagnetizing field in the x direction is $-N_x M_x$, where the minus sign denotes that the field is opposed to M_x. One of the properties of the demagnetizing factors is that they sum to unity.

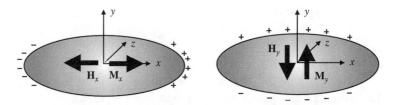

Figure 2.9 Demagnetizing fields of an ellipsoidal shape.

$$N_x + N_y + N_z = 1 \qquad (2.13)$$

If we imagine the ellipsoidal figure on the left in Figure 2.9 to be stretched in the x direction to make a long thin rod, then in the limit the demagnetizing factors are $N_x = 0$, $N_y = 0.5$, and $N_z = 0.5$. In this case, since the magnetic charge is only on the ends of the rod, and since these ends are very far away from most of the rod, the demagnetizing field in the x direction in the limit must be zero. The lack of a demagnetizing field in this direction makes it easier to magnetize this ellipsoidal shape in this direction (for H applied in the positive x direction). We could have deduced these demagnetizing factors since we know from the foregoing argument that $N_x = 0$ and by symmetry, $N_y = N_z$, so it must be from equation (2.13) that $N_y = N_z = 0.5$. We can imagine making a very thin plate by collapsing the ellipsoidal shape on the left in Figure 2.9 along the x axis. In this case, we also could deduce the demagnetizing factors. Since in the limit of a very thin disk, there is no magnetic charge on the edges of the disk, $N_y = N_z = 0$, and therefore by equation (2.13), $N_x = 1$. Here, all other things being equal, $\mathbf{M}$ lies in the y–z plane. Another example of demagnetizing factors is a sphere that by symmetry and equation (2.13) must have $N_x = N_y = N_z = 1/3$. In this case, $\mathbf{M}$ has no preferred direction.

2.7 AMPERE'S LAW

Ampere's law is used in many areas of magnetics. This law states that if we choose any closed path and integrate the flux density **B** around that path l, the result will equal the total current i_{total} passing through the closed path.

$$\oint \mathbf{H} \cdot dl = i_{\text{total}} \tag{2.14}$$

As an example of the use of Ampere's law for the calculation of magnetic fields, we calculate the magnitude of the **H** field around a straight wire. Although it is not proven here, the magnetic field lines for a straight wire lie in concentric circles around the axis of the wire as shown in Figure 2.10. In this case, **H** is parallel to the path parameter l, and so equation (2.14) gives

$$\mathbf{H} \oint dl = \mathbf{H} 2\pi r = i \tag{2.15}$$

or

$$\mathbf{H} = \frac{i}{2\pi r} \tag{2.16}$$

The current is in amperes, the radius r in meters, and the magnitude of the field H is in amperes per meter. As one might expect, the magnitude of H increases with increasing current and decreases as one gets farther away from the wire.

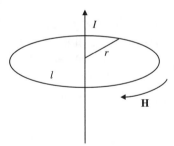

Figure 2.10 Magnetic field and path around a straight current-carrying wire.

2.8 FARADAY'S LAW

The use of Faraday's law of induction to describe electrical power generators is well known. It is also important in magnetic recording. It is used to understand the voltage induced in a read head by data bits recorded on a magnetic disk. All our previous discussion has been regarding static phenomena. Faraday's law allows us to calculate some time-dependent phenomena.

Faraday's law says that the electromotive force, or emf, induced in a conducting loop of n turns is proportional to the time rate of change of flux ϕ through that loop

$$V = -n\frac{d\phi}{dt} \tag{2.17}$$

The unit of emf is the volt, the unit of flux is the weber, and the unit of time is the second. Therefore, the unit of volt is the same as webers per second.

The flux through the area of the conducting loop may be calculated from the flux density **B** using equation (2.8). The negative sign in equation (2.17) means that the induced voltage is in such a direction as to create a current in the loop that will oppose or try to reduce the change in flux.

2.9 INDUCTION

We have noted that an electrical current will create a magnetic field. There are several relations between the current and its magnetic field that will be useful in later discussions. Suppose we have a single-turn coil carrying a current i. From Figure 2.5, we might imagine that the magnetic field **H** created by this current will be as shown in Figure 2.11. For a coil in air where $M = 0$ and $B = \mu_0 H$, equation (2.8) says the flux ϕ through this coil may be obtained by integrating the field **H** over the cross-sectional area of the coil

$$\phi = \mu_0 \int \mathbf{H} \cdot dA \tag{2.18}$$

We will see in the next section that flux is the magnetic analog to electrical current. We can visualize this flux as *something* like a "magnetic current," which, in this case, is flowing through the coil.

From Ampere's law (equation 2.14) we note that fields are proportional to current. Therefore, by equation (2.18) the flux will also be proportional to the current, and so we may write

$$\phi = Li \tag{2.19}$$

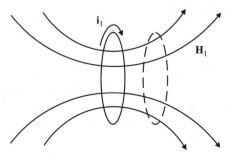

Figure 2.11 Field $\mathbf{H}_1$ created by current $\mathbf{i}_1$ through single-turn coil. A second coil is shown by the dashed line.

where L is a constant of proportionality. L is called the *self-inductance* or often just the *inductance*. The unit of inductance is the henry (H). Since flux is in webers, and current is in amperes, the henry is the same as weber per ampere (Wb/A). It is a constant that depends on the geometry of the circuit.

In the previous section on Faraday's law, we saw that if the flux through a closed path changes (such as the coil in Figure 2.11), then an emf is induced on that path. Substituting equation (2.19) into (2.17) and setting $n = 1$, we find that

$$V = -L\frac{di}{dt} \tag{2.20}$$

since L does not change with time. This equation will be important when we calculate the read voltage created in a magnetic head by the changing flux from a disk transition. We have considered the case where a current in a coil creates a flux passing through the same coil. Equation (2.19) gave us the ratio of flux to current. What about the case where we have another single-turn coil nearby as shown by the dashed line in Figure 2.11? The current i will create a flux through this second coil as well. Let's call it ϕ_2. Using the same arguments as for self-inductance, we can define a constant of proportionality between the flux induced in coil 2 by the current in coil 1:

$$\phi_2 = M_{21}i_1 \tag{2.21}$$

M_{21} is called the *mutual inductance* between the two circuits. The unit is the henry. In addition, a current in coil 2 will create flux in coil 1, which will be described by equation (2.21) with the subscripts 1 and 2 interchanged.

2.10 MAGNETIC CIRCUITS

Electrical circuits usually consist of voltages, currents, and resistances such as is illustrated in the simple series circuit shown on the left in Figure 2.12. Some magnetic circuits may be represented in a way that is analogous to the electrical circuit case. The magnetic analog of the electrical circuit on the left of Figure 2.12 is the loop of magnetic material on the right of that figure. The right side of Figure 2.8 suggests that the analog of electrical current should be something related to **B** since it is a continuous field.

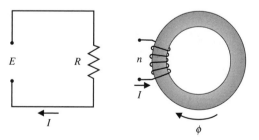

Figure 2.12 Electric and magnetic circuit analogs.

The analog of electrical current i is, in fact, magnetic flux which is **B** times an area (equation 2.8). In an electrical wire, current flows in the wire because the electrical conductivity of the wire is much higher (many orders of magnitude higher) than that of the media (usually air) surrounding the wire—current flows in regions of high conductivity. In a similar manner, flux "flows" in regions of high magnetic permeability. The permeability of the magnetic material, for example, the magnetic yoke on the right of Figure 2.12, is perhaps two or three orders of magnitude higher than free space ($\mu_r = 100$, or 1000), and so there is little leakage of flux outside the yoke. Most of the flux will lie inside the yoke on circumferential circles. If the flux density inside the yoke is B, the flux through a cross-sectional area A of the yoke will be $\phi = BA$.

The way to create a driving force similar to electrical voltage is to wrap a coil of current-carrying wire around the yoke as shown. The magnetic analog to voltage is magnetomotive force (mmf) which, in the case shown in the right side of Figure 2.12, is the product Ni (the number of turns in the coil times the current through the coil). Combining these quantities gives the magnetic analog of Ohm's law (resistance = voltage ÷ current) as

$$\mathcal{R} = \frac{ni}{\phi} \tag{2.22}$$

where $\mathcal{R}$ is defined as the magnetic *reluctance*. If we now apply Ampere's law to a circular path l_m that lies inside the magnetic yoke shown in Figure 2.12, we find

$$Hl_m = ni \tag{2.23}$$

where the total current through the path is n times the current through a single turn. This may be rewritten using the preceding relations as

$$\mathcal{R} = \frac{Hl_m}{BA} = \frac{Hl_m}{\mu_r\mu_0 HA} = \frac{l_m}{\mu_r\mu_0 A} \tag{2.24}$$

where A is the cross-sectional area. This may be compared with the electrical case in which the resistance is given by

$$R = \frac{l_r}{\sigma A} \tag{2.25}$$

where l_r is the length of the resistor, A is the cross-sectional area of the resistor, and σ is the conductivity. Comparing quantities shows that the corresponding quantities in the electrical case and in the magnetic case are as follows in Table 2.2.

TABLE 2.2 Electric and Magnetic Analogs

Electrical	Magnetic
Voltage E	Magnetomotive force mmf $= nl$
Current I	Flux $\phi = BA$
Resistance $R = l/(\sigma A)$	Reluctance $\mathcal{R} = l/(\mu_r\mu_0 A)$
Conductivity σ	Permeability $\mu_r\mu_0$

2.11 UNITS AND CONVERSIONS

Since cgs units are often used for certain quantities in practical magnetics work, we will take a short diversion now to review the relationship between SI and cgs units. Furthermore, we will show how some of the fundamental equations appear in cgs units.

There are three principal systems of cgs units: electrostatic units (esu), electromagnetic units (emu), and Gaussian units. Electrostatic units are used primarily with electrostatic quantities such as charge and current. Electromagnetic units are used primarily with electromagnetic quantities such as magnetic field and permeability. Gaussian units are a combination of the two, using esu for electrical quantities and emu for magnetic quantities. For magnetic quantities, Gaussian and emu units are the same. We will be using Gaussian units in this section. Conversion factors between units are sometimes confusing because of not knowing whether to multiply or divide. The convention followed here is that conversions are formatted as follows:

$$1 \ \text{unit}_{\text{cgs}} = k \cdot \text{unit}_{\text{SI}} \tag{2.26}$$

From this format one can calculate k. Then, to convert a cgs quantity to an SI quantity, multiply the cgs quantity by k. To go the other way, divide by k. For example, the length conversion is formatted as $1 \ \text{cm} = 10^{-2} \ \text{m}$. From the form of equation (2.26), $k = 10^{-2}$. To convert 15 centimeters to meters, multiply 15 cm by k to give 0.15 meters.

Another way to do this conversion is to multiply 15 cm by unity, that is, by $10^{-2} \ \text{m}/1 \ \text{cm}$, cancel units, and multiply out the numbers:

$$15 \ \text{cm} \left(\frac{10^{-2} \ \text{m}}{1 \ \text{cm}} \right) = 0.15 \ \text{m} \tag{2.27}$$

The base units in cgs are centimeters for distance, grams for mass, and seconds for time. Starting with the magnetic form of Coulomb's law (equation 2.1), the cgs form of this law is

$$F = \frac{m_1 m_2}{r^2} \tag{2.28}$$

The unit of force is the dyne ($1 \ \text{dyne} = 10^{-5}$ newtons), and distance is in centimeters ($1 \ \text{cm} = 10^{-2} \ \text{m}$). The unit of pole strength does not have a name but is defined in terms of the equation (2.28). One feature of cgs units is that μ_0 does not appear.

The magnetic field (equation 2.2) is defined again in terms of the force (in dynes) on a unit pole, but without the μ_0

$$\mathbf{H} = \frac{\mathbf{F}}{m_{\text{test}}} \tag{2.29}$$

The unit of magnetic field is called the *oersted* (1 Oe = $(1/4\pi) \times 10^3$ A/m, which is approximately 80 A/m). The field around a single magnetic pole m_1 (equation 2.3) is

$$\mathbf{H} = \frac{m_1}{r^2} \tag{2.30}$$

All these equations look simpler than the corresponding equations in SI units. However, now we come to the field of a solenoid (equation 2.4). In cgs Gaussian units, n_l is the number of turns per centimeter of solenoid, i is the current in statamperes [1 statampere $= (1/3) \times 10^{-9}$ A], and c is the velocity of light (3×10^{10} cm/s).

$$\mathbf{H} = \frac{4\pi n i}{c} \tag{2.31}$$

This equation is more complicated than its counterpart in SI units.

The cgs unit of dipole strength, or dipole moment, is the erg/G, commonly referred to as the "emu". The conversion is 1 emu $= 10^{-3}$ Am^2. As discussed earlier in connection with Table 2.1, the cgs unit of magnetization is commonly referred to as "emu/cm^3." However, often in the literature one will find values of "magnetization" quoted that are actually $4\pi M$ instead of M. To be sure which parameter one is dealing with, one must look carefully at the data. The formula relating $\mathbf{H}$, $\mathbf{M}$, and $\mathbf{B}$ (equation 2.7) in cgs units is

$$\mathbf{B} = \mathbf{H} + 4\pi\mathbf{M} \tag{2.32}$$

The cgs unit of flux density is gauss (1 G $= 10^{-4}$ T or 10^{-4} Wb/m^2). Formulas for flux (equation 2.8) and magnetic susceptibility (equation 2.9) are the same in both units. In cgs units the permeability (equation 2.10) is simply

$$\mathbf{B} = \mu\mathbf{H} \tag{2.33}$$

where μ is a unitless quantity just like μ_r in SI units (equation 2.11). For the case where $\mathbf{M} = 0$, equation (2.33) shows that $\mu = 1$.

Regarding the demagnetizing field, the formulas are the same except that in these formulas N should be multiplied by 4π. The maximum value of the resulting cgs value of N is then 4π rather than unity. In equation (2.13), the sum of the three components of demagnetizing factors is not one but 4π. Ampere's law (equation 2.14) in cgs units is

$$\oint \mathbf{H} \cdot dl = \frac{4\pi i_{\text{total}}}{c} \tag{2.34}$$

TABLE 2.3 Unit Conversions

Quantity	cgs (Gaussian)	Conversion Factor, k	SI
Distance, l	centimeter	10^{-2}	meter (m)
Mass, m	gram (g)	10^{-3}	kilogram (kg)
Time, t	second (s)	1	second(s)
Force, **F**	dyne	10^{-5}	newton (N)
Pole strength, m	cgs	$4\pi \times 10^{-8}$	ampere-meter (A-m)
Dipole moment, p	emu	10^{-3}	ampere-meter^2 (A-m^2)
Magnetic field, **H**	oersted (Oe)	$(1/4\pi) \times 10^3$	ampere/meter (A/m)
Magnetization, **M**	emu/cm^3	10^3	ampere/meter (A/m)
Magnetization, **M**	emu/cm^3	1	kiloampere/meter (kA/m)
Flux density, **B**	gauss (G)	10^{-4}	tesla (T), weber/m^2 (Wb/m^2)
Flux, ϕ	maxwell (Mx)	10^{-8}	weber (Wb)
Energy, E	erg	10^{-7}	joule (J)
Current, i	statampere	$(1/3) \times 10^{-9}$	amperes (A)
Inductance, L	esu	9×10^{11}	henry (H)
Capacitance, C	cm	$(1/9) \times 10^{-11}$	farad (F)
Potential, V	statvolt	300	volt (V)
Permeability, μ	dimensionless	$4\pi \times 10^{-7}$	henry/meter (H/m)
Anisotropy, K	erg/cm^3	10^{-1}	joule/meter^3 (J/m^3)
Susceptibility, χ	dimensionless	4π	dimensionless

where i_{total} is in statamperes. Table 2.3 summarizes conversions between SI units and cgs Gaussian units. To use this table, multiply the cgs Gaussian value of a quantity by the conversion factor k to get the value of the quantity in SI units.

2.12 CGS–SI CONVERSION TABLE

Multiply the value of quantity in cgs by k to get the value in SI. For example, 15 cm $= 15k = 15 \times 10^{-2} = 0.15$ m. The conversion would be read as 1 cm $= 10^{-2}$ m. Remember $\mu_0 = 4\pi \times 10^{-7}$ volt-second/ampere-meter. It is also convenient to remember for field conversions that $(1/4\pi) \times 10^3 = 79.6$.

Prefixes that are often used with units are the following: giga- (10^9), mega- (10^6), kilo- (10^3), centi- (10^{-2}), milli- (10^{-3}), micro- (10^{-6}), nano- (10^{-9}), and pico- (10^{-12}). Some commonly used lengths are 1 angstrom (Å) $= 10^{-8}$ cm $= 10^{-10}$ m, 1 micrometer (micron) $= 10^{-4}$ cm $= 10^{-6}$ m, and 1 micro-inch (1 μ-in.) $= 254$ angstroms.

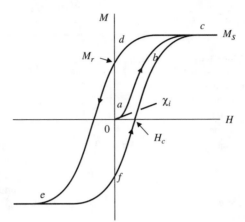

Figure 2.13 Hysteresis loop.

2.13 HYSTERESIS LOOPS
AND MAGNETIC MATERIALS

Returning now to the general subject of magnetism, we shall explore in some detail the way in which magnetic materials respond to a magnetic field. A plot of the magnitude of magnetization or flux density as a function of applied magnetic field is called a *hysteresis loop*. A typical hysteresis loop is shown in Figure 2.13. In this case, a magnetic field **H** has been applied to a sample of magnetic material, and the component of magnetization in the direction of H has been plotted. Such a loop could be directly plotted, for example, by an instrument often used in the analysis of magnetic materials called a *vibrating sample magnetometer* (VSM). The VSM mechanically oscillates a magnetic sample in a static magnetic field, measuring the component of M in the direction of H as H is slowly varied in magnitude.

Another common method of producing hysteresis loops is by placing the sample in a long solenoid. The solenoid creates a rapidly oscillating magnetic field H. The sample flux density is read from a small pickup loop placed near the sample. Since even without a sample, the pickup coil will pick up the field of the solenoid, two identical pickup coils are used with the sample mounted inside one of them. The signal is the difference between the output of the two coils.

In Figure 2.13, starting in zero H field with a demagnetized sample, the field is gradually increased in the positive H direction. The path the magnetization initially takes, the initial magnetization curve, is *0-a-b-c*. The initial slope is called the *initial susceptibility* χ_i. If we were plotting B versus H instead of M versus H, the initial slope would be called the *initial permeability*. The maximum value of magnetization reached is called the *saturation magnetization*, M_s, where application of additional H will yield no appreciable increase in M. When the field is now reduced and reversed, the magnetization will take the path around the loop labeled *c-d-e-f-c*. The value of M at zero field on this major loop is called the *remanent magnetization* M_r. The value of H for zero magnetization on this major loop is called the *coercive force* or *coercivity* H_c. The early part of the initial magnetization curve from 0 to *a* is nearly linear and is reversible. The next section, from *a* to *b*, is irreversible. The final section from *b* to *c* is reversible again. We will explain these features of the hysteresis loop in a later section in terms of domain wall motion and magnetization rotation.

Ferromagnetic materials are divided into two broad classes: soft magnetic materials and hard materials. Hard magnetic materials show low initial permeability (or susceptibility) and high coercive force. Figure 2.13 shows a hysteresis loop that is characteristic of a hard magnetic material that might be used for disk media or for a permanent magnet application. Soft magnetic materials exhibit high initial permeability (or susceptibility) and also low coercive force. Figure 2.14 shows a hysteresis loop that is characteristic of a soft magnetic material that might be used for a transformer or a magnetic head application.

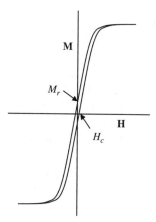

Figure 2.14 Hysteresis loop of soft magnetic material.

Figure 2.15 shows values for permeability and coercive force for some representative magnetic materials.

Supermalloy and 78 Permalloy may be considered soft magnetic materials, and Alnico V and ferroplatinum may be considered hard magnetic materials. This figure shows a rather clear inverse relationship between permeability and coercivity. It also should be noted that both of these parameters vary over a remarkably large range—five to six orders of magnitude.

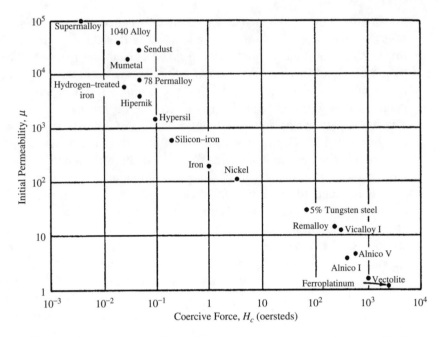

Figure 2.15 Initial permeability and coercive force for representative materials [2].

2.14 MAGNETIC ANISOTROPY

Central to an understanding of hysteresis loops is the subject of anisotropy. This term refers to the fact that even when no magnetic fields are applied to a magnetic material, the direction of magnetization prefers to point in certain directions called *easy axes*. In Figure 2.16 for zero applied field, all other things being equal, the magnetization **M** would point along the easy axis shown ($\alpha = 0$). When a field **H** is applied, the magnetization is pulled toward the field direction. As the field is increased, **M** points closer to the field direction. At an intermediate value of α, **M** is being attracted in opposite directions—up by the field **H** and down by the anisotropy.

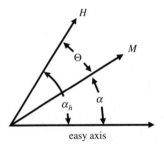

Figure 2.16 Magnetization **M** pulled away from easy axis of anisotropy by field **H**.

If all the magnetization is pointing in the same direction in a magnetic material, and if this material exhibits an easy axis of magnetization, we may describe the energy per unit volume of the magnetization of this material by

$$E = K \sin^2 \alpha \qquad (2.35)$$

K is called the *anisotropy constant* and is in units of energy per unit volume (SI: J/m^3; cgs: ergs/cm^3). E is also energy per unit volume. The usual way to describe the magnitude of uniaxial anisotropy is in terms of the *anisotropy field* which is defined as

$$H_k = \frac{2K}{\mu_0 M} \qquad (2.36)$$

In cgs units, the μ_0 is missing. For Permalloy films, values of $\mathbf{H}_k$ are typically in the range 80–800 A/m (1–10 Oe). We may calculate the equilibrium angle of the magnetization as follows. The energy of magnetization is given by

$$E = K \sin^2(\alpha) - \mu_0 M H \cos(\alpha_h - \alpha) \qquad (2.37)$$

where the first term is the anisotropy energy (equation 2.35). The second term is the energy due to the magnetic field from equation (2.6) with B replaced by $\mu_0 H$, and $\alpha_h - \alpha$ is the angle between $\mathbf{H}$ and $\mathbf{M}$. For equilibrium, we require that the first derivative be zero

$$\frac{\partial E}{\partial \alpha} = 2K \sin \alpha \cos \alpha - \mu_0 M H \sin(\alpha_h - \alpha) = 0 \qquad (2.38)$$

For the simple case where $\mathbf{H}$ is directed at right angles to the easy axis, $\alpha_h = 90°$, one finds for the equilibrium angle for the magnetization relative to the easy axis

$$\sin \alpha = \frac{H}{H_k} \qquad (2.39)$$

For $H = 0$, $\mathbf{M}$ points along the easy axis. For $H = H_k$, $\mathbf{M}$ points along the direction of H ($\alpha = \alpha_h = 90°$). For intermediate values of H, $\mathbf{M}$ points at the value of α given by equation (2.39) rotating smoothly between the easy axis and the applied field. We have spent time on this calculation because it is one that is repeated often in many different situations.

2.14.1 Magnetocrystalline Anisotropy

If one were to look at the atoms in a typical metal, one would find that they are not randomly arranged, but instead, exhibit a very regular, periodic structure. Figure 2.17 shows one common structure, the *body-centered cubic* (bcc) structure. Imagine the corner atoms of this structure as replicated throughout space to form a perfect cubic lattice. This is called a *simple cubic lattice*. Add the atom in the center of each cube, and you have a body-centered cubic lattice. The other common cubic lattice is the *face-centered cubic* (fcc) lattice in which, rather than

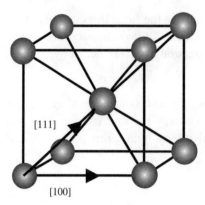

[111]

[100]

Figure 2.17 Body-centered cubic unit cell.

an atom at the cube center, atoms are added at the center of each of the cube faces. Associated with these atomic arrangements are special directions. In all these cubic lattices, the direction that points along any of the cube edges is called a *[100] direction.* The direction that points from any cube corner to the cube center is called a *[111] direction.*

If the material contains magnetic atoms, it turns out that the atomic dipoles on these atoms prefer to point in certain directions in the crystal lattice. For example, in bcc iron the preferred directions of magnetization, the easy axes of magnetization, lie along the [100] crystallographic directions.

All other things being equal, the magnetization in iron will lie along a [100] direction. In iron, the *magnetocrystalline anisotropy energy* is lowest when the magnetization points along a [100] direction. In nickel, which is fcc, the easy axes lie along the [111] crystallographic directions. We have been discussing the case of a single crystal of material. However, most materials are usually polycrystalline. This means that in a small region of the material, a crystalline *grain* of the material, all the atoms will exhibit the foregoing periodic structure. In fact, all grains will exhibit a periodic structure. The difference between one grain and the next is the crystallographic orientation of the grain; the [100] and [111] directions, for example, will be different from one grain to the next. Typical grain sizes for materials range from 10 nm to 100 μm (100 Å to 100 μm). Since the magnetization prefers to lie along a particular direction in each grain, the magnetization may point in different directions from one grain to the next. For uniform magnetization, when averaged over randomly oriented grains in a polycrystalline material, the magnetocrystalline anisotropy energy is independent of the direction of magnetization. If for some reason there is a nonrandom or preferred crystalline orientation in the polycrystal, then the crystalline anisotropy must be considered. In most cases of thin film materials, the crystallographic grain size is very small and randomly oriented in the plane of the film, so crystalline anisotropy is not very important.

2.14.2 Field-Induced Anisotropy

In some materials, it is possible to induce a magnetic anisotropy with a magnetic field. This may be done in two ways. One way is to deposit a film in the presence of a magnetic field. A second way is to heat the material in the presence of a magnetic field. In either case, after such treatment, the material may exhibit an easy axis of magnetization that points in the direction of the magnetic field that was applied. This induced anisotropy is independent of any crystalline anisotropy or any other form of anisotropy that might be present. The classic material that exhibits this phenomenon is Permalloy. Permalloy is a metallic magnetic alloy that consists of approximately 80% nickel and 20% iron. This material and variations on it are probably the most popular magnetic materials in use today. This is because of exceptionally high permeability and low coercivity (Figures 2.14 and 2.15). Permalloy is so sensitive to the induction of an anisotropy by a magnetic field that even if no magnetic field is applied during film deposition, the resulting film will exhibit a uniaxial anisotropy. If there are no stray magnetic fields present in the deposition chamber, the easy axis of anisotropy will be found to be in the direction of the earth's magnetic field.

2.14.3 Shape Anisotropy

We have already discussed the manner in which demagnetizing fields are created when a component of the magnetization lies perpendicular to a free surface of the material. Creation of this demagnetizing field expends energy since there is an energy associated with any magnetic field. All other things being equal, if the direction of magnetization is free to change, the magnetization will change direction in order to minimize demagnetizing fields. The shape of the sample, then, is creating a magnetic anisotropy. The lowest energy direction for the magnetization is called the *easy axis of magnetization.* In Figure 2.9, for example, the easy axis of magnetization due to shape anisotropy will lie in the horizontal direction, since this is the direction that minimizes the demagnetizing field and demagnetizing field energy.

2.14.4 Magnetostrictive Anisotropy

Another important form of anisotropy in magnetic materials is due to magnetostriction. Magnetostriction relates the stress in a magnetic material to an anisotropy created by that stress. The magnetostriction constant λ (no units) is the constant of proportionality. The exact form of the equation depends on the geometry, but a common geometry is a rectangular bar of material such as in Figure 2.18. If the magnetostriction constant is positive, then application of a tensile (stretching) stress to the bar will create an easy axis in the direction of the applied stress. If a compressive stress is applied, then the direction of the easy

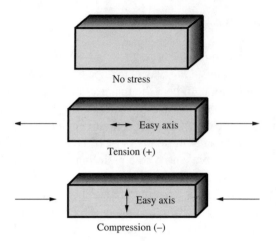

Figure 2.18 Inducing an easy axis with tension and compression for a material with positive magnetostriction.

axis created will be perpendicular to the stress direction (Figure 2.18). On the other hand, if the magnetostriction constant for the material is negative, then this is all reversed: a tensile stress will create an easy axis perpendicular to the stress direction, and a compressive stress will create an easy axis in the direction of the applied stress. The magnitude of the anisotropy constant for uniaxial anisotropy arising from magnetostriction is

$$K = \frac{3}{2}\lambda\sigma \tag{2.40}$$

where λ is the magnetostriction constant and σ is the applied stress (a positive value of σ corresponds to a tensile stress).

The magnetostriction constant is defined in the following way. Suppose one has a given length of nonmagnetic material. If the material has a positive value of λ, then causing the material to become magnetic will cause the material to lengthen or stretch in the direction of the magnetization. The fractional increase in length is defined as the magnetostriction constant λ. If the material has a negative value of λ, then the material will shorten in the direction of the magnetization. One may be able to see in a crude way that these two descriptions of λ are consistent with each other.

Suppose that λ is positive. Then, assuming that the magnetization is horizontal in Figure 2.18, the material will try to expand in the horizontal direction. Thus, tension in the horizontal direction helps in this effort to expand, and the magnetization is quite content to lie in the horizontal direction; that is, the horizontal direction is an easy axis of magnetization. Typical values of λ are $1–10 \times 10^{-6}$. For a value of λ of 1×10^{-6}, the increase in length will be 1 part per million. This is a small effect, but it is nevertheless very significant in the design and processing of heads containing thin film elements.

2.15 DOMAINS

Now that we understand anisotropy, we can discuss the hysteresis loop behavior in more detail. A typical magnetic material will in general consist of many *magnetic domains*. A *domain* is a local region of the material in which all atomic moments are pointing in the same direction. However, the moment in one domain will not be parallel to the moment in a neighboring domain. For example, in the upper part of Figure 2.19 we show the directions of magnetization in a rectangular slab of material.

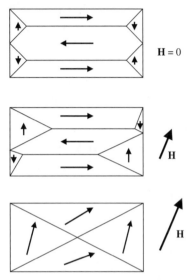

Figure 2.19 Wall motion and domain rotation under application of an external magnetic field.

Each arrow shows the magnetization direction in a particular domain. The lines between domains represent *domain walls*. These walls are very narrow regions—in iron, they are approximately 100 nm (1000 Å) thick—in which the magnetization changes from its direction in one domain to its direction in the adjacent domain. Thus, the magnetization in a magnetic material does not change directions gradually over large distances. The changes in magnetization direction are confined to the very small volume of the material consisting of domain walls.

We have assumed in Figure 2.19 that this material has a uniaxial anisotropy with a horizontal easy axis. Why is not all the magnetization in this figure directed horizontally? The pattern of domains in the top of Figure 2.19 is a particular arrangement that minimizes demagnetizing energy. We saw in our earlier discussion of demagnetizing fields that when the magnetic moment is pointing toward a boundary where the magnetization changes, such as at the edge of the sample, uncompensated magnetic poles appear. These poles create a magnetic field, and this field contains energy. To reduce the demagnetizing energy, the domains try to arrange themselves in such a way as to reduce the number of these poles. In this figure, we note that at all edges of the sample, the magnetization is parallel to the edge. Therefore, no poles are created at the edges. We also note that all magnetization vectors intersect domain walls at the same angle (45°). Thus, the perpendicular components of magnetization on entering and leaving a domain wall are equal, and so there is no net magnetic charge built up at a domain wall. The particular magnetization configuration shown in the figure results in no magnetostatic energy being created by demagnetizing poles on surfaces or on domain walls. Therefore, it is a low-energy configuration.

If a field is applied as shown in the figure, the domain magnetization tries to line up with the field (like the dipole in Fig. 2.7). The first thing that happens is the domain walls begin to move. With very small fields, domains may move reversibly since they sit in small potential wells. This reversible region is shown as the 0-*a* section on the initial hysteresis loop of Figure 2.13. At higher applied fields, as in the middle panel of Figure 2.19, the domains move irreversibly in such a way as to enlarge the domains that are favorably oriented with respect to the field and diminish the domains that are unfavorably oriented. This corresponds to the section *a-b* on the initial hysteresis curve of Figure 2.13. Finally, at large fields, rotation of the domains occurs and domain rotation is reversible (section *b-c* of Fig. 2.13). At a still higher field, all the magnetization points in the field direction, there are no more domain walls, and the sample is said to be saturated ($\mathbf{M} = M_s$ in Fig. 2.13).

How much magnetization switching is due to wall motion and how much is due to domain rotation depends upon the field orientation. If $\mathbf{H}$ is oriented parallel to the easy axis direction, the sample switches entirely by wall motion. If $\mathbf{H}$ is oriented perpendicular to the easy axis, the sample switches entirely by domain rotation. For intermediate fields, the sample switches by a combination of wall motion and domain rotation.

2.16 EXCHANGE

We have discussed that in certain materials like iron and nickel, atomic magnetic dipoles tend to line up with each other to produce an overall magnetization for the material. Materials in which adjacent dipole moments tend to line up in the same direction are called *ferromagnetic*. The occurrence of ferromagnetism is relatively rare—looking at the periodic table, we see that only a few of the pure elements (iron, nickel, cobalt, and gadolinium; see Table 2.1) exhibit ferromagnetism at room temperature. Without this tendency for atomic dipoles to line up parallel to each other, we would not have magnetic recordings, or electric motors, or many of the devices to which we have grown accustomed.

The tendency for neighboring atomic dipoles to line up parallel or antiparallel to each other is called *exchange*. The detailed description of exchange can be given only in terms of quantum mechanics. Basically, exchange results from the overlap of orbiting electrons on adjacent atoms. The atomic moment of an atom is proportional to the angular momentum of the atom. This angular momentum consists of orbital angular momentum due to the rotation of electrons in their orbits and spin angular momentum (called *spin* for short) which is due to the rotation of electrons about their own axes. If we let the spin angular momentum of two electrons on neighboring atoms be s_1 and s_2, we may describe the energy of this pair of electrons in an approximate sense by the following equation:

$$E = -2Js_1 \cdot s_2 \tag{2.41}$$

where J is a constant called the *exchange integral*. If J is positive, the energy is lowest when the two spins are parallel to each other. Therefore, ferromagnetic materials are those in which atoms exhibit a positive value of the exchange integral. For J negative, another type of magnetism results, called *antiferromagnetism*. In an antiferromagnet, the moments of adjacent atoms point in opposite directions and, thus, there is no net macroscopic moment in the material. An example of this type of material is MnFe which has been an important material in the fabrication of MR heads. Still a third type of magnetism is called *ferrimagnetism*. In this case, J is also negative, but the atomic moment on atom A is not equal to the moment on adjacent atom B, so the moments do not completely cancel each other; in this case, the material does exhibit a net (but reduced) magnetic moment. Examples of the spin directions in the three types of magnetic materials are shown in Figure 2.20.

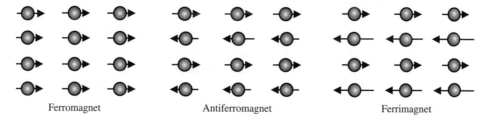

Ferromagnet   Antiferromagnet   Ferrimagnet

Figure 2.20   Atomic moments for three types of magnetism.

The exchange thus far discussed is between spins all in the same material. What about spins between two different materials? Exchange also may occur in this case. However, since exchange is largely a nearest-neighbor phenomenon that occurs across distances typical of the distance between atoms in a solid (a few angstroms), the interface between the two materials must be clean at the atomic level to see such exchange. If there is one atomic layer of oxide between the two materials, that may be enough to destroy the exchange.

An example of exchange between an antiferromagnet such as MnFe and a ferromagnet such as Permalloy is shown in Figure 2.21. In this example, a ferromagnetic film has been deposited first (lower part of figure), followed immediately by an antiferromagnetic film (upper part of figure). The first (lowest) layer of the antiferromagnet has aligned itself by exchange with the topmost layer of the ferromagnet. Such an arrangement is discussed in connection with the MR head; in this case, the antiferromagnet acts as a permanent biasing layer that keeps the ferromagnet pointed in a constant direction (to the left in this figure).

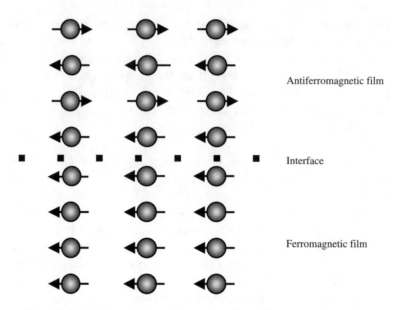

Antiferromagnetic film

Interface

Ferromagnetic film

Figure 2.21 Exchange across a ferro-magnetic–antiferromagnetic interface.

If one measures a hysteresis loop on a sandwich consisting of a ferromagnetic layer and an antiferromagnetic layer, and if exchange across the interface is taking place, then one will probably see a shifted hysteresis loop similar to the one shown in Figure 2.22. The amount of the shift, shown as H_x in the figure, is a direct measure of the exchange coupling across the interface.

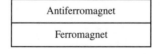

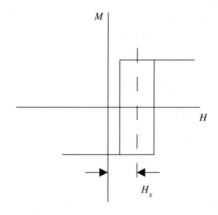

Figure 2.22 Shifted hysteresis loop due to exchange coupling between a ferromagnetic layer and an antiferromagnetic layer.

2.17 MAGNETORESISTANCE

One of the more exciting developments in magnetic recording on rigid disks in recent years is the development of magnetoresistive (MR) heads. The phenomenon of magnetoresistance has been known for a long time. The basic effect is that when a magnetic field is applied to an MR material, like Permalloy, the resistance of the material changes. The phenomenon may be described by

$$R = R_0 + \delta R \cos^2 \theta \tag{2.42}$$

where θ is the angle between the direction of the electrical current and the magnetization, R_0 is a constant independent of θ, and δR is the change in resistance between having the field parallel to the current and having the field perpendicular to the current. When the magnetization is parallel to the current direction ($\theta = 0$), the resistance is a maximum ($R = R_0 + \delta R$). When the magnetization is perpendicular to the current direction ($\theta = 90$ degrees), the resistance has fallen to the value R_0. For Permalloy, the value of $\delta R/R_0$ is about 2%. The effect does not depend directly on H, but only on the direction of M relative to the current direction. The effect of H is simply to change the direction of M. Application of this discussion of magnetoresistance to MR sensors is given in Chapter 6.

REFERENCES

[1] R. M. Bozorth, *Ferromagnetism*, D. Van Nostrand Company, Inc, Princeton, NJ, 1951, p. 2.

[2] C. Kittel, *Introduction to Solid State Physics*, John Wiley & Sons, NY, 1956, p. 425.

3

Disk Drive Magnetic Recording

3.1 INTRODUCTION

Multitrack magnetic audio recording in cassette and open-reel form is universally well known. The drawback of this form of recording is a long access time to a selected section on the tape. In the past, phonograph recording and, now, compact discs are preferred for quick access to a desired selection. In the 1950s, digital magnetic tapes predominated in providing on-line data storage although, for a few years in the late 1950s, expensive and complex drums were employed for critical applications requiring fast access to the data. For reasons analogous to those for the audio recording—that is, access to random data—the evolution of the rigid disk drive began in 1956. In a sense, the disk drive is a hybrid of a digital tape recorder and a phonograph jukebox. Figure 3.1 shows the parts of a disk drive. The disk is often referred to as a *platter*. Disk drive parts and their functions are given in the list that follows.

- The purpose of the disk drive is to store data over a long period of time and retrieve it reliably.
- The head writes and reads data from the disk.
- The head is part of a slider. A slider has a flexible connection to the actuator, and it has a profiled surface facing the medium that forms an air-bearing surface (ABS) allowing the head to "fly" at a close distance from the medium.
- An actuator provides a means of moving the head/slider from one track to another and produces motions to retain the head in the center of the track under servo electronics commands.

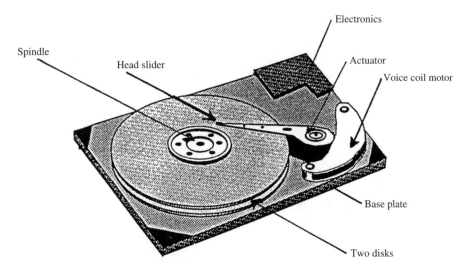

Figure 3.1 Schematic drawing of a disk drive and its parts.

■ A channel converts the digital data to be stored into write currents and supplies them to the head coil. It receives signals read by the head from the medium and translates them to data or usable bit patterns.

For disk drives equal to or larger than 130 mm (5.25 in.) in diameter, linear actuators with comblike head accessing arrangements have been used. For disk diameters of 95 mm (3.5 in.) and smaller, rotary actuators are utilized. Figure 3.1 shows a rotary actuator. To shorten the latency or time of accessing on a given track, the drive rotates between 1800 and 7200 revolutions per minute (RPM). The relative velocity between head and disk is in tens of meters per second. For instance, for a 76 mm diameter track of a disk rotating at 7200 RPM, relative velocity between head and disk is about 29 m/sec (64 mi/hr). To ensure sufficiently long life for the head and magnetic medium on the disk, the head slider attached to the actuator aerodynamically "flies" at close distance of less than 100 nm (4 microinches).

After reviewing the principles of writing and reading, we shall focus on the magnetic writing of data by the head on the medium (magnetic thin layer on a substrate). The magnetic writing process is strongly tied to the recording performance of the disk drive system. Because of its importance, the discussion on writing is divided into parts. The beginning part is simple and fairly intuitive, yet it points out the limitations of the head and medium components, which has led to the evolution of recording technology. Additional topics on writing are described in the last two sections of the chapter. These issues are important for the comprehensive understanding of disk drive recording. The middle sections are dedicated to the reading processes. The significant aspects of reading are how the signal voltages and signal pulse widths vary with the head and medium parameters and the spacing between head and medium. The principles and procedures used in deriving useful equations are explained. As much as possible, simple equations are used for illustrations and clarification of concepts. More complex equations are not derived here, but their applications and simplifications are reviewed and references are pointed out where more details can be found. An inductive head is assumed for most of the discussion. Where appropriate, the comparison of inductive and MR heads is considered, but details of the MR signal characteristics are treated in Chapter 6.

3.2 WRITING AND READING

First, we shall review the writing and reading processes. Figure 3.2 shows a schematic of a ring head and a disk. The head consists of a ring or yoke of magnetic material with a coil of wire wrapped on the core. The coil is connected to the channel electronics. There is a gap at the bottom of the head, close to the medium. The writing sequence is as follows:

1. The channel receives data to be stored from the computer, and after some processing (explained in Chapter 8), generates currents in circuits called *write drivers*.
2. The write driver supplies current to the head coil.
3. The coil current results in magnetization of the "core" of the head. Near the gap, the magnetic field spreads out.
4. Some of the fringe or stray field near the gap reaches the medium and magnetizes it in one direction as seen in Figure 3.2.

As the data changes, depending on the coding rules, the current in the coil is reversed, and the field near the gap reverses, reversing the magnetic poles in the medium. The sequence of data from the channel electronics thus gets translated into magnetized poles in the medium. During reading, the write drivers are switched off and are virtually isolated from the head coil. The reading preamplifier is connected to the head. Assuming that the disk track has previously written data, the following sequence of events or *reading* converts them into *user* bits.

1. As the magnetic poles pass near the head gap, the core of the head becomes magnetized.
2. The direction of magnetization of the core will depend on the direction of the magnetization of the medium.
3. The change in magnetization in the core results in a voltage across the head coil.

Note that only a *change* in magnetization in the medium and, hence, a *change* in magnetic flux through the coil, produces a voltage. According to Faraday's law (Sec. 2.8), $V = -d\phi/dt$ or voltage is generated if the flux changes with time. This is what happens during changing of the magnetization pattern under the head gap. At transitions, where the magnetizations in the medium change, voltage outputs result. Depending on the data, there are two types of transitions possible: north poles facing north poles or south poles facing south poles. These transitions create positive- or negative-going voltage pulses in the head coil. These voltage pulses

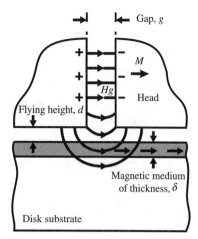

Figure 3.2 Head gap region and head fields.

get amplified and, after a series of detection steps (discussed in Chapter 8), result in usable data supplied to the computing processor.

Figure 3.3 illustrates write and read sequences. Figure 3.3a shows a sequence of data in the form of a series of "ones" and "zeros." In one method of storing this sequence of data, the current through the head coil must reverse at each "one" and not reverse at each "zero" (Fig. 3.3b). When this is done during disk rotation, the magnetization of the disk medium along a disk track looks as in Figure 3.3c. A magnetic transition occurs at each "one" and not at each "zero."

Let's turn now from *writing* data to *reading* data. The operation occurs in reverse. As a written transition passes under the head, a small change in the yoke magnetization occurs (Fig. 3.3d). This change in yoke magnetization induces a voltage in the coil that is sensed by the disk drive electronics (Fig. 3.3e). This occurs each time a transition passes under the head.

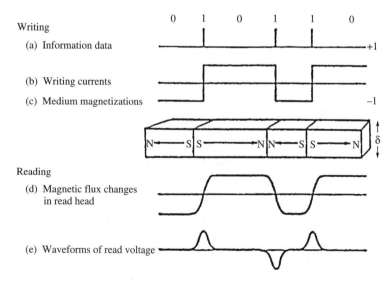

Figure 3.3 Writing and reading data.

From an energy standpoint, the writing and reading of information in the disk drive is highly inefficient. For writing, one needs currents—on the order of a few tens of milliamperes—so that the writing field at the disk medium is high enough to write. On the other hand, for reading, one only has voltages in the range 0.1 to 1 millivolts, and this requires complex external detection and amplification to extract usable data out of such low signals. However, the merit of this technology lies in its ability to store data indefinitely without power, and retrieve it inexpensively and reliably.

3.3 FIELD FROM THE HEAD

The preceding discussion gave a qualitative picture of how data are written to and read from a disk. However, to understand general design principles as well as recent improvements in head and disk designs, one needs to have a quantitative understanding of the factors involved in the writing and reading processes.

A sufficient writing field must be applied to the disk medium to write magnetic transitions. More specifically, the field produced by the head at the medium must at least exceed the coercivity of the medium. However, applying a field equal to H_c to a typical medium as shown in Figure 2.13 will reverse only half the magnetization. Due to the nonsquare nature of these loops, a field equal to two or three times H_c is applied to reverse all the magnetization. A factor of 2.5 is commonly used and will be used in illustrative examples. The stray magnetic field near the gap of an inductive head looks like that shown in Figure 3.4. This figure gives a more detailed (and inverted) picture of the head stray field previously illustrated in Figure 3.2.

The arrows indicate field direction with the length representing the magnitude of the field strength. Notice that arrow directions are effectively horizontal at the

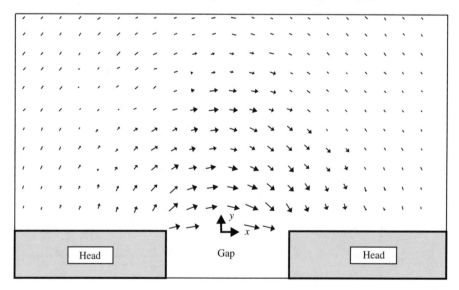

Figure 3.4 Head field and contours of equal fields.

center of the gap above the gap center. Everywhere else, they are at various angles with respect to the horizontal or x axis. First, we obtain a simple equation of the head field based on an intuitive argument and later we discuss a more accurate one. In Figure 3.4, it seems that the field contours are circular; that is, equal fields are located on the circumference of a circle. Recalling Ampere's law (refer to Sec. 2.7), the magnetic field surrounding a straight conductor with current is radially distributed, and the field is given by $I/2\pi r$, where r is the radius of the circular path. In the limiting case for the head where the gap becomes very small, the field contours become circular and the value of the field at radius r approaches $ni/\pi r$ amperes/meter. Here, i is the current in the coil, n is the number of coil turns, and ni is the ampere turns or approximately the magnetomotive force at the gap. The denominator has πr instead of $2\pi r$ because the field is integrated over a semicircle instead of a full circle as is done in the definition of Ampere's law (refer to Sec. 2.7). For longitudinal recording, our main interest is the magnetic field in the x direction. Converting the foregoing field from cylindrical (r, θ) coordinates to cartesian (x, y) coordinates, x and y components of the field are given by

$$H_x = \frac{ni}{\pi} \frac{y}{(x^2 + y^2)}, \qquad H_y = \frac{ni}{\pi} \frac{x}{(x^2 + y^2)} \tag{3.1}$$

The x field equation will be used several times in the text since it allows usable voltage signal equations and simplifies the understanding of recording concepts. Strictly speaking, the validity of the equation requires that the gap is negligible or very small compared to the distance y. In many cases, the equation is usable even when y is only slightly larger than gap g. However, as relatively smaller flying heights are used, there is a need for an accurate field equation including gap parameter for design.

More general equations for the x and y fields of a ring head of infinite poles have been derived [1] and are

$$H_x(x, y) = \frac{H_g}{\pi} \left(\arctan \frac{x + g/2}{y} - \arctan \frac{x - g/2}{y} \right) \tag{3.2}$$

$$H_y(x, y) = \frac{-H_g}{2\pi} \ln \left[\frac{(x + g/2)^2 + y^2}{(x - g/2)^2 + y^2} \right] \tag{3.3}$$

In these equations g is the gap and H_g is the magnetic field strength inside the head gap due to current in the coil (Fig. 3.2). The units of H_x and H_y are the same as the units of H_g. Since equation (3.2) plays a major role in longitudinal recording, let us examine it more closely. There is a simple way of visualizing equation (3.2). The difference of the two arctangent functions in the parentheses is nothing more than the angle θ subtended by the gap at a location x, y, where the value of field is required. The geometric construction is illustrated in Figure 3.5.

Accordingly, equation (3.2) can be simply written as

$$H_x(x, y) = \frac{H_g}{\pi} \theta \tag{3.4}$$

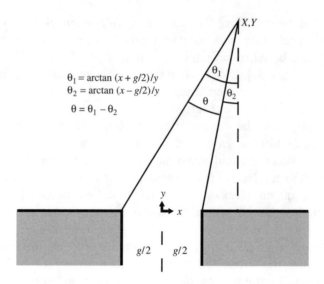

Figure 3.5 Karlqvist head field in terms of an angle.

where θ is as defined in the last paragraph and is in radians. $H_x(x, y)$ is the largest
where θ is the largest; that is, from Figure 3.5 where the point of interest x, y is
closest to the gap and directly over the gap ($\theta = \pi$ and $H_x = H_g$). Using the angle
θ, one can qualitatively plot the contours of equal fields surrounding the gap of a
ring head.

Figure 3.6 shows plots of H_x and H_y along the x and y axes. The x-axis values are divided by g, and head fields H_x and H_y are divided by H_g to make these uni-

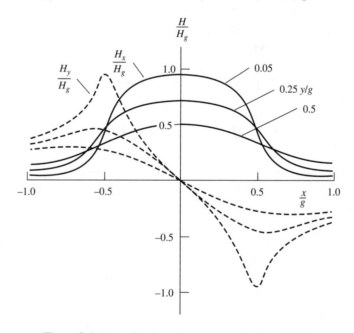

Figure 3.6 Normalized x and y components of head field.

versal plots, that is, independent of particular g and H_g values. Three field contours are shown for y/g values of 0.05, 0.25, and 0.5. As illustrated earlier in Figure 3.4, the H_x component of the field (solid lines in Fig. 3.6) is maximum along the vertical axis. H_x also is shown growing larger as y becomes smaller, that is, nearer the head. H_y, on the other hand (dashed lines), is zero at the gap center; there is no vertical component of the field along the vertical center line (see Fig. 3.4). However, this field peaks at some distance from the center line. It turns out that the locations on the x axis, where the H_y field is a maximum or a minimum in Figure 3.6, are the points where the H_x field is 50% of the maximum value of H_x. The values of x, where H_y has a maximum and a minimum, are obtained by differentiating it with respect to x on the right-hand side of equation (3.2) and equating the result to zero. We define the distance between these two x values, where H_x is 50% of its peak value as the half width (Δx) of H_x. The value of Δx can be obtained in equation form by manipulating equations (3.2) and (3.3).

$$\Delta x = 2\left[\left(\frac{g}{2}\right)^2 + y^2\right]^{1/2} \tag{3.5}$$

The equation gives the half width of the x component of the head field. In Section 3.7, it will be seen that under certain conditions, the shape of the read voltage pulse becomes identical to that of the head field, and the same equation (3.5) gives a pulse half width of the read voltage. Note that in the close vicinity of the gap ($y = 0$), Δx becomes equal to the gap size g. Putting $x = 0$ in equation (3.2), we get the (peak) horizontal field along the y axis. This equation is plotted in Figure 3.7.

$$H_x(0, y) = \frac{2H_g}{\pi} \arctan \frac{g}{2y} \tag{3.6}$$

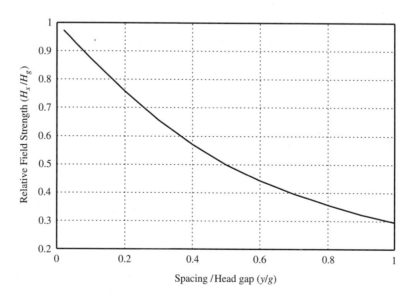

Figure 3.7 Peak head field as a function of the ratio of spacing and gap.

The following example is given to demonstrate the use of this equation and increase familiarity with the nomenclature. The example also points out the importance of parameters that lead to head and medium technology enhancements.

3.4 EXAMPLE: HEAD FIELD CALCULATION

The objectives are, first, to calculate the head gap field, which allows writing magnetic transitions on the medium and second, to calculate the current required in the head coil to produce this field. The following parameters are assumed:

1. The medium has a coercivity of 1600 Oe (127 kA/m).
2. A field H_x equal to 2.5 times the coercivity of the medium is required for proper writing.
3. Head gap $g = 400$ nm.
4. Flying height (magnetic distance between head and medium, Fig. 3.2) $y = 100$ nm.
5. Medium thickness is considered negligibly small compared to the flying height.

Solving equation (3.6) for H_g results in $H_g = 5666$ Oe (451 kA/m).

More easily and less accurately, Figure 3.7 may be used to calculate the same quantity. For $y/g = 100$ nm/400 nm $= 0.25$, $H_x/H_g = 0.7$. For a field at the medium of 1600 Oe (127 kA/m) $\times 2.5 = 4000$ Oe (318 kA/m), a gap field of 4000 Oe/0.7 $= 5700$ Oe (454 kA/m) is required.

This field in the gap is generated by the head coil current. It is assumed that all the ampere turns (current multiplied by number of turns) are utilized to produce a head gap field. This happens if the permeability of the head material is very high. The magnetomotive force (refer to Sec. 2.10) required to produce a gap field is given by $H_g \times g = (451 \times 10^3) \times (400 \times 10^{-9}) = 180.4$ ma for a single-turn head. For a 20-turn head a current of 9 ma would be required. In practice, the permeability of the material is finite, and not all the field generated by the coil reaches the head gap. To account for the geometry of the head and permeability of the head core, the term "head efficiency" is introduced. The next section describes a formula to calculate head efficiency for a ring head structure.

3.5 HEAD EFFICIENCY AND FIELD IN THE GAP

The magnetic circuit of the ring head can be approximated by two reluctances in series: that of the head gap and that of the head core (see Sec. 2.10 for a discussion of magnetic circuits). These reluctances are given by $\mathcal{R}_g$ and $\mathcal{R}_c$ as

$$\mathcal{R}_g = \frac{g}{\mu_0 A_g}, \qquad \mathcal{R}_c = \frac{l_c}{\mu A_c} \tag{3.7}$$

where g and l_c = the lengths of the gap and head core
A_g and A_c = the gap and head core areas, respectively
μ = the permeability of the head core material.

The magnetomotive force provided by the coil current is divided between these two reluctances. Since the magnetomotive force (mmf) across the gap results only in a gap field, the efficiency of the head is given by

$$\eta = \frac{\mathcal{R}_g}{\mathcal{R}_g + \mathcal{R}_c} = \frac{1}{1 + (l_c\mu_0/g\mu)(A_g/A_c)} \tag{3.8}$$

The total mmf is the ampere turns ni which is the summation of mmfs across the head core and the gap; that is, $ni = H_g\, g + H_h\, l_c$. Hence, efficiency in terms of ampere turns or mmf is defined as

$$\eta = \frac{H_g g}{H_h l_c + H_g g} = \frac{H_g g}{ni} \tag{3.9}$$

Solving equation (3.9) for H_g gives

$$H_g = \eta\frac{ni}{g} \tag{3.10}$$

Substituting equation (3.8) into (3.10) gives

$$H_g = \frac{ni}{g + (l_c\mu_0/\mu)(A_g/A_c)} \tag{3.11}$$

Equation (3.11) is the final equation, giving the head gap field in terms of the geometry of the head (n, g, l_c, A_g, A_c), head material (μ), and current (i) through the head coil. Substituting this into equations (3.2) and (3.3) allows us to calculate the head field at a given location x, y near the head gap.

Equation (3.10) has a limitation. Increasing the current in a ring head coil does not increase H_g indefinitely. Once the magnetization of the yoke reaches its saturation value M_s, no additional field may be created on the gap surface and the H_g attains its maximum value, which turns out to be M_s. The highest value of saturation magnetization M_s for ferrite material is obtained in hot-pressed MnZn ferrite and is about 6000 gauss (480 kA/m); hence, this is the maximum value of H_g. This points out a limitation of ferrite heads and suggests a motivation for the development of metal-in-gap (MIG) and thin film heads.

3.6 READING OF MAGNETIC DISK DATA

Writing and reading processes are qualitatively discussed in Section 3.2. The next few sections describe reading in more detail. When a magnetic transition on the disk medium (Fig. 3.3c) passes under the ring head, a voltage is induced in the coil of the head (Fig. 3.3e). This voltage constitutes the read signal from the disk. The objective now is to formulate equations for this induced voltage as a function of head parameters, media parameters, and flying height. These equations are used by the designer to arrive at appropriate compromises in selecting components and channel electronics. Some of these results point out the evolution of new technological developments toward high-density disk drive recording.

Sections 3.3, 3.4, and 3.5 discussed the head field as a function of head geometry and current through the coil. In this section, a voltage equation is derived by relating the head field to the medium magnetization. In this discussion, only the x component of the field and medium magnetizations are considered; hence, the subscript y is omitted in their representations. The longitudinal head field $H(x)$ creates a magnetic flux $\phi_m(x)$ in the media

$$\phi_m(x) = \mu_0 H(x) w \delta \tag{3.12}$$

where w is the track width and δ is the medium thickness. The current in the head coil generates the magnetic field, and it magnetizes the medium. For reading, it is useful to formulate how the magnetized transitions in the medium result in flux changes in the head coil, which in turn produces an output signal. Every element of the magnetized medium contributes to flux change in the head gap and generation of voltage pulse. If contributions of all the elements of the medium are integrated, total flux changes and output voltage pulse can be obtained. However, this procedure is difficult to carry out analytically. There is a shortcut method known as the *principle of reciprocity,* which simplifies the mathematical derivation. Those familiar with the concept of mutual inductance between two coils already know the reciprocity principle. Figure 3.8 shows two coils, one of the head and the other (virtual coil) of medium magnetization. When current i_h flows through the head coil, flux ϕ_m is generated in the section of the medium and is given by

$$\phi_m = L_{hm} i_h \tag{3.13}$$

where L_{hm} is the mutual inductance between two coils.

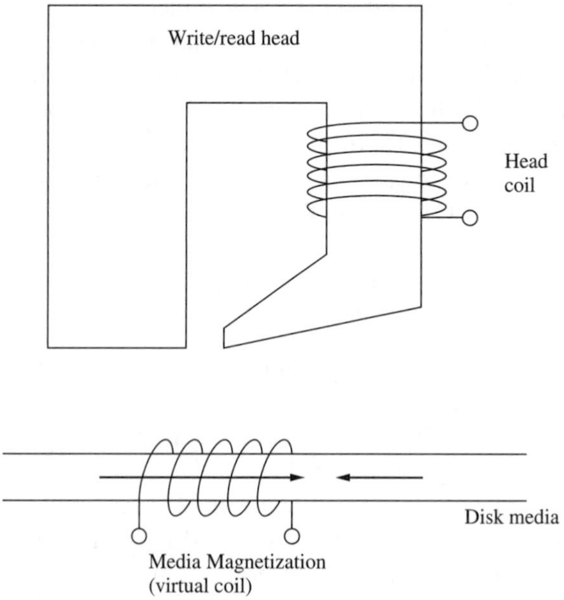

Figure 3.8 Principle of reciprocity applied to head and magnetic media.

Likewise, under the influence of medium magnetization (virtual current), flux ϕ_h is generated in the head coil and is given by

$$\phi_h = L_{mh}i_m \tag{3.14}$$

The reciprocity principle simply states that these mutual inductances are equal. With this consideration, flux in the head coil due to medium magnetization is given as

$$\phi_h = i_m \frac{\phi_m}{i_h} \tag{3.15}$$

Now at any point in the medium, the track is rotating at a velocity v; hence, location of a point in medium with reference to center line of the head ($x = 0$) is given by $x - x'$, where x' is equal to vt. Medium magnetization at a point is given by $M(x - x')$. This magnetization along the length of distance dx for an area of $w\delta$, where δ is the medium thickness and w is the track width, can be treated as a source of current with magnitude:

$$i_m = M(x - x')dx \tag{3.16}$$

Combining equations (3.15), (3.16), and (3.12), the head field due to an element of medium magnetization is given by

$$d\phi_h = \mu_0 w\delta M(x - x')dx\frac{H(x)}{i_h} \tag{3.17}$$

The total field in the head coil due to medium magnetization is given by the integration

$$\phi_h(x') = w\delta\mu_o \int_{-\infty}^{\infty} M(x - x')\frac{H(x)}{i_h}dx \tag{3.18}$$

The reciprocity relation utilized in the preceding derivation is a basic technique frequently used in magnetic recording; hence, we give here a slightly modified example from [2] that illustrates the principle of reciprocity very well. Interference from a local FM station at a frequency range in excess of 88 MHz is often experienced by engineers during tests on test stands. The noise of several microvolts in the head output signal from such a source is observed if the room is poorly shielded. Let us say that a 100-ampere current in a station antenna creates 10 μV of noise in the head under test. If we were to pass a 100-ampere current through the head (not practical!), the radio station would experience 10 μV of noise on its signal. If we know the result of transmission in one direction, the outcome for the reverse condition can be predicted.

Equation (3.18) is often stated as a three-dimensional integral [4]. However, in practice, medium magnetization in the x direction is the most important one. Assumption of uniform magnetization along the z direction results in track width w in the equation, and summation of fields in the y direction results in the medium thickness δ. It is also implied that the head to medium spacing d is large compared to medium thickness δ. The next step is to obtain the voltage equation as a function of t or x', which is vt, where v is the velocity of disk rotation:

$$V(x') = V(vt) = -n\frac{d\phi}{dx'}\frac{dx'}{dt} = -nv\frac{d\phi}{dx'} \tag{3.19}$$

Note that n is the number of head turns. Combining equations (3.18) and (3.19), we obtain

$$V(x') = -\mu_o nvw\delta \int_{-\infty}^{\infty} \frac{dM(x - x')}{dx'}\frac{H(x)}{i_h}dx \tag{3.20}$$

For an explicit analytical function of the voltage, it is necessary to define the slope of medium magnetization within the transition. For a qualitative look at voltage generation as a result of medium transitions, see Figure 3.3.

3.7 READING WITH STEP-FUNCTION MAGNETIC TRANSITIONS

In equation (3.20), the voltage of a ring head is expressed as a function of the derivative of medium magnetization. This derivative can be evaluated if the magnetization and its changes in the x direction are known. Magnetization and its transitions in magnetic recording are widely studied subjects and are reported in many textbooks and papers. Three types of transitions have been studied in detail:

1. An ideal step-function transition (Fig. 3.9).
2. A transition with magnetization in the transition region obeying an arctan function of distance (Fig. 3.10).
3. Transitions with magnetization varying as a sinusoidal function in the x direction (Fig. 3.18).

First, assume that the magnetization change or transition is a step function, that is, the magnetization in the transition, M_x, that goes abruptly from $-M_r$ to $+M_r$ at location $x = x'$ (Fig. 3.9), where M_r is the remanent magnetization of the medium. The derivative of a step function is known as a *Dirac delta function* and is designated by δ (we will call it δ_D to distinguish it from our medium thickness). Differentiation of M_x will be given by

$$\frac{dM_x(x - x')}{dx} = 2M_r\delta_D(x - x') \tag{3.21}$$

By substituting equation (3.21) into equation (3.20) and using the standard property of integrals involving the delta function, equation (3.20) becomes

$$V(x') = -2\mu_o nvw(M_r\delta)\frac{H(x')}{i_h} \tag{3.22}$$

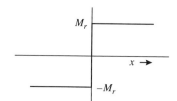

Figure 3.9 Step-function transition of
medium magnetization.

This equation suggests a number of important points.

1. The voltage output of an inductive head is directly proportional to $H(x')$. Because of this proportionality, measurement of the voltage pulse waveform reflects the head field characteristics. This could be used to characterize head geometry.

2. The voltage is proportional to $M_r\delta$, which contains all the medium parameters. This quantity indicates medium *strength*. For example, in the case of a particulate medium, the particles of the magnetic material are relatively far apart and have low magnetization; hence, it is difficult to obtain a high M_r. For thin magnetic coatings, 100% of the medium material is magnetic, so M_r can be quite large. The film thickness can be very small, yet the product $M_r\delta$ can be sufficiently large to give adequate signal voltage.

3. The voltage output of an inductive head is also proportional to the number of coil turns n, the velocity of the disk v, and the track width of the head w.

Until now, we have not considered the efficiency of the head, but that term also directly multiplies to the right-hand-side function of the voltage. Substitution of equations (3.2) and (3.10) in (3.22) gives analytical function of the voltage,

$$V(x') = -2\mu_o \left(\frac{\eta n v w}{\pi g}\right)(M_r\delta)\left(\arctan\frac{x' + g/2}{d} - \arctan\frac{x - g/2}{d}\right) \quad (3.23)$$

where d is the flying height (parameter y). The peak voltage can be obtained by putting $x' = 0$ in equation (3.23) and P_{50}, or the half width of the voltage pulse is the same as the half width of the field and is given by equation (3.5).

3.8 READING ARCTANGENT MAGNETIC TRANSITIONS

The most widely used assumption in digital recording about the shape of the magnetization is an arctan function of x [3]. This is given as

$$M_x = \frac{2}{\pi}M_r\left(\arctan\frac{x}{a}\right) \quad (3.24)$$

At large values of $+x$ and $-x$, the arctan function approaches $+\pi/2$ and $-\pi/2$, respectively, making M_r and $-M_r$ limiting values for M_x (Fig. 3.10). Only one

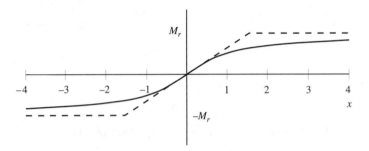

Figure 3.10 Arctan magnetic transition.

parameter a is needed to specify the transition characteristics. The parameter a is known as the *transition parameter* and is a measure of the width of the transition. The voltage equation is obtained by substituting arctan function for the magnetization transition in equation (3.20) and integrating. We shall not go into this process but simply give the result.

$$V(x',d) = -2\mu_0 \left(\frac{\eta n \upsilon w}{\pi g}\right)(M_r \delta)\left(\arctan \frac{x' + g/2}{a + d} - \arctan \frac{x' - g/2}{a + d}\right) \qquad (3.25)$$

This equation has the same form as that of equation (3.23), except that in place of d, $a + d$ is substituted. This is interesting and important, as the effect of transition broadening from width 0 (step function) to width a is equivalent to adding a to flying height d, making effective flying height as $a + d$. Substituting $x' = 0$ in equation (3.25), the peak voltage for this case is obtained,

$$V_{p-p} = 8\mu_0 \left(\frac{\eta n \upsilon w}{\pi g}\right)(M_r \delta) \arctan\left(\frac{g/2}{a + d}\right) \qquad (3.26)$$

and substituting $a + d$ in place of y in equation (3.5), the half width of the voltage pulse is given by

$$P_{50} = 2\left[\left(\frac{g}{2}\right)^2 + (a + d)^2\right]^{1/2} \qquad (3.27)$$

Note that a and d in equations (3.26) and (3.27) always occur as a summation $a + d$. Decreasing $a + d$ increases peak voltage and reduces the half width of the voltage pulse or slims the pulse. Narrow pulses allow increased linear density. Much research is directed toward (1) decreasing d by innovations in the head-disk interface and (2) improving medium to achieve shorter a. Sections 3.11 and 3.12 discuss plots of these parameters and engineering optimization of the system using these equations. Derivation of equation (3.27) assumes that the thickness of the medium is very small compared to flying height. However, the equation can be generalized, including medium thickness, and the result is given as [4].

$$P_{50} = 2 \left[\left(\frac{g}{2} \right)^2 + (a + d)(a + d + \delta) \right]^{\frac{1}{2}}$$ (3.28)

$$= [g^2 + 4(a + d)(a + d + \delta)]^{\frac{1}{2}}$$

3.9 TRANSITION PARAMETER *a*

Achieving the narrowest possible transition (smallest *a* value) allows placing recorded bits close together and hence results in high linear density. Until now, we have not defined how one can find this parameter. Several authors have reported the derivation of *a* by taking into account a detailed writing process using nonlinear B–H loop (refer to Sec. 2.13) characteristics of the medium [2–5]. The most practical equation used for head-disk modeling studies is given by

$$a = K \left(\frac{M_r \delta d_{eff}}{H_c} \right)^{1/2}$$ (3.29)

where $M_r \delta$ has the same meaning used in this chapter. H_c is the coercivity of the medium. In the equation, M_r and H_c are expressed in SI units (A/m). If M_r and H_c are expressed in cgs units, that is, emu/cm^3 and Oe, M_r is multiplied by 4π as ampere/meter. *K* is a constant derived analytically after several considerations, some of which are

1. The head field applied during writing is optimized for shortest transition distance.
2. The demagnetization field is taken into account.
3. Head imaging into the medium is included.
4. Finite remanent coercivity of the medium is also included.

The approximate value of *K* from [3] and [6] is 0.87. With simplifications of a Lorentzian pulse form in place of the Karlqvist field function and other assumptions [4], the value of *K* turns out to be $1/\sqrt{\pi}$, or 0.565. In case of cgs values for M_r and H_c, *K* modifies to 3.1 and 2, respectively. The d_{eff} is the geometrical mean distance from head to medium and is expressed by

$$d_{eff} = [d(d + \delta)]^{1/2}$$ (3.30)

Equation (3.29) indicates that the reduction in *a* and increased linear density may be achieved by decreasing the effective flying height d_{eff}, increasing the coercivity H_c of the medium, and decreasing the thickness δ of the magnetic medium. Smaller M_r could also reduce *a*, but as seen in equation (3.26), a smaller $M_r \delta$ would reduce the signal voltage, and so there must be a compromise.

Increasing the coercivity H_c of the medium requires a larger write field from the head. This has motivated the development of MIG heads, thick-pole thin-film heads, and high-magnetic-moment materials for MR-head write elements.

3.10 EXAMPLE: CALCULATIONS OF TRANSITION PARAMETER a, V_{p-p}, AND P_{50}

This example is chosen to put some real dimensions into the use of the preceding equations. One of the problems in making calculations of recording parameters is mixed units. We intend to use SI units as much as possible. However, some scientists and engineers are not going to abandon the use of cgs units, so one objective of this exercise is to practice conversions of popular units into SI units to arrive at useful, final results. A discussion of units will contribute to an understanding of the concepts. So clarification of ideas is yet another goal of the example. The following parameters are assumed for this exercise:

$\eta = 0.8$ efficiency of the head

$n = 30$ head coil turns

$v = 20$ meters per second, velocity of the medium under head

$w = 8$ μm, track width of the head

$g = 0.25$ μm

$M_r = 800$ kA/m (800 emu/cm^{-3})

$\delta = 30$ nm (300 A°), medium thickness

$d = 100$ nm (4 μin.)

$H_c = 130$ kA/m (1600 Oe)

$\mu_0 = 4\pi \times 10^{-7}$ Vs/Am (H/m)

$M_r\delta$ in SI units is $800,000 \times 30 \times 10^{-9} = 24 \times 10^{-3}$ A (2.4×10^{-3} emu/cm^{-2}). Note that in SI units, medium strength is expressed in the unit of current. Treatment of medium strength as a coil current is exemplified by the unit dimension. One can express $M_r\delta$ as 24 milliamperes of current.

Next, a is calculated from equation (3.29). Since we want an answer for a in nanometers, δ and d_{eff} can be retained in nanometers for the calculation. Using the value of K as 0.87, a is computed to be 119 nm. Equation (3.26) is used for the calculation of peak-to-peak voltage V_{p-p}. $M_r\delta$ should be expressed in amperes, as shown earlier. The ratio of track width to gap need not be converted into meters and can be written in micrometers. The quantities in the ratio of gap to the summation of d and a within the arctan function can also be totally expressed in nanometers and need not be converted to meters. The V_{p-p} is calculated to be ($1180 \times$ arctan function value of 0.518) $\times 10^{-6}$ volts, or 616 μV. It is common practice to express head

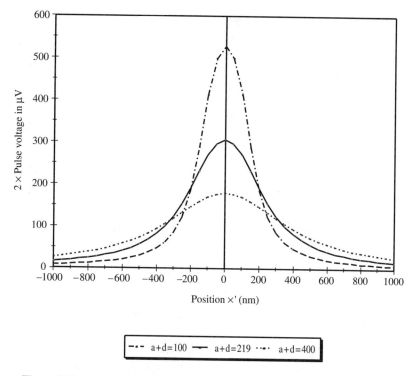

Figure 3.11 Isolated pulse voltage variations with spacing and transition parameters.

voltage in nanovolts per 1-μm track width, per meter/sec velocity, and per turn. This quantity is calculated as 127 nV/μm per m/sec per turn. This method of normalizing signal voltage is useful in comparing heads. Half-pulse width P_{50} is calculated from equation (3.28): $P_{50} = [(250)^2 + 4(119 + 100)(119 + 100 + 30)]^{1/2} = 530$ nanometers. P_{50} is an important parameter that determines the ability of the system to achieve high densities. These topics are discussed in Chapter 8, Section 8.18.

3.11 SIGNAL VOLTAGE PARAMETERS AND ENGINEERING APPROXIMATIONS

Voltage pulses described in equations (3.25) and (3.26) and half-width expressions (3.28) are now analyzed as functions of a head/disk system. The parameters used in the example in Section 3.10 are also used in plotting the graphs discussed later in this chapter. It should be noted that much of this discussion applies to inductive (ferrite, MIG, and film) heads. A similar analysis is carried out for MR heads in Section 6.18. Certain parameters like gap, g, get modified for MR head, and there is no velocity dependence for the magnetoresistive heads. Figure 3.11 shows three pulses

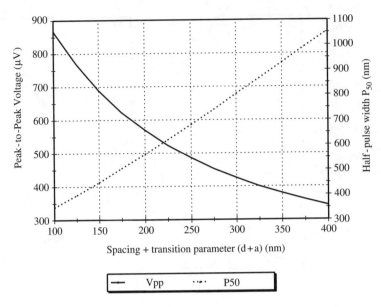

Figure 3.12 Peak-to-peak voltages and half-pulse widths versus $d + a$.

calculated using equation (3.25) with variations in parameter $d + a$. As described earlier, d is the head-medium spacing, and a is the transition parameter. In the equations these parameters always occur as a summation, so conclusions drawn from the figure are valid if only one parameter is varied at a time or both the parameters are changed simultaneously. As $a + d$ is increased, the voltage peak decreases. Also the pulse gets widened, making P_{50} larger as a function of $a + d$. This is further illustrated in Figure 3.12. In Figure 3.12, peak-to-peak voltage (equation 3.26) and P_{50} (equation 3.28) are plotted as continuous functions of $a + d$. The message is clear that low-flying heights and narrow transitions are important to get adequate signal and short-pulse widths.

The signal voltage is related to thin film medium saturation magnetization M_r in two ways. Higher M_r results in increased signal strength and hence an increase in output voltage. However, a large M_r increases the transition parameter a, which tends to reduce voltage. Figure 3.13 shows the cross-over in case of M_r versus isolated peak-to-peak signal voltage. The figure also shows the increase in P_{50} as a function of M_r because of increasing values of a.

Practitioners prefer simple expressions for quick derivations and comparisons with experimental results. Here are some ideas which may be helpful. Section 3.3 indicated that if the gap of the head is very small, an approximate $H_x(x, y)$ field is obtained as given by equation (3.1). If this approximation is used instead of the Karlqvist equation in the integration of equation (3.20), a simple voltage pulse form can be given as

$$V(x) = \frac{V_{\max}}{1 + (2x/P_{50})^2} \tag{3.31}$$

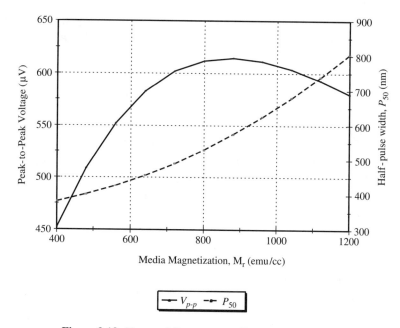

Figure 3.13 V_{p-p} and P_{50} versus media magnetization M_r.

where P_{50} is given by $a + d$. This equation is known as a *Lorentzian pulse,* and one can see that at $x = \pm P_{50}/2$, the voltage is half its peak value, which confirms the definition of P_{50}.

To verify the degree of validity and usefulness of equation (3.31), the normalized value of equation (3.25) is compared with the normalized value of equation (3.31) in Figure 3.14.

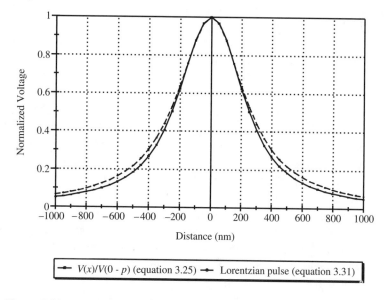

Figure 3.14 Comparison of normalized voltage waveform with Lorentzian pulse.

Normalization of equation (3.25) means that the equation is divided by zero-to-peak voltage (1/2 of peak-to-peak voltage of equation 3.26) so that the peak value of normalized voltage is 1. Normalization of equation (3.31) is obtained by dividing the right side of the equation by V_{max}. The correlation between these two cases is good. One application of this form of equation is to compute the roll-off curve to obtain resolutions of the overlapping pulses at high densities. This is described in Chapter 8.

Equation (3.31) would be more useful if there were some way of estimating V_{max}. Here we suggest an approximate procedure useful for a rough estimate. Observation of Figure 3.12 suggests reciprocal relationship between P_{50} and V_{p-p}. Utilizing this observation and information from the accurate equations described, V_{max} may be derived from

$$V_{max} \propto \frac{\mu_0 n v w (M_r \delta)}{P_{50}} \tag{3.32}$$

where all the variables are as discussed earlier. So the task boils down to finding the proportionality constant, which may be obtained experimentally.

3.12 DIGITAL WRITING PROCESS: DISCUSSION AND GRAPHICAL ILLUSTRATION

A large amount of experimental and analytical or numerical modeling has been done on the subject of the write process in magnetic recording. However, the complete solution of the process has not been attained, as it involves nonlinear and complex medium magnetization processes, transition formation details, and dynamics of head and medium interactions.

Here we shall describe only the qualitative principles of the writing procedures to understand interactions among component properties and parameters. Two parameters of interest involve how the transition of magnetization from one direction to the other is formed: what contributes to the variability in its length, and what contributes to the variation in distance (length jitter) between such transitions. The first parameter is useful in designing for high linear density, and the second pertains to error-free detection of the signal. The writing process includes application of current to the head coil, which produces a field in and near the gap of the head. The field reaching the medium either supports the existing direction of magnetization direction or opposes it, creating a reversed magnetized region in the medium. The process of medium magnetization follows the M–H (medium magnetization as a function of applied field H, see Section 2.13) hysteresis loop curve. The magnetization reversal in the medium happens in the spread-out region, and this is the transition region we referred to in the last few sections. Going through the step-by-step understanding of the writing process will help the practitioner know the measures used to design the write/read electronics as well as appreciate the measurement practices used in the industry.

Figure 3.15 shows the building blocks of the writing process. The writing process is complex, due to time and distance factors becoming intermingled along with nonlinear magnetization process in the medium. However, it is possible to develop a sufficient qualitative understanding of the process. When digital data is written on a disk track, the medium is magnetized to saturation in one or the other direction. Incomplete or nonsaturated writing results in uneven signal outputs and causes errors. The process of writing involves a head that provides a magnetic field sufficient to reverse magnetizations in selected locations of the track. This is called *overwriting*, and its measurement is discussed in Section 8.16.

In Figure 3.15 a head and medium are shown. The medium has a magnetization in the direction of the arrow on the right-hand side of the head gap center. A current is applied instantaneously (step function) in a direction to produce a field that reverses the magnetization in the medium. Instantaneous application of current is assumed in order to clarify the basic concept. The influence of finite-time current application is considered later. The nature of the head field is described in Section 3.3, and it is shown that the x component of the head field in medium is strongest in the center line of the gap. This is also illustrated in Figure 3.15b. The field in the medium varies from x_1 to x_2. At x_1 the field is weak, while at x_2 it is strong. Corresponding to locations x_1 and x_2 in the medium, the head fields are shown as H_1 and H_2 in Figure 3.15b, and these fields are applied to the medium, resulting in magnetizations M_1 and M_2, as shown on the M–H loop in Figure 3.15c. The medium M–H loop is shown rotated 90° to simplify drawing and explanation. The magnetization M_1 at distance x_1 is too small, and only weak reverse magnetization results. At field H_2 magnetization is almost reversed close to the saturation in the reverse direction. In Figure 3.15d medium magnetization values from location x_1 to x_2 are plotted. This is the same as the transition region, and the shape of the change in magnetization is simulated by equation (3.24).

With the foregoing visualization of writing in a magnetic medium, the following points can be made:

1. The steepness of the change in the head field would influence the transition length.

2. A steep M–H loop slope can reduce transition length (a perfectly square loop is ideal).

3. The current applied to the coil to generate the H field is a function of time. If the current versus time has a shallow slope, the H field generated will be gradual. Inductance and capacitance of the head writing circuit contributes to delays in generation of fields. These factors adversely contribute to the field generation and result in elongation of transition time and length of magnetic transition. These issues become more acute at high medium velocity (RPM) and high data rates.

4. Whenever a magnetic field is changed in magnetic material, a demagnetizing field is set up in the material, and this reduces the influence of the applied field trying to magnetize the material. This is manifested in the

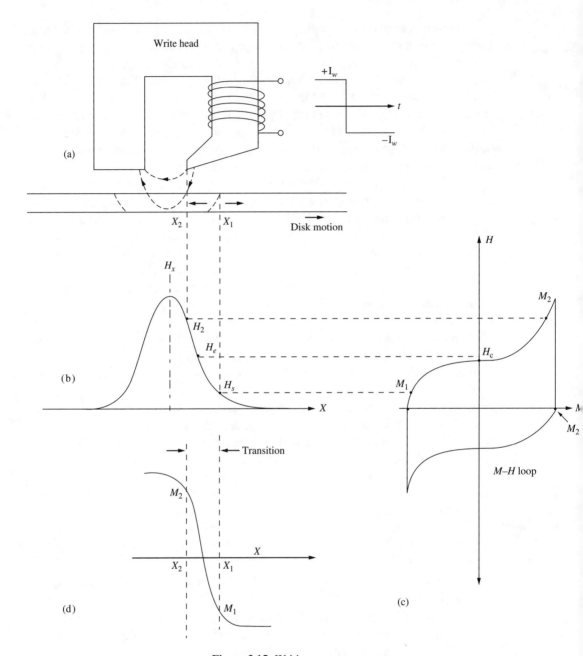

Figure 3.15 Writing process sequence.

phenomenon of "like poles repel each other." Section 2.6 describes demagnetizing fields.

Due to demagnetization fields, when the head field is supporting an already existing direction, the length of magnetization tends to elongate, and when the head field opposes the existing magnetization direction, the length of that section tends to become narrower. The discrepancies in the lengths of the segments result in variations in locations of transition regions and create what is known as *peak jitter* in resultant sequence of signal pulses. This adversely affects linear density. As a matter of fact, the derivation of transition parameter a is based on equating a demagnetizing field slope to the applied field of the head.

3.13 SIDE WRITING, READING, ERASING, AND FRINGING FIELDS OF HEADS

In all the discussion of the magnetic field from the head and its influence on the medium so far, we have considered x and y directions. Direction x is where the head poles and gap are located, and y is the direction from the head toward the medium, as shown in Figure 3.16. For the third direction, z, we have assumed that writing and signal production occur only in the width of the head. This is a reasonable assumption for wide tracks. However, as track densities increase and tracks get narrower, the influence of fringing fields beyond the physical track width becomes important. We review this subject qualitatively with the help of Figures 3.16 and 3.17. Reference [7] gives quantitative discussion of this topic. In Figure 3.16, the axes x, y, and

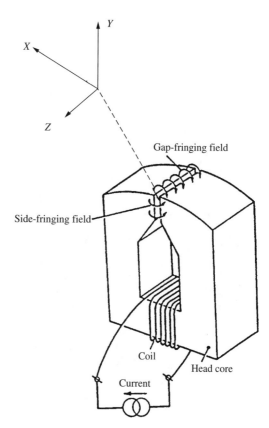

Figure 3.16 Side-fringing field of a head. [7]

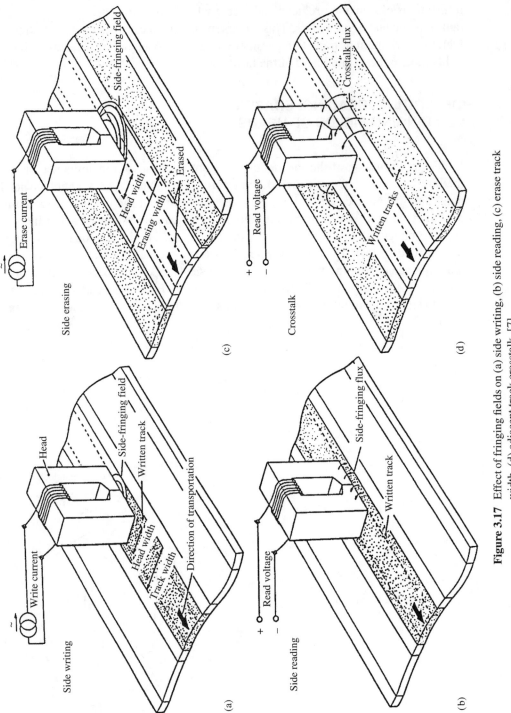

Figure 3.17 Effect of fringing fields on (a) side writing, (b) side reading, (c) erase track width, (d) adjacent track crosstalk. [7]

z are indicated. In Section 3.4, the head field in the medium at distance d is calculated. The field of at least H_c is required to reverse magnetization in the medium. However, 2.5 H_c is provided to fully saturate the medium and allow for variations in the field due to flying height, partial head saturation, and so on. For the calculation of this field, it is assumed (implicit in the Karlqvist equation) that the head is infinitely long in the $\pm z$ direction. Now if the fringe field in z at the end of the track width is viewed in a similar manner, it is seen that only half of the head surface contributes to the field, that is, the $-y$ direction. There is no head material in the $+y$ direction to add to the field. So the $H_x(0, d)$ in the z direction will be half as much as $H_x(0, d)$ in the y direction. Thus, we expect to see as much as 1.25 H_c field at distance d from the head surface in the z direction.

Currently, d, the flying height, is on the order of 100 nanometers (0.1 μm). The fringing magnetic field of $1.25 H_c$ in the z direction reaches as far as 0.1 μm on both sides of the track width. Hence, the magnetic track width is effectively increased by 0.1 μm on each side of the physical track width. For writing, at least a field H_c is needed; however, the written track can be partially erased at much lower fields. So fringing fields result in erased bands on two sides of the written tracks. Influence of erase bands in the track-pitch determination are addressed in Section 9.11.

Figure 3.17 shows the influence of fringing fields during writing and reading of a magnetic track. The figure originally related to the study of fringing fields in a tape but is equally applicable to disk recording. Figure 3.17a shows how the written track width is increased from the physical head width during writing. Figure 3.17b indicates pickup of fringing fields by the read head. Figure 3.17c shows increased erase track width, which results in erase bands adjacent to written track. Figure 3.17d shows how the adjacent track signals may generate noise in the signal of a track being read. It should be noted that media parameters such as coercivity, head geometry, and the degree of asymmetry in head write and read responses influence fringing fields at track ends. Measurements of track profiles and microtrack profiles are usually carried out to relate influence of fringing fields for component integration in a drive. Chapters 8 and 9 detail some of these measurements and error rate studies.

3.14 READING SINUSOIDAL MAGNETIC TRANSITIONS

Most of the pioneering work on magnetic recording has been done on sinusoidal recording. Consumer electronics and recording utilize sine-wave signals for audio and video recording. This is changing with more and more digital techniques being used in consumer applications. For disk applications, sinusoidal signals are not used directly. However, the study of sinusoidal magnetization is useful in fundamental studies in disk recording and provides a useful insight into disk design. At

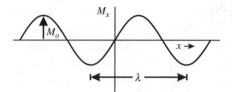

Figure 3.18 Sine-wave function.

high linear densities, digitally recorded signals become almost sinusoidal. More-over, sinusoidal functions are convenient for analytical studies, separating the con-tributions of different system parameters and for referring to the literature on mag-netic recording practices.

For a sinusoidally varying medium, we may write the magnetization as

$$M_x(x) = M_0 \sin(kx) \tag{3.33}$$

where x is the distance along the track and k refers to the periodicity of the magne-tization and is defined by $k = 2\pi/\lambda$, where λ is the wavelength of the sine wave (Fig. 3.18). Substituting the magnetization function equation (3.33) and the Karl-qvist expression for H_x from equation (3.2) into equation (3.20) and with quite a bit of algebra, Wallace [8] obtains the voltage output of the coil as

$$V(x') = -\mu_o nvw(M_r\delta)k[\eta][e^{-kd}]\left[\frac{1 - e^{-k\delta}}{k\delta}\right]\left[\frac{\sin(kg/2)}{kg/2}\right]\cos(kx') \tag{3.34}$$

where $x' = vt$.

This equation explicitly separates out four loss factors as indicated by the four quantities in square brackets. The reason these terms are called "losses" is that each of these terms is smaller than unity and reduce the output voltage by a corresponding fraction. The first term is the head efficiency η and has been discussed earlier.

The second term shows that the voltage decreases very rapidly—in fact, ex-ponentially, as the flying height d increases. This term is also known as *Wallace's spacing loss factor.* The number of decibels of power reduction due to spacing loss can be calculated using

$$\text{Spacing loss} = 20\log_{10}(e^{-kd}) = -55\left(\frac{\lambda}{d}\right)\text{dB} \tag{3.35}$$

This means that as the sinusoidal signal wavelength approaches the head-disk spac-ing (high frequency), the signal suffers a loss of -55 dB or the signal is reduced to less than 0.2% of its value. One practical application of the loss factor [9] is the experimental determination of flying height d in a disk drive by observing the ratio of voltages for two sinusoidal wavelengths on the disk.

The third term relates to the dependence of voltage on the medium thickness δ. The slope of this loss with increasing thickness is not as steep as that of spacing loss but is significant. This is somewhat like a spacing loss for magnetization in the medium layer. Regions of magnetization in the medium that are farthest from the

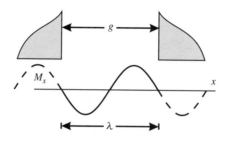

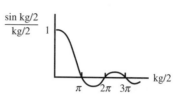

Figure 3.19 Gap loss factor.   **Figure 3.20** Gap nulls.

head contribute relatively little to the signal voltage. The last term in parentheses is referred as the *gap loss factor.* For a very small gap, this term is unity, and as the gap increases, the gap loss factor decreases and oscillates around zero (Fig. 3.19). The first zero corresponds to having the gap length equal to the wavelength of magnetization reversal. When this happens, there is equal positive magnetization and negative magnetization under the gap, and therefore no signal is generated (Fig. 3.20). No practical application has been considered beyond this first null. However, it has been demonstrated [10] that in the case of closely-spaced perpendicular recording transitions, a fifth null has been seen at as high as 650 kiloflux reversals per inch. This means that magnetic recording is capable of showing observable voltage signals up to very high linear densities.

REFERENCES

[1] O. Karlqvist, *Trans. R. Inst. Technol. (Stockholm),* vol. 86 (1954), p. 3.

[2] John C. Mallinson, *The Foundations of Magnetic Recording,* p. 92. New York: Academic Press, 1993.

[3] M. L. Williams and R. L. Comstock, *A.I.P. Conf. Proc.,* vol. 5 (1972), p. 738.

[4] B. K. Middleton, Chapter 2, in C. D. Mee and E. D. Daniel, eds., *Magnetic Recording Handbook.* New York: McGraw-Hill, 1990.

[5] A. S. Hoagland and J. E. Monson, *Digital Magnetic Recording,* Chapter 4. New York: John Wiley & Sons, Inc., 1991.

[6] T. Arnodussen, private communication, San Jose, (1992).

[7] A. van Herk, *"Three Dimensional Analysis of Magnetic Fields in Magnetic Recording Heads,"* Philips Research Laboratories, Eindhoen, The Netherlands, (1980), p. 40.

[8] R. L. Wallace, "The reproduction of magnetically recorded signals," *Bell Syst. Tech. J.,* vol. 30 (1951), p. 1145.

[9] B. R. Brown, H. L. Hu, K. L. Klaassen, J. J. Lum, C. L. Jacobus, J. C. L. Van Peppen, and W. E. Weresin, U.S. Patent No. 4,777,544 (1988).

[10] S. Yamamoto, Y. Nakamura, and S. Iwasaki, "Extremely high density recording with single pole perpendicular head," *IEEE Trans. Magn.,* MAG-23 (1987), p. 2070.

4

Ferrite and MIG Heads

4.1 INTRODUCTION

Ferrites used in magnetic recording applications are compounds of iron oxide and materials such as manganese, nickel, and zinc. Magnetic ferrites have properties of high resistivity (see Table 4.1), ruggedness, and extremely low wear-out, making them ideal core materials for heads in all recording applications.

During the early 1960s, prior to the emergence of semiconductor memories, ferrite cores were used as high-speed (2 microsecond cycle time) memory elements for computers. Early digital data recorders used nickel-zinc-ferrite heads. In the 1970s, large disk drives such as the IBM 3350, 3370, and 3375 all used ferrite heads. The emergence of small disk drives in the mid-1970s became a driving force for additional innovations in ferrite head technology. Meanwhile in the 1970s and 1980s, rapid progress in consumer electronics—VCRs and audio recorders—resulted in a substantial boost in ferrite head technology. The large production volume of these applications resulted in lowering the cost of disk drive heads. Metal-in-gap (MIG) heads were first developed for analog tape recording on a metal medium. In the late 1980s, MIG heads were introduced for rigid-disk drive applications. The low cost of heads and adequate performance of these heads with newly available metal medium generated an accelerated growth in the disk drive industry. For very high areal

TABLE 4.1 Properties of Materials Commonly Used for Heads

Material	B_s, T (kG)	μ_r	ρ, $\mu\Omega$-cm	H_c, A/m (Oe)	Vickers hardness
Hot-pressed NiZn Ferrite	0.4–0.46 (4–4.6)	300–1,500	10^{11}	11.8–27.6 (0.15–0.35)	900
Hot-pressed MnZn Ferrite	0.4–0.6 (4–6)	3,000– 10,000	5×10^6	11.8–15.8 (0.15–0.2)	700
Single crystal MnZn Ferrite	0.4 (4)	400–1,000	0.5×10^6	3.96 (0.05)	—
Sendust	1 (10)	8,000	85	2 (0.25)	480
Plated (81–19) NiFe Permalloy	1(10)	1,500– 3000	20	0.1–0.5	120

densities, thin film heads were used. However, due to low cost, MIG heads were often substituted in place of thin film heads for 95 and 65 mm diameter disk drives. In 1993, more ferrite heads and their extension, metal-in-gap heads, were used in rigid-disk drives than all other types of heads combined. Non-MIG ferrite heads are virtually phased out of rigid-disk drive applications, whereas MIG heads are still used in low-density drives. Flexible (floppy) disk drives use ferrite heads. This chapter begins with a discussion of the two types of ferrite materials used for digital recording heads. Their properties and limitations are described following a discussion on ideal recording-head characteristics of a disk drive head.

Figure 4.1a shows a monolithic ferrite-head slider. Figure 4.1b shows the two-dimensional enlarged view of the gap region. The gap of the head is made of glass. The track of the head is defined by the top flat part of the central rail of the air-bearing surface (ABS) of the head, Figure 4.1a. Figure 4.2 shows the near-gap region of a monolithic MIG head. A MIG head differs from the standard ferrite head by the additional layer of Sendust (an alloy of iron, silicon, and aluminum) metal on the trailing side of the gap region [1]. Details of the construction process and properties of MIG heads are discussed in Section 4.7.

Properties of ferrites make them attractive as a base material for other types of heads: the MIG head is an extension of the ferrite head. The MR tape heads use a ferrite substrate. Several patents on MR heads indicate the use of ferrite as a substrate material. Alloy-laminated heads combine the use of a ferrite substrate in conjunction with thin film depositions. These heads are considered for applications associated with digital VCRs and camcorders. Materials, properties, and limitations of ferrite heads are covered in the next three sections. Subsequently, process steps in the construction of the two types of MIG heads—monolithic and composite—are discussed. After considerations of the performance and limitations

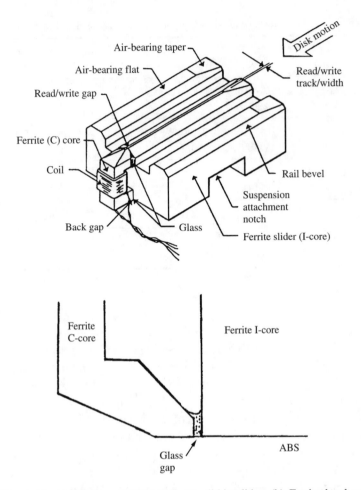

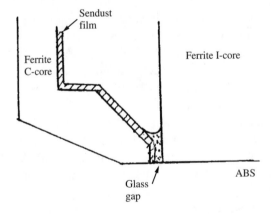

Figure 4.1 (a) Ferrite or MIG trirail monolithic slider; (b) Ferrite head gap closeup.

Figure 4.2 Metal-in-gap closeup.

of MIG heads, material from several references is summarized to describe the state of the art of these devices. Lastly, material advances and future applications of MIG heads are described.

4.2 FERRITE MATERIALS

Permalloy and ferrites are the primary materials used in the construction of disk-drive heads. The first heads for the IBM 350 drive RAMAC (1957) were made of sheets of Permalloy that were used at that time for digital and instrument tape recorders. In the mid-1960s, ferrite heads were developed for disk drives. The major advantage of the ferrite at that time was its high resistivity, which prevented eddy currents and did not require laminations for high-frequency applications. With thin film (1971) and magnetoresistive (1989) heads, we return to Permalloy, but in a significantly different (thin film) form.

Ferrites are magnetic ceramics composed of oxides of iron and other metals. Earlier heads were made with nickel-zinc ferrite (for example, $Ni_{0.3}Zn_{0.7}Fe_2O_3$ [2]. These heads have excellent wear resistance—about 20 times better than Permalloy—and high electrical resistivity—between 5 and 10 orders better than Permalloy and Sendust (see Table 4.1); hence, they inhibit eddy currents up to high frequencies (several megahertz). In addition, retention of high permeability in the megahertz range made their use almost universal in tapes and disks for two decades. Features such as high durability and absence of corrosion combined with excellent head-disk interface properties, that is, low friction and low stiction (tendency of the head to stick to disk surface) during start-stops, make ferrites very suitable for recording applications. However, ferrites have high porosity, a tendency to pitting, and crystal pullout at gap edges. This poses serious problems for narrow-track disk applications. Hot isostatically pressed (HIP) ferrites with finer grain structures along with improved glass bonding techniques have reduced some of these problems. Early use of nickel–zinc gave way to MnZn ferrites for disk drive applications. The MnZn ferrite (for example, $Mn_{0.7}Zn_{0.3}Fe_2O_4$) has higher permeability (see Table 4.1) and high saturation induction (approaching 6000 gauss); as a result, it became the preferred material in most disk-drive applications. However, MnZn ferrite has a higher electrical conductivity than that of NiZn; hence, NiZn is still preferred for some applications. As stated earlier, the problems of chipping at the ferrite poles near the gap were controlled with HIP-processed fine-grain materials and diffused glassing processes. However, as the tracks get progressively narrower in disk applications, problems often continue to recur. Polycrystalline ferrites in common use have a grain size of 5 to 6 μm, larger than the size of track widths currently used. Up to 6-μm-track ferrite-MIG heads became available in 1993, and narrow tracks as small as 2 μm are claimed to have been demonstrated in the research environment.

4.3 RECORDING HEAD CHARACTERISTICS

Here we define the desirable properties of a good head for disk drive applications:

1. *Magnetic "softness."* The ease with which magnetization in the material can be increased linearly with application of a magnetic field, which also implies low coercivity. This point is discussed in Section 4.4.

2. *High permeability in the frequency range of interest.* Efficiencies of the writing and reading processes depend on the permeability of the core material, equation (3.8). Permeability should be high throughout the applicable frequency range.

3. *High electrical resistivity in the core material.* The inhibition of eddy currents at several megahertz frequencies is a desirable property in nonlaminated bulk material for head cores. Existence of excessive eddy currents results in phase shifts in read signals and distorts output. Heads made of metallic sheets were laminated to prevent eddy currents.

4. *High-saturation flux density (B_s).* Writing on a high-coercivity medium requires high fields at reasonable currents from the head. This is the most important property of a head for disk drive applications. This requirement has resulted in the transition of head technology from ferrite to MIG-ferrite and Permalloy thin films.

5. *High material denseness and low porosity in the core material.* This inhibits chipping at the corners of the tracks.

6. *Corrosion resistance during fabrication and use.* Metals like Permalloy tend to corrode when parts are kept on the shelf for prolonged periods without environmental protection. Handling, packaging, and storage of these parts require a controlled environment.

7. *Wear resistance.* Compared with tapes and floppy drives, rigid-disk drives with flying heads have less tendency to wear. However, the head should be able to withstand start-stops and occasional contacts between head and disk. The generation of debris during such contacts is a major concern for the disk drive operation. Ferrites have excellent wear resistance and are not susceptible to corrosion problems.

8. *Low magnetostriction.* The magnetic properties of heads change when under stress. During processing, head materials go through stress cycles. Materials with low magnetostriction (tendency of material to generate internal magnetic field while mechanically stressed) can withstand these stresses without affecting the head performance. Thin film heads and MR heads are particularly sensitive to this property and require careful considerations during preparation of materials and subsequent processes.

Figure 4.3 shows a comparison of head and medium B–H loops. For the head, a narrow loop with negligible coercivity is required to ensure high reading sensitivity to

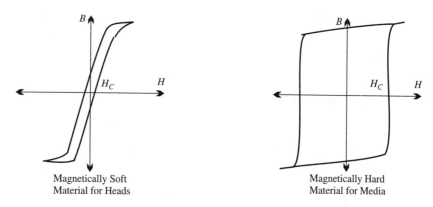

Magnetically Soft
Material for Heads

Magnetically Hard
Material for Media

Figure 4.3 Differences in B–H loops and coercivities of head and media materials.

the field from the medium. The remanence should be low, so that the head does not retain memory of earlier information. Saturation flux density should be as high as possible for the head to write on a high-coercivity medium. Also, the slope of the B versus H curve should be steep (i.e., permeability should be high). For the medium, a square loop with large H_c and sufficiently high M_r are required so that written magnetizations will remain unperturbed for years and can be detected successfully without errors.

4.4 LIMITATIONS OF CONVENTIONAL FERRITE HEADS

Ferrites have a major disadvantage in comparison with metals like Permalloy or Sendust. They have almost half the saturation flux density (B_s) of metals. Moreover, the change in flux density with the current or field is an "S"-shaped curve with gradual slope. When a ferrite-head coil current is increased to about half the saturation field strength, the pole tips start to saturate, which requires a gradually increased rate of current change for further increase in the field [3], and the efficiency of the head suffers as a result. For the ferrite head to write successfully on a film medium, the field produced by the head must be approximately 2.5 times the medium coercivity field within the medium. With the best MnZn ferrite saturation induction reported 0.6 T (6 kG), the field at the medium will be less than 200 kA/m (2500 Oe); see equation (4.1) and the example in Section 4.8. This indicates that the maximum medium coercivity practically usable with the head is about 80 kA/m (1000 Oe). One would not expect dramatic improvement in the value of B_s in ferrites since they are ferrimagnetics. Ferrimagnetics have inherent saturation flux limit of a factor of less than 2 compared to ferromagnetic metals such as Sendust and Permalloy [2]. Prior to the use of MIG structures, ferrite heads were often made with epoxied or bonded pieces of bulk Sendust close to the gap area facing the air-bearing surface. Sendust is a hard material and does not fracture; moreover, high-saturation flux density writes better. These attached pieces were mechanically weak, and at high frequencies eddy currents on the surface of the metal pieces resulted in unacceptable phase shifts in signal pulses.

4.5 METAL-IN-GAP HEADS: MOTIVATION

The development of important steps in technology often happens by the coincidence of contributing factors rather than by preplanned research and development. In the mid-1980s, thin film disk development reached the product application stage. This immediately led to the availability of high-coercivity media. Ferrite heads simply could not handle writing on metal films above 1000 Oe. In practice, the weakness of the ferrite head becomes apparent beyond 750 Oe. The concept of adding a metal layer in the gap of a ferrite head to increase magnetization saturation value is as old as 1970 [4]. The deposition of Sendust metal on ferrite heads was practiced for writing on metal tapes in audio and video applications in the mid-1980s. The use of the MIG head for the digital tape recording application has been described [3]. Several companies took initiatives to develop Sendust-deposited MIGs for disk drives in 1986. New drives with these heads were announced in 1988 and 1989. High cost and limited availability of film heads contributed to the upsurge of MIG heads. During 1992, over 120 million MIG heads of monolithic and composite types were sold for disk drive use. This was probably the peak use of MIG heads for disk drives within a period of one year.

There are several technical advantages of MIG heads, and they are discussed in the section on performance of these heads (Section 4.8). The emergence of a high-coercivity medium, constraint in supply of thin film heads, and low cost made MIG heads the favorite for disk drive applications.

4.6 TYPES OF FERRITE AND MIG HEADS

Four categories of ferrite heads have been developed and are used in varying quantities.

1. *Monolithic ferrite head.* This is the lowest-cost head extensively used in files made for PCs and low-performance applications. The entire monolithic ferrite head sliders and active write/read elements are made of ferrite (except the gap, which is glass, and the coil, which is copper). The head structure is seen in Figures 4.1a and 4.1b.

2. *Composite ferrite head.* This is a hybrid head with a slider being made of nonmagnetic ceramic material; the active elements are made out of ferrite and are inserted and bonded into a slot in the slider. Due to higher costs,

use of these heads never became very popular. Technology developed for this head has been applied to the composite MIG head (see item 4), which has enjoyed some following in the disk drive industry.

3. *Monolithic MIG head.* This head is similar to the monolithic ferrite head except that one or both sides of the poles near the gap are sputtered with high-magnetic-saturation material. Currently, Sendust is commonly used for this purpose. Sendust is an alloy of iron (85%), silicon (9.6%), and aluminum (5.4%), and it is electrically (9 orders of magnitude) more conductive than ferrite; hence, the name "metal" in the gap.

4. *Composite MIG head.* The composite MIG head is basically the same as the composite ferrite head except for the intermediary Sendust metal in the gap. Construction details of this head in Section 4.7 will clarify the structure. The large nonmagnetic slider helps to reduce head inductance and allows improved efficiency. Also, the tracks are better defined in these heads; hence, narrower tracks than those for monolithic MIG heads are feasible with the structure. These heads have been sometimes used in medium- and high-capacity or high-performance drives. These heads are between 20 and 40% more expensive compared to monolithic MIGs.

4.7 MIG-HEAD CONSTRUCTION STEPS

Figure 4.4 shows the steps used in the construction of the MIG head. The steps exemplify general manufacturing practice; exact construction details vary with manufacturers. A large ferrite brick is sliced into bars. Two bars of different widths are shown in Figure 4.4a. The smaller bar is cut/profiled to a C-shape on one side and is called a *C-bar.* The wider bar is called an *I-bar.* After bevel profiling and lapping, a layer of Sendust (1 to 2 μm thick) is sputter deposited on the inner surface of the C-bar. Next a layer of glass is deposited on top of the metal. The glass thickness defines the gap thickness of the head. Note that the C-core forms the trailing edge of the completed head and is used for writing data on a medium. Figure 4.4b shows a C-bar with deposited layers. C- and I-bars are then bonded together. Figure 4.4c shows the bonded bar. The long structure of connected C and I portions is cut into smaller slices. C-core profiling of the single head is shown in Figure 4.4d. The top surface of the separated individual head becomes the air-bearing surface when the head flies over the disk. This surface of the slider is profiled into three rails with tapered front ends for improved stability during flying. The slider is now ready for conductor winding in an automated machine. Figure 4.1 shows a complete slider with three rails and tapered segments on the rails. The width of the central rail defines read/write track width. The finished C bar is referred to as the ferrite (C) core. Coil winding, read/write gap, and back gap are also indicated in the figure. The figure also shows the suspension attachment notch at the bottom of the slider. A

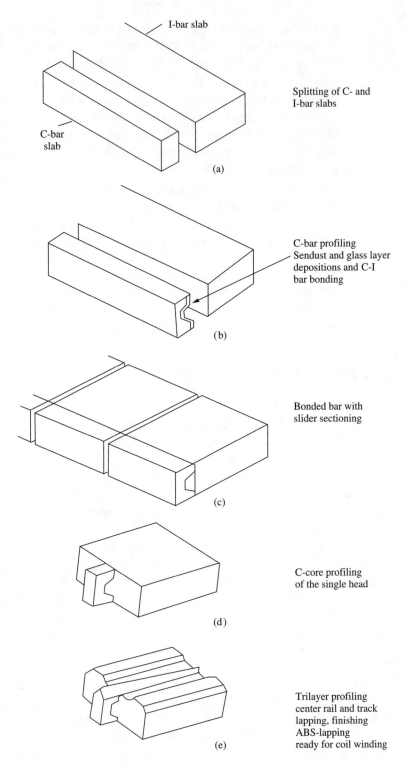

I-bar slab

C-bar
slab

(a)

Splitting of C- and
I-bar slabs

(b)

C-bar profiling
Sendust and glass layer
depositions and C-I
bar bonding

(c)

Bonded bar with
slider sectioning

(d)

C-core profiling
of the single head

(e)

Trilayer profiling
center rail and track
lapping, finishing
ABS-lapping
ready for coil winding

Figure 4.4 Monolithic trirail MIG head construction [5].

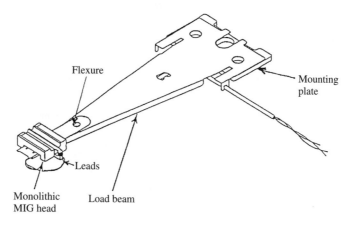

Figure 4.5 Ferrite-head suspension assembly.

completed head with suspension and flexure is shown in Figure 4.5. Recent practice with mini-monolithic MIG sliders uses a two-rail structure with the C part profiled at one of the two end rails. The top of the rail may be protected by an additional step of glassing to prevent chipping at track boundaries.

Figure 4.6 shows the schematic of a commercially available composite MIG head.

The body section is made of a ceramic substrate such as calcium titanium oxide ($CaTiO_3$). It has a two-rail structure. Ferrite C- and I-sections are separately fabricated and bonded as blocks for inserting in the slots prepared in the ceramic substrate. The following steps are described to illustrate the construction process. Figure 4.7a shows a profiled slider strip produced from a bar of ceramic material. The strip has slots prepared for receiving small ferrite-head blocks. It also has coil-winding windows cut out to ease the winding of conductors through head cores. In Figure 4.7b, C- and I-bars are shown prepared in a manner similar to that discussed for monolithic MIG heads, except the bars are very small compared to those used for making monolithic heads. A pair of bars produce many more C and I parts. Metal, such as Sendust, is sputtered on the C-cores of the bar. Glass forming the gap is sputtered on the Sendust layer. These bars are glass bonded, and the bonded bar is cut into small individual ferrite sections, Figure 4.7c. Two elements with profiled tracks are shown in Figure 4.7d. Each of the ferrite elements is inserted into a slot of the ceramic body of the head and is bonded with a low-temperature glass into

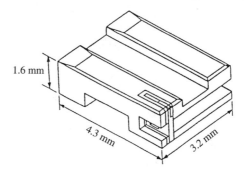

Figure 4.6 Composite MIG slider.

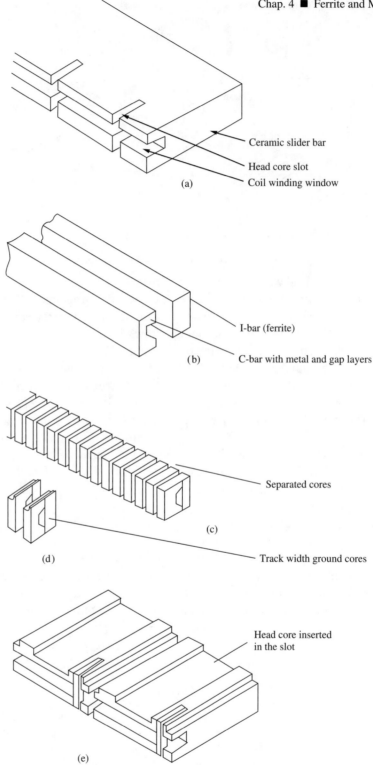

Ceramic slider bar
Head core slot
(a) Coil winding window

I-bar (ferrite)
(b) C-bar with metal and gap layers

Separated cores
(c)
(d) Track width ground cores

Head core inserted
in the slot
(e)

Figure 4.7 Composite MIG head slider construction steps [5].

the slot. The reason for using a low-temperature glass bonding is that the gap glass used between C- and I-sections should not melt during this operation. Next, the air-bearing surface of the composite structure is lapped and finished. Figure 4.7e shows a pair of completed head sliders. The low-temperature glass used for bonding ferrite blocks also protects the fragile narrow tracks of ferrites.

4.8 PERFORMANCE ADVANTAGES OF MIG HEADS

The following are the specific advantages of MIG heads:

- The Sendust provides high-saturation magnetization of 10–11 kG (1 to 1.1 T).
- The steep B–H curve implies high magnetic permeability (see Table 4.1).
- Desirable mechanical, chemical, and electrical attributes make it suitable as a disk drive head.
- The metal used in the MIG head can be changed while retaining the ferrite body. Advantages of the ferrite substrate with the possibility of improving the metal give an extra degree of freedom in the construction of MIG heads.

MnZn ferrite can have a saturation gap flux (B_s) of 6 kG (0.6 T). If the whole structure of the head is made of Sendust, the flux can be as large as 11 kG (1.1 T). The MIG head structure is a hybrid of ferrite and Sendust. The top of the ferrite head poles begin saturating at half the B_s value [3]. At this point, the permeability in the core drops below 50%, and the head field gradient starts to decrease. The high-frequency content of the writing pulses starts degrading. The Sendust B–H loop is sharper, and the flux at the tip of the Sendust pole can rise up to 90% before degrading surrounding field or field gradients. So a layer of Sendust film in the trailing edge of the head provides a flux approaching 8 kG (0.8 T) or a magnetic field of 8 kOe (640 kA/m) in the gap. Recalling equation (3.6),

$$\frac{H_g}{H_x\,(0,\,d)} = \frac{\pi}{2\arctan\,(g/2d)} \tag{4.1}$$

where d is the spacing between head and disk, H_x is the field in the media, and H_g is the field in the gap. For a gap of 200 nm and spacing (d) of 200 nm, the ratio H_g/H_x from Figure 3.7 is observed to be 3.33. A gap field, H_g of 640 kA/m (8000 Oe), results in a medium surface field of 192 kA/m (2400 Oe).

The differences in fields and field gradients near the gap of MnZn ferrite and one-sided metal-in-gap heads have been computed [6]. Figure 4.8 illustrates the differences. Two factors are important in writing: high field intensity in the medium and a high rate of change of field intensity in the medium. The transition parameter a is a strong function of these two factors. Larger write fields and steep field gradients result in a shorter transition parameter a. Output signal amplitude increases with shorter a. The writing abilities of the ferrite head, MIG head, and MIG head with separately optimized write and read head gaps were computed [7]. Figure 4.9 shows

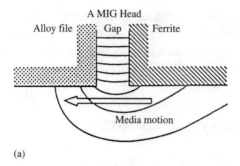

(a)

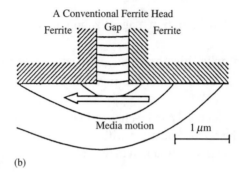

(b)

Figure 4.8 Distribution of magnetic flux in the gap region with magnetomotive force = 0.8 AT [6].

$d = 0.3 \ \mu m$ A: All-ferrite, $H_g = 3693$ Oe

$\delta = 0.05 \ \mu m$ B: MIG, $H_g = 7386$ Oe

$4\pi Ms = 7500$ G C: MIG Write, Separate Read, $g_r = 0.25 \ \mu m$

$S^* = 0.85$

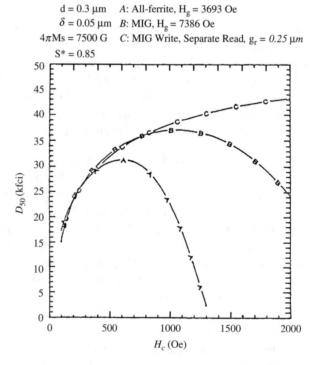

Figure 4.9 Ferrite, MIG, and dual-head comparison of linear densities [7].

the results. Flux changes per inch, which are proportional to linear bit density at a 50% drop in amplitude, are plotted on the y axis, and coercivity of the media is plotted on the x axis. Plain ferrite-head density (A) starts dropping at over 600 Oe coercivity, while MIG values (B) do not drop until a coercivity of 1200 Oe. The plot (C) in the figure illustrates the advantage of the MIG write head and separate read head. Another way to look at ferrite versus MIG performance is to compare the optimization of the gap for writing and reading for each of these heads:

1. Higher bit densities require reading with narrow gap heads.
2. Wide gaps write with higher fields and steeper field gradients.

A compromise is made for every inductive head designed for both these functions. What happens to the writing and reading abilities of the heads as gaps are varied from large to small values, given the measure of the head "goodness"? The read/write performance comparison of the minicomposite MIG head against the minimonolithic ferrite head has been made [8]. Pertinent results are shown in Figures 4.10 and 4.11. Gap length versus output voltage for the MIG head remains fairly constant, with gap variations suggesting that the high field of the MIG head is sufficient to write well even with relatively narrow gaps. The ferrite head has a reduced signal due to weak writing, which increases transition widths and hence decreases output voltage. Figure 4.11 shows clearly that overwrite capabilities of the MIG head are superior as expected from the higher-saturation magnetization of the Sendust.

The composite MIG head has a potential advantage of narrow track widths and hence higher track densities. The track edges in composite structures are supported by bonding glass, and hence narrow tracks can be produced with higher reliability. Work has been done on making glass-supported two-rail monolithic MIG heads that could also support narrow tracks. Tracks as narrow as 5 μm have been reported for double-sided MIG heads [9]. The nonmagnetic ceramic slider of the composite head reduces stray losses resulting in higher efficiency. The inductance of the composite head is likely to be lower than that of the monolithic MIG. Whereas composite MIGs are more expensive than monolithic types, composite MIGs may have an advantage over their monolithic counterparts for critical applications.

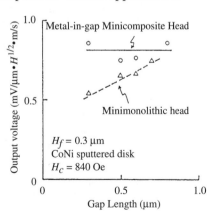

Figure 4.10 Output voltage versus gap length of MIG composite head at 20 kfci.

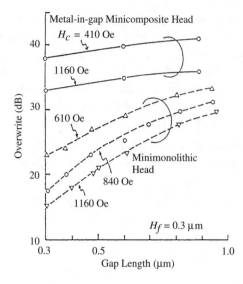

Figure 4.11 Overwrite versus gap length of MIG composite head with varying H_c.

4.9 LIMITATIONS OF MIG HEADS

In the early stages of development, the MIG head had serious problems with the existence of secondary gap (or pseudogap) between the Sendust and the ferrite body. Figure 4.12 shows the air-bearing surface structure of a MIG head and signal output from the head with a significant secondary gap. The roll-off curve or plot of frequency (or flux changes per millimeter) versus signal becomes wavy or may show humps depending on the length of the gap, the Sendust film, and the thickness of the secondary gap. The severity of the effect of pseudogap is measured by the ratio of amplitudes a_2/a_1 as a percentage. Head manufacturers often report this number in MIG head specifications, and 5% is considered acceptable. The effect of the secondary gap on composite MIG head performance has been reported [10].

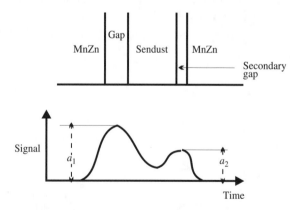

Figure 4.12 Secondary gap distortion in MIG head.

Figure 4.13 shows the effect of a secondary gap (pseudogap) on (1) density versus amplitude and (2) density versus bit shift. There are several reasons for the occurrence of a nonmagnetic layer between metal and ferrite. It could be due to interdiffusion during metal deposition or during subsequent process steps. Some authors [11] attribute the secondary gap to the formation of a reactive layer of $Al_2O_3 + SiO_2$ between the ferrite and Sendust during the annealing process. An additional sputtered barrier layer of 5–6 nm silicon dioxide or silicon nitride prevents the reaction between Sendust and MnZn ferrite. Other manufacturers have contained the problem of the secondary gap by using a variety of interfacial treatment prior to metal depositions. With a better understanding of the interface between Sendust and ferrite, much of this problem has been resolved; however, difficulties do recur when manufacturing processes are changed.

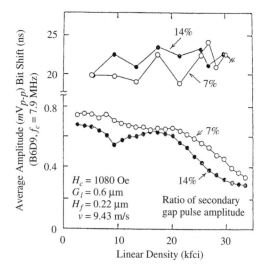

Figure 4.13 Amplitude and bit density as functions of linear density for composite MIG head [10].

The inductances of ferrite and MIG heads are an order of magnitude larger than thin film heads (see Section 5.7). The head inductance along with the preamplifier input capacitance results in a resonant frequency. If the data frequency approaches resonance, excessive phase shifts occur in the signal, which could cause data errors. With higher inductance the resonance frequency occurs at lower value and constrains the upper frequency of the data. Reduction of head inductance is one of the primary challenges for the advancement of MIG heads. The equivalent circuit of a ferrite head is described in Section 5.7, where performances of ferrite, film, and MR heads are compared. Ferrite and MIG head track widths are defined by grinding of the central rail or some other mechanical processes. Attempts to obtain narrow track widths using metal masking and ion etching or laser trimming are being investigated. The control of track widths under 4 μm is another objective for the future development of MIG heads.

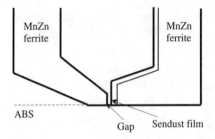

Figure 4.14 Double-apex MIG structure.

4.10 IMPROVEMENTS AND INNOVATIONS IN MIG HEAD STRUCTURES

Several structural and material innovations beyond conventional C- and I-bar types of MIG heads are already incorporated in the production of the heads and are being pursued by several laboratories. Among these ideas are

- Double-apex-gap structure
- Dual-sided metal (Sendust) depositions
- Use of single-crystal ferrites
- Double-gap structure
- Replacement of Sendust with high-magnetization material to write on very-high-coercivity media—160 kA/m (2000 Oe) and beyond.

The double-apex structure in Figure 4.14 provides a wider space for conductor windings. It also results in higher efficiency, since stray fields between two poles away from the throat (or gap height) are reduced. The conductor is placed closer to the gap, making the flux generation and its flow to the gap more efficient.

A double-sided metal-in-gap head for 150 Mb/in.^{2} recording has been reported [9]. The gap area of the head structure is shown in Figure 4.15, with conditions of measurements indicated in the legend. Plots of linear-bit density and track

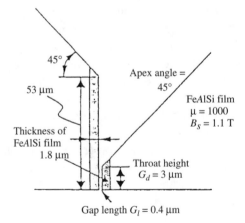

Figure 4.15 Double-MIG computation model [9].

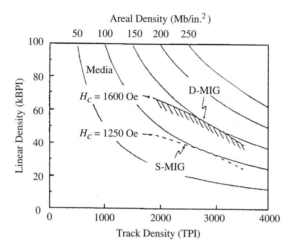

Figure 4.16 Double- and single-sided MIG head areal density projections [9].

density for single-sided MIG and double-sided MIG are shown in Figure 4.16. The D-MIG and S-MIG contours are drawn for the conditions of -28 dB overwrite and 31 dB signal-to-noise ratio.

The use of single-crystal ferrites in place of polycrystals for disk drives has several advantages. The track width of the polycrystal ferrite head is defined by trapezoidal-shaped grinding of the bar material. Dimension of the depth is often 10 times as deep as its width [12]. Ten-μm and smaller tracks may have only one or two ferrite grains at the top. With further processing, there are chances of track degradation, pullout of material, and other breakdowns. Moreover, dimensions of width and height of the track area are poorly controlled with purely mechanical processes. Polycrystalline ferrites do not lend themselves to the use of photolithography and controlled etching of material depth. The pattern definitions are difficult to control on multigrain boundaries of polycrystalline surfaces. Single-crystal ferrites allow controlled patterning and etching depth control of the material. Photolithography, which defines track width and air-bearing surface contours, results in better process controls and potential for narrow tracks. Single-crystal heads also provide higher signal output, consistent permeability under stress, and better overwrite capabilities [13]. It is also reported that the single-crystal MIG head resulted in 25% less bit shift and close to 100% less jitter in peak timings. This is attributed to the low Barkhausen noise of the single-crystal head.

Another possibility of improving the performance of the MIG head being discussed is the use of double gap. Figure 4.17 shows a schematic of the head. The head gap is made partly of a low-saturation magnetic material g_1 and glass g_2. During writing, the magnetic material saturates at a low current, and the effective gap increases to the sum of g_1 and g_2. During reading, the flux from the medium is much smaller, and gap 1 behaves as a magnetic material of high permeability. Thus, writing with wide gap and reading with narrow gap are accomplished. Such heads have been in use in floppy-disk drives.

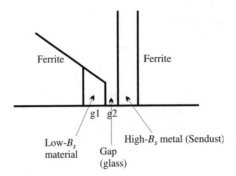

Figure 4.17 Double-gap ferrite MIG structure.

Saturation-flux density of Mn-Fe range 0.5– 0.6 T (5– 6 kG) and Sendust B_s vary between 1 and 1.1 T (10–11 kG). Higher B_s materials can advance the capability of heads to write on metal films of coercivities beyond 160 kA/m (2000 Oe). Considerable research for materials with higher B_s is in progress. Table 4.2, based on [14] and [15], shows the list of materials and their properties. Appropriate material should have acceptable writing and reading properties after passing through the processes and fabrication cycles.

TABLE 4.2 Properties of High B_s Materials for Enhancing the MIG Head Technology [14], [15]

Material	B_s, (T) 1 T = 10 kG	H_c (A/m), 80 (A/m) = 1 Oe	μ_r
Sendust (Fe Al Si)	1.1	80	1000 at 5 MHz
Super Sendust (SiAlNiFe)	1.4	80	800 at 5 MHz
FeZrN	1.7	80	1000 at 5 MHz
FeY	2.0	80	1500 at 5 MHz
FeGaSi	1.3	7.2	2000 at 1 MHz
FeAlGe	15	16	1800 at 1 MHz
FeCoGaSi	12	14	1900 at 1 MHz
FeCoAlGe	14	32	1600 at 1 MHz
FeGaSiRu	12	8.8	2000 at 1 MHz

REFERENCES

[1] F. J. Jeffers, R. J. McClure, W. W. French, and N. J. Griffith, "Metal-in-gap head," *IEEE Trans. Magn.,* MAG-18 (1982), p. 1146.

[2] M. Camras, *Magnetic Recording Handbook,* p. 192. New York: Van Nostrand Reinhold, 1988.

[3] F. Jeffers, "High density magnetic recording heads," *Proceedings of the IEEE,* vol. 74, no. 11 (1986), p. 1540.

[4] W. Nystrom, IBM technical disclosure bulletin, May 1970.

[5] H. H. Gatzen, "Ferrite heads" tutorial at Recording Head, Technology and Applications, University of Santa Clara, CA, 1989. Figures 4.4 and 4.7 are based on figures presented at the meeting.

[6] M. Iizuka, Y. Kanai, T. Abe, M. Sengoku, and K. Musaka, "Analysis and design of a metal-in-gap head for rigid disk files," *IEEE Trans. Magn.,* MAG-24 (1988), p. 2623.

[7] G. Winson Kelley, "Write-field analysis of metal-in-gap heads," *IEEE Trans. Magn.,* MAG-24 (1988), p. 2392.

[8] T. Nishiyama, K. Noguchi, K. Mouri, H. Iwata, and T. Shinohara, "Recording characteristics of metal-in-gap mini composite head," *IEEE Trans. Magn.,* MAG-23 (1988), p. 2931.

[9] T. Nishiyama, R. Goto, M. Yamazaki, I. Sakaguchi, S. Suwabe, and A. Iwama, "A double-sided metal-in-gap head for 150 Mb/in.^{2} recording," *IEEE Trans. Magn.,* MAG-28 (1992), p. 2632.

[10] M. Nakao, K. Noguchi, S. Suwabw, and T. Nishiyama, "Bit shift characteristics of MIG heads," *IEEE Trans. Magn.,* MAG-25 (1989), p. 3704.

[11] K. Kajiwara, M. Hyakawa, Y. Kunito, Y. Ikeda, K. Hayashi, K. Aso, and T. Ishida, "Analysis of metal-ferrite interface layers in metal-in-gap heads," *IEEE Trans. Magn.,* MAG-26 (1990), p. 2978.

[12] M. Ichinose and M. Arnoff, "Single-crystal ferrite technology for monolithic disk heads," *IEEE Trans. Magn.,* MAG-26 (1990), p. 2972.

[13] H. Iwata, K. Noguchi, S. Suwabe, and T. Nishiyama, "MIG minicomposite head using single crystal Mn-Zn ferrite," *IEEE Trans. Magn.,* MAG-26 (1990), p. 2394.

[14] K. Hayashi, M. Hayakawa, W. Ishikawa, Y. Ochiai, H. Matsuda, Y. Iwasaki, and K. Aso, "New crystalline soft magnetic alloy with high saturation magnetization," *J. Appl. Phys.,* vol. 61, no. 8 (1987), p. 3514.

[15] Masao Kakizaki, presentation at Discon Conference, San Jose, CA, 1991.

5

Thin Film Heads

5.1 INTRODUCTION AND HISTORICAL PERSPECTIVE

In the mid-1970s only ferrite heads were used for disk drive recording. Progressively increasing areal densities in disk drives required (1) reductions in head gaps and track widths and (2) materials with high saturation magnetization. It became apparent that for a long run, ferrite heads could not meet these challenges due to the following reasons:

1. Ferrite head gap is formed by placement of a glass layer between two separate pieces of ferrite slabs (Section 4.7). Submicron gaps for increasing linear densities could not be produced by these procedures.
2. Track widths of early ferrite heads were defined by careful grinding of the trapezoidal shape of the central rail of the ferrite slider. Track widths of less than 25 micrometers with adequate tolerances were difficult to produce by these procedures.
3. Inductance of hand- or machine-wound multiturn ferrite heads ranged in several microhenries. It was clear that writing and reading at several tens of MHz frequencies needed methods of decreasing head inductance.

4. As new media were developed with increasing coercivities, ferrite heads with saturation magnetization (B_s of 4–6 KG) would be inadequate, and new materials needed to be explored. The move to thin film heads provided solutions to all these issues.

With semiconductor technology developing at a rapid pace in the mid-1960s, it was natural for head manufacturers to consider adopting some of the new tools and techniques developed for semiconductor processing. These tools included lithographic processes to define the small geometries necessary for head miniaturization. Other techniques included vacuum deposition processes such as evaporation and sputtering for depositing thin films. Considerable work was also being done in the area of magnetic thin film memories that stored information magnetically in thin films of Permalloy (nickel-iron). These films were often made by electroplating, and therefore expertise was built up in thin film fabrication by this method. A thin film head yoke made of Permalloy would allow higher magnetization and higher permeability than ferrites.

Besides miniaturization and ease of fabrication, other benefits from thin film technologies included:

1. Precise control of the submicron head gap.
2. Thin poles that would result in narrow read-back pulses.
3. Excellent frequency response due to low inductance.

Also, the smaller geometry and mass of the head and slider would result in shorter access times by allowing faster track-to-track response of the head in accessing data. Figure 5.1 compares ferrite and film head geometries. The substrate or bulk of the slider is ferrite in the case of the monolithic or MIG ferrite head, while the thin film head substrate is ceramic. The gap for ferrite is defined by a bonded glass layer

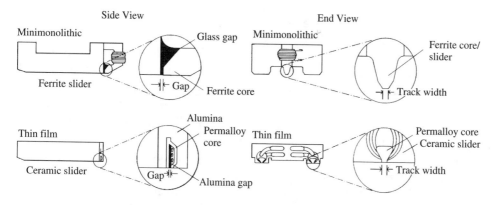

Figure 5.1 Schematic comparison of ferrite and thin film heads.

between C and I bars, while deposited film of aluminum oxide forms the gap of a film head. The track width of a ferrite head is fabricated by mechanically grinding and polishing ferrite material, while track width of the film head is formed photolithographically. The head coil is manually or automatically wound for the ferrite head and the film head coil consists of lithographically defined layers of copper.

Economic considerations also played an important role. The ability to make many elements simultaneously on a single wafer was a strong attraction. However, the lower cost of the thin film head compared to the ferrite head has been rarely realized since a significant part of the head cost is in fabrication and assembly after thin film processes.

Several groups of researchers attempted to fabricate thin film heads in the early 1960s. The first head with relatively small geometry was reported in 1970 [1]. The dimensions of this head were 2 μm gap, 200 μm track width, and overall head measurements of approximately 250 μm by 250 μm by 500 μm. The first head to appear in a commercial disk drive (IBM 3370 and 3380) was reported in 1980 [2]. This film head featured eight turns with Permalloy poles and copper conductors. This was the beginning of the thin film head era in the magnetic-recording industry. Table 1.2 indicates the gap and track dimensions of the head.

5.2 FILM HEAD STRUCTURE

The thin film head is very similar to the ferrite-ring head and MIG heads of Chapter 4 in the sense that it consists basically of a magnetic yoke and a coil. The main difference is that in the thin film head, in one of the dimensions (thickness), all the parameters are very small. Figure 5.2 shows the principal parts of the head—the yoke consisting of Permalloy films P_1 and P_2 and the pancake-shaped copper coil. These films are all deposited on a substrate or base that is commonly a ceramic compound of alumina (aluminum oxide or Al_2O_3) and titanium carbide (TiC).

Ignoring insulating layers for a moment, the first film to be deposited on the substrate is P_1 (upper part of Figure 5.2). Next, the coil is deposited on top of P_1 (middle part of Figure 5.2). And finally, film P_2 is deposited on top of the coil. To complete the magnetic circuit of the yoke, P_1 and P_2 are connected near the coil center (the connection is made under the small oblong shape shown in the upper right of the P_2 layer). Figure 5.2 shows the gap between the P_1 and P_2 layers at the air-bearing surface (ABS) of the slider. (The air-bearing surface is the surface of the slider, which is parallel to the disk surface and rides on a cushion of air between the head and the disk.) The width of the trailing layer (P_2, in this case) is often smaller than the leading layer (P_1) and defines the writing track width of the head. The copper coil of several turns passes between the Permalloy sheets P_1 and P_2. A number of insulation layers are included and are discussed in the next section.

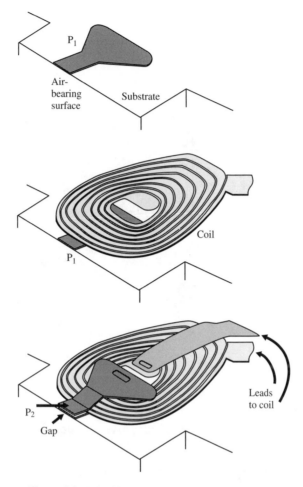

Figure 5.2 Thin film head coil and yoke construction.

5.3 FILM HEAD CONSTRUCTION

A schematic of the first commercial thin film head, the IBM 3370 head, is shown in Figure 5.3. The view of the head from the top is shown in Figure 5.3b. The section at left, Figure 5.3a, is a cross section through the center of the head; note, however, that this section is expanded to show detail from the air-bearing surface *only* up to the center of the coil (only the lower coil turns are included). Permalloy layers are labeled P_1 and P_2 in this figure; the pole tips are labeled (B), the coil is labeled (C), the gap is labeled (D), and the insulation layers are labeled (I_1, I_2, and I_3). A view of the pole tips as seen from the air-bearing surface is shown below the right-hand portion, Figure 5.3c. On top of Figure 5.3b two wide conductors are shown that connect the coil turns to pads.

Most manufacturers use wet processes to fabricate thin film heads. The term *wet process* refers to the use of the electroplating for the deposition of the metals

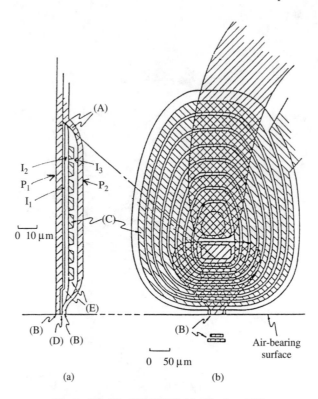

I_2
I_3
P_1
P_2
I_1
(A)
(C)
0 10 μm
(E)
(B)
(D) (B)
(B)
Air-bearing
surface
0   50 μm
(a)   (b)

Figure 5.3 The IBM 3370 thin film head [2].

(Permalloy and copper). The alternative *dry process* uses sputtering for deposition
of the metals. The following sequence gives the steps in the construction of a typical
thin film head:

1. The alumina-TiC substrate is a disk or a square wafer approximately
   2.5–4 mm thick and 4–6 in. in diameter (see Figure 5.4a, for example).
   The layers are built up one at a time on the surface of this wafer. The circular wafer is usually preferred so that standard semiconductor wafer handling equipment can be used for the various processing steps, but square
   wafers are also used. After all film depositions, the wafer is sliced up into
   rows of many sliders. Each slider may have one or two heads. Between
   3000 and 6000 potential minisliders of one head each can be produced on
   a large-size wafer.

2. The first film to be deposited on the alumina-TiC wafer is a thin film of
   alumina. This layer provides a smooth surface for further processing and
   insulates the heads from the conductive slider body.

3. The next layer is the P_1 Permalloy layer (Figures 5.2 and 5.3). This
   layer actually consists of two individual layers of Permalloy that are deposited using conventional lithography and plating processes. The first
   layer makes the P_1 pole tip at the air-bearing surface. The second layer
   is deposited over the first everywhere except near the pole tip (Figure 5.3).

The net result is that a thin layer is obtained at the pole tip for high resolution, while a thicker layer is obtained everywhere else to achieve more efficiency in carrying flux from the inside of the head to the gap at the air-bearing surface.

4. The read/write gap layer, (D) in Figure 5.3a, is usually alumina. This layer is deposited on top of P_1. A hole in this insulation layer is made (during the lithography) in the back-gap area (near the coil center). When the P_2 layer is eventually deposited, this hole allows the P_2 layer to make physical contact with the P_1 layer to make a complete yoke. Subsequent layers of insulation must also provide a hole for this purpose.

5. Another insulating layer (I_1 shown as (E) in Figure 5.3a) is deposited on top of the gap layer prior to the coil deposition. A photoresist or compatible resin is chosen for this layer because these materials tend to planarize the surface. The photoresist is poured onto the surface of the wafer as a liquid. The wafer is then spun rapidly. This allows the photoresist to flow outward toward the edges of the wafer to achieve a uniform thickness of photoresist. The photoresist is then baked to harden it. In addition to creating a level surface, the photoresist creates a relatively strain-free layer that reduces stress on the Permalloy films. Stressed Permalloy films often cause unstable electrical performance of the head.

6. Next, the coil layer is lithographically patterned, and the copper is usually put down by a wet (plating) process.

7. A second layer of photoresist (I_2) now follows to provide insulation between the coil and the upper P_2 Permalloy sheet. Again, photoresist planarizes the surface. A hole in this layer allows connection of the center of the coil to the coil lead.

8. Deposition of the P_2 layer, (B) in Figure 5.3a, is next. Again, as in the P_1 case, this is a two-layer deposition to allow relatively thin Permalloy near the gap and thick Permalloy elsewhere for efficient flux flow.

9. Large copper pads (see Figure 5.4b) are deposited near the head, and they are covered later with gold for ultrasonic bonding. These pads are connected to the head coil thin film leads to allow the connection of wires to the head coil.

10. The last film deposition is a covering of alumina to provide protection to the sensitive film layers from chemical or mechanical attack during further wafer processing and use.

11. The wafer with deposited thin film heads is now cut into rows as shown in Figure 5.4a. One side of the row cut during row separation will eventually become the air-bearing surface of the slider. These row surfaces are mechanically ground and lapped to provide smooth air-bearing surfaces. Rails or more complex patterns of air-bearing surface are mechanically profiled, or a reactive ion etching process may be employed. The design of the air-bearing surface is one of the most critical steps in head design

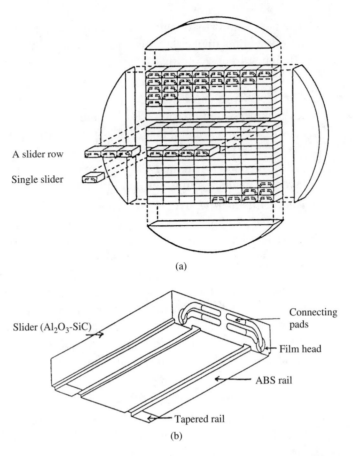

A slider row

Single slider

(a)

Slider (Al_2O_3-SiC)

Connecting
pads

Film head

ABS rail

Tapered rail

(b)

Figure 5.4 (a) Wafer showing a row of sliders cut out and a single slider cut out
from this row. Each slider has two heads deposited on it. (b) Completed
slider showing two heads with four pads for electrical connections.

and performance. Flying height variations over the inner to outer diameter of the disk, head stability during flying, and the reliability of the head
and disk during starts and stops depend on the design of the head-surface
facing media. This subject is detailed further in Chapter 10. After rows
are lapped and polished, individual sliders are cut and finished as shown
in Figure 5.4b. Another parameter, called the *throat height*, of the head
is carefully controlled during lapping of head air-bearing surface. Throat
height is the length of head poles near the gap that defines gap height
(Figure 5.3a). Shorter throat height is desirable for the head to write with
maximum head field. On the other hand, the mechanical process of lapping
a row has tolerances; hence, there are trade-offs between shortest throat
heights and the possibility of yield loss due to lapping through gaps. Special resistance patterns on the wafers and numerous electrical and mechanical tools are designed to achieve maximum controls of these processes.

12. The slider is mounted on a suspension arm as shown in Figure 5.5.

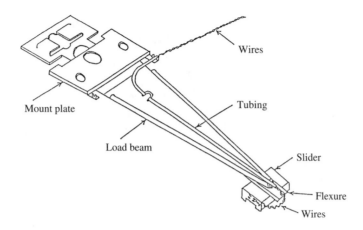

Figure 5.5 Head suspension assembly.

5.4 THIN AND THICK POLE HEADS

There are two types of film heads: thin-pole, thin-film heads and thick-pole, thin-film heads. The disk files with film heads during the decade from 1979 to 1989 were made almost exclusively with thin pole film heads. Pole thicknesses of thin pole heads ranged from slightly under 1 μm to 1.5 μm. Thin poles were able to deliver sufficient flux density for writing on relatively low-coercivity ($<$ 40 kA/m, 500 Oe) particulate media. Thin poles provided a built-in "equalization" or slimming of the output voltage pulses. As discussed in Section 8.18, slimmer pulses result in higher linear densities. Figure 5.6 shows calculated pulses for a single transition from film

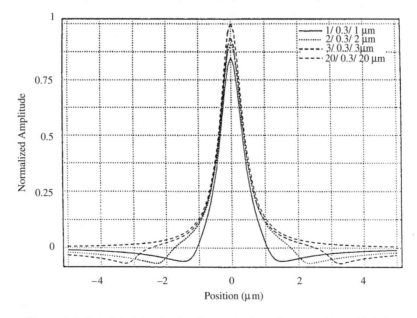

Figure 5.6 Calculated signal pulses from a single medium transition with 1-, 2-, 3-, and 20-μm thick poles.

heads of 1-μm , 2-μm, 3-μm, and 20-μm pole thicknesses. The pulse from 1-μm thick poles has undershoots close to the main pulse that sharpen the pulse, making pulse widths narrow. The 20-μm thick poles closely simulate ring or MIG head response which is given here for comparison. Notice that the peaks of the undershoots correspond roughly to the pole thicknesses. These undershoots result in a wavy output in the linear density versus voltage signal plot, which is called the *roll-off curve* (Section 8.18).

The reason for the use of thick poles in place of thin poles has been motivated by the ability of thick poles to deliver a higher magnetic field to the media during the writing process. As the current through copper conductors in the film head is increased, the magnetic flux through the Permalloy core increases proportionally. However, if the cross-sectional area through which the flux propagates is not large enough, the flux density will reach a limit M_s called *saturation magnetization*. For 81/19 Permalloy, the saturation magnetic field intensity is about 1 T (10 kG). After saturation occurs in any part of the magnetic flux path, the reluctance of the head circuit increases, and the efficiency of the head decreases. After this point, the field in the gap virtually stops increasing with increased currents. Thin poles of 1 μm will reach that limit at a lower field compared to thicker 3-μm thick pole heads. One way this limit is observed is in the overwrite capability of the head. Overwrite measurement is described in Section 8.16, and it relates to the ability of the head to erase existing information by writing new information on top of it and is measured in negative decibels, see equation (8.10). Higher overwrite reduces error rates and is desirable. Good overwrite capability can allow use of a high-coercivity medium, which in turn allows higher linear bit densities.

Advantages of thick pole, thin film heads were reported in 1982 [3]. It was shown that thick pole film heads were more suitable for writing on sputtered γ-Fe_2O_3 disks of coercivity H_c = 56 kA/m (700 Oe). Figure 5.7 shows the overwrite performance of 1-, 2-, and 3.5-μm thick pole heads. Overwrite of higher than −40 dB is obtained for 3.5-μm thick poles. For most disk drives, numbers between −25 dB and −30 dB are considered acceptable. This suggests that higher coercivity

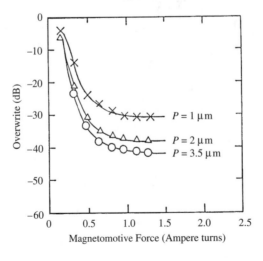

Figure 5.7 Overwrite of film heads with 1-, 2-, and 3.5-μm thick poles [3].

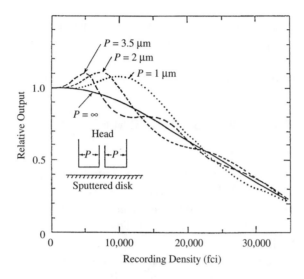

Figure 5.8 Roll-off curves of film heads with varying pole thicknesses [3].

disks can be used with these thick pole heads. Heads with 3- to 4-μm thick Permalloy poles are currently used with thin film disks of coercivities between 128 and 160 kA/m (1600 and 2000 Oe), depending on the flying height. Roll-off curves of 1-, 2-, and 3.5-μm and infinitely thick (ferrite head) pole thicknesses are shown in Figure 5.8. The waviness in the curves for 1-, 2-, and 3.5-waveforms, as described earlier. An infinitely thick pole curve simulates a ferrite head signal and is given here for comparison. Similarly, wavy outputs are observed in the outputs of these pole thicknesses when peak shift is measured against recording density (Figure 5.9). These curves suggest that for specific linear

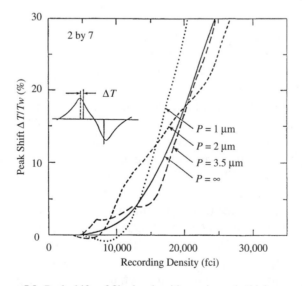

Figure 5.9 Peak shifts of film heads with varying pole thicknesses [3].

density, the pole thickness needs to be designed to optimize appropriate signal resolution and peak shift. Roll-off is described in Section 8.18, and peak shift is described in Section 8.3. With the introduction of thin film, high-coercivity disks,
thick pole film heads have become standard in the industry.

5.5 WRITING AND READING WITH FILM HEADS

In Sections 5.5 through 5.9, writing and reading performance of film heads is discussed. Section 5.6 describes *writing* issues related to the thin film head. Section
5.7 describes an equivalent circuit. This circuit applies to ferrite or MIG head, thin
film head, and also to the MR head. The characteristics of all three types of heads
can be studied and compared with this circuit by simply changing input parameters
for each type of head. Input parameters of interest are head resistance, inductance,
capacitance, number of turns, preamplifier loading, and damping resistance. The
output parameters of interest are the real part of head impedance as a function of
frequency and head resonance frequency. The first parameter relates to noise of a
head, and resonance frequency sets a high-frequency operation limit on the head.

Sections 5.8 and 5.9 discuss the modeling and performance of the thin film
head as they relate to film-head efficiency, film-head inductance, and signal-voltage
calculations. Details of equation derivations are minimal here. An appendix gives
the format for calculating the voltage of a thin film head, which may be useful for
computer modeling of a head-disk system.

5.6 FILM HEAD WRITING

The current through the conductors of the thin film head should generate sufficient
magnetic flux in the Permalloy core of the head and deliver it to the gap of the head at
the air-bearing surface. Two factors influence this process. One is the effectiveness
or efficiency of the head to convert electrical current into magnetic flux; the other
is the ability of the flux to produce field in the gap with minimum obstruction or
saturation in the Permalloy magnetic path. Saturation in the yoke, back gap (the
small area connection between lower and upper yoke plates), and the region close to
the beginning of the throat area are commonly known to prevent application of flux
to the front poles. The objective of film-head structure and process development is
to avoid saturation in these areas. In the absence of these problems, the pole corners
near the gap saturate first when sufficient current is applied. The writing takes place
at the trailing edge of the pole; hence, the construction process is designed to avoid
kinks or thinning of the upper yoke near the throat region.

Figure 5.10 shows the schematic of the write driver and a slightly under-
damped current waveform of the output. The current peak and the rise time of
the waveform are important parameters, since overwrite of the head, off-track side

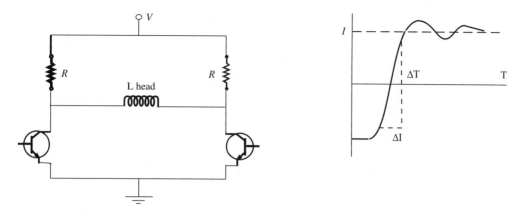

Figure 5.10 Write current circuit and current waveform.

writing, and peak shift or transition shifts in the written data are dependent on the write pulse and are governing factors in the error-rate performance of the system. The write rise time is a strong function of the inductance of the head. As an example, consider the approximate rise time of the head given by

$$\Delta t = -\frac{L}{V}\Delta I \qquad (5.1)$$

where L and V are inductance and voltage, respectively, and ΔI is the current change. For a 5-volt supply and current rise of 50 ma, a MIG head with an inductance of 3 μH will have a rise time of 30 nsec. A typical 30-turn film head with 0.5-μH inductance would result in a rise time of 5 nsec. In an application with a linear density of 68,000 b/i (2677 b/mm), assuming 1,7 coding (explained in Section 8.6), flux change per mm is 2000. For a typical disk linear velocity of 20 m/sec, the time between flux changes is calculated as 25 nsec. Obviously, a MIG head with 30-nsec rise time is unacceptable for the application while the film head is usable.

5.7 EQUIVALENT CIRCUIT OF INDUCTIVE AND MR HEADS

The equivalent circuit of a head is shown in Figure 5.11a. While most of the discussion here relates to inductive heads, the MR head is included for comparison. The circuit is applicable to all heads; only component values differ according to the type of the head. The R_h, L_h, and C_h in each case are the resistance, inductance, and capacitance of the head. R_d is an external resistance used in the circuit and is called the *damping resistance*. The purpose of the damping resistance is to reduce transients in drive current waveform during writing. For ferrite heads with large inductance, such damping is a necessity. Since writing and reading in an inductive head are performed by the same element, the secondary effect of damping resistance during reading is to reduce the resonance of the circuit and also to reduce

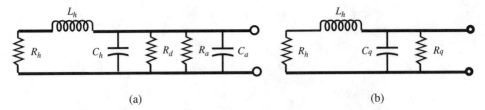

Figure 5.11 (a) Equivalent circuit of a head; (b) simplified equivalent circuit of a head.

the steep rise in equivalent resistance of the circuit near the resonance frequency. There is a limit to how much damping can be used. Too much damping distorts the write current pulse and contributes to bit shifts. For an MR head, the write head element is inductive, and it has a separate drive circuit so damping influences only the write process and can be optimized accordingly. The R_a and C_a are the equivalent resistance and capacitance of the preamplifier, and they significantly modify the response of the head equivalent circuit.

The equivalent circuit gives quantitative assessment of two factors:

1. The noise of the head can be calculated from the equivalent resistance of the head. The ratio of signal to noise is a determinant in controlling error rates in the disk drive.

2. The resonance frequency of the circuit can be computed. Resonance frequency sets the upper limit on the usable bandwidth of the head in a system. The highest frequency of the signal being detected by the detecting preamplifier should be less than the resonance frequency of the equivalent circuit. The equivalent circuit of Figure 5.11a is first simplified to fewer elements by combining two parallel resistances (R_d and R_a) and two capacitances ($C_h + C_a = C_q$) (see Figure 5.11b).

The next three impedances in parallel can be combined by usual circuit manipulation techniques to obtain the following expression for $Re(Z)$, the real part of the impedance.

$$Re(Z) = \frac{R_q[R_h(R_h + R_q) + (\omega L_h)^2]}{[(R_h + R_q) - R_q L_h(C_h + C_a)\omega^2]^2 + [L_h + R_h R_q(C_h + C_a)]^2 \omega^2}$$
(5.2)

where $\omega = 2\pi f$, f = frequency, and $R_q = R_a R_d/(R_a + R_d)$. Table 5.1 describes typical values for two film heads, one MIG head and an MR head. The data for the MIG and one of the film heads comes from [4].

TABLE 5.1 Comparison of Electrical Parameters of Various Head Types

Head	No. of Turns	R_h (ohms)	L_h (nH)	R_d (ohms)	C_h (pF)	f_R (MHz)
MIG	34	4.4	1580	2800	5	25
Film	30	31	475	292	5	46
Film	50	50	1000	500	5	32
MR	1	25	40	Open	5	159

The lead wires from the head to the preamplifier also contribute to the R, L, and C of the equivalent circuit. For this illustration, a 2-cm, long twisted pair of lead wires is assumed which has typical parameters of $R = 1$ ohm, $L = 40$ nH, and $C = 2$ pF. These values are included in the corresponding head parameters in the table. For the MR head, the single turn of the MR stripe contributes negligibly to the inductance; hence, only lead inductance is included in the circuit. Following the preamplifier parameters used in [4], resistance of 750 ohms in parallel with 20-pF capacitance is assumed for all head circuits. Resonance frequencies f_R of the head circuits are calculated using head inductance and total capacitance of the circuit and using equation (5.3). Figure 5.12 displays plots of $Re(Z)$ for the four heads calculated with the use of equation (5.2) and circuit parameters of the heads from the table. Notice that the peaks of $Re(Z)$ for each head coincide with the calculated resonance frequencies of the respective head.

5.8 NUMBER OF TURNS AND RESONANCE FREQUENCY OF INDUCTIVE HEADS

Two key figures of merits for inductive heads are

1. Signal-to-noise ratio.
2. Resonance frequency of the head circuit.

Simple considerations indicate that the signal-to-noise ratio can be increased with an increased number of turns. To a first approximation, the signal S is proportional to

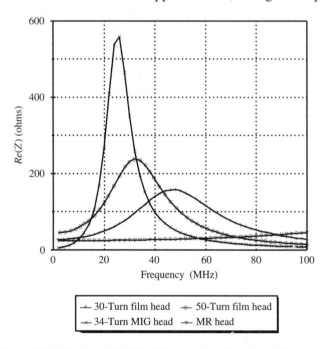

Figure 5.12 "Real part" $Re(Z)$ of four heads as functions of frequency.

the number of turns n. The resistance of the head is also proportional to n. The noise N of a resistance is proportional to the square root of the resistance. Hence, the ratio signal-to-noise S/N is proportional to $\sqrt{n}$. Increasing the number of turns increases the signal-to-noise ratio. The subjects of signal-to-noise ratio and error rates are discussed in Sections 8.19 through 8.23. However, one adverse effect of increasing the number of turns is the decrease in resonance frequency. Equation (5.3) describes resonance frequency in terms of circuit parameters. Since L is proportional to n^2, f_R (resonance frequency), according to the equation, is proportional to $1/n$. The increase in turns thus reduces f_R.

The resonance frequency of the head imposes a limit on the frequency of operation. The bit shift of the head output increases severely as the upper-bandwidth frequency of the application approaches resonance frequency. A general practice for the inductive head has been to use up to one-half, or at most two-thirds, the value of resonance frequency as an upper limit of the application frequency. Resonance frequency is calculated from the equation

$$f_R = \frac{1}{2\pi\sqrt{L_h(C_h + C_a)}} \tag{5.3}$$

Notice the importance of head inductance from this equation. One of the major motivations behind the development and use of the thin film head in place of ferrite and MIG heads has been the lower head inductance. One way of prolonging the use of inductive heads for disk drive technology is to increase its number of head turns. The increase in number of turns increases the head inductance. Advancements in processing technology and new designs such as the diamond head, flat head, planar construction, and multilayers permit increasing the number of turns with smaller inductance per n^2. This ratio of head inductance to n^2 can be considered as a figure of merit of inductive head technology so it is interesting to explore it in some detail. The ratio (L/n^2) is designated as a factor k in nanohenries per square turn. The inductance of the head L is then given by kn^2. Head designers attempt to decrease k of the head by clever designs and process advancements. From a survey of recent publications, it is observed that film head k appears to range between 0.5 and 0.7. A few designs are under development that suggest that it may be possible to improve k to between 0.3 and 0.4. For comparison purposes, a film head k factor of 0.6 will be used as state of the art, while 0.3 is used as a future potential. For MIG head, k values of 2.6 and 1.3 are used to represent current status and future advancement, respectively. Using these values, the inductances of heads with a varying number of turns are calculated. With these inductance values and a constant capacitance of 25 pF, four resonance frequency plots are made as functions of the number of turns. These are shown in Figure 5.13. The two lower curves provide boundaries for MIG head high-frequency capability, while the two upper curves indicate the range for thin film heads. The uppermost curve corresponds to the thin film head with $k = 0.3$, with the highest resonance frequencies, while the lowest curve corresponds to the MIG head with state-of-the-art $k = 2.6$.

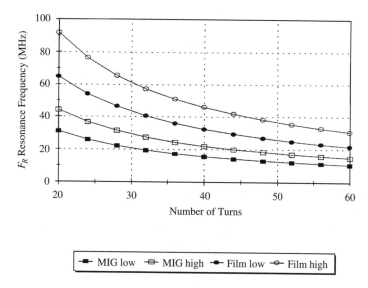

Figure 5.13 Resonance frequencies of inductive heads as functions of number of turns.

The highest required frequency f_H of a drive can be calculated for given linear density, linear velocity, and code. For example, with 1,7 code (Section 8.6), f_H is given by

$$f_H = \left(\frac{1}{33.87}\right)(\text{bpi})(v)\left(\frac{1000}{2}\right) \tag{5.4}$$

where bpi is bits per inch and v is the velocity in meters per second. The first term relates bpi to flux changes per mm. The last term is due to conversion of velocity from m/sec to mm/sec, and the factor 2 is due to 2 flux changes per cycle of frequency. As an example, for 68,000 bpi and velocity of 20 meters/sec, $f_H = 20$ MHz. Assuming the ratio of resonance frequency to f_H of 3/2, improved MIG heads may be usable with up to 30 turns. With the current technology, thin film heads can be used up to 40 turns, while improved designs may allow over 50 turns to meet the design criteria.

5.9 THIN FILM-HEAD EFFICIENCY AND INDUCTANCE MODELING

Voltage read by the film head is directly proportional to the efficiency of the head. The efficiency of a ring head was discussed in Chapter 3, Section 3.3. For clarity, let us recap the definition of efficiency. The current I through the head coil of n turns results in the magnetic field in the gap of the head. Ideally, $nI = H_g g$ on both sides represented by ampere-turns. However, due to losses in the process of delivering ampere-turns from the coil to the gap, the flux is reduced by a factor η or head efficiency. During reading, the magnetic flux reversals in the medium are sensed by the poles of the head, and these fields are sensed by the coil. The signal generated in the coil depends on the efficiency, η, of this process as well.

The following discussion relates to finding η or "efficiency" in terms of the geometry of the head and magnetic parameters. There are three approaches to estimating and using an efficiency factor. Most practical thin film heads have an efficiency between 0.6 and 0.9. Fairly rigorous formulations of efficiency are discussed in Refs. [5–8]. An intermediate approach is used here for appreciating the effects of head geometry parameters on thin film head efficiency. This approach results in a relatively simple equation for calculating head efficiency. In Chapter 3 (equations 3.8–3.11) ring head efficiency was derived in terms of magnetic reluctances of the magnetic field paths. In the case of the film head, the coil turns are spread out between two layers of Permalloy magnetic path. Hence, each turn is not equally effective in contributing to the field in the gap; a coil turn close to the gap contributes more to the gap field than a remote turn. The calculation of the efficiency should include the distributed nature of the conductors. The distributed nature of the currents and magnetic fields results in a structure analogous to a transmission line. The expressions for efficiency and inductance of a thin film head are obtained [5] by considering pieces of transmission lines for each conductor turn and accounting for changes in the geometry of the Permalloy path. The method includes solving separate transmission-line equations with connecting sections represented by matching boundary conditions. This concept has been extended [6] to a quasi-three-dimensional analysis by including linearly varying geometries of the Permalloy path in two dimensions. For accurate treatment of the topic, one of these two analyses can be programmed on a computer. The simplest model of a film head was proposed [7] where the head was simulated by a single section of a transmission line. This model is useful for "back of the envelope calculation" and a stepping-stone to more complex efficiency models. The low-frequency efficiency of a film head with a single section is given by [7]

$$\eta_1 = \frac{\tanh(k_1 l_1)}{k_1 l_1} \qquad (5.5)$$

where $k_1 = 1/(\mu_r p_1 g_1)^{1/2}$
        $p_1 = $ the thickness of the Permalloy core
        $\mu_r = $ the permeability of the Permalloy
        $g_1 = $ the gap width.

As a by-product of the efficiency calculation, distributed inductance of the single-section transmission line is also calculated as

$$L = \frac{\mu_0 \mu_r w p_1 n^2}{2 l_1}(1 - \eta_1) \qquad (5.6)$$

where $\mu_0 = $ the permeability of free space and has a value of $4\pi 10^{-7}$ H/m
        $\mu_r = $ the relative permeability of Permalloy poles and ranges between
                500 and 4000
        $w = $ the track width of the head
        $n = $ the number of turns.

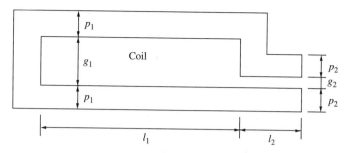

Figure 5.14 Two-section transmission line model of a film head.

Strictly, these two equations are applicable only for low frequencies. The transmission line analytical model, including quasi-three-dimensional geometry and complex effective permeability applicable at high frequencies has been reported [8].

A reasonable approximation for the efficiency of the film head can be obtained with a two-section transmission line model. This analysis follows the basic procedure of Ref. [5] and considers a two-section transmission line. The two-section model is shown in Figure 5.14. The length l_1 is assumed to have a single conductor carrying current equal to the ampere-turns of a multiconductor head. It has a wide gap, g_1, to accommodate conductors and insulating layers. Section l_2 has a narrow gap g_2. This section is often referred to as a *throat height* of the film head. Using two transmission line sections and applying appropriate boundary conditions, an analytical equation for efficiency is obtained as

$$\eta = \left[\frac{\tanh(k_1 l_1)}{k_1 l_1}\right]\left[\frac{1}{\cosh(k_2 l_2) + (k_2/k_1)^{1/2}\tanh(k_1 l_1)\sinh(k_2 l_2)}\right] \quad (5.7)$$

where
$$k_1 = 1/(\mu_r p_1 g_1)^{1/2}$$
$$k_2 = 1/(\mu_r p_2 g_2)^{1/2}$$
$$p_1 \text{ and } p_2 = \text{thicknesses in respective sections.}$$

We assume thicknesses of both poles at the air-bearing surface as p_2 and thicknesses of Permalloy yoke plates in length l_1 as p_1. μ_r is the relative permeability of all the Permalloy parts. Figures 5.15, 5.16, and 5.17 are plotted to study the sensitivity of head efficiency when only one parameter is varied at a time. Nominal values assumed for this example are

$$\mu_r = 1600$$
$$g_1 = 5\ \mu m$$
$$g_2 = 0.4\ \mu m$$
$$p_1, p_2 = 3\ \mu m$$
$$l_1 = 80\ \mu m$$
$$l_2 = 1\ \mu m$$

Nominal efficiency for these parameters is calculated to be 0.8.

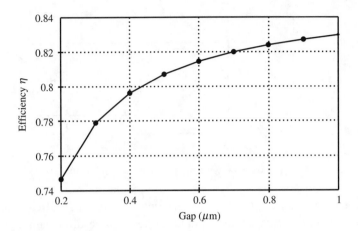

Figure 5.15 Gap versus efficiency of a film head.

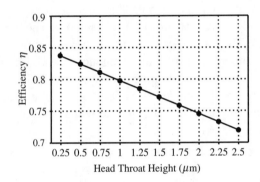

Figure 5.16 Throat height versus efficiency.

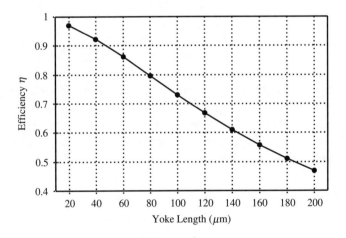

Figure 5.17 Yoke length versus efficiency.

According to Figure 5.15, a wide gap results in high efficiency and is desirable for writing. However, larger gaps result in increased P_{50}, the half-pulse width of the voltage signal, equation (3.27). Since small P_{50} is preferable for high linear density (see Section 8.18), the gap size determination is a compromise. Separate write and read heads on a slider can allow individual optimizations of these functions but at a cost of increased process complexity.

Figure 5.16 describes a drop in efficiency with increasing throat height l_2. A small throat height is preferable. Attainment of small throat height requires close control of mechanical lapping and polishing processes during slider fabrication. Submicrometer tolerances during mechanical operations are difficult to achieve and require carefully designed electrical lapping guides and tight process controls during lapping operations. As the state of the art advances, throat heights are decreasing from a few micrometers to submicrometer lengths.

Figure 5.17 indicates that high efficiency requires the yoke region covering the coil conductor (l_1) to be small. The read signal from the gap is directly proportional to the number of turns. Increase in number of turns can be achieved through (1) longer l_1, (2) multiple layers, or (3) smaller size conductors and smaller spacings between conductors. Having multiple layers for a given number of turns will make a head more efficient. As deposition and photolithography processes improve, more turns are accommodated in a given length l_1 of the head. A 50-turn head with four layers has been reported.

The inductance formula for a two-section transmission line is derived using the procedure of Ref. [5], and the result is

$$
L = \frac{\mu_0 \mu_r w p_1 n^2}{2l_1} \left\{ 1 - \left[\frac{\tanh(k_1 l_1)}{k_1 l_1} \right] \frac{1}{1 + (k_1)/(k_2)^{1/2} \tanh(k_1 l_1) \tanh(k_2 l_2)} \right\}
\tag{5.8}
$$

The formula gives the inductance of the part of the coil covered by Permalloy poles. There is a second component of the coil inductance corresponding to the coil conductor outside of the Permalloy sandwich. The first part is generally much larger and is sufficient for engineering estimates.

5.10 APPLICATIONS OF FILM HEAD INDUCTANCE MEASUREMENTS

As seen in Section 5.9, the efficiency and inductance of a head are functions of the head internal geometry and permeability. Moreover, head operating conditions, such as saturation of the head in some part of its geometry, would also affect these parameters. Efficiency is not observable directly, but inductance can be measured. Since inductance and track width are correlated (equation 5.8), measurement of inductance reveals a lack of uniformities in track widths for a set of heads. Also, measurement of inductance versus head gap reveals permeability variations [9].

Measurement of inductance as a function of DC current through the coil reveals the onset of saturation. The current at which the inductance shows signs of saturation may exhibit location of the saturation in the head flux circuit. The shorting of coil turns may be more sensitively detected with measurement of inductance rather than by resistance [9]. A method of controlling throat-height lapping end points by measuring inductance as a function of current through the coil has been reported [10]. Detection accuracy of 0.6 μm in throat height was obtained using this method.

5.11 READING WITH THIN FILM HEADS

We have already seen some characteristics of reading with film heads. Figure 5.6 showed voltage pulses computed for an isolated transition in the media. The voltage equation in terms of the head field with the same assumptions as used for equation (3.22) but usable for computing thin film head response is

$$V_x(x\prime, d) = -2\mu_0 n\upsilon w\eta(M_r\delta)\left[\frac{H_x(x, d + a)}{gH_g}\right] \tag{5.9}$$

Szczech [11] formulated a field equation for thin film heads and used measurements on a large-scale physical model of a film head to fill in boundary conditions. The field derived in this way is described by the summation of four parts:

$$H_x(x, y) = A + B + C + D \tag{5.10}$$

These terms are given in the appendix to this chapter, and they can be used for a complete pulse waveform calculation as well as for estimating roll-off characteristics and peak shifts. The voltage pulses shown in Figure 5.6 were calculated using these terms. The results of Figure 5.6 indicate that at $x = 0$, the difference between the peak voltage of a 3-μm thick pole head and a 20-μm thick pole head (which simulates a semi-infinite pole ring head) is relatively small. The first term, A, of equation (5.10) turns out to be the solution of a semi-infinite pole head (sometimes referred to as a *Karlqvist head*). Consider equation (3.25) and term A in the appendix. For the peak voltage calculation of a thick pole head, equation (3.25) may be a good approximation for practical purposes. It is also seen that the half-pulse widths of a thick pole head and a semi-infinite pole head are fairly close, and equation (3.27) may be used to approximate the half-pulse width of a thick pole head (see Fig. 5.6). With these considerations, the results of parameter variations in Figures 3.11 through 3.14 may be applied to thick pole heads. The terms B, C, and D of equation (5.10) are the result of interactions of undershoots at the boundaries of the finite poles. In the case of thin-thin (one micrometer size) pole heads, these undershoots play an important role in equalizing the pulse, reducing the pulse width, and decreasing peak voltage at $x = 0$; hence, these terms cannot be neglected. In the case of 3-μm and thicker pole heads, the undershoots are far away from the center of the voltage pulse and their influence may be neglected for engineering estimates.

5.12 PROCESSES AND MATERIALS FOR THIN FILM HEADS

The performance of a thin film head is strongly tied to its magnetic characteristics, which in turn are a function of the materials and processes used for its construction. The future improvements or breakthroughs in film head technology depend heavily on newer concepts as well as handling of new materials. This section is aimed at providing first-pass understanding of these factors and appreciation of research in the field.

The required characteristics and reasons behind applications of specific materials for film head poles are given in Tables 5.2 and 5.3 and are from [12].

TABLE 5.2　Ideal Pole Material Characteristics for Inductive Thin Film Heads [12]

Characteristic	Advantage
High permeability	High efficiency
Large saturation magnetization	Large gap field
Low magnetostriction	Low media contact noise
Wear and corrosion resistance	Long life
Small non-zero anisotropy	Domain structure control
High resistivity	Minimization of eddy currents
Low hysteresis loss	Low thermal noise

The effect of permeability on the efficiency of the head was covered in the earlier sections. Pole saturation magnetization was also discussed in Section 5.4. Medium noise due to low magnetostriction is not a major issue for flying-head rigid disk drives, but it is important for "in-contact" flexible-medium recording and may become important with in-contact rigid-disk recording. The control of anisotropy in material to control domain noise, often referred to as *Barkhausen noise,* is very important and plays a major role in the design and processing of narrow-track thin film heads. As frequencies of operation increase, eddy currents become an important problem, particularly with low-resistivity Permalloy material. At some stage, laminations will be needed to reduce eddy currents and excessive phase shifts in data, in the case of Permalloy pole heads. Hysteresis loss in heads contributes to the head circuit as an effective resistance that gives rise to thermal noise. As signal-to-noise ratio becomes critical with high-density recording, this factor gains in importance. The materials in Table 5.3 are either already used or are being considered for future applications for film head poles.

Most heads today use Permalloy as the pole material. Wet processes or electroplating is commonly used in the deposition of Permalloy. The logical reasons for these choices have to do with an existing knowledge base, economy of scaling production, and the ability of electroplating experts to keep up with the need for advances in the technology. Several manufacturers have developed commercial

TABLE 5.3 Important Material Characteristics [12]

	Permalloy	Sendust	CoZr
Composition (wt%)	$Ni_{81}Fe_{19}$	$Al_{5.4}Fe_{65}Si_{9.6}$	$Co_{90}Zr_{10}$
Relative permeability μ_r (at 10 MHz)	~ 1000	~ 1000	~ 1500
Saturation magnetization T (kG)	1 (10)	1.1 (11)	1.4 (14)
Uniaxial anisotropy (ergs/cm^3)	2×10^3	Unknown	4×10^3
Magnetostriction	$< 10^{-6}$	$< 10^{-6}$	2×10^{-6}
Resistivity ($\mu\Omega$-cm)	18	> 85	> 100
Recrystallization temperature °C	~ 425	~ 700	~ 450
Thermal stability	Excellent	Excellent	Uncertain
Corrosion resistance	Poor	Unknown	Uncertain
Wear resistance	Poor	Better	Best

production of Permalloy pole structures with dry-process deposition and subtractive photolithographic processes to make yokes and poles of thin film heads. There are definite advantages of using dry processes in the future for the processing of thin film heads. Materials like Sendust and CoZr and a large number of alloy and amorphous materials are deposited only by dry processes. For the future, high-B_s materials will be sputtered or evaporated. Laminated structures of all materials require dry deposition. The control of magnetic domains (see Section 2.15) requires specific parameter controls, and dry processes have more flexibility to be adaptable for changing requirements. There is a continual knowledge gained in deposition and subtractive milling of structures in semiconductor technology that disk drive technology may be able to use.

5.13 PROGRESS AND RESEARCH ON THIN FILM HEADS

Early film heads [2] had 8-turn coils and track widths of 30–38 μm. Both the Permalloy poles/yoke and copper conductors were electroplated. The insulation layers between coil and yoke were made of photosensitive resins. With time, these processes have progressed to the development of 24 turns and 31 turns in two layers. Track widths have shrunk to under 4 μm. There is an abundance of published papers describing incremental progress in the technology of film heads. Highlights of a few that were either pacesetters or have strategic importance in the future progress of film heads (either as complete film heads or as a write element of MR heads) are presented here.

Dry-processed CoZr pole heads with a 17-turn plated copper coil, 15-μm track width, and 0.2-μm gap were developed in 1984 [13]. These heads had relative permeability of 3500, at 10 MHz, a B_s of 14 kG (1.4 T), and coercivity of 0.05 Oe. D_{50} of 36 K flux reversals per inch with overwrite of -34 dB were observed, proving the superiority of CoZr material over conventional NiFe heads. Four-layer laminated CoZr/Ta heads were fabricated in 1988 [14], which showed high B_s of 14 kG (1.4 T) compared to 10 kG (1 T) for Permalloy heads. However, it was observed that the signal decreased with subsequent annealing with or without an applied field. The decrease in signal is attributed to a decrease in permeability of the material. The instability of some of the magnetic properties has been the major roadblock in use of amorphous materials for thin film heads. Heads with CoZrRe amorphous pole and yoke were developed in 1989 [15]. These heads were found to be more stable and had near-zero (less than $+2, 5 \times 10^{-7}$) magnetostriction. A B_s of 12 kG (1.2 T) was obtained. However, a limitation on the material is that the maximum process temperature should not exceed 200°C.

The paper on gigabit recording [16] describes the use of a plated Permalloy inductive head for writing. Reading in this case was accomplished by an MR head. The write head had 8 turns and 4-μm thick poles. Track widths of 2.5 to 4.5 μm were achieved by ion milling of pole thicknesses near the air-bearing surface. A 2-gigabit-per-square-inch demonstration [17] also used separate read and write heads to achieve 17,000 tracks per inch. The write head was a 17-turn thin film inductive head using 2-μm thick, Fe-based multilayered films. The multilayers consisted of 480-nm-thick magnetic layers and 20-nm thick nonmagnetic intermediate layers. The head poles had B_s of 2 T (20 kG). The track width of 1 μm was achieved using a focused ion beam (FIB) etching process.

From the foregoing summary of inductive thin film head activity, it can be concluded that the major research in the field is directed toward

1. Achieving high B_s in head poles with stable magnetic performance and manufacturable processes and learning to control materials and processes for high-yield manufacturing.
2. Understanding domain mechanisms that cause wiggles and other forms of noise in the output signal.

5.14 INSTABILITY, WIGGLES, AND MULTIDOMAINS IN FILM HEADS

Figure 5.18 shows pulse outputs of the same isolated transition before and after a film head was excited by writing on a remote track [18]. This is an example of the irregularity in a thin film head output. It has been observed that under conventional writing and reading processes, film head outputs often exhibit the following characteristics (1) extra "wiggles" as seen in the trailing side of the pulse in Figure 5.18, (2) variations in signal peak amplitude or (3) variations in signal width. This unpredictable reading of the same data by a head contributes to the total head noise and an increase in the error rate of the head-disk system. Existence of extra wiggles is referred as "domain noise," "popcorn noise," or "Barkhausen noise" in the literature. The unpredictability and distortion of the head-disk output are referred to as *head instability*. The

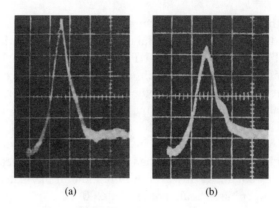

(a)   (b)

Figure 5.18 Thin film head isolated pulses before and after writing on a remote track [18].

subject of understanding and then eliminating these problems has been studied in detail. The factors that influence this noise source and precautions taken by design and process engineers to reduce it are summarized.

The conventional theory of magnetics indicates that given a field H at the tip of the head pole from a medium transition, a flux density $B = \mu_0\mu_r H$ is generated inside the pole and transmitted along the magnetic path, μ_r being the relative permeability of the pole material. In reality, the process of transmitting flux within magnetic material is complex. Figure 5.19 shows the domains of magnetization in a pole and yoke region of a head. During the construction of the head pole, a large field is applied to establish an easy axis or the preferred direction of magnetization. Ideally, the majority of domains tend to align with this easy axis. However, as pointed out in Section 2.15, establishment of domains follows the rule of minimizing energy by forming closed circuits for flux. So the domain patterns like those shown in Figure 5.19 are established. Each domain has walls or boundaries known as *Bloch walls* for thick (greater than 100 nm) films. Also, each domain has a local magnetization equal to the saturation magnetization of the material. When an external field from the medium is applied perpendicular to the pole surface, the magnetization inside the material is propagated by rotation of the domain magnetizations and motion of the domain walls. If all these processes of transmitting flux inside material were fully reversible, an ideal linear head performance would result. However, inherent (or process-generated) material defects, variation in material compositions, and a number of other factors can randomly pin the wall motion in one or more directions and a noisy and unpredictable signal is often generated in the head output.

Domain patterns in the pole and yoke structures of film heads have been observed and measured [19] by a magneto-optical method. Figure 5.20 shows the difference between two structures with different magnetostriction constants and corresponding domain patterns. It is concluded that the domain patterns with negative magnetostriction (Section 2.14) provide more stable heads. During the development

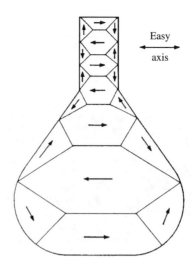

Easy
axis

Figure 5.19 Domain configuration in an inductive film head.

of dry-processed heads, researchers [20] observed that negative λ's of the pole material resulted in wiggle-free readouts (Figure 5.21a). They also pointed out that there is a window of NiFe composition (see Figure 5.21b) within which high permeability and wiggle-free output are obtained.

5.15 SILICON PLANAR THIN FILM HEAD

A new method of processing a thin film head was reported at Intermag 1989 [21]. This method constructs the planar head on top of a silicon wafer (see Figure 5.22). The slider air-bearing surface is also constructed on the same surface. Conventional film head processes involve two different phases:

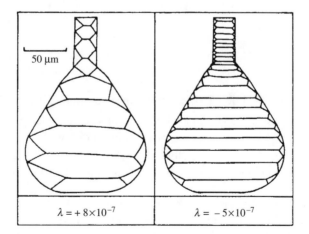

50 μm

$\lambda = + 8 \times 10^{-7}$ $\lambda = -5 \times 10^{-7}$

Figure 5.20 Domain configurations in the positive and negative magnetostrictive Permalloy films [19].

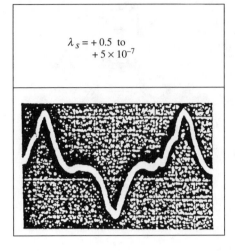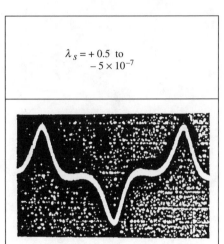

(a)

(b)

Figure 5.21 (a) Correlation between head readout wiggles and magnetostriction constants λ_s; (b) the term λ_s versus composition of Ni [20].

1. Thin film depositions on top of a ceramic substrate.

2. Construction of an air-bearing surface on a face perpendicular to the deposition surface after the wafer is cut into rows (see Figure 5.4a). This second phase includes a number of mechanical steps such as grinding, lapping, polishing, and the like. They add substantial cost to the head manufacturing.

One objective of the planar process is to carry out both the depositions and fabrication of the slider air-bearing surface in a continuous semiconductorlike processing. Figure 5.22, on the right, shows the air-bearing surface and the location of the heads on the same surface. Figure 5.23 shows the schematic of the head. The magnetic

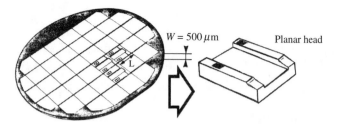

Figure 5.22 Silicon planar head wafer and slider [21].

layers form a ring structure with a gap on the top. Each of the two connected coils surrounds the two sides of the Permalloy path. For connecting the coil to the external circuit, a hole is created in the silicon substrate by laser drilling, and conductor deposition in the hole is done by a vacuum deposition process. There are several advantages of this structure:

1. The whole process is carried out on a silicon wafer; hence, all the semiconductor processing tools are directly applicable to the head making. Since the silicon wafer size is rapidly increasing (approaching 8 inches in diameter), head manufacturing directly benefits from increasing production efficiencies of the scaled-up wafer sizes.

2. The cost of second-phase fabrication operations of current manufacturing may be reduced with silicon planar processes.

3. Throat height of the head is now controllable through the deposition process; hence, a much more uniform head-to-head performance is possible.

4. Two divided conductor coils are more efficient and provide double the flux for a given number of turns compared to a conventional film head, and this results in half the head inductance for a given number of turns.

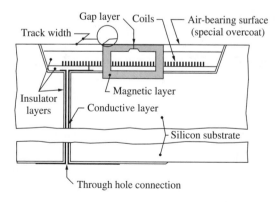

Figure 5.23 Schematic view of silicon planar thin film head [21].

Some of the challenges of the head structure are

1. A through-hole connection and conductor layer deposition in the hole (see Figure 5.23) appear to be an unconventional and challenging process.
2. The gap is defined by photolithographic processes.

The resolution of the best conventional lithography is currently about 0.36 μm and is expected to decrease to 0.2 μm by the year 2000. The current film heads achieve 0.2 μm in manufacturing by the deposition process. High linear densities require 0.2 μm and shorter gaps.

APPENDIX: HEAD GAP FIELD FOR A THIN FILM HEAD

The gap field of a thin film head is given by the following expression of four parts. The first term A is exactly the same as equation (3.2), that is, the field equation for the semi-infinite pole (attributed to Karlqvist and discussed in Chapter 3). Section 5.11 comments on application of this equation.

$$H_x(x, y) = A + B + C + D \qquad (A.1)$$

$$A = \frac{H_g}{\pi}\left(\arctan\frac{v}{y} - \arctan\frac{w}{y}\right)$$

$$B = \frac{0.59gH_gy}{2\pi}\left[\frac{1}{y^2 + (P_2 + v)^2} + \frac{1}{y^2 + (P_1 - w)^2}\right]$$

$$C = \frac{gH_gP_2}{4\pi}\left(\frac{v^2 - y^2}{v^2 + y^2}\right)\left[\arctan\left(\frac{P_2 + v}{y}\right) - \frac{\pi}{2}\right]$$

$$- \frac{(P_2 + 2v)y}{(v^2 + y^2)(y^2 + (P_2 + v)^2)} - \frac{yv}{(v^2 + y^2)^2}\ln\left(\frac{P_2^2}{y^2 + (P_2 + v)^2}\right)$$

$$D = \frac{gH_gP_2}{4\pi}\left(\frac{w^2 - y^2}{w^2 + y^2}\right)\left[\tan^{-1}\left(\frac{P_1 - w}{y}\right) - \frac{\pi}{2}\right]$$

$$- \frac{(P_1 - 2w)y}{(w^2 + y^2)(y^2 + (P_1 - w)^2)} + \frac{yw}{(w^2 + y^2)^2}\ln\left(\frac{P_1^2}{y^2 + (P_1 - w)^2}\right)$$

In this appendix, $v = x + g/2$, $w = x - g/2$, P_1 and P_2 are the pole thicknesses of the film head, and g is the gap. For a specific flying height d and transition parameter a, substitute $y = d + a$.

REFERENCES

[1] L. T. Romankiw, I. Croll, and M. Hatzakis, "Batch-fabricated thin-film magnetic recording heads," *IEEE Trans. Magn.,* MAG-6 (1970), p. 597.

[2] R. E. Jones, Jr., "IBM 3370 film head design and fabrication," *IBM Disk Storage Technology GA* 26-1665-0 (1980), p. 6.

[3] A. Kakeshi, M. Oshiki, T. Aikawa, M. Sasaki, and T. Kozai, "A thin film head for high density recording," *IEEE Trans. Magn.,* MAG-18 (1982), p. 1131.

[4] E. M. Williams, Chapter 7, in T. C. Arnoldussen and L. L. Nunnelley, eds., *Noise in Digital Magnetic Recording,* Word Scientific Publishing Co. (1992), p. 235.

[5] R. E. Jones, Jr., "Analysis of the efficiency and inductance of multi-turn thin film magnetic recording heads," *IEEE Trans. Magn.,* MAG-14 (1978), p. 509.

[6] T. C. Arnoldussen, "A modular transmission line/reluctance head model," *IEEE Trans. Magn.,* MAG-24 (1988), p. 2482.

[7] A. Paton, "Analysis of the efficiency of thin-film magnetic recording heads," *J. Appl. Phys.,* vol. 42 (1972), p. 5868.

[8] Erich P. Valstyn and Houblin Haung, "An extended dynamic transmission line model for thin film heads," *IEEE Trans. Magn.,* MAG-29 (1993), p. 3870.

[9] R. C. Anderson and R. E. Jones, Jr., "Substrate testing of film heads," *IEEE Trans. Magn.,* MAG-17 (1981), p. 2896.

[10] K. Kawakami, M. Suda, M. Aihara, M. Fukuoka, Y. Hagiwara, and K. Takeshita, "Electrical detection of end point in polishing process of thin film heads," *IEEE Trans. Magn.,* MAG-28 (1992), p. 2109.

[11] T. J. Szczech, "The use of equations for the field components of a thin film head for calculating isolated pulse output," *IEEE Trans. Magn.,* MAG-16 (1980), p. 985.

[12] W. D. Doyle and T. Jagielinski, "Magnetic materials in thin-film inductive heads," *Physics of Magnetic Materials,* edited by W. Gorzkowski, World Scientific Publishing Co. (1992), p. 235.

[13] K. Yamada, T. Maruyama, H. Tanaka, H. Kaneko, I. Kgaya, and S. Ito, "A thin film head for high density magnetic recording using CoZr amorphous films," *J. Appl. Phys.,* vol. 55 (1984), p. 2235.

[14] James L. Su, Mao-Min Chen, Jerry Lo, and Rod E. Lee, "Laminated CoZr amorphous thin-film recording heads," *J. Appl. Phys.,* vol. 43 (1988), p. 4020.

[15] C. Nishimura, K. Yamagisawa, A. Tago, and J. Kishigami, "CoZrRe amorphous film heads for high density magnetic recording," *IEEE Trans. Magn.,* MAG-25 (1989), p. 3683.

[16] C. Tseng, M. Chen, T. Yogi, and K. Ju, "Gigabit density recording using dual element MR/inductive heads on thin film disks," *IEEE Trans. Magn.*, MAG-26 (1990), p. 1689.

[17] H. Takano, H. Fukuoka, M. Suzuki, K. Shiiki, and M. Kitada, "Submicrometer-trackwidth inductive/MR composite head," *IEEE Trans. Magn.*, MAG-27 (1991), pp. 4678–4683.

[18] R. E. Jones, Jr., "Domain effects in the thin film head," *IEEE Trans. Magn.*, MAG-15 (1979), p. 1619.

[19] S. Narishige, M. Hanazono, M. Takagi, and S. Kuwatsuka, "Measurements of magnetic characteristics of thin film heads using magneto-optical method," *IEEE Trans. Magn.*, MAG-20 (1984), p. 848.

[20] M. Hanazono, S. Narishige, S. Hara, K. Mitsuka, K. Kawakami, and Y. Sugita, "Design and fabrication of thin-film heads based on a dry process," *J. Appl. Phys.*, vol. 61 (1987), p. 4157.

[21] J. P. Lazzari and P. Deroux-Dauphin, "A new thin film head generation, IC head," *IEEE Trans. Magn.*, MAG-25 (1989), p. 3190.

6

MR Heads

6.1 INTRODUCTION

The search for sensitive magnetic transducers has been going on since the beginning of magnetic recording. The success of tape recording and the subsequent emergence of drum and disk devices in the late 1950s provided further motivation for the search for high-sensitivity reading elements. There are numerous patents and publications advocating semiconductor devices, such as "Hall effect" transducers and arrays of transistors for use as magnetic heads. However, efforts to use these devices have not proven successful. A magnetic recording sensor must meet at least three requirements:

1. It should efficiently convert medium magnetization changes into sufficiently high current or voltage with a minimum amount of noise.
2. It should detect signals at high densities with a negligible loss in signals.
3. It should be cost-effective.

The magnetoresistive (MR) sensor qualifies well on all three counts. Moreover, MR-sensor technology is extendable to very high disk drive densities. The term "magnetoresistance" refers to the change in resistivity of metals in the presence of a magnetic field. This effect has been known since 1857 [1]. Relatively high magnetoresistance is known to exist in ferromagnetic materials such as nickel, iron, and cobalt; hence, these metals and their alloys have been studied extensively. The alloy of Ni and Fe in 81/19 composition is called Permalloy. Thin film stripes of Permalloy exhibit magnetoresistivity between 2 and 3% of the intrinsic resistivity of the material. The first published suggestion for the use of MR for magnetic recording came in 1971 [2]. Magnetic and physical properties as well as methods of deposition and characterization of Permalloy films were extensively studied during thin film memory activity in the late 1960s. Because of the accumulated knowledge and significant magnetoresistance, a thin film of Permalloy became the material of choice for the research on MR sensors for recording applications. Between 1970 and 1980, several important issues related to the making of MR heads, such as different biasing schemes, shielding for high linear density, and processing techniques, were investigated.

The thrust of the sensor for recording applications began in early 1980, and the first MR read head for digital tape recording was introduced in 1985 with the announcement of the IBM 3480 tape drive system. Compared to film-head poles, which are 1–3 μm thick, MR-sensor thickness is on the order of 0.03 μm (30 nm) or thinner, and it is susceptible to electrical, mechanical, and chemical damages. The successful uses of the MR head for tape recording led to increased confidence for its application to disk applications. There is a major difference in operation of the sensor for wide-track tape recording compared to narrow tracks in a disk drive. The wide track of tape uses a long stripe of MR film, and long MR stripes are less susceptible to signal instability (waviness) than short-length MR film. This topic is discussed further in Section 6.12. MR sensors for narrow tracks of disk drive applications suffered from these signal instabilities. The early 1980s through 1990 was a period of solving magnetic and physical problems of MR heads and converting research findings into manufacturable processes. IBM's announcements of disk drives in 1991 using MR sensors paved the way for rapid increases in areal densities.

The following attributes of the MR read sensor give it significant advantages over inductive heads. (We use the words "sensor," "element," and "head" for a magnetoresistive device corresponding to a stripe of MR, an electrically testable part, and a complete structure capable of read and write, respectively.)

1. The MR-sensor signal is independent of the velocity of the disk medium. It measures the flux from the medium, while the inductive head measures the change in flux with time. This has important implications in disk-drive applications. For example, the MR-head signal is equally large when it is used in the high-velocity (high-RPM) drive as when it is used for the slowly rotating portable-notebook drive. The following illustration will clarify this point. Signal responses of 30- and 60-turn inductive heads are plotted as functions of disk velocity in Figure 6.1. The voltage (V_{p-p}) of an inductive head was calculated (about 127 nV per μm of track width, per meter per second velocity, per turn of the head) in Section 3.10. The marked point at velocity of 2.26 m/sec on the x axis is the velocity of a 1.8-in. disk inner diameter at 3600 RPM, and another point at 9.43 m/sec corresponds to a 3.5-in. disk inner diameter velocity at 7200 RPM. These two points cover the range of disk drive applications. In the same figure a range of MR-head response is also shown by a cross-hatched region. A

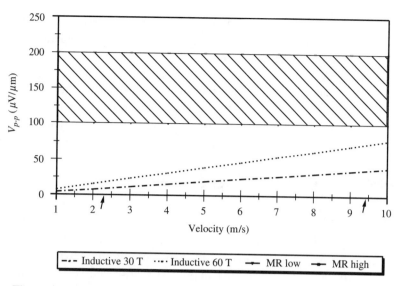

Figure 6.1 Comparison of inductive and MR-head signals as functions of medium velocity.

typical MR head response under similar flying height condition may range from 100 to 200 μV per micron of track width depending on the current through the sensor (Section 6.18). The MR-sensor signal is velocity independent. It provides the same large signal for both these applications. An inductive head can be employed for high-velocity applications but would require a wider track for increasing signal or would have to fly closer to the disk for a signal voltage comparable to an MR head.

2. An MR sensor is virtually a single-turn device; hence, it has very low inductance. The resonance frequency of its inductance in conjunction with circuit capacitance is very high. Unlike an inductive head, there is no barrier to the high-frequency performance of an MR head. Section 5.7 compares MR and inductive head equivalent circuits and resonance frequencies. Inductive head noise increases with its number of turns. MR noise is purely resistive and depends on the sensor dimensions.

3. The preceding example shows that the MR sensor exhibits a higher signal per unit track width compared to an inductive head (in a velocity range of 1 to 10 m/sec). The large signal per unit track width permits smaller track widths with an MR head. The error rate of a drive depends on its SNR (signal-to-noise ratio, Section 8.23). A high MR-sensor SNR ratio is a major reason why several gigabit per in^2 density products are now possible.

4. The MR sensor is an active device. The signal of the sensor can be increased by increasing current through it. The inductive head is a passive device, and its signal output depends on the parameters discussed previously. There are limits to currents through an MR sensor, and these are discussed in this chapter (Section 6.15).

5. The MR sensor is only a read element. For writing, an inductive write head is constructed on top of the read element. This separation of read and write functions allows independent optimization of each element for its respective function. One important consequence of the separation of write and read elements is that it allows "write wide, read narrow" operation. Since the MR read sensor can be made narrow compared to written track, it is less susceptible to picking up adjacent track noises. This capability translates into reductions of track widths and consequent increases in track densities.

6.2 PRINCIPLES OF THE MR SENSOR OPERATION

Figure 6.2 shows the track of a disk medium and two head elements. The read element is a single stripe of MR material within the gap of two shields. The write element is a thin film head of 8–17 turns. Joining these two elements makes a complete MR head. The structure and processes are discussed in Section 6.4. Figure 6.2 shows that the MR stripe is perpendicular to the track direction. Its long dimension w is directed across the track, and its height h is perpendicular to the disk.

Looking at the magnified MR sensor in Figure 6.3, we note that the current comes down one vertical (nonmagnetic) thin film conductor, across the horizontal MR stripe, and back up the other conductor. The magnetization of the MR stripe is shown directed at about 45° to the current direction in the stripe. In this chapter we shall use the same conventions for the dimensions as shown in this figure.

When a thin Permalloy film is deposited on a nonmagnetic substrate for making a magnetoresistive sensor, a magnetic field is typically applied during film deposition in a direction parallel to the plane of the film. This magnetic field induces a uniaxial anisotropy (preferred direction of magnetization) with an easy axis of magnetization that lines up parallel to the field. Figure 6.3 shows an MR sensor with this easy axis aligned parallel to the direction of current in the MR stripe.

The magnetization M in Figure 6.3 would normally line up parallel to the easy axis. However, in this case there is also an external magnetic field H_y applied in the

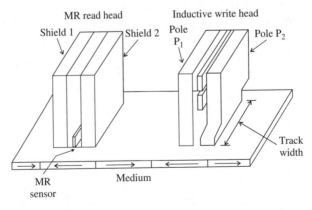

Figure 6.2 MR read head, inductive (film) write head.

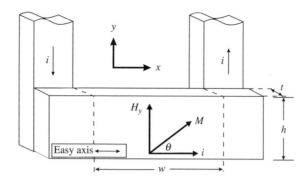

Figure 6.3 MR element schematic and dimensions.

up direction that causes M to rotate to some intermediate angle θ with respect to the easy axis.

When a current is flowing through an MR stripe and M is rotated with an applied external field H_y, the resistivity ρ of the MR stripe changes. This change is a function only of the angle θ between the magnetization and the current direction as shown. The exact relation is given by

$$\rho = \rho_0 + \Delta\rho_m \cos^2 \theta \qquad (6.1)$$

When the magnetization is parallel to the current ($\theta = 0°$), the resistivity is at its maximum, $\rho_0 + \Delta\rho_m$. When the magnetization is perpendicular to the current ($\theta = 90°$), the resistivity is a minimum, ρ_0. The maximum change in resistivity is $\Delta\rho_m$. The topic of magnetization direction is examined in Section 2.14, and it is shown that by minimizing the magnetic energy, the angle of the magnetization as a function of the applied field H_y can be found; see equation (2.39).

$$\sin \theta = \frac{H_y}{H_0} \qquad (6.2)$$

where $H_0 = H_k + H_d$, H_k is the anisotropy field related to the easy axis shown in Figure 6.3, and H_d is the demagnetizing field that is related to the shape of the MR stripe and is given approximately by tM_s/h. For the case of a stripe with height much longer than thickness, $H_0 = H_k$. Assuming this condition, equations (6.1) and (6.2) then can be combined to give

$$\rho = \rho_0 + \Delta\rho_m \left[1 - \left(\frac{H_y}{H_k}\right)^2 \right] \qquad (6.3)$$

The plot of ρ versus H_y, Figure 6.4, is a parabola of magnetoresistivity change on top of a constant resistivity value. Only the changing part is shown in the figure. The parabola has limiting values of $H_y = \pm H_k$ and a maximum change in resistivity $\Delta\rho_m$ of about 2.5% of the resistivity of Permalloy ($\rho_0 = 20 - 25 \ \mu\Omega$-cm). The equality $H_y = \pm H_k$ agrees with the usual definition of H_k as the field required to rotate the magnetization vector through a right angle from the easy axis direction $\theta = 0$ to $\theta = \pi/2$. The value of H_k is about 400 A/m (5 Oe).

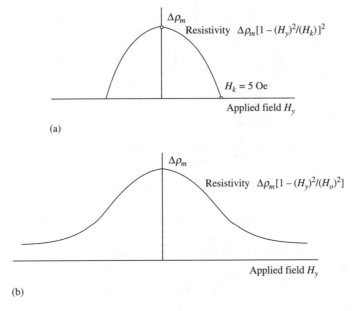

(a)

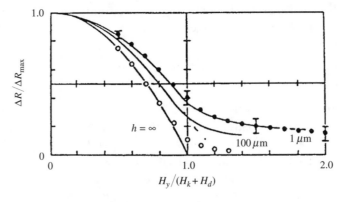

(b)

Figure 6.4 (a) The magnetoresistive effect: plot of resistance versus applied field. (b) The magnetoresistance characterization curve for a short-height MR stripe.

Actual experimental curves of magnetoresistance versus H_y deviate from the parabola as shown in Figure 6.4b. The resultant curve is more like a bell shape. Such a specific curve for a large population of head sensors reveals many details of design and process deviations; hence, its measurements and interpretation of features are used in testing and diagnostics of the MR heads. Because of its importance in diagnostics, the curve is often named as the characterization curve of an MR element.

Figure 6.5 shows the experimental and computed plots of magnetoresistance of Permalloy stripes of three different heights as functions of the applied field H_y in the hard axis [3]. The graph corresponding to $h = \infty$ is equivalent to the ideal

Figure 6.5 MR versus H_y field of MR films with varying heights [3].

parabola of Figure 6.4a. Practical MR sensor heights for disk drives range between 1 and 3 μm. The parabolic curve gets broad near the base as stripe height decreases. There are two contributing factors for the broadening and gradual spreading of the curve, resulting in an inflection of the slope as shown in Figures 6.4b and 6.5.

The broadening of the curve at the bottom is due to the demagnetization field generated at the boundary of the film that opposes the applied field H_y. So more and more H_y is required to produce equal changes in resistivity as the value of H_y increases. The demagnetizing field H_d for an MR stripe is given by $H_d = M_s(t/h)$. For Permalloy film $M_s = 800\,kA/m$ (10 kG). Assuming a stripe height of 3 μm and a stripe thickness of 30 nm, $H_d = 8\,kA/m$ (100 Oe) is obtained. An approximate fit to bell-shaped experimental curves can be obtained by fitting the parabola of Figure 6.4a between $H_y = 0$ and $H_y = H_k$ (≈ 400 A/m or 5 Oe) and replacing H_k by $H_0 = H_k + H_d$ for the rest of the curve. The demagnetization field just discussed is highest at the boundaries, that is, at $y = 0$ and $y = h$ in Figure 6.3. The resultant field, which is the summation of applied and demagnetization fields, is near zero at these points; hence the rotation of M is very small at these points. On the other hand, H_d is negligibly small at the center of the height and the applied field is most effective in rotating M at $h/2$.

In Figure 6.6 the rotation of M is varied across the height to indicate this variation in resultant fields. The center of the stripe saturates first when an applied field H becomes large enough. Further increases in H cause smaller changes in resistivity, and this causes the broadening of the MR characteristic curve of Figure 6.4b. The curve has an inflection point. In the vicinity of the inflection point, the relation between applied field and sensor signal (resistance change) will be nearly linear for small changes in the field ΔH. The sensor may be biased with a constant field H_b. Now when the sensor receives small field ΔH_y, the resistivity change in the sensor will be "linear" and symmetrical (see Figure 6.7). If a sense current is applied to the sensor at the same time, a symmetrical voltage signal across the stripe will result. The biasing of the sensor means application of a constant field H_b in the direction transverse to the flow of current in the sensor. Hence, this bias field is called the transverse bias. The transverse bias shifts the characterization curve such that the field from the media now applies to the head where its characteristic curve is most

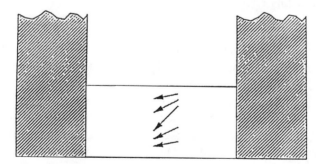

Figure 6.6 Magnetization directions in an MR stripe due to boundary demagnetizations.

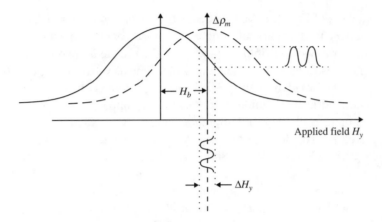

Figure 6.7 Biasing of an MR sensor for the signal linearity.

linear. A variety of biasing schemes is possible, and they are discussed in Sections
6.5–6.11.

The DC voltage across the MR stripe is given by $V = IR_0 = Jth \times (\rho_0 w/th) = J\rho_0 w$, where J is the current density in A/cm^2 and ρ_0 is the resistivity in micro-ohm-centimeters, w is track width in centimeters, and voltage V is in microvolts. The maximum small-signal voltage v_m possible from the sensor can be obtained using equation (6.3) as

$$v_m = Jw\Delta\rho_m = J\rho_0 w \left(\frac{\Delta\rho_m}{\rho_0}\right) \tag{6.4}$$

As an example, let us assume that $J = 10^7$ A/cm^2, $w = 8 \times 10^{-4}$ cm (8 μm), $\rho_0 = 20$ μΩ-cm, and $\Delta\rho/\rho_0 = 2.5\%$. The signal voltage is calculated as 4 mV. Considering the response within the linear section of the curve, a practical device may have a signal of about 1 mV. This corresponds to a 125 μV/μm track width. Formulas are provided in Section 6.18 for calculating voltages with the inclusion of flying height and head and medium parameters.

6.3 SHIELDED MR HEADS

For high-density recording in disk drives, shields are required on both sides of the MR sensor. These shields—each 1–3 μm thick—create a gap within which the MR sensor, biasing arrangement, and conductors are located. Figure 6.8 shows the shielded MR element. The purpose of shields along the track width of the head and perpendicular to the rotating track is not only to protect the MR sensor from external fields but also to provide a focused entry to confined fields from closely spaced magnetic transitions from the disk. Only medium transitions close to the MR gap regions are influential in producing voltage. Faraway transitions are shielded from the active sensor. The shielding also results in slimmed or equalized pulses. The equaliza-

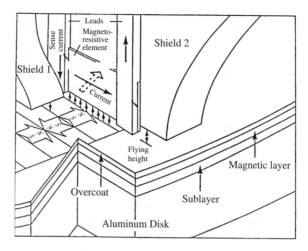

Figure 6.8 Shielded MR sensor structure [5].

tion is mechanical; hence it does not vary with the velocity of the medium. Additional shaping of the pulses can be done with electrical filtering for meeting the constraints of peak detect or partial response maximum likelihood (PRML) channels. Shields can be made of Permalloy (NiFe), ferrites, Sendust (FeSiAl), or amorphous materials such as CoTaZr. Many other materials may qualify. For proper shielding, the shields must have a high permeability within the applicable frequency range. Shields also provide mechanical protection to the MR head during head/disk contacts and start-stops. When the head comes in contact with disk asperities, there is a potential for conductive material being scratched or smeared on the head surface, which in turn can cause electrical shorts. This can be avoided by using either ferrite or Sendust for the first shield and Permalloy or another high-permeability material for the second shield [4].

6.4 STRUCTURE AND PROCESSING CONSIDERATIONS OF THE MR HEAD

Figure 6.2 shows separate MR read and thin film inductive write elements. In principle the complete MR head is simply the superposition of the write head on top of the shielded MR structure. The first heads, known as *PMR* or *piggyback magnetoresistive heads,* had two separate shields with the gap accommodating the MR sandwich structure. The MR part was insulated, and then a complete film head was constructed on the top. This was a conservative structure to minimize interaction between write and read processes. The structure had two disadvantages:

1. A lengthy process sequence was required to complete the head.
2. The distance between write and read head gaps was relatively large for accurate alignment between the two elements.

As a second generation of MR heads, a new head structure called a *merged head* has been developed. Figure 6.9 shows such a merged MR head design. The second shield of the MR sensor is also the first pole of the inductive write head. The second pole of the film head P_2 controls the writing field and write track width. The distance between read and write gaps is considerably shorter than a piggyback MR (PMR), which improved photolithographic alignment between read and write elements.

The short box named *MR read element* includes the thin film sensor, transverse and longitudinal biasing arrangements, and conductors to carry current to the sensor as well as sensing voltage. A short description of the process steps used in manufacturing of the device is described next.

MR heads are generally built upon the same substrates as film heads. Al_2O_3-TiC is the commonly used material, but a nonconducting ferrite may also be used with the advantage of reduction in potential shorts between MR and substrate or between shields. The choice of substrate material for the slider is also governed by the processes that form the air-bearing surface (ABS).

The conducting surface is insulated with a layer of alumina (Al_2O_3) before the first shield material is deposited. Next, a thin layer of insulator forms half the gap of the MR sensor. This is followed by depositions of a sandwich structure to provide the sensor, transverse and longitudinal biases, and conductor metallurgy. The details of this structure depend on the specific transverse bias scheme used for the MR. The reason for longitudinal bias is to reduce Barkhausen noise in the sensor output voltage. This topic is discussed in Sections 6.12 and 6.13. The second half of the gap is deposited next. Then, the second shield material, which is also the first pole of the write head, is plated or sputtered. The gap for the write function is formed with another insulating layer. The conductor coil is deposited in a manner conventionally used in processing the inductive thin film head. For the write function a single

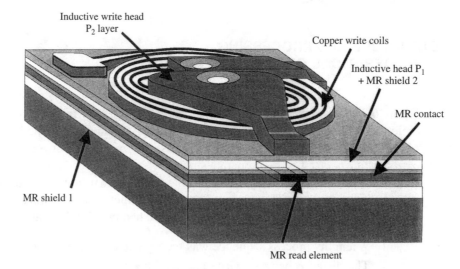

Figure 6.9 Merged MR head: Second MR shield and first write head pole P1 are merged [6].

layer of coil is generally sufficient. The write pole, P_2, does not require the thick and thin shaping sections that are used in the thin film head for both write and read functions. The coil connectors and MR connectors require a minimum of four pads. The shunt-biasing scheme using independent current supply for biasing may need six contact pads. Recall that an inductive read/write head required only two contact pads.

In terms of total number of process steps, the MR head is no more complicated than a thin film head with a multilevel coil. The inductive-write part of MR-head processing is considerably simpler with one thickness per pole and a single coil of few turns. MR processing, quality controls, and diagnostics are the major issues requiring the coordination of a knowledge of physics, material characteristics, and processes during the development and manufacturing of MR heads.

6.5 BIASING OF AN MR HEAD

The thin-film inductive head has a linear-reading characteristic. The signal produced in the head coil is proportional to the energy or strength of the flux changes from the media. The MR head is primarily a nonlinear device, as its response to input magnetic flux is governed by the parabolic shape of the characterization MR curve as described in Section 6.2. The possibility of biasing the sensor to achieve partial linearity considerably simplifies the use of the sensor. The next few sections are dedicated to different biasing schemes used or being developed for future MR heads.

The biasing of the MR sensor merely shifts the initial condition for applying an external field coming from the disk medium. Figure 6.7 showed this shift of the characterization curve. This shift should be such that the applied field is converted into an MR sensor signal as linearly as possible so as to obtain as much of a symmetric output as possible. A generally accepted criterion is to provide a bias so that the angle θ of equation (6.2) is close to $45°$, which means that the bias field, H_b, should be about $0.707 H_0$. In practice the biasing angle may be decided depending on the biasing scheme and trade-offs to maximize signal amplitude and minimize signal asymmetry. Figure 6.10 shows three cases of biasing. Underbiasing and overbiasing result in asymmetric signal outputs. Electronics can handle some degree of asymmetry, but in general a symmetrical signal is the most desirable for digital-signal processing and detecting signals. The choice of biasing scheme, the process controls in making the sensors, the stability of the MR sensor domains, and magnitudes of the head and medium parameters influence the signal characteristics of the sensors.

In estimating the voltage output due to medium magnetizations in equation (6.4), a reduction factor (of 4) from the maximum possible magnetoresistance change of MR has been assumed. A more accurate estimate of this factor depends on the magnitude of the flux from the medium along the height of the sensor and effectiveness of the bias field to rotate magnetic field along the sensor height. For

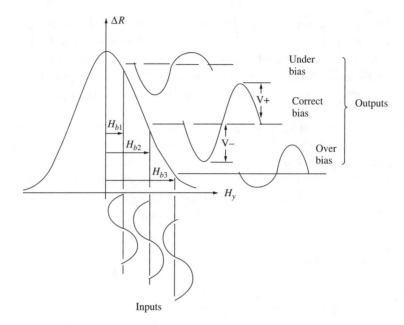

Figure 6.10 Biasing and symmetry of an MR-element signal.

the comparison of biasing efficiency and for calculating the MR-sensor voltage as a function of head and medium parameters, consider the following equations. In equation (6.3), for the short-height sensor, H_0 is substituted for H_k. Also note that the part that is variable with the external magnetization field is only the last term $(H_y/H_0)^2$.

The magnetization M_y in the sensor is proportional to the field H_y of equation (6.3), and H_0 corresponds to saturation magnetization M_s in the sensor. The ratio H_y/H_0 can be approximated by M_y/M_s. Actually, M_y along the direction of sensor height y consists of two components, the magnetization caused by the media and the magnetization due to the biasing field; that is, $M_y = m_b + m_s$, where m_b is the magnetization caused by the biasing field and m_s is the sensor magnetization due to the field from the medium. In the absence of medium magnetization, $M_y = m_b$ and $m_b/M_s = \sin\theta$. From these substitutions voltage proportionality equation follows as

$$V_{mr} = v_m \left(\frac{H_y}{H_0}\right)^2 = v_m \left(\frac{M_y}{M_s}\right)^2 = v_m \frac{1}{h} \int_0^h \left(\frac{m_b + m_s}{M_s}\right)^2 dy$$

$$= v_m \frac{1}{h} \int_0^h \left(\frac{m_b^2 + 2m_b m_s + m_s^2}{M_s^2}\right) dy \qquad (6.5)$$

v_m is given in equation (6.4). The term multiplying v_m is less than one; hence, it is a reduction factor from possible maximum voltage. The reduction factor can be viewed as biasing and flux propagation efficiency of the sensor. Focusing on the last term of the equation, biasing condition m_b^2 is a constant and m_s^2 is the contributor of the second harmonic distortion. In a well-biased system the nonlinear term should be small, so it is neglected for further derivations. The equation simplifies to

$$V_{mr} = v_m \frac{2}{hM_s^2} \int_0^h m_b(y)m_s(y)dy \qquad (6.6)$$

This equation quantifies the effect of bias and signal magnetization in the sensor at every point along the height of the sensor and integration of the effect results in total efficiency of the process to estimate the signal. The signal may be assumed linearly proportional to the biasing and signal changes along the y direction of the sensor. The derivation of the voltage for biased sensor is discussed in Section 6.18. This equation will be used to discuss the differences among biasing schemes and how the signal is affected by the biasing. This is done by studying variation in $m_b(y)$ as a function of y for each biasing scheme.

6.6 PERMANENT-MAGNET-BIASED SHIELDED MR HEAD

The application of a permanent-magnet bias for a shielded PMR head has been described [7]. The principle of the operation is illustrated in Figure 6.11. The MR sandwich consists of three thin films—MR film, insulator film, and a permanent-magnet film. The permanent-magnet flux fringes through the Permalloy and biases it. The advantage of the permanent-magnet scheme is that the transverse field created by flux from the permanent-magnet scheme the MR element uniformly across the height of the MR element. The condition for biasing at 45° is provided by controlling the thicknesses of the MR film and the bias film [7],

$$t_H M_H \simeq \frac{t_s M_s}{\sqrt{2}} \qquad (6.7)$$

where t_H and t_s are permanent magnet and MR film thicknesses, respectively. M_H is the bias magnetization, and M_s is the saturation magnetization of Permalloy film. The bias film material chosen for the experiment [7] was α-Fe$_2$O$_3$. The paper also points out the use of slanted magnetization in the biasing stripe so the stripe can have a dual function of transverse biasing and partial longitudinal biasing, which could help in maintaining a single domain in a narrow MR stripe and reduce Barkhausen noise. The details of the permanent-magnet film and the difficulty of using it are given in [8]. It was pointed out that a minimum separation of 75 nm was required to prevent inhomogeneities of a permanent magnet from creating domain walls in an MR stripe and resultant noise in its output. Later experiments with permanent magnet films of CoPt and CoIr have been carried out, but the difficulties of controlling film thicknesses and closeness of gap between shields have prevented the use of this scheme of biasing. Also, there is a possibility that the medium magnetization may be erased

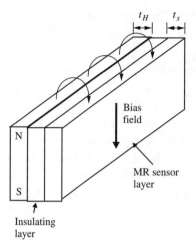

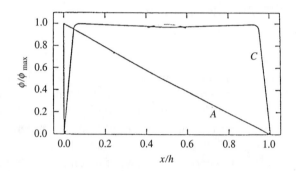

Figure 6.11 Permanent-magnet biasing.

Figure 6.12 Permanent-magnet-biasing profile along the sensor height [9].

or altered by the permanent magnet in low-flying-height conditions. On the other hand, fields from a high-coercivity magnetic medium may alter permanent magnet film properties, creating additional noise in Permalloy film output.

The advantage of permanent-magnet biasing is the uniformity of bias field along the height of the sensor. This can be seen from Figure 6.12 [9]. The x axis in the figure represents the direction of the MR stripe height. The y axis denotes the flux (or field) from either the bias or the medium. The plot A shows how the flux from the medium penetrates the sensor in the direction of its height. The plot C indicates constancy of the bias field due to permanent-magnet bias. The product of these two fields integrated along the y axis from 0 to h gives the signal sensitivity of this biasing scheme (refer to equation 6.6).

6.7 SHUNT-BIASED SHIELDED MR HEAD

The concept of biasing an MR head by current through a parallel conductor stripe is illustrated in Figure 6.13. Voltage is applied across the parallel circuit of an MR stripe and a conductor. The current is divided in two paths. A part flows through

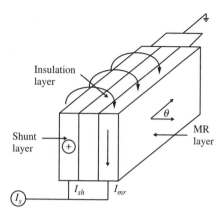

Figure 6.13 Shunt biasing of an MR element.

MR to sense the signal (I_{mr}), while the remaining current (I_{sh}) passes through the conductor. The field generated by the DC current through the conductor shunt layer enters the MR sensor transversely, in a direction perpendicular to the direction of current in the MR sensor. The amounts of biasing current and MR current are defined by the resistances of the parallel paths. This is a flexible scheme since a current through the pair is controllable after the device is made. One disadvantage of the scheme is the loss of power in the shunt path, which also contributes to the generation of heat in the structure. The major drawback of shunt biasing is that some of the signal generated in the MR sensor is shunted by the conductor parallel path, resulting in a smaller output signal.

The first extensive use of an MR head in digital recording came with IBM 3480 tape drives. Figure 6.14 shows the schematic of a shielded head [10] with a pair of thin films, one of which is an MR film (NiFe) while the other is a conductor film (titanium). This application has several interesting features. The MR sensor was divided into two parts along the track direction by providing a center-tap conductor and utilizing a differential signal from the MR stripe. The currents through the two sections formed by the center tapping are in opposite directions, while the bias applied to both the sections is in one direction; hence, the small signal outputs of the two sections are reversed. The differential voltage that results is free of second harmonics, and thus it is more linear and less asymmetrical. The center-tapping conductor reduces an effective track width of the sensor, but for a relatively wide track in tape application, this is a minor disadvantage.

Note that the location of the MR element and shunt layer are off center between shields. The reason for this is to obtain part of the biasing field. This is explained next. Consider only an MR element in the center of the gap. When the current passes through the sensor, it causes a surrounding field. Two shields provide easy paths for the flux. The sensor receives the total flux as a return path. For the centrally located sensor, the flux incoming and outgoing are equal, and no residual flux enters or leaves the MR sensor. However, if the sensor is placed asymmetrically between the shields, there will be a residual field that tends to bias the sensor in the

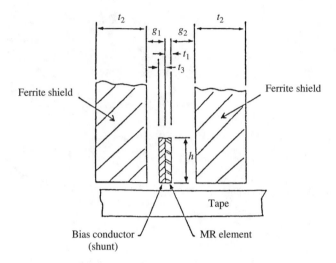

Figure 6.14 Shunt-biased MR for tape application [10].

vertical or transverse direction. Theoretically, an MR sensor can generate its own bias this way. However, this biasing by itself is too small, so in this application both shunt and self-bias are provided.

6.8 SHIELDED SHUNT-BIASED MR HEAD FOR 2 GB/IN.^{2} DENSITY

A head using the shunt-bias scheme was developed as a part of 2 Gb/in.^{2} density demonstration in 1991 [11]. Figure 6.15 shows the head structure.

The write-head poles were made of an Fe-based multilayer (laminated) material that has B_s of 2 T (20 kG) field strength. The shields for the MR head are made of 1-μm thick CoTaZr amorphous material for obtaining a smooth planar surface for thin film MR head processing. Permalloy of 15 nm is used for the MR stripe, and the shunt conductor is made of niobium. The MR had a sheet resistivity of 30 μΩ-cm and a magnetoresistivity of 2%. The MR track width is about 0.8 μm, obtaining a track density of 669 t/mm (17 ktpi) and a linear bit density of 4724 b/mm (120 kbpi). An MR head current density of 3×10^7 A/cm^2 was used. To stabilize such a narrow track, an antiferromagnetic layer of FeMn was used. The gap was 0.3 μm. A low-frequency signal of 420 μV per μm track width was obtained. Roll-off density of 3543 fc/mm at −6 dB was measured. A partial response 8/9 coded channel was used, which helps to increase linear density. Comparisons of 1 Gb/in.^{2} (IBM SAL-biased MR), 2 Gb/in.^{2} (Hitachi shunt-biased MR), and 3 Gb/in.^{2} (IBM SAL-biased MR) demonstrations are made in Section 11.3.

The biasing profile for the shunt-biasing scheme is given in Figure 6.16 [12]. Plot A gives the bias magnetization field variations along the direction of the sensor height. Plot B is the medium field drop along the height of the sensor. Plot C gives the summation of these two magnetizations. The shunt-bias profile is more variable

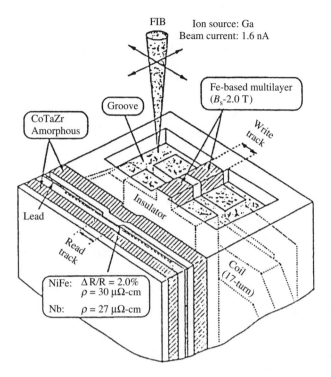

Figure 6.15 A 2-gigabit-density MR head with shunt biasing [11].

compared to the permanent-magnet or the soft-adjacent-layer (SAL) biasing methods. The plots indicate that either at high shunt current or increased initial ($y = 0$) medium magnetization, the MR would saturate somewhere along the sensor height. The inflection of the characterization curve and location of bias are determined by this point. The location of this point is a strong function of the biasing current through the shunt conductor.

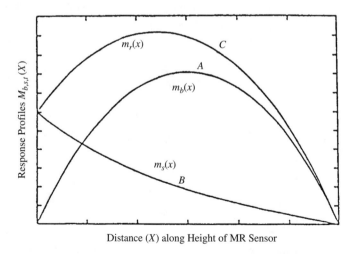

Figure 6.16 Shunt-bias profile along the sensor height [12].

6.9 SOFT-ADJACENT-LAYER BIAS FOR THE MR HEAD

The soft-adjacent-layer is the most preferred biasing technique and has been used in the MR head products produced by IBM since 1989. This biasing is also employed in 1 Gb/in.^{2}, (1990 [13]) and 3 Gb/in.^{2} presentations (1995 [14]). Figure 6.17 shows a SAL method of biasing an MR head. A three-layer sandwich consists of an MR stripe A, an adjacent layer B, and an intermediate, electrically insulating layer separating stripes A and B.

When a DC sense current passes through the MR stripe, it generates a magnetic field that surrounds itself. Part of the flux reaches the adjacent stripe B, which is magnetically soft (i.e., its coercivity is low, and it has a high permeability) and magnetizes easily by the field. The magnetized adjacent layer now provides the field to the MR itself in a transverse direction and biases it. Once thicknesses of these three layers are properly designed, the SAL magnetically saturates at moderate currents in the MR element. Increases in current in the MR sensor beyond this value do not increase SAL's magnetization anymore; hence, it provides constant biasing to the sensor. The saturated SAL provides relatively uniform biasing across the MR height. These are important advantages of SAL compared to the shunt-bias scheme. The difference between the adjacent permanent-magnet stripe and soft-adjacent-layer biasing is that the SAL magnetizing stripe is active only so long as there is a current in the MR stripe. Also the SAL sandwich can be fabricated more simply in a few process steps.

The selection of a soft film material is a critical component in this biasing scheme. It should be magnetically "soft," and it should have small magnetostriction. It should not be magnetoresistive; otherwise, it will add noise to the MR film magnetic response. It should have high resistivity so that it has minimum current shunting effect. Films of amorphous material CoZrMo [15] and ternary alloys NiFeX [16], where X may be Al, Au, Nb, Pd, Pt, Si, Cr, Zr, or Re, have been published in the literature for this application.

The soft-adjacent-layer-biasing profile for unshielded MR heads has been analyzed [17]. Figure 6.18a depicts characteristics of SAL biasing for variations in ratio

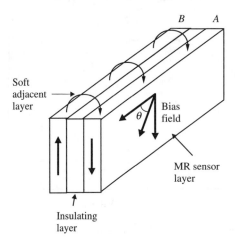

Figure 6.17 Soft-adjacent-layer biasing of an MR sensor.

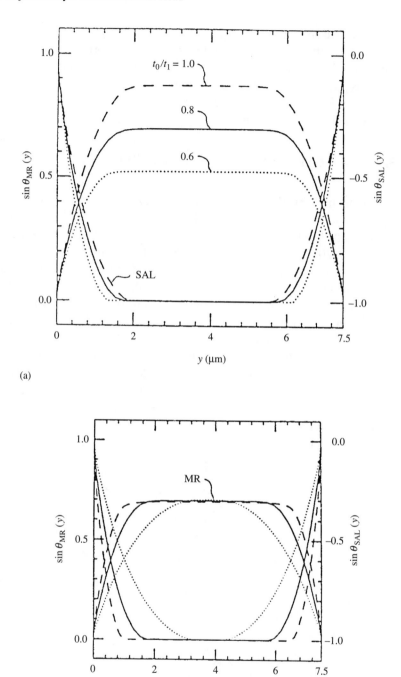

(a)

(b)

Figure 6.18 (a) SAL-bias profile as a function of MR and SAL thicknesses; (b) SAL-bias profile as a function of MR current [17].

of SAL/MR thicknesses, t_0/t_1. Note that the $\sin\theta_{MR}(y)$ is the same as m_b/M_s on the axis. At saturation, $\sin\theta = 1$ and $\theta = 90°$. The ratio of 0.7 may be considered close to theoretically ideal 0.707 or $\theta = 45°$. Figure 6.18b shows the effect of variability in bias profile due to changes in current density through MR stripe. Notice that once the adjacent layer is saturated, the bias profile remains close to constant across the sensor height for the changes in current densities.

6.10 BARBER-POLE BIASING FOR AN MR SENSOR

This method for biasing has been extensively studied and reported on [18, 19], primarily for use as an unshielded MR sensor. Analytical expressions for shielded MR heads and heads with yoke structures have also been published [19]. There is a patent [20] depicting a narrow-track shielded MR head version. The concept of barber-pole biasing is unique and interesting. Figure 6.19a describes the principle. In all the other schemes of biasing, current flows in the long-track-width direction, and bias is produced by applying a constant magnetic field perpendicular to the direction of easy axis or direction in which the current flows. In the barber-pole-biasing method, conductors are deposited at a 45° angle to the direction of the easy axis or track width side of the MR sensor. The effect of these striped conductors is that the current from one end of the sensor tends to flow at an angle of 45° with respect to the easy axis or long direction of the sensor. Thus, there is a built-in bias angle of 45° between current flow and magnetization direction that meets the requirement of biasing the sensor.

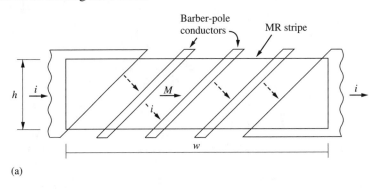

(a)

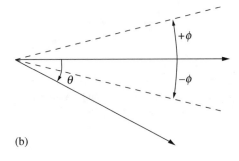

(b)

Figure 6.19 (a) Barber-pole biasing; (b) The biasing and applied-field angles for the barber-pole-biasing method [18].

When the alternating external field from the medium is applied, the magnetic field in the sensor rotates from its initial easy axis direction and the angle between current and magnetization direction becomes $\theta + \phi$, (see Figure 6.19b). Equation (6.3) for the barber-pole biasing modifies to

$$\Delta \rho = \Delta \rho_m [1 - \sin^2(\theta + \phi)] \tag{6.8}$$

and

$$\sin(\phi) = \frac{H_y}{H_0} \tag{6.9}$$

After substituting $\theta = \pi/4$ for built-in bias, trigonometric manipulations, and substitution of H_y/H_0 for $\sin(\phi)$, equation (6.10) for the characterization curve for barber-pole biasing is obtained.

$$\Delta \rho = \Delta \rho_m \left\{ \frac{1}{2} - \frac{H_y}{H_0} \left[1 - \left(\frac{H_y^2}{H_0^2} \right) \right]^{1/2} \right\} \tag{6.10}$$

Figure 6.20 compares the characterization curves of barber-pole ($\theta = \frac{\pi}{4}$) versus other biasing schemes ($\theta = 0$). Note that in the absence of an external magnetic field, there is a resistivity change to one-half the maximum value. It would appear that there is a large segment of the barber-pole characterization curve that is linear; hence, a possibly higher $M_r \delta$ medium can be used, resulting in a higher signal voltage. Another possible advantage of the structure is that the current passing through slanted conductors results in longitudinal (in the direction of track width or easy axis) bias, which can provide some domain stability and reduction of Barkhausen noise. The presence of conductors in the middle of the track width is an undesirable aspect of this design. Conductors reduce the effective track width and hence reduce

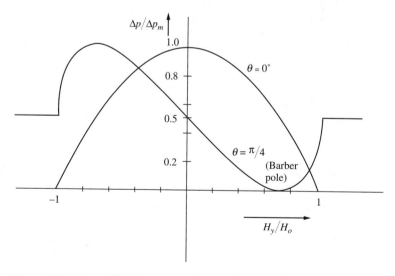

Figure 6.20 Comparison of characterization curves of barber-pole versus other biasing schemes [18].

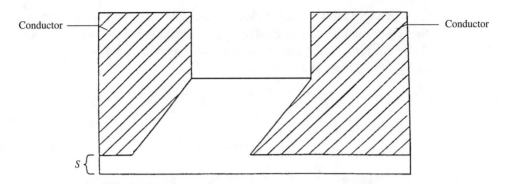

Figure 6.21 Narrow-track barber-pole structure [20].

the signal. It is difficult to expect micrometer-size tracks with such a structure. There is a quasi-barber-pole structure shown in Figure 6.21 that may allow a narrow-track version of this biasing scheme [20]. However, lack of current-carrying conductors would require additional longitudinal biasing for signal stability and elimination of Barkhausen noise.

6.11 DUAL-STRIPED MR-HEAD BIASING

Dual-striped or paired magnetoresistive biasing [21] is shown in Figure 6.22a. It is conceptually a very simple and elegant scheme, and it has several important advantages. Two identical MR elements, M_1 and M_2, are separated by a thin insulating layer. These two resistive elements are connected in parallel to a source of current I_s. The current $I_s/2$ passing through each MR results in a magnetic field surrounding itself. The fringe field of each sensor biases the other as indicated by shown arrows. The strengths of biasing depend on the insulator spacing. Figure 6.22b indicates the biased characterization curves of sensors. Each of the elements acts as a separate MR sensor. Medium transitions passing under the dual sensors generate signals in the elements. The signal at the differential preamplifier (Figure 6.22a) is twice the drive current times the change in resistance of one element. The same currents $I_s/2$ perform the dual function of biasing the elements and sensing the signals. Two sensors are close enough to be magnetostatically coupled and hence require relatively smaller current to bias adjacent elements.

The differential sensing provides common mode rejection of thermal noise since changes in temperature produce equal resistance changes in the elements. Also, closely coupled magnetic sensors reduce the magnetic demagnetizations at the stripe boundaries, enhancing the sensitivity of the device. Some of the challenges with this form of biasing are

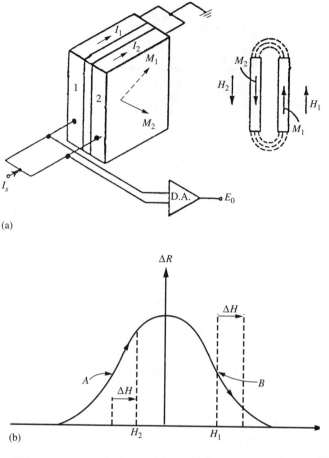

Figure 6.22 (a) Dual-stripe MR biasing; (b) characterization curves of dual-stripe biasing [21].

1. Requirements for matching the elements in thicknesses, resistances, MR properties, thermal properties, and so on.
2. Processing of pinhole-free insulating layer between two elements.
3. Accommodating triple-layered sensor with leads within narrow space between shields.

6.12 BARKHAUSEN NOISE AND INSTABILITIES IN MR SENSORS

One of the major problems faced by researchers in the early development of the MR sensor was the occurrence of jumps in the response characteristics of MR sensors. This is often referred to as *Barkhausen noise* (BN). The phenomenon is named

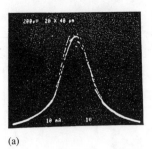

(a)

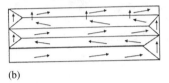

(b)

Figure 6.23 (a) Noisy response of a 20 × 80-μm 400 Å-thick MR element; (b) Buckling domain patterns in a small MR element [22].

after Barkhausen, who discovered (1919) the irregular magnetization in iron due to irreversible breaking of magnetic domain walls. Long MR stripes reduce this problem significantly to allow their applications for cash register stripe readers and wide-track tape recording. For narrow-track disk recording, the problems of electrical signal spikes and instabilities are serious concerns. Here instability refers to lack of repeatability in output waveforms during repeated write/read cycles. The cause of these jumps or irregularities in output is attributed to the existence of multidomains in short thin films. Figure 6.23a shows the BN irregularities in the signal output of a relatively narrow MR stripe with multidomains. Figure 6.23b shows buckling multidomains in the MR stripe. So the solution to the problem exists in providing operating conditions conducive to single-domain films for MR sensor and ensuring that this domain configuration remains unperturbed after the sensor goes through processing and fabrication steps.

6.13 PREVENTION OF BARKHAUSEN NOISE: LONGITUDINAL BIASING OF MR HEADS

There are two known methods to reduce or eliminate BN. One is to increase the effective magnetic length of the MR stripe. Long stripes have reduced stripe demagnetizations at stripe ends and hence a tendency to retain single magnetic domain in the stripe. As a second method, the application of a small magnetic field in the easy axis direction of the sensor results in a single domain and reduces BN. But there is an adverse effect of adding this longitudinal field: this field reduces the sensitivity of an MR sensor to the transverse field. The reduced sensitivity causes lower signal output. A solution to this problem was proposed [23] as follows. Apply the longitudinal bias only in two edge regions as shown in Figure 6.24a. The longitudinally

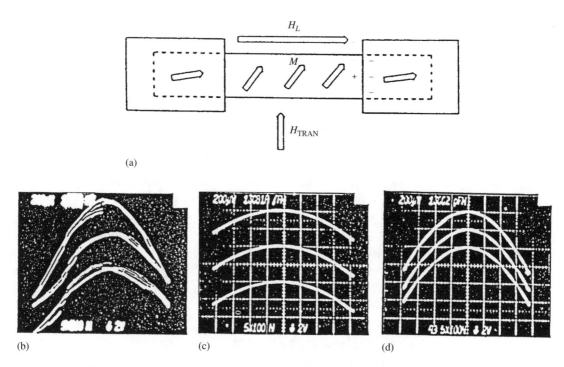

Figure 6.24 Pattern exchange bias for elimination of Barkhausen noise [23].

biased edge sections would provide a small field to the sensor, eliminating BN while retaining the signal sensitivity of the central region. To provide this selective bias at the edges, a layer of exchange material like MnFe is deposited on top of the MR-stripe edge sections. The principle of exchange is described in Section 2.16. The selective longitudinal field forces a single domain in the edge region and tends to maintain a single domain in the central section due to magnetostatic and exchange interactions between the edges and the central section. Figure 6.24a shows an MR stripe with edge regions covered by a film of an exchange material. This longitudinal biasing scheme is called *pattern exchange biasing*. Note that the middle section of the stripe is free of exchange material; this allows the magnetization vector in the active track region to rotate freely with the applied transverse field. The difference in magnetization rotation between the middle and tail regions creates positive poles at the boundaries, as shown, and promotes longitudinal biasing to the middle region. Figures 6.24b–d show three experimental transverse MR (characterization curves) responses: (b) nonexchange-biased MR stripe, (c) uniformly covered exchange bias layer on top of the sensor layer, and (d) pattern exchange-biased case. Figure 6.24b shows high response but noisy output due to BN. In Figure 6.24c, the response is dampened down due to the fully covered exchange layer. Figure 6.24d shows a pattern-biased case; the signal response is noise free and has not suffered signal loss.

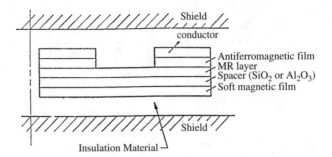

Figure 6.25 MR head cross section with SAL transverse-biased sensor and pattern exchange longitudinal biasing [24].

The patent [24] describes the details of pattern exchange biasing on an SAL transverse-biased sensor. Figure 6.25 shows the concept. The multilayered structure of the head consists of

1. The bottom soft-bias layer for the transverse biasing
2. A high-resistivity spacer layer
3. An MR sensor layer
4. An exchange layer covering the end areas of the structure
5. An electrical conductor layer to carry sensing and biasing currents.

The MR layer is biased longitudinally in the end regions by exchange bias developed by a thin film of antiferromagnetic material. The bias is of sufficient magnitude to provide single-domain configuration in the MR track sensor area. Thus a single-domain sensor combined with a sensitive central MR track width region is obtained. The temperature sensitivity of FeMn exchange-bias material and potential corrosion for unprotected exchange layer material have prompted ideas of new longitudinal biasing approaches.

A permanent-magnet or hard-bias layer for longitudinal biasing has been suggested [25]. Figure 6.26a indicates the arrangement. The end portions of the MR layer are covered by the ferromagnetic hard-bias film. The materials suitable for the application are suggested as NiCo, NiCoP, CoP, Fe_2O_3, etc. The high coercivity of the material provides a permanent exchange magnetization in the longitudinal direction of the MR film to retain single domain in the central active track area.

Another interesting and useful method of hard biasing was patented [26] and is shown in Figure 6.26b. The hard-bias material is deposited on the sides of the MR sandwich structure such that abutting junctions of the shape shown are formed. The central active soft film/insulator/MR region has just the dimensions of the track width to be read. Confinement of the MR active region to track width dimension removes some of the problems encountered when using previously described longitudinal-biasing methods. The extra MR regions in other methods have a tendency to add side-reading noise, which is eliminated in this design. Such a structure has decided advantages for very narrow tracks. The abutting junction between the sensor and biasing material is an important aspect of this invention. The lead

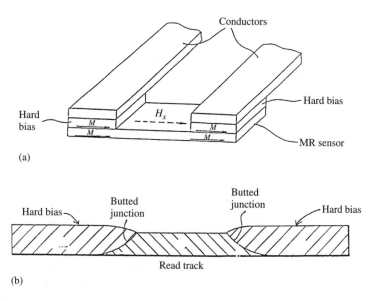

(a)

(b)

Figure 6.26 (a) Exchange, hard longitudinal bias for the MR sensor [25]. (b) In plane hard longitudinal bias with butted MR and bias film junctions [26].

conductor can be deposited on top of the hard-bias film in the same sequence of the process. Hard-bias materials indicated in the patent are CoCr, CoPt, and CoCrPt, the same materials used for high-coercivity-disk media.

6.14 ELECTROMIGRATION IN MR SENSORS

According to equation (6.4), the signal voltage of the MR sensor can be increased by increasing current density through it. However, the sensor would get overly heated at high current density and could result in electromigration that can cause failure of the sensor. Electromigration is the transport of metal material when the metal is stressed by high current densities along with high temperatures. The phenomenon has been known for several decades, but its occurrence in aluminum metal in semiconductor circuits in the 1960s resulted in significant research. The high-speed circuits for fast computers demanded high currents through narrow lines of aluminum. It was observed that the metal in several locations erodes while it is deposited in other places. The detail of erosions and depositions varied with the polarity of the local fields and flow of currents. In the early 1970s, electromigration in Permalloy (NiFe) became important due to its use in bubble memory detectors and later as MR sensors for tape and disk drive applications. The equation that relates mean time to failure (MTF) of a metal due to electromigration as a function of temperature and current density is

$$\text{MTF} = AJ^{-n}\exp\frac{\Delta E}{kT} \tag{6.11}$$

Here A is a constant and function of the cross-sectional area of the film, and it depends on the failure mechanism. ΔE is the activation energy of the metal in electron volts, k is Boltzman's constant, and T is film temperature in degrees kelvin.

The following failure modes are observed for the Permalloy films under high current and temperature conditions:

1. Increase in coercivity ($H_c \geq 800$ A/m, 10 Oe) of the stripe due to low-temperature oxidation (in a one-year period) at 85°C [27].

2. Decrease in MR coefficient from 2.5 to 0.7% after 100 hours at 5×10^6 A/cm^2 and 200°C [28].

These studies report that the change in magnetoresistance was due to microsegregation or changes in the Ni/Fe ratio as a result of electromigration.

The limiting current density largely depends on two parameters:

1. Control of rise in temperature, which varies inversely with thermal resistance of the sensor. Most heat from the sensor diffuses away from two flat surfaces (stripe height $h \times$ sensor width w). Since h depends on the lapping process, there is more variation in its value. The variations in thermal path and rise in temperature can be reduced if these factors can be made independent of h. It is shown that this is possible with constant voltage biasing instead of constant current biasing [29].

2. Duty cycle of the MR reading. The head used for reading only data has a low duty cycle. The MR sensor reading both data and servo information continuously will have a long duty cycle. The sensor for this application may be limited to relatively low current density. Special thermal path designs may be needed for designing heads with current densities far beyond 10^7 A/cm^2.

6.15 TOPICS RELATED TO RELIABILITY OF MR HEADS

When an MR head comes in contact with asperities on the disk, momentary friction can generate high-temperature pulses, which in turn create pulsed variations in resistance of the sensor. These variations will superimpose on the signal pulses and become noise. Normally, these noises are confined to low frequencies and hence are filterable from the signal pulses. Also, special circuits are designed to eliminate these thermal spikes [29]. Several materials used in the exposed MR heads may be subject to corrosion at the air-bearing surface of the heads. In addition, smearing and scratching of the conductive materials can cause shorts between the sensor and other conductive surfaces exposed on the air-bearing surface. This demands careful engineering of materials and processes unheard of in the manufacture of other types of heads. Heads are often coated with a hard material at the ABS to protect them from chemical, electrical, and mechanical damage.

Yoke-type structures have been attempted to eliminate these problems at several companies in the United States and Japan and in Europe. There is potential for their use so we review the topic in the next section.

6.16 YOKE-TYPE MR-HEAD STRUCTURES

Yoke structures for high-density applications [9], barber-pole structures [19], and high track density [30] have been published. Figure 6.27 illustrates the yoke structure for a shielded head application. The MR sensor and its biasing layers are removed from the air-bearing surface and encapsulated; hence they are protected against scratches, smearing, and surface electrostatic charges. The potential of corrosion of sensitive layers due to exposure to disk environment is also eliminated. The yoke may consist of thick NiFe or other magnetically soft material and provides conduit to flux from the head air-bearing surface to the sensor. An interesting yoke structure [30] is shown in Figure 6.28. The yoke has two parts: the front yoke collects magnetic flux and transfers the flux to two MR sensors differentially; the back yoke is separated from the front yoke by the MR elements. The thickness of the yoke, which is controlled by the deposition process, defines the track width. Hence a head with submicrometer track widths is possible with this structure. However, the read gap is controlled by the lithographic process and is limited to a fraction of a micrometer.

In principle, yoke structures have the following advantages:

1. They protect the MR sensor against mechanical and electrical surface problems.

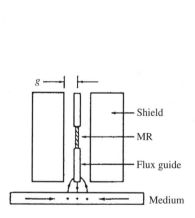

Figure 6.27 Yoke structure for shielded MR head.

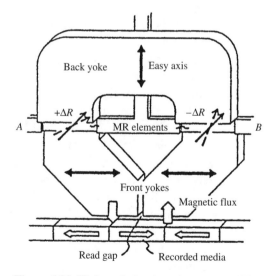

Figure 6.28 High-track-density yoke structure [30].

2. They offer several choices in optimizing transverse biasing and domain noise-control schemes once the MR is located far away from the surface.

3. They increase material options for these functions since corrosion and surface-wear issues are removed from the MR structure itself.

However, yoke structures are inefficient. The flux reaching the MR element is severely reduced. It is difficult to place a yoke between shields since the gap size has to be increased, which in turn reduces the high-frequency performance of the head. The yoke itself is a generator of BN due to multidomain wall movements within itself. In case of relatively long tracks and unshielded sensors, yoke structures are usable (e.g., the digital compact cassette DCC tape recorder employs a yoke MR sensor), but for narrow tracks, shielded-head yokes are difficult to realize.

6.17 NOVEL MR-HEAD STRUCTURES

The results of a study of a vertical shielded MR structure for longitudinal recording on a rigid disk have been published [31]. Figure 6.29a indicates the principle of operation. The MR sensor width w is along the track width direction as shown, while the current flows perpendicular to the track width direction. The current produces a magnetic field in a direction parallel to the track that is also the easy axis direction of the MR element. This self-produced magnetic field gives longitudinal bias to the sensor and tends to create a single domain in the MR sensor. Thus the MR current itself provides BN control. Figure 6.29b shows the shielded structure. A transverse field for biasing the sensor is provided by a separate shunt conductor (not shown). The MR film consists of a laminated structure of two films with intermediate nonmagnetic aluminum oxide film. One objective of such a laminated structure is to provide a closure path between two layers at the track width ends. This should reduce track-to-track crosstalk and provide sharper track width reading. A track width as small as 3 μm showed a noise-free characteristic. To pass current through the MR sensor, one lead is at or close to the ABS, while the other end is at the top. The lead structure and its control in practice may be the weak points of the structure. The structure certainly provides a new way of approaching narrow track reading with MR heads.

A horizontal MR structure for planar processing of heads has been described [32]. Figures 6.30a and 6.30b show the concept. Actually, there are two MR stripes center connected (shown in the front of Figure 6.30a) and sensed differentially by an amplifier. The air-bearing surface of the head has a magnetic surface layer with a gap defined by lithography. The field from the medium passes between two poles on the sides of the gap and equally divides between two sensors. The biasing scheme is not reported in the paper, but shunt or SAL biasing can possibly be designed.

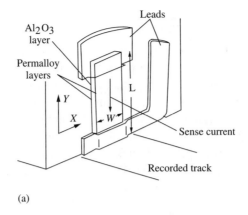

(a)

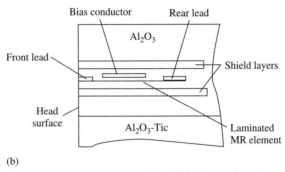

(b)

Figure 6.29 (a) Vertical, shielded, coupled MR head for longitudinal recording; (b) Schematic cross section of the shielded vertical head [31].

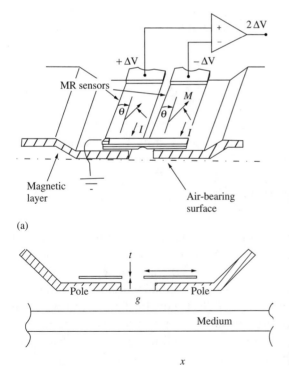

Figure 6.30 (a) Planar MR head for longitudinal recording; (b) cross section of the planar MR head [32].

151

Differentially sensed signals eliminate common mode noise. It turns out that the poles at the ABS provide partial shielding and partial yoke-type effect. The output pulse shape is a strong function of the length of the MR sensors since the field from the transition permeates through pole material. For a high magnetization medium, higher signals compared to a conventionally shielded sensor are claimed. One problem of the structure is the limitation of gap definition by lithography rather than deposition processes, which are finer and more controllable. The existence of a large pole structure at the ABS could pose wear and reliability problems unless protected.

6.18 MODELING OF SHIELDED AND BIASED MR HEADS

Signal voltage equations for an inductive head were described in Sections 3.6–3.11. Similar equations for an MR head are discussed here. Maximum possible voltage of an unshielded MR sensor has been addressed in Section 6.2. It is possible to calculate MR performance parameters using complex computer modeling. However, simplified analytical expressions are useful for an MR head design and head-disk system optimizations. Such equations for an MR head peak-to-peak voltage and pulse width P_{50} are derived by taking into account (1) the sensor characteristics (i.e., stripe dimensions), gap between shields, and saturation magnetization; (2) the medium parameters, M_r, δ, and the transition parameter a and (3) the flying height d. It is interesting to compare basic voltage equations of an inductive head and an MR head

$$\text{Inductive} \qquad\qquad \text{MR}$$
$$V_i = nvw\frac{d\phi}{dx} \qquad V_{mr} = Jw\Delta\rho_m F \tag{6.12}$$

where F is a factor smaller than 1 and multiplies v_m of equation (6.6). Substituting for F from equation (6.6), the voltage equation is given by V_{mr} in terms of head geometry and material parameters:

$$V_{mr} = [Jw\Delta\rho_m]\left[\frac{2}{M_s^2 h}\int_0^h m_b(y)m_s(y)\,dy\right] \tag{6.13}$$

The first bracketed term gives the maximum voltage obtained in terms of current density, track width, and maximum sheet resistivity change for the sensor. The second bracketed term is the factor F, and it is an efficiency factor that relates to the efficacy of the biasing—through $m_b(y)$—and second to the sensitivity function of the sensor $m_s(y)$. The sensitivity function reflects how the field of transitions in the disk medium are captured by the sensor and converted into a resistance change.

For the derivation of the voltage equation, a simplification is made that a constant idealized bias is applied so that magnetization angle $\theta = 45°$ or $m_b(y)/M_s =$

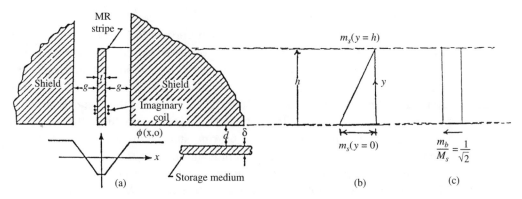

Figure 6.31 Shielded MR sensor modeling: (a) Head and media representation;
(b) Stripe magnetization profile; (c) Bias profile [33].

$\sin \theta = 1/\sqrt{2}$. Figure 6.31 illustrates (a) the shielded sensor and segment of storage medium; (b) stripe magnetization profile along the y direction; and (c)bias profile along the y direction. The assumption of constant biasing would be applicable to permanent biasing, partly true for the soft film biasing, and somewhat less applicable for the shunt biasing. Another simplification is that the magnetization due to medium flux varies linearly along y and reduces to zero at the end of the stripe height h. The condition under which this assumption is strictly true is explained in Section 6.19. With these assumptions, equation (6.13) simplifies to

$$V_m = [Jw\Delta\rho_m]\left(\frac{2}{M_s}\right)\left(\frac{1}{\sqrt{2}}\right)\left[\frac{m_s(y=0)}{2}\right] \tag{6.14}$$

The only quantity now needed for the voltage equation is $m_s(y = 0)$, which is the magnetization in the sensor due to media flux. For this derivation it is convenient to express $m_s(y = 0)$ in terms of the flux entering the MR sensor $\phi(x)$.

$$m_s(y=0) = \frac{\phi(x)}{\mu_o tw} \tag{6.15}$$

The flux per unit area is actually proportional to B, but inside the sensor H is very small compared to M and hence M can be approximated by B. The voltage equation now becomes

$$V_m = [Jw\Delta\rho_m]\left(\frac{1}{\sqrt{2}}\right)\left[\frac{\phi(x, y=0)}{\mu_o M_s tw}\right] \tag{6.16}$$

A popular paper on MR head theory [33] derives an expression for $\phi(x, y)$ at $y = 0$ and explains advantages of the shielded MR head sensor with approximate voltage calculation. In Section 3.7, we discussed an expression for $H(x)$ in terms of medium parameters by invoking reciprocity principle. The MR sensor is only a reader, and hence the conventional method of invoking reciprocity for the writing and reading process is not possible. So a conceptual technique of an imaginary coil surrounding the MR sensor is used (see Figure 6.31). The field created by such a coil for a two-gap structure formed between the sensor and the shields could in principle magnetize the medium. The application of reciprocity then allows calculation of the sensor magnetization at the air-bearing surface in terms of the field due to the medium transitions. From the conceptual arguments, the two-gap MR structure is treated as a summation of two inductive heads displaced from each other. The following expression for $\phi(x)$ in the case of the shielded MR head is obtained, and we shall use it without derivation [33].

$$\phi(x) = \frac{2\mu_o M_r \delta w}{\pi}\left[\frac{d+a}{g}\right]\left[f\left(\frac{x+g+t/2}{d+a}\right) - f\left(\frac{x+t/2}{d+a}\right)\right.$$
$$\left. + f\left(\frac{x-g-t/2}{d+a}\right) - f\left(\frac{x-t/2}{d+a}\right)\right] \tag{6.17}$$

where

$$f(u) = u\tan^{-1}u - \frac{1}{2}\ln(1+u^2) \tag{6.18}$$

In this equation, d is the head-to-medium spacing, a is the transition parameter as discussed in Section 3.9, g is half the gap between shields, w is the track width, and M_r and δ represent medium magnetic moment and thickness, respectively. Making a realistic assumption that thickness of the sensor t is much smaller than $d+a$ and g, the flux equation at $x = 0$ simplifies to

$$\phi(x=0, y=0) = \left[\frac{4\mu_o M_r \delta w}{\pi}\right]\left[\tan^{-1}\left(\frac{g}{d+a}\right) - \frac{d+a}{2g}\ln\frac{g^2+(d+a)^2}{(d+a)^2}\right] \tag{6.19}$$

The peak-to-peak voltage $V_{p-p} = 2V_m$ is obtained by substituting equation (6.19) in equation (6.16), as

$$V_{p-p} = \left(\frac{4\sqrt{2}}{\pi}\right)(Jw\Delta\rho_m)\left(\frac{M_r\delta}{M_s t}\right)\left[\tan^{-1}\frac{g}{d+a} - \frac{d+a}{2g}\ln\frac{g^2+(d+a)^2}{(d+a)^2}\right] \tag{6.20}$$

In spite of a number of assumptions, this equation is useful for obtaining an understanding of the influence of head/media parameters on signal output.

Another important parameter is the width of an isolated pulse. The equation applicable for the case is derived in [34] and stated as follows:

$$P_{50} = [g^2 + 4(d + a)^2]^{1/2} \qquad (6.21)$$

This is the same equation as equation (3.27) for an inductive ring head except that g, or the gap in this case, is half the gap between shields. For an inductive head, g is the gap between two poles. Applications of equations (6.20) and (6.21) are exemplified with three graph plots, Figures 6.32, 6.33, and 6.34. The nominal parameter values assumed in this example are as follows:

J, current density $= 10^7$ A/cm^2

ρ_0, sheet resistivity of the MR film $= 20$ $\mu\Omega$-cm, $\Delta\rho/\rho_0 = 2\%$

w, read track width $= 4$ μm

M_s, MR saturation magnetization, 800 kA/m (800 emu/cc)

t, MR film thickness $= 20$ nm

g, half gap between shields $= 200$ nm

M_r, medium magnetization $= 400$ kA/m (400 emu/cc)

δ, medium magnetic film thickness $= 20$ nm

d, head medium spacing $= 75$ nm

$H_c = 128$ kA/m (1600 Oe)

a, the transition parameter, is calculated using equation (3.29) with the value of $K = 3.1$. Figure 6.32 shows how the flying height between head and medium and transition parameter singly or together influence the magnitude of the voltage and pulse width of an MR head response of an isolated transition. As in the case of an

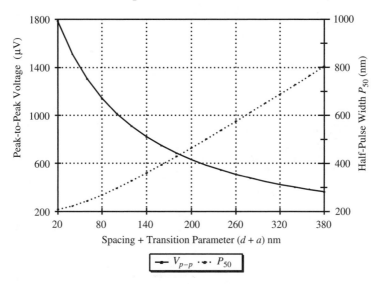

Figure 6.32 Plots of V_{p-p} and P_{50} of the MR head as functions of $d + a$.

inductive head (Chapter 3), a small head-disk spacing and small transition parameters are desirable for the high output voltage and narrow pulses. Figure 6.33 indicates dependence of V_{p-p} and P_{50} on medium magnetization. Between high peak voltage and short pulse width there would be a compromise for the selection of M_r. It is also known that too high M_r tends to produce MR head saturation. For these

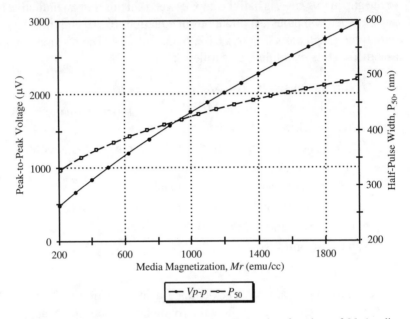

Figure 6.33 Plots of V_{p-p} and P_{50} of the MR head as functions of M_r (media magnetization).

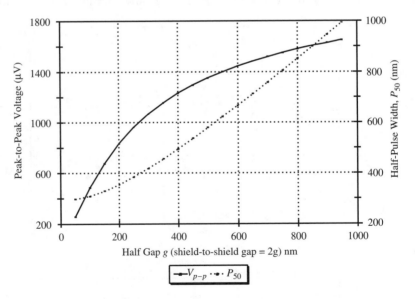

Figure 6.34 Plots of V_{p-p} and P_{50} of the MR head as functions of (g) head half gap.

reasons, 1 and 3 Gb/in.^{2} demonstrations use $M_r\delta$ of less than 1×10^{-3} emu/cm^3. The medium for use with an inductive head employs three times larger $M_r\delta$ so as to produce a large signal. Note that contrary to the maximum observed for inductive head for a similar curve (see Figure 3.13), no such maximum is observed here within the range of selected values of parameters. Figure 6.34 shows the head gap versus V_{p-p} and P_{50}. The wide gap is desirable for the high output of an isolated voltage pulse, but high density requires short pulse width. So there is a compromise in selection of the gap. Generally, narrow pulse widths for high linear density take precedence, and progressively shorter gaps are developed for new generations of MR heads.

6.18.1 MR Head Equivalent Circuit

Basically, there is no difference between the equivalent circuit of an MR head and that of an inductive head; hence, they are both described in Section 5.7. The MR sensor stripe and two leads form a closed circuit, so for circuit representation, it is a single-turn head. Table 5.1 describes comparable parameters of three inductive heads and an MR head. The single-turn MR sensor has a very low equivalent inductance, and the calculated value of its resonant frequency is very high. Figure 5.12 shows the plot of the real part of sensor impedance, which largely depends on its resistance. The $Re(Z)$ peak and resonance frequencies are outside the range of the plot. The integrated average value of $Re(Z)$ along the frequency range within applicable bandwidth can be used to calculate the noise due to head circuit. This topic is discussed further in Section 8.18. As seen in Figure 5.12, the MR head has a distinct advantage with a consistently low resistance in a broad frequency range. The large signal and low noise are the key parameters of an MR head since the SNR exponentially relates to error rates. A large SNR allows wide bandwidth applications, resulting in high linear densities with the MR sensor.

6.19 MEDIUM FIELD DISTRIBUTION OF A SHIELDED MR HEAD

In the preceding section, the assumption was made that the flux and magnetization distribution along the y direction was represented by a straight line. This is not strictly true, and it is useful to know the condition when it is applicable. In [9] the flux path is considered as a transmission line, and a more accurate generalized equation is obtained as

$$\phi(y) \simeq \phi(y = 0)\left[\frac{\sinh(h - y/\lambda)}{\sinh(h/\lambda)}\right] \tag{6.22}$$

where $\lambda = \sqrt{(\mu_r tg/2)}$ and is called the *characteristic length*. μ_r is the relative permeability of Permalloy or MR material used. For $h/\lambda < 1/2$, the equation is close to linear; that is,

$$\phi(Y) \simeq \phi(0)\left(\frac{1 - y}{\lambda}\right) \tag{6.23}$$

With a tendency toward short MR stripe heights, this equation is applicable in most cases. For $h/\lambda > 2$, the equation becomes exponential; that is,

$$\phi(y) \simeq \phi(0)e^{-y/\lambda} \tag{6.24}$$

6.20 SINUSOIDAL TRANSITION RESPONSE OF THE SHIELDED MR

For the reasons considered in evaluating sinusoidal response of an inductive head (Section 3.14), we likewise give here the voltage equation for the sinusoidal magnetization in the case of a shielded MR sensor. The flux at the entry of the shielded MR from sinusoidal medium transitions is given by [34]

$$\phi(x, y = 0) = 2\mu_o M_r \delta w \sin \frac{\pi(g + t)}{\lambda} e^{-kd} \left(\frac{1 - e^{-k\delta}}{k\delta}\right)\left(\frac{\sin kg/2}{kg/2}\right) \sin kx \tag{6.25}$$

Substituting this value of ϕ in equation (6.16), the voltage equation for sinusoidal magnetizations is obtained

$$V_{MR} = \sqrt{2} I R_o \left(\frac{\Delta\rho_m}{\rho_o}\right)\left(\frac{M_r \delta}{M_s t}\right)\sin \frac{\pi(g + t)}{\lambda} e^{-kd} \left(\frac{1 - e^{-k\delta}}{k\delta}\right)\left(\frac{\sin kg/2}{kg/2}\right) \tag{6.26}$$

Removal of $\sqrt{2}$ in the front of the equation makes the equation valid for a shielded barber-pole configuration [19]. It may be instructive to compare inductive and MR response to the sinusoidal magnetization in the media. In Chapter 3, equation (3.34) gives inductive head response to a sine wave medium magnetization.

6.21 ASYMMETRIC TRACK READING OF THE SHIELDED-BIASED MR HEAD

It has been observed that the track profile of the MR sensor is asymmetric. This is evident when a microtrack profile is measured. A track profile is the measurement of a signal voltage as a function of the distance, w, along the sensor track. These measurements are discussed in Section 9.8. The reason for this asymmetry is explained [35] by the influence of sections of track magnetizations on a biased MR sensor. Figure 6.35a shows the MR bias angle (designated M_s) and field from the portion X_R of one side of the track. This field can be viewed as being made up of two components H_x and H_y along the x and y directions. The field torque of both x and y components tends to increase the bias angle θ, resulting in an increase in resistivity change and hence increased signal. Figure 6.35b shows the portion of track on the left of the track center. The H_x and H_y components of the field from this track portion are shown. Here the x component H_x produces the magnetization torque, which tends to reduce the angle θ, while the y component H_y tends to increase the angle. Because of the effect of differences in fields from different locations of the track, the microtrack profile is asymmetric and looks as shown in Figure 6.36. The field components (x and y) from the left side of the track interact with each other, and at some point they become equal. At this location minimum signal is obtained, as indicated in the figure.

The asymmetrical profile has several consequences:

1. Asymmetry is increased when an MR sensor has exchange-bias or hard-bias wings on the top.

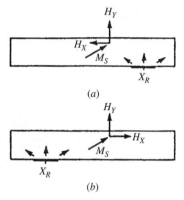

Figure 6.35 Asymmetric influence of track magnetizations on the sensor magnetization angle [35].

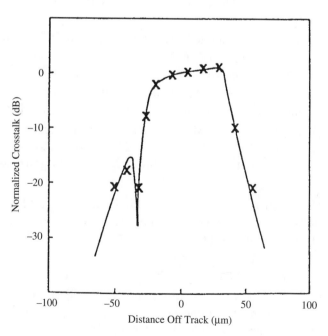

Figure 6.36 Asymmetric track profile of the shielded MR sensor [35].

2. Track profile depends on the bias angle of each head and thus introduces additional variability in track density design.

3. The misalignment between write and read elements inherent in separate read/write functions is further accentuated with the addition of this variability and requires offset correction by design or through software solution.

4. This asymmetry depends on the domain states within the sensor; hence track profile also becomes the function of sensor domain states. The microtrack profile is an excellent diagnostic tool for assessing the impact of this effect.

REFERENCES

[1] R. M. Bozorth, *Ferromagnetism*, New York: IEEE Press, 1993. p. 745.

[2] R. P. Hunt, "A magnetic readout transducer," *IEEE Trans. Magn.,* MAG-7 (1971), p. 150.

[3] R. Anderson, C. Bajorek, and D. Thompson, "Numerical analysis of a magnetoresistive transducer for magnetic recording applications," *AIP Conf. Proc.,* Vol. 10 (1972), pp. 1445–1449.

[4] C. Bajorek, C. T. Horng, and T. Yen, "Process for making shielded magnetoresistive sensor," U.S. Patent No. 4,918,554 (1990).

[5] Roger Wood, "Magnetic megabits," *IEEE Spectrum* (May 1990), p.32.

[6] R. A. Scranton, "The era of magnetoresistive heads," presented at the IDEMA Symposium, Santa Clara, CA, February 1994. (Figure 6.9 courtesy of E. Grochowski.)

[7] C. Bajorek, S. Krongelb, L. Romankiw, and D. Thompson, "An integrated magnetoresistive read, inductive write high density recording head," *Magnetism and Magnetic Materials,* (1974), p. 548.

[8] C. H. Bajorek and D. A. Thompson, "Permanent magnetic films for biasing of magnetoresistive transducers," *IEEE Trans. Magn.,* MAG-11 (1975), p. 1209.

[9] D. A. Thompson, "Magnetomotive transducers in high-density magnetic recording," *AIP Conf. Proc.,* Vol. 24 (1975), pp. 528–533.

[10] F. Shelledy and G. Brock, "A linear self-biased magnetoresistive head," *IEEE Trans. Magn.,* MAG-11 (1975), p. 1206.

[11] H. Takano, H. Fukuoka, M. Suzuki, K. Shiiki, and M. Kitada, "Submicrometer-trackwidth inductive/MR composite head," *IEEE Trans. Magn.,* MAG-27 (1991), pp. 4678–4683.

[12] C. Tsang, "A theoretical study of the signal response of a shielded MR sensor," *IEEE Trans. Magn.,* MAG-26 (1990), p. 3016.

[13] C. Tsang, M. Chen, T. Yogi, and K. Ju, "Performance study and analysis of dual element head on thin film disk for gigabit density recording," *IEEE Trans. Magn.,* MAG-26 (1990), p. 2948.

[14] C. Tsang, D. McCown, H. A. Santini, J. Lo, and R. Lee, "3Gb/in.^{2} recording demonstration with dual element heads and thin film disks," *Digests of the Magnetic Recording Conference* (1995), p. A0.

[15] T. Maruyama, K. Yamada, T. Tatsumi, and H. Urai, "Self-adjacent layer optimization for self-biased MR elements with current shunt layers," *IEEE Trans. Magn.,* MAG-24 (1988), p. 2404.

[16] M. Chen, N. Gharsallah, G. Gorman, and J. Latimer, "Ternary NiFeX as soft biasing film in MR sensor," *J. Appl. Phys.,* Vol. 69 (1991), pp. 5631–5633.

[17] N. Smith, "Micromagnetic analysis of a coupled thin-film self-biased magnetoresistive sensor," *IEEE Trans. Magn.,* MAG-23 (1987), p. 259.

[18] K. Kuijk, W. Van Gestel, and F. Gorter, "The barber pole, a linear magnetoresistive head," *IEEE Trans. Mag.,* MAG-11 (1975), p. 1215.

[19] W. F. Druyvesteyn, J. A. C. van Ooyen, L. Postma, E. L. M. Racemakers, J. J. M. Ruigrok, and J. de Wilde, "Magnetoresistive Heads," *IEEE Trans. Mag.,* MAG-17 (1981), p. 2884.

[20] G. S. Mowry, "Magnetic head with magnetoresistive sensor, inductive write head, and shield," U.S. Patent No. 4,967,298 (1990).

[21] O. Voegeli, "Magnetoresistive head assembly having matched elements for common mode rejection," U.S. Patent No. 3,860,965 (1975).

[22] C. Tsang, "Magnetics of small magnetoresistive sensors" *J. Appl. Phys.,* vol. 55, no. 6 (March 15, 1984), p. 2226.

[23] C. Tsang, "Unshielded MR elements with patterned exchange biasing," *IEEE Trans. Magn.,* MAG-25 (1989), p. 1149.

[24] C. Tsang, "Patterned exchange bias," U.S. Patent No. 4,663,685 (1987).

[25] T. Kira, T. Miyaguchi, and M. Yoshikawa, "Thin film magnetic head having a magnetized ferromagnetic film on the MR element," U.S. Patent No. 4,639,806 (1987).

[26] M. Kroumbi, "Magnetoresistive read transducer having hard magnetic bias," U.S. Patent No. 5,018,037 (1991).

[27] C. Bajorek and A. F. Mayadas, "Reliability of magnetoresistive bubble sensors," *AIP Conf. Proc.,* Vol. 10 (1973), p. 212.

[28] G. E. Moore, Jr., P. A. Turner, and K. L. Tai, "Current density limitations in Permalloy magnetic detectors," *AIP Conf. Proc.,* Vol. 10 (1973), p. 217.

[29] K. B. Klaassen, "Magnetic recording channel front-ends" *IEEE Trans. Magn.,* MAG-27 (1991), p. 4503.

[30] T. Maruyama, K. Yamada, H. Tanaka, S. Ito, H. Urai, and H. Kaneko, "A yoke magnetoresistive head for high track density recording," *IEEE Trans. Magn.,* MAG-23 (1987), p. 2503.

[31] H. Suyama, K. Tsunewaki, H. Fukuyama, N. Saito, T. Yamada, and H. Karamon, "Thin film MR head for high density rigid disk drive," *IEEE Trans. Magn.,* MAG-24 (1988), p. 2612.

[32] D. W. Chapman, D. E. Heim, and M. L. Williams, "A new horizontal MR head structure," *IEEE Trans. Magn.,* MAG-25 (1989), p. 3689.

[33] R. I. Potter, "Digital magnetic recording theory," *IEEE Trans. Magn.,* MAG-10 (1974), p. 502.

[34] A. V. Davies and B. K. Middleton, "The resolution of vertical magneto-resistive readout heads," *IEEE Trans. Magn.,* MAG-11 (1975), p. 1689.

[35] N. H. Yeh, "Asymmetric crosstalk of magnetoresistive head," *IEEE Trans. Magn.,* MAG-18 (1982), p. 1155.

7

Thin Film Media

Kenneth E. Johnson
IBM Corporation

7.1 INTRODUCTION AND HISTORICAL PERSPECTIVE

The recording medium for disk drives, simply described, is a film of magnetically hard material on a circular substrate. The substrates in use are classified into two formats: flexible and rigid. Flexible media, or *floppy disks,* are based on polyester film substrates. This nonrigid substrate limits storage capacity but allows for an easy means of transferring data from one machine to another. The prevalent rigid-media substrate is an aluminum-magnesium alloy (Al-Mg) of various diameters and thicknesses. Disks are stacked in an assembly of 1 to 12 platters and permanently encased in the disk drive structure. The rigidity of the substrates allows servo mechanisms to accurately follow very narrow tracks, resulting in high track and areal densities. This chapter will discuss rigid-disk technology.

Rigid-disk drives and disks have shrunk in size over the years. The first rigid disks, manufactured in 1957, were 24 in. in diameter. During the 1960s and 1970s, 14-in.-diameter, 0.075-in.-thick disks with 6.625-in. holes dominated the industry. Disk sizes decreased rapidly during the 1980s. The 210-mm- (8-in.-) diameter disk survived the entire decade. 130-mm- (5.25-in.-) diameter disks with 40-mm holes were introduced in the early 1980s. 95-mm (3.5-in.) disks with 25-mm holes were first seen mid-decade and dominate the disk volumes to this day. The late 1980s saw the thickness of the 95-mm disk drop to 0.8 mm. 65-mm- (2.5-in.-)

diameter, 0.635-mm-thick disks with 20-mm holes emerged in the early 1990s. 48-mm disks are just now emerging for laptop applications. Currently made 48-mm disks are 0.635 mm thick, but designs as thin as 0.38 mm are being developed. Hewlett-Packard introduced a 33-mm-diameter disk in 1992, but it was later discontinued.

After a brief discussion of particulate media, the remainder of this chapter will focus on the structure, properties, manufacturing, magnetic performance, and mechanical performance of thin film disks.

7.2 PARTICULATE MEDIA

The magnetic coating used exclusively for the first 25 years of rigid-disk technology was based on magnetic particle dispersions coated onto rotating substrates forming polymer-particle composite structures similar to paint. The magnetic particles were made of γ-iron oxide (γ-Fe_2O_3) developed for tape recording at the end of World War II. The gamma form of iron oxide has the similar brown color of rust, α-iron oxide, but is ferromagnetic and magnetically hard. Particle shapes were acicular with aspect ratios of approximately 6:1. Around 1970 technology improvements allowed the introduction of improved particles with better dispersibility and aspect ratios of approximately 10:1. Higher coercivity values were reached through the increased shape anisotropy of these more acicular particles. Particle sizes were originally 1–2 μm in length, but today, 0.5-μm length is common, giving higher packing volumes and lower read-back noise supporting higher bit densities.

γ-iron oxide was partially displaced by other materials in flexible-media recording, and this also affected rigid-disk designs in the late 1980s. The addition of a surface layer of cobalt to γ-iron oxide adds a magnetocrystalline contribution to the total anisotropy, increasing coercivity and magnetic recording performance. Particle developments such as CrO_2, metal particles, and barium ferrite ($BaFe_{12}O_{19}$) have furthered recording technology on flexible substrates, but the introduction of thin film technology to rigid substrates closed the further development of particulate rigid-disk media.

The method of creating a particulate film is based on chemical engineering principles. Magnetic particles are dispersed in polymer resins and solvents using milling techniques. For rigid disks, the dispersion or magnetic "ink" is applied to a rotating substrate through a nozzle. A rapid angular acceleration spins off excess ink, leaving a thin polymer-particle film behind. The film, while still fluid, is passed under a magnetic field to circumferentially align the acicular particles, thereby improving magnetic properties. The wet film is then baked in an oven, initiating a cross-linking chemical reaction that creates a very hard structure that locks the particles into a thin film on the substrate. A postbake buffing process thins the hard coating to the desired thickness, also leaving a smooth finish. After lubrication with a perfluoropolyether lubricant, the disk is ready for testing and eventual shipment.

7.3 THIN FILM MEDIA STRUCTURE AND MANUFACTURE

Particulate film technology is limited in its areal density and is no longer used in rigid-disk drives. Today, all rigid disks are made using thin film technology. Magnetic metallic thin films are deposited using vacuum-deposition technology. Metal films have higher magnetization than particulate thin films. This is because the magnetic moment is not diluted by nonmagnetic polymer constituents and also because pure ferromagnetic metals are magnetically much stronger than their oxides. This high magnetization allows the use of thinner films on the rigid substrate. Very thin layers, currently as low as 20 nm, are necessary to write very narrow transitions. Thin metal films also can be endowed with much higher coercivity values than particulate films, and as will be seen later, high coercivity is critical to increasing areal density. Vacuum deposition has other benefits that will be discussed later.

7.3.1 Disk Structure

Figure 7.1a shows a schematic cross section and Figure 7.1b an actual cross section of a typical thin film disk. The substrate of choice is aluminum because of its low density, rigidity, and low cost. A smooth surface is required for a rigid disk to give uniform read-back signals from low-flying heads. Aluminum by itself is quite soft and cannot be polished to a smooth enough finish. A technique called *diamond turning* was used successfully for many years to produce mirrorlike surfaces on aluminum substrates for particulate coatings. But this surface preparation technology is not adequate for high-areal-density thin film disks. A modification of the aluminum substrate to give a hard surface for thin magnetic film structural support and to supply a surface capable of being polished to a high degree of smoothness for low-flying recording heads is needed. Electroless nickel-phosphorus-plated aluminum is universally used today to provide this hard surface. Its hardness is measured at approximately 550 kg/mm^2 on the Brinell scale, almost equivalent to that of a cutting steel. The Ni-P surface is abrasively polished to a 1.0-nm root-mean-square (RMS) finish followed by a texturing process resulting in circumferential grooves. The surface finish measured with a stylus profilometer orthogonal to the ridges measures 3–5 nm RMS. The grooves serve two purposes: the added roughness

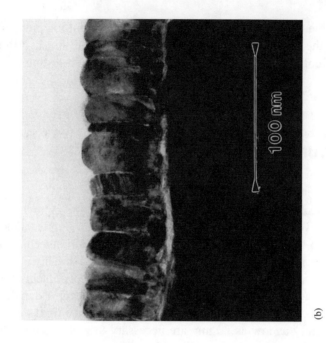

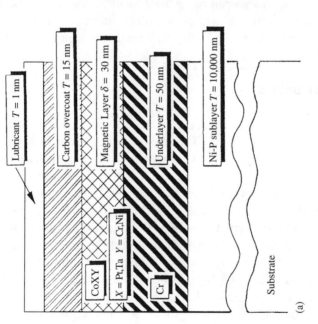

(b)

Lubricant $T = 1$ nm

Carbon overcoat $T = 15$ nm

Magnetic Layer $\delta = 30$ nm

CoXY

$X = $ Pt,Ta $Y = $ Cr,Ni

Underlayer $T = 50$ nm

Cr

Ni-P sublayer $T = 10{,}000$ nm

Substrate

(a)

Figure 7.1 Cross section of typical thin film disk: (a) schematic view; (b) transmission electron micrograph (M. Mirzamaani, IBM). For the film structure in this micrograph, close examination shows the interface between the 15-nm Cr underlayer and the 50-nm magnetic layer.

minimizes head stiction to the disk surface, and the grooves induce a circumferential magnetic anisotropy on the disk, resulting in uniform magnetic read-back signals during the course of a disk revolution. Figure 7.2 shows AFM pictures of a circumferentially textured thin film disk.

Thin film disks require an underlayer to help nucleate and grow microstructures giving appropriate magnetic properties. Chromium is the most often-used underlayer and is useful because of an epitaxial match of the chromium planes to preferred ones in the cobalt-based magnetic alloys used in thin film media. This epitaxy allows for alignment of the easy axes of magnetization in the plane or close to the plane of the disk. Underlayers also present a microstructure that is replicated by the superimposed magnetic thin film. Grain structures are critical in determining thin film disk noise, and the structure can be controlled in the magnetic film by modifying the underlayer template.

Ferromagnetic materials are needed for the magnetic layer. Cobalt-based binary and ternary alloys are suitable because of the large magnetocrystalline anisotropy giving high coercivity. Three alloys are in general use in the production of current thin film disks: CoCrTa, CoPtCr, and CoPtNi. Cobalt by itself provides too low a coercivity. By forming alloys with large-diameter transition elements such as Pt, Ta, Ir, and Sm, coercivity values can be tailored to cover a range from 1000 Oe to values in excess of 3000 Oe.

Chromium is a crucial second or third element in sputtered magnetic films, and it serves two purposes. First, the presence of chromium in the alloy reduces corrosion potential. It is thought that the chromium oxidizes and passivates the surface from further degradation. Second, the presence of chromium in the magnetic alloy allows for precipitation of other crystalline phases at grain boundaries, or within grains, that can aid in noise reduction.

Thin film disks have a need for protection of the magnetic layer from the recording head, which makes surface contact during turn-on and shutdown of the disk drive. The use of hard-sputtered overcoats has become universal, and amorphous carbon has been the overwhelming choice of the thin film disk industry. Material properties of amorphous carbon can be tailored by incorporation of dopants such as hydrogen or nitrogen. Carbon overcoats are on the order of the thickness of the magnetic layer, and 10–15 nm thickness is typical. The overcoat serves to protect the magnetic layer and also acts as a support structure for the lubricant.

The final layer in the thin film disk structure is the lubricant. The lubricant is a perfluoropolyether organic polymer. Lubricants serve to reduce friction and wear between the carbon overcoat and the recording head. Important lubricant properties embodied in the perfluoropolyethers are chemical inertness, low vapor pressure to prevent evaporative loss, a low contact angle allowing uniform wetting of the carbon overcoat surface, and a chemical affinity for the overcoat, preventing spin-off and desorption. Lubricant thickness is between 1 and 3 nm. The lubricant's affinity for the carbon surface seems to be rooted in physisorption rather than chemisorption, as noted by the strength of the lubricant-overcoat bonding.

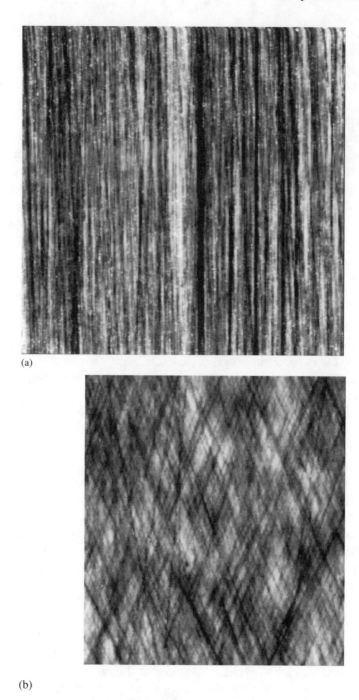

(a)

(b)

Figure 7.2 AFM pictures of textured thin film disk surfaces. The traces are 100 μ by 100 μ. The general circumferential nature of the texture is observed convoluted with a cross-hatched pattern; (a) shows a cross-hatched angle close to 0° while (b) is about 45°.

Figure 7.1b shows a cross-sectional transmission electron micrograph of a thin film disk. No carbon is present. The columnar nature of the underlayer and magnetic layer is observed. Close examination shows the interface between the 15-nm Cr underlayer and the 50-nm magnetic layer [1].

7.3.2 Disk Manufacture

The Al-Mg substrates supplied to disk manufacturers are cut to the appropriate dimensions. This includes making the thickness and outside and inside diameters to tolerance and imparting a chamfer on the outside edge of the disk. The rough-surfaced Al-Mg blank is ground to a smooth surface using abrasive techniques. The substrate is next plated using an electroless plating process. Disks are placed on mandrels and dipped into a tank containing a variety of chemicals, but principally a dissolved Ni salt. The electroless process is an oxidation-reduction reaction that spontaneously occurs in solution without the aid of external electrical power supplies. The electrons needed for the chemical reduction of Ni^{2+} come from hypophosphite ions (H_2PO^{-2}). The phosphorus from the hypophosphite is incorporated into the final plated film at about 10 atomic percent. The resulting Ni-P of 10 μm thickness is not ferromagnetic and is very hard, giving the desired surface to support the magnetic layer.

Vacuum deposition, or physical-vapor deposition techniques, as opposed to solution deposition methods such as electroless plating, is used to deposit the underlayer, magnetic films, and overcoat materials. One can evaporate metallic thin films onto a substrate by heating a crucible with the desired material in a vacuum. Evaporation is an effective way to deposit large quantities of material rapidly, but lacks versatility in process control. Vacuum deposition of magnetic thin films through sputtering is the preferred method used in the rigid-disk industry. Sputtering is accomplished by applying a voltage between the target material and the substrate to be sputtered in a vacuum vessel containing a sputtering gas (Figure 7.3). Argon is universally used because of its low cost and large atomic mass, leading to good sputtering yields. A plasma of electrons and Ar ions is spontaneously generated upon voltage application and the Ar gas glows purple from the electronic excitations. Argon ions are accelerated onto the target material, and by momentum transfer, atoms are displaced from the target and transferred to the substrate. Thin film composition replicates the target composition in the sputtering process.

Sputtering can be done in several modes. Perhaps the simplest configuration is DC diode sputtering, where a DC potential is placed between the target and substrate. Another mode, magnetron sputtering, has been introduced to increase sputtering rates. In one common configuration, a magnetic field in the form of a racetrack is placed on the target by placing magnets on the target backside (Figure 7.4). Electrons are trapped close to the sputtering target, increasing argon ion production and subsequent sputtering rate. Indeed, DC magnetron sputtering is the most common method to sputter thin film disks. Radio frequency (RF) sputtering is also possible where a high-frequency RF voltage is capacitively coupled to the

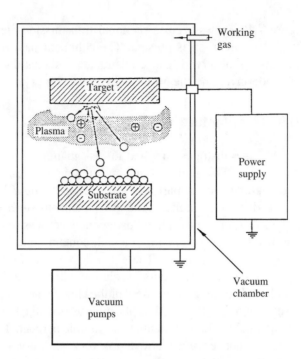

Figure 7.3 Schematic diagram of the sputtering process. A voltage is applied between the target and substrate in several mTorr of Ar gas. A plasma of
Ar ions is created. The Ar ions are attracted to the voltage-biased target and collide with the target material. Through momentum transfer,
target atoms are transferred to the disk substrate.

target. The RF sputtering allows for the deposition of nonconducting oxides and
other materials that are possible candidates for thin film disk overcoats and recording layers.

Figure 7.5 shows two manufacturing methods used to sputter thin film disks.
Figure 7.5a is an in-line approach where a pallet containing the substrates moves
on a drive mechanism past sets of targets. The pallet of disks first enters the sputtering system through a load-lock chamber and is preheated to drive off surface
contaminants and to aid in film nucleation. The pallet then proceeds into the sputtering chamber. Pallets have been designed to hold up to fifty-three 95-mm-diameter
disks. The capacity for smaller diameters is even greater. Some drawbacks of in-line
machines are a lack of magnetic uniformity over the pallet and a slight magnetic
anisotropy in the direction of pallet motion that can cause read-back modulation
around the disk.

Figure 7.5b shows the other common approach to sputtering thin film disks.
Disks are sputtered one at a time, stationary between two concentric sputtering targets. Consistency of properties from disk to disk is excellent and magnetic circumferential variation is low. However, throughput of disks is lower in the single-disk

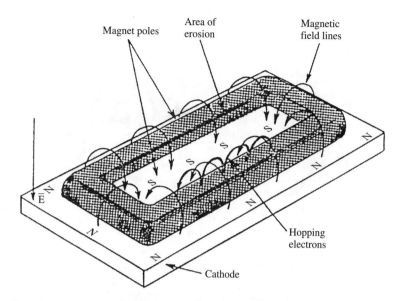

Figure 7.4 Sputtering target used in magnetron sputtering. Magnetic field lines from magnets placed in a racetrack pattern on the backside of the target trap electrons in a localized region on the target. The number of ionizations of the Ar gas increases, consequently greatly increasing sputtering rate.

sputtering machines compared to pallet systems. Both methods are in common usage.

The next step in disk manufacture is lubrication. The standard process is to dip the disks into solutions of perfluoropolyethers in Freon or Freon-like solvents. Upon emerging from the solution, the solvent rapidly evaporates, leaving a uniform lubricant film. The lubricant is sometimes bonded to the surface by heat treatment. The thickness of the lubricant can be controlled by adjusting bath concentration, dip rate, and heating conditions.

Finally, the disk surface is lightly burnished to remove any asperities that may interfere with the flying head. An abrasive tape is passed over the surface lightly enough to avoid scratching. The disk is now ready for testing (see Section 7.6).

7.4 DISK MAGNETICS

Rigid-disk media magnetic properties can be conveniently subdivided into macroscopic and microscopic properties. An understanding of each is needed to design thin film media for the desired signal-to-noise ratio, S_0/N, required by the magnetic recording system. Macroscopic properties such as coercivity (H_c), remanence-thickness product ($M_r\delta$), coercive squareness (S^*), and squareness (S) determine

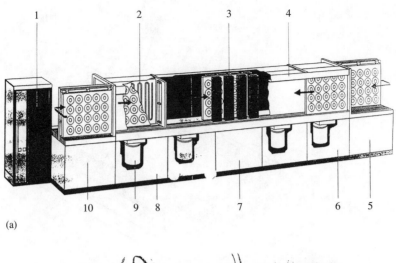

(a)

(b)

Figure 7.5 (a) In-line manufacturing sputtering system used to sputter thin film disks (Leybold Technologies, Inc.). In the in-line approach, a pallet containing the substrates moves on a drive mechanism past sets of targets. These targets contain the underlayer, magnetic, and overcoat material. (b) Stationary manufacturing sputtering system used to sputter thin film disks (Intevac, Vacuum Systems Division). Disks are sputtered one at a time stationary between two concentric sputtering targets. Consistency of properties from disk to disk is excellent and magnetic circumferential variation is low.

read-back signal (S_0) variables such as pulse shape, amplitude, and resolution. These disk parameters are indicated in Figure 7.6, which shows an **M–H** hysteresis curve (see Section 2.13) taken with a vibrating sample magnetometer (VSM) of a thin film disk suitable for readback with a magnetoresistive (MR) head. Microscopic properties such as grain size, grain coupling, and grain crystallographic

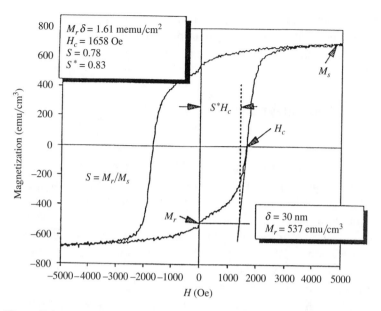

Figure 7.6 Hysteresis curve of a thin film disk sample taken with a vibrating sample magnetometer.

orientation determine the noise properties (N) of the films. An optimization of macromagnetics for signal and micromagnetics for noise is necessary.

7.4.1 Macromagnetics

Theoretical work was presented in 1971 that allows one to calculate recording responses of media knowing H_c, M_r, δ, and S^* in conjunction with head fly height (d) [2]. From their analysis, the Williams-Comstock parameter a has been derived that relates macromagnetic properties of the disk and the field distribution of an inductive recording head to isolated pulse widths. The original expression can be simplified to the following, assuming S^* values close to unity:

$$a = \left[\frac{4M_r\delta[d + (\delta/2)]}{H_c} \right]^{1/2} \qquad (7.1)$$

Combining this factor with the formula for pulse width at 50% amplitude,

$$PW_{50} \cong \sqrt{g^2 + 4(d + a)(d + a + \delta)} \qquad (7.2)$$

where g is the gap length of the head, one can approximate the read-back pulse shape for any head/disk combination. The general design criteria for rigid-disk media is to minimize PW_{50} and a by increasing the coercivity H_c as much as possible without exceeding the writability of the head, keeping S^* high for narrow switching field distributions, leading to narrow transitions, and keeping δ very low for high-frequency output. The M_r has to be adjusted to give adequate signal output without sacrificing resolution. These topics are discussed in detail in Sections 3.8 and 3.9.

7.4.2 Micromagnetics

Thin film media are comprised of grains between 20 and 50 nm in diameter. As seen in the transmission electron micrographs in Figure 7.7, the grains can be very close together, leading to strong magnetostatic and intergranular exchange interactions. The exchange forces fall off rapidly with separation distance and are ignored in particulate media because of the large particle separations. In thin film media, grains are closely packed and at separation distances where exchange forces are very strong. Exchange interactions are of ultimate importance in the understanding of macromagnetic and micromagnetic properties of thin film media. During the magnetic recording process, exchange interactions cause the grains to act cooperatively. In a DC-erased state, the magnetization direction over a large scale is constant. The DC erase noise is low in thin film media. However, transition noise is higher due to zig-zag walls or sawtooth transitions (Figure 7.8). The wall is irregular across the track width, and this nonuniformity in the zig-zag leads to noise in the transition.

The consequences of having highly coupled thin films with zig-zag walls in the recorded transition were demonstrated in 1983 [3]. Noise power in thin film alloys of CoNi, Co, and CoRe was investigated to densities of 1500 flux changes/mm, as shown in Figure 7.9. The noise power increases with recording density. The key development that has occurred for the extendability of thin film media is the understanding of how to minimize exchange interactions through microstructural modifications giving low noise medium while at the same time keeping the macromagnetic properties in the desired ranges.

7.4.3 Low-Noise Fabrication Techniques

There are three major approaches to thin film disk noise reduction: physical grain separation, compositional segregation, and multilayers. Physical grain segregation has been observed in TEM micrographs in low-noise thin film media, as seen in Figure 7.7a. There are several means to achieve voided grain structures within the control of the thin film disk fabricator. Sputtering process effects on thin film disk microstructure and media noise have been interpreted using adatom kinetic energy arguments initially put forth by Thornton [4, 5]. Figure 7.10 shows a zone diagram for sputter deposited metal films showing the effect of temperature and sputtering pressure on film structure. The substrate temperature is T, and T_m is the melting point of the thin film material. Sputtered films deposited at low temperatures

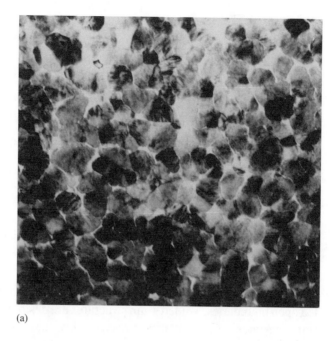

(a)

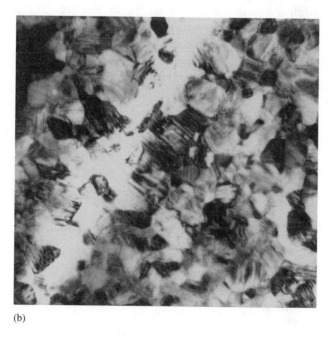

(b)

Figure 7.7 Transmission electron micrographs of two different thin film disk structures at 200,000×
magnification: (a) Grains are noticeably voided, leading to reduced magnetic interactions
and lower disk noise. (b) Voids are lacking. This type of structure can be highly magnetically coupled, leading to high noise.

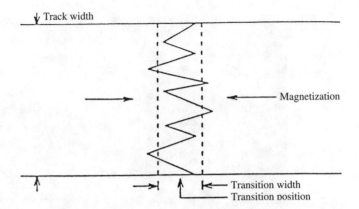

Figure 7.8 Zig-zag transition between regions of opposite magnetization in a thin film disk. The wall is irregular across the track width, and this nonuniformity in the zig-zag leads to noise in the transition.

and high pressures fall into zone 1 and exhibit a columnar growth structure defined by voided open boundaries. Voided grain structures are desired for low-noise media. Low sputtering rates, high sputtering pressure, low sputtering temperatures, and the absence of bias are low-mobility sputtering conditions that rob the sputtered atoms of their kinetic energy during atom transport and film growth, allowing the formation of the voided structures.

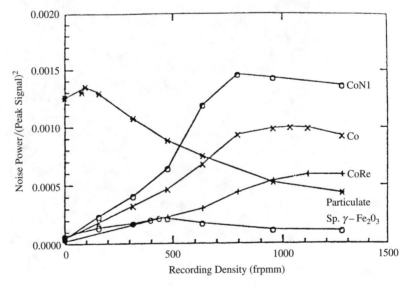

Figure 7.9 Noise versus recording density for different thin film media [3]. Depending on the fabrication process and the resulting microstructure, different noise contents are observed.

The nature of the underlayer has a large effect in determining noise performance. Magnetic films tend to replicate the underlayer structure below; thus, forming segregated underlayer structures should lead to segregated magnetic film structures. Work by Yogi et al. and Natarajan and Murdock in 1988 revealed the reduction of noise with increasing chromium thickness for sputtered films of CoNiCr and CoP [6, 7]. It is observed that chromium underlayer grains enlarge and segregate with increasing thickness and propagate these properties to the magnetic layer.

Compositional segregation of grains in thin film disks is another effective way to minimize interactions giving low-noise disks. Experimental evidence has been obtained using X-ray fluorescence (XRF) and wet-etching techniques. Figure 7.11a shows a structure of chromium precipitation to the grain boundaries consistent with the TEM/XRF mapping work by Chapman and Rogers [8, 9]. Wet-etching work by Maeda has led to a slightly different interpretation of the microstructure [10]. In this technique, cobalt regions are preferentially dissolved, leaving patterns designated as CP structures (chrysanthemum-like pattern). Figure 7.11b shows a CP grain model where each magnetic grain shows internal composition fluctuations.

Substrate temperature and chromium alloy concentration on sputtered CoPtCr/Cr longitudinal films have been recently reported as a means to effect composition segregation [11]. High chromium content and higher temperatures lead to lower-noise films, and it is speculated that these variables accelerate the chromium segregation to grain boundaries, forming nonmagnetic phases. Choosing an alloy composition that can undergo a phase change at elevated temperatures

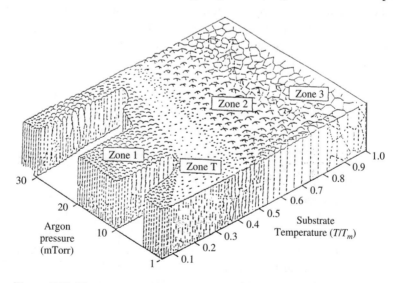

Figure 7.10 Thornton zone diagram showing thin film microstructure as a function of sputtering temperature and pressure [4]. Zone 1 structures are voided and lead to low disk noise.

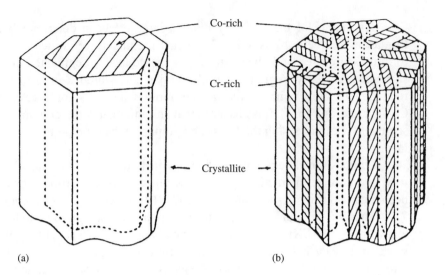

Figure 7.11 Grain structure showing chromium segregation to (a) the boundaries and (b) internal chrysanthemum structures [10].

is necessary to induce compositional segregation. It is suggested that based on equilibrium phase diagrams, certain binary and ternary alloys can be two-phase alloys. Noise performance is better using the alloys that allow two phases such as CoCr and sputtered CoP. Such phase separation may be particularly true for the CoCrTa alloy. At above 2% Ta, the H_c value drops precipitously, suggesting that the hcp phase of this composition becomes unstable and that the precipitation of a different phase may be starting. Compositional segregation may help explain why CoCrTa alloys (see Figure 7.7b), often lacking any evidence of a physically voided structure, are less noisy compared to other ternary alloys used for longitudinal recording.

Sputtering quaternary alloys such as CoPtCrTa and CoPtCrB is proving to be an effective way of producing low-noise thin film media, particularly with films containing boron. It is postulated that the low solubility of boron in the cobalt alloy leads to composition segregation of the grains [12]. Fabricating new alloys with constituents having limited solubilities may be the key to the next generation of low-noise alloys.

There has been much interest recently in the use of magnetic multilayers as a means to decrease noise in thin film media. By depositing two or more magnetic films separated by a thin nonmagnetic material to create the same $M_r\delta$ product, noise reductions have been observed. This is a statistical result based on the increased number of noise sources per unit volume. Noise is reduced by the square root of the number of layers. Figure 7.12 shows the cross section of a typical bilayer disk with a nonmagnetic chromium interlayer.

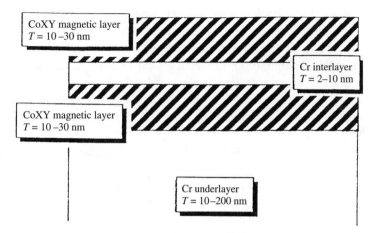

Figure 7.12 Schematic diagram of a bilayer disk. The nonmagnetic Cr interlayer serves to decouple the two magnetic layers, leading to lower disk noise.

7.5 DISK TRIBOLOGY

Tribology refers to the study of friction, wear, and lubrication. Significant head/disk interactions occur when disk drives start and stop. Even during the normal flying of the head, interactions can occur, particularly for the small head-medium spacings seen in current products. Severe head/disk interaction can result in head crashes where disk material is physically abraded and data are lost. Thus, tribological design of thin film disks is critical to the usable life of a disk drive. Historically, this effort has been greater than the effort needed to produce good disk magnetics. The key to developing the best tribological materials lies in understanding the physics and chemistry of the head/disk interface.

There are three key variables in disk tribological design: surface texture, overcoat material and thickness, and lubricant material and thickness. The textured surface of the disk, described in Section 7.2, serves a function of alleviating stiction of the recording head when the disk drive is turned off. Stiction forces (static coefficient of friction) are proportional to the contact area, and roughening the disk surface reduces contact surface area between the head and the disk. A rough surface may reduce stiction, but it demands that the head fly higher to avoid surface asperities, and large fly height, as seen in equation (7.2), is detrimental to magnetic performance. The stiction–magnetic performance trade-off dilemma is of major concern in tribology design.

The magnetic film sputtered on a textured surface cannot, by itself, withstand the friction and wear forces from the recording head. Overcoat materials that have been developed, along with the application of a topical lubricant, reduce wear and friction to an acceptable level. The overcoat material in general use is sputtered carbon (α-C). Sputtered carbon is amorphous but can be endowed with properties during sputtering similar to carbon in bulk form, that is, graphite or diamond. Diamondlike properties such as high hardness, chemical inertness, optical transparency, and high electrical resistance are desirable and have been observed in sputtered carbon films, particularly with the addition of H during the process. Diamondlike carbon (DLC) or α-C:H overcoats are widespread in the disk industry [13].

Thicknesses of sputtered carbon films were about 25 nm for many years, but there have been recent activities to make the thickness lower. The design of the head/disk interface focuses on the head-to-overcoat spacing; on the other hand, the design of the head/disk magnetics focuses on the head-to-magnetic layer spacing. Carbon overcoats contribute to the magnetic fly height of the head. With heads currently flying below 100 nm, an overcoat thickness of 25 nm can subtract substantially from the total head/medium spacing budget and widen read-back pulses limiting areal density. Efforts are under way to develop coatings with thicknesses of less than 10 nm.

There are other natural candidates for overcoat materials, but none has emerged as a viable thin film disk overcoat. The hardest materials available belong to the oxide, nitride, and carbide families. ZrO_2 has been tried as a disk overcoat using RF sputtering methods. Tribology results were mixed, and the extra difficulty and loss of manufacturing throughput from using RF techniques squelched further developments. Other hard materials require high deposition temperatures that can adversely affect the magnetic and Ni-P underlayer.

The use of lubricants on interacting surfaces reduces wear and friction, and this general tribological principle is applied to thin film media. On top of the carbon overcoat, liquid perfluoropolyether (PFPE) films are applied. The several polymer structures in use are shown in Figure 7.13. These materials are the most suitable lubricants for disk applications because of their thermal stability, lubricity, and low vapor pressure. Several monolayers are left on the disk after dipping in the lubricant/solvent tank. In some manufacturing approaches, the lubricant bonding to the surface is enhanced by baking [14].

The amount of lubricant applied to the carbon surface is critical. Too little can lead to excessive wear, while too much can lead to large stiction values. The optimum value is about one to three monolayers but depends strongly on the roughness of the surface.

Thin films can react chemically with a variety of materials in the environment, and thus, corrosion resistance is a concern for thin film disk manufacturers. The design of magnetic alloys and the overcoat/lubricant system has been successful in alleviating this concern. High humidity, particularly at high temperatures, is one of the most severe environments. To minimize surface degradation from water condensation at temperature and humidity extremes, the use of chromium in the magnetic layer is crucial. Chromium readily forms a thin, nonmagnetic oxide layer, which protects the rest of the disk structure. Some

$$F-(CF-CF_2-O-)m-CF_2-CF_3$$
$$CF_3$$

$$CF_3-O-(CF-CF_2-O-)m-(CF_2-O-)n-CF_3 \qquad m/n > 40$$
$$CF_3$$

$$CF_3-O-(CF_2-CF_2-O-)p-(CF_2-O-)q-CF_3 \qquad p/q < 1$$

$$F-(CF_2-CF_2-O-)m-CF_2-CF_3$$

Figure 7.13 Schematic diagram of perfluoropolyether thin film disk lubricants. Several structures are in use, but they all are polymers with all hydrogen atoms replaced by fluorine atoms.

early thin film disk Co-P-plated magnetic films were very susceptible to corrosion. Figure 7.14 shows a corrosion-rate comparison between a plated CoP thin film disk with a carbon overcoat and a sputtered CoPtCr thin film disk with and without a carbon overcoat. Corrosion occurs at a much greater rate on the CoP film system. Bare CoPtCr shows a corrosion improvement. The presence of carbon on top of the sputtered CoPtCr diminishes the corrosion rate even further. The C layer serves as a protective barrier between the environment and the thin film.

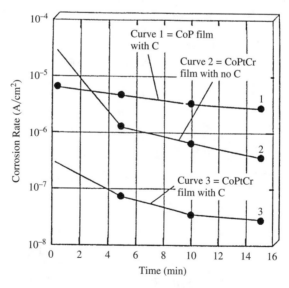

Figure 7.14 Corrosion rate of thin film disks made by plating (CoP) and sputtering (CoPtCr). For the sputtered media, results with and without a carbon overcoat are shown. The CoPtCr film is more corrosion-resistant because of the presence of chromium. The carbon overcoat enhances corrosion-resistance further.

7.6 DISK TESTING AND CHARACTERIZATION

Many sophisticated techniques are employed to characterize, test, and certify thin film disk media. The development of thin film structures demands an understanding of materials and their magnetic properties. The development of thin film disk candidates involves mechanical testing of the head/medium interface for durability and friction. The manufacture of a finished thin film disk requires that every surface be certified asperity-free and pass basic magnetic recording performance tests.

7.6.1 Materials Characterization

Magnetic property measurements are done to determine the hysteresis parameters H_c, $M_r\delta$, and S^*. The standard research tool to measure hysteresis curves is a VSM. Figure 7.15 shows the fundamental setup, and Figure 7.6 is an example of a VSM hysteresis curve. A sample is cut from a disk, typically on the order of 1 cm^2, and placed on the bottom of a vibrating rod. The sample is sanded on one side so that contributions from magnetic properties of both sides are not confused. The vibrating rod is placed in a DC magnetic field of an electromagnet that slowly sweeps the magnetization from positive to negative saturation, typically ±5000 Oe. The magnetization of the vibrating sample, through Faraday's law, induces flux in pick-up coils placed on the poles of the electromagnet. Knowing the area of the sample, the result is a plot of the sample magnetization-thickness product ($M\delta$) versus applied field. If the magnetic layer thickness is known, M can also be calculated. The intrinsic coercivity, H_c, is measured at the point where $M = 0$. The VSM can also record

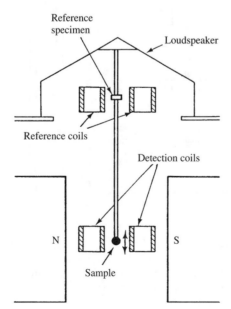

Figure 7.15 Diagram of a vibrating sample magnetometer used to measure magnetic properties of thin film disks. A small sample is placed on the bottom of a vibrating rod immersed in a magnetic field generated by an electromagnet. The magnetization **M** of the sample induces a signal in the detection coils. Here, **M** is plotted versus the applied field **H**. The result is a hysteresis curve [22].

several types of remanence curves. A DC demagnetization remanence curve is the result of saturating the sample and then noting the remanence M_r, the magnetization in the zero field, after a sequence of increasing fields in the opposite direction to the initial magnetization. The field necessary to bring the sample to $M_r = 0$ is called the *remanence coercivity H_r*. The process used to measure H_r resembles the process of magnetic recording and is thus a slightly more meaningful characterization of the disk coercivity. The VSM is the primary calibration tool from which others are correlated.

A VSM gives the most magnetic information about disk hysteresis but is destructive to the disk and is time-consuming. Other techniques have been developed that are rapid and nondestructive. Magnetic induction measuring techniques are used in several instruments. Figure 7.16 shows the heart of a transfer-curve magnetometer used by IBM that is based on the writing and reading of pulses by heads on a spinning wheel several thousandths of an inch above the disk surface. This instrument can measure $M_r\delta$, H_c, and S^* in about a minute [15]. A commercial

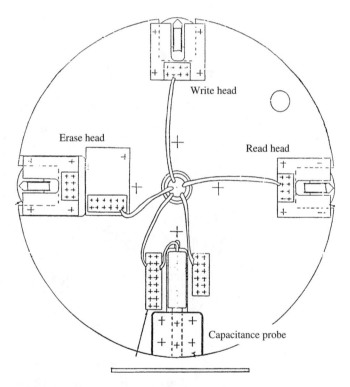

Figure 7.16 Transfer curve magnetometer used to measure magnetic properties of thin film disks rapidly and nondestructively [15]. After an initial erasure, a pulse is written by the write head. By plotting pulse height with the read head versus current to the write head, a remanence transfer curve is obtained containing $M_r\delta$ and H_r values.

instrument is available that also measures these same quantities using pulse writing and reading methods [16]. This instrument keeps the head stationary and moves the disk.

Less often used are **B–H** (see Section 2.13) looping techniques. These have been applied to thin film media both in the sample and full-disk measurement modes. Here, a sample or disk is placed inside a 60-Hz AC magnetic field and the induction is measured. A hysteresis curve trace can be monitored on an oscilloscope. This approach is fast, but for full disks, a complication arises from the existence of eddy currents in the conductive Al-Mg substrate that influences induction measurements.

Magneto-optical Kerr effect instruments have also been designed [17]. Hysteresis curves can be obtained from plots of rotation angle versus applied field by taking advantage of the rotation of the plane of polarization of light by materials in a magnetized state. A laser beam is placed on a spot of the disk in question that is subject to an alternating applied magnetic field of about 5–10 Hz. A particular advantage is the possibility of mapping H_c on the surface of the disk because of the small size of the laser beam probe. Figure 7.17 shows an H_c map of a thin film disk showing the variation possible across one surface [18]. A drawback to such instru-

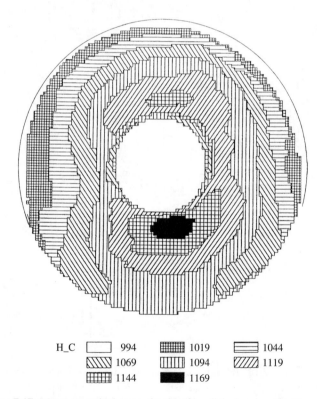

H_C	994	1019	1044
	1069	1094	1119
	1144	1169	

Figure 7.17 Magneto-optical map of a thin film disk showing the H_c variation possible on a single disk surface.

ments is that they are sensitive only to H_c; the measurement of M_r is complicated by overcoat and surface-roughness effects. The product $M_r\delta$ is not measurable.

Hysteresis properties can be obtained using a recording head on a thin film disk. By writing a series of pulses and noting their height, the field required to erase them to half height, $M_r\delta$ and H_c can be obtained. For calibration purposes, the applied field is done using a macroscopic magnetic head with repeatable gap/disk spacing for repeatable and controllable fields. Each read back head must be calibrated for voltage readback versus $M_r\delta$.

The thickness of magnetic films and underlayer films is measured by XRF. By monitoring the intensity of Co, the primary constituent of the magnetic film, and Cr, the typical underlayer material, correlations to thin film thicknesses can be established. X-ray fluorescence is also useful in establishing composition of the sputtered binary, ternary, or quaternary magnetic films. In a similar manner, carbon overcoat thickness can be measured by measuring the carbon excitation intensity. Another technique for determining carbon overcoat thickness is ellipsometry. If one knows the optical properties (index of refraction n and absorption coefficient k) of the magnetic layer and the carbon layer, the ellipticity of a reflected laser beam can be analyzed and a thickness calculated. Lubricant thickness can also be accurately measured by using ellipsometry. More common, however, for lubricant thickness quantification is the use of Fourier transform infrared (FTIR) *spectroscopy.* The perfluoropolyethers have very specific molecular vibrations in the infrared region at about $1250 \, \text{cm}^{-1}$. The intensity of these bands is proportional to thickness. Figure 7.18 shows an FTIR spectrum of a disk lubricant.

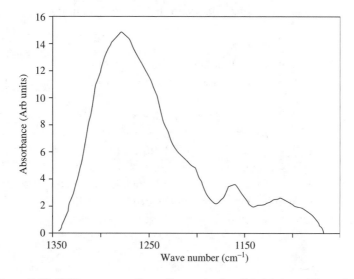

Figure 7.18 FTIR spectrum of a perfluoropolyether disk lubricant. The carbon-fluorine vibrations are active at about $1250 \, \text{cm}^{-1}$ and absorb infrared radiation. Lubricant amount can be quantified by noting the peak height of the absorption.

Materials structure information is very important to understanding thin film properties. Although tedious, TEM is used to probe the grain structures of thin films. From these micrographs (see Figure 7.7), one can induce the nature of the grain sizes, shapes, and their proximities, which affect magnetic interactions. Also obtainable through TEM work is structural information from electron diffraction. Electron diffraction patterns give understanding of the phases present in grains and their orientations. Figure 7.19 shows an electron diffraction ring pattern indicative of an hcp cobalt structure. X-ray diffraction is another probe for phase and crystalline orientation. Figure 7.20 shows a series of patterns of thin film disk structures with different chromium underlayer thicknesses. At low chromium underlayer thickness, the easy axis of magnetization, the c axis, of CoPtCr is parallel to the substrate surface. Diffraction patterns are not present for the carbon overcoat or lubricant, which are amorphous and show no long-range order.

Scanning electron microscopy (SEM) is widely used for thin film disk surface characterization. High-resolution SEM is capable of seeing grain structure directly on the surface of the disk, eliminating the painful sample preparation techniques. A scanning electron micrograph also has XRF capability, allowing the identification of composition and contaminants.

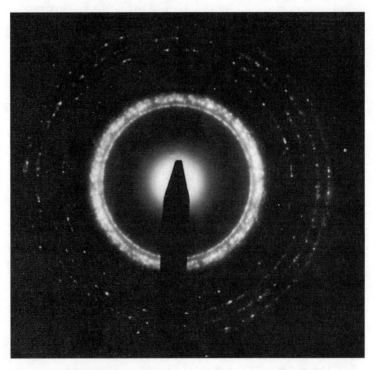

Figure 7.19 Transmission electron diffraction pattern from the magnetic film of a thin film disk. The three bright rings are indicative of a cobalt alloy with a hexagonally closed packed structure. The intensities are suggestive of an in-plane c axis.

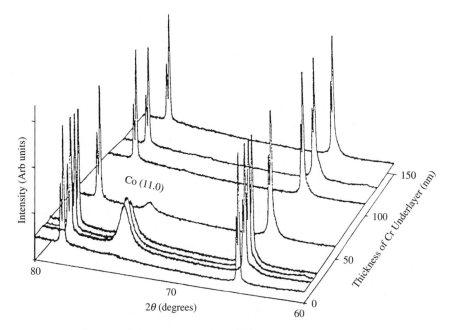

Figure 7.20 X-ray diffraction spectrum of a thin film disk structure with different chromium underlayer thicknesses. The disks with chromium underlayers below 50 nm show a preferred orientation of the c axis in plane. This is indicated by the growing intensity of the Co (11.0) diffraction line.

Sophisticated techniques are used occasionally to probe composition and contamination of thin film disk structures. Auger electron spectroscopy and electron spectroscopy for chemical analysis (ESCA) allow the identification and quantification of constituents on the surface and in the layers of thin film structures. This can be particularly useful when trying to understand the interface between the many layers of a thin film disk.

Surface topography characterization is important to understanding many aspects of thin film disks. Stylus techniques involve the dragging of a small-dimension probe over the surface and interpreting the trace. Surface roughness and peak heights can be determined. More recent scanning tunneling microscopy (STM) and atomic force microscopy (AFM) instruments allow a higher-resolution study of the surface and a better understanding of the texture process.

7.6.2 Finished Disk Testing

After a thin film disk is lubricated, it proceeds on to a burnish process and glide height test. As mentioned in Section 7.3, surface asperities need to be removed or burnished from the disk surface to eliminate potential head/disk interactions in the disk drive. The glide height test (GHT) has been designed to check for the effectiveness of the burnishing step. Special precision test stands have been developed where a glide head with an imbedded piezo-crystal (PZT) is flown over the disk. If a head bumps into an asperity, a signal is induced in the crystal and the electronics recording system makes note of the size and location. Depending on specific disk program criteria, disks will be rejected for glide failure. Current thin film disks have heads flying at less than 100 nm. The glide test checks at 20–40 nm below the nominal fly height for asperities.

Usually on the same test stand as the GHT is the single-disk magnetic test apparatus. This consists of a magnetic head and channel that writes and reads signals on a sample of tracks on the disk surface, checking for basic magnetic recording parameters and defective surface sites. Signal amplitudes are measured at two frequencies and the resolution, defined as the ratio of the two amplitudes, is carefully monitored. Dropouts in the read back signal train are recorded. Only so many dropouts, or missing bits, are allowed on a disk surface before rejection. Missing bits are the result of defects on the disk surface typically originating in surface contamination, sputter spitting, or texture irregularities. Figure 7.21 shows a defect on a thin film disk that caused a missing bit.

There are other magnetic parameters of great importance that are not measured on every disk but deserve mention. The effectiveness of writing one frequency signal over a previously written pattern of a different frequency is called *overwrite* and should exceed 30 dB in magnitude. This parameter is of importance in determining whether the disk coercivity is too high. As defined in equation (7.2), PW_{50} can be measured on isolated written pulses. The ratio of disk signal to noise as described in Section 7.4 is measured on thin film media using several techniques. The most common approach is to write a square wave on the surface at the high-frequency design point. By using spectral analysis, one can eliminate the contribution of the discrete written frequency and quantify the area of the resultant trace for media noise content. A faster technique that has proven highly effective is to write a track to saturation in one polarity and then DC erase the track in the opposite polarity until the track is in the state of zero remanence ($M_r\delta = 0$). The RMS read voltage of the erased track is proportional to the high-frequency noise content.

The magnetic measure of importance in the actual disk drive is the error rate. Such an analysis can be done on a precision test stand or in the drive itself. A data pattern is written on the disk track and then read back, checking for data integrity. An incorrectly read bit due to bit shift, noise, or defects is an error. Error rate is measured logarithmically as errors per total read bits. The raw error rate ratio specification in common usage is 10^{-10}. Read-back errors can be detected by the read-back channel and corrected giving an actual error rate better than 10^{-14}, essentially error-free.

7.6.3 Mechanical Testing

During the course of thin film disk development, several mechanical tests evaluating the robustness of the head-disk interface are checked. Contact start-stop (CSS) testing is routinely done. In this test, the disk is started and stopped thousands

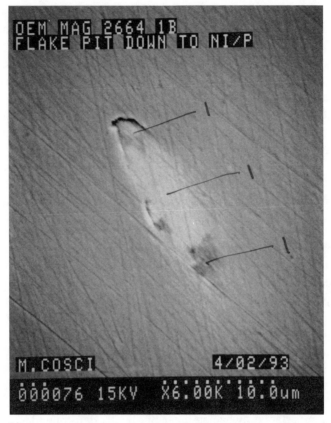

(a)

(b)

Figure 7.21   (a) Multiple defects observed on a thin film disk surface; (b) a defect resulting in a missing bit during testing. (C. H. Moy, IBM)

of times, resulting in many head take-offs and landings. Friction is monitored as a function of CSS cycles. Coefficients of friction < 1.0 are typically demanded after 20,000 cycles. Stiction forces are tested on disks by checking the static coefficient of friction. This value cannot be too large, or the motor torque will be insufficient to start the disk drive. Stiction can be altered by adjusting texture roughness and lubricant thickness. These tests are often done in extreme cases of temperature and humidity to ensure that the head-disk interface will be functional in different environments. Current file designs are requiring that the mean time between failures (MTBF) should exceed 800,000 hours.

7.7 DISK TECHNOLOGY DIRECTIONS

Discussions and technology development are under way to demonstrate recording system feasibility of 10 Gb/in.^{2} by the end of the decade [19]. Technology improvements in all aspects of disk design will be introduced, but the most important advances will come in the areas of substrate, magnetic film, and head/disk interface.

7.7.1 Substrates

The substrate material and substrate surface description are evolving to allow for new function, capacity, and areal density demands. Aluminum has been the substrate in general use since the inception of rigid-disk technology, but aluminum has an important drawback—it can plastically deform under mild strain conditions. New drive designs for laptop and notebook computers require shock resistance in excess of 100 times the force of gravity. Such forces can occur when a device is dropped from a desk. Ceramic and glass materials can withstand such deceleration and are being used in disk designs to increase shock resistance. These materials break rather than deform like aluminum, but at levels of strain much greater than aluminum and suitable for the new drive formats. The elasticity and high yield strengths of glass and ceramic materials will also allow rigid-disk thicknesses to decrease, allowing more disks to be placed in a drive for a greater data capacity. The 65- and 48-mm disks of 0.38 mm thickness are thought to be viable designs. It is unlikely that aluminum will be usable at these thickness levels.

Other important substrate demands for future drive technologies are high stiffness, low density, flatness, low surface roughness, and low cost. Although glass and ceramic materials have great promise for improved deformation characteristics compared to aluminum, they show no particular advantage over Ni-P-plated aluminum in these other categories. There is a great opportunity for new materials development for disk substrates. Table 7.1 compares physical properties among leading candidates for disk substrate materials.

A critical demand for the next generation of substrates is an extremely smooth surface finish. The reason for this is twofold. First, the largest magnetic recording

TABLE 7.1 A Comparison of Physical Properties for Disk Substrate Materials

Property	NiP	Soda Lime Glass	Aluminosilicate Glass	Glass-Ceramic	Carbon	SiC
Density (g/cm^3)	2.7	2.5	2.5	2.7	1.8	3.2
Young's modulus (GPa)	72	75	85	83	35	460
Surface hardness (kg/mm^2)	500	540	590	650	650	2500
Yield strength (MPa)	117	37	—	>200	90	400

gains come from reducing fly height. Asperities arising from surface roughness must be eliminated so that the head/media spacing can be small without any tribological risk. Current state-of-the-art head/media spacings are < 75 nm and require surface finishes of R_q (root-mean-square) less than 4 nm. Projected head/media spacings of 25 nm demand substrate surfaces with finishes below 1 nm. The second reason smooth surfaces are necessary is because of the noise contribution to the error rate. Fluctuations arising from the local variation in spacing and coercivity inherent in nonsmooth surfaces must be minimized. Superfinish technologies on Ni-P-plated aluminum along with smooth glass offer recording surfaces capable of achieving much higher areal densities. Figure 7.22 compares an AFM picture of a superfinished substrate with a conventionally finished surface in general use today [20].

Landing on such a superfinished surface as in Figure 7.22 will not be allowed because of the great stiction forces that will be generated. To get around this problem, zone texture technologies are being developed. Figure 7.23 shows a schematic of how this may work. Here, a textured landing zone is prepared, usually at the inner radius of the disk, where the head can land without sticking. The remainder of the disk area serves as the data zone. Head load/unload solutions are also being contemplated where the head never lands on any part of the disk when power is turned off. In any case, substrate materials capable of achieving atomically smooth surfaces are necessary for the next generation of disk technology.

7.7.2 Magnetic Film

One debate that has been going on since the mid-1970s is the preferred orientation of the magnetic anisotropy for optimum magnetic recording. Iwasaki proposed that a CoCr perpendicular magnetic medium would be optimum [21]. Theoretically, this is desirable because of the nature of the demagnetizing fields associated with recorded transitions. In longitudinal recording, where the bits are recorded head to head, demagnetizing forces emanating from the bit oppose the magnetization direction of the next bit and limit the sharpness of the transition and the ultimate recording density (see Figure 7.24). These considerations lead to equation (7.1) for the transition parameter in longitudinal media. In perpendicular recording,

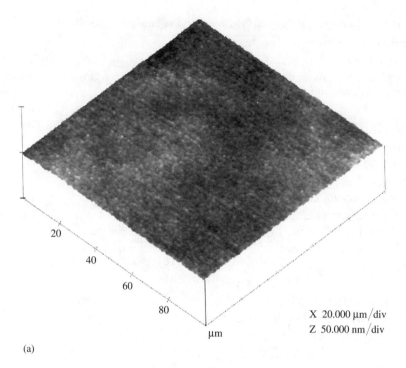

X 20.000 µm/div
Z 50.000 nm/div

(a)

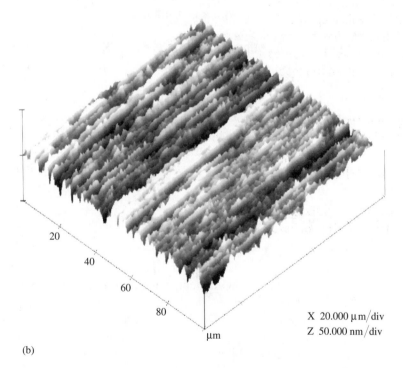

X 20.000 µ m/div
Z 50.000 nm/div

(b)

Figure 7.22 AFM pictures comparing a superfinished polish surface (a) with a
standard finished surface of a thin film disk (b).

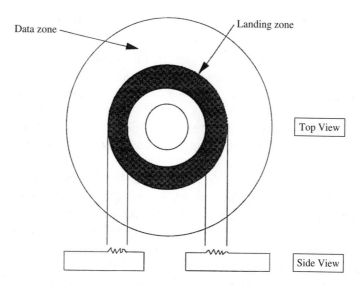

Figure 7.23 Zone-textured disk having a rough zone for head landing and a smooth zone for data recording.

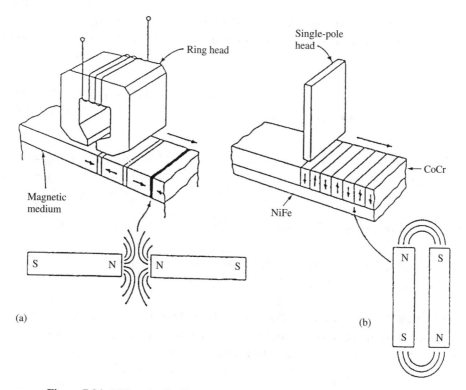

Figure 7.24 (a) Longitudinally recorded transactions; (b) perpendicularly recorded transactions.

adjacent bit magnetic fields are magnetizing rather than demagnetizing and transition widths can be theoretically smaller. But complications in the write process and the apparent necessity of almost zero head/media spacings for sufficiently high write gradients has clouded technological advantages for perpendicular recording, and indeed, no rigid-disk drive system has yet been manufactured.

It is generally thought that great technological gains in longitudinal media are still possible [18]. From a macromagnetic view, requirements will demand coercivity values in excess of 2000 Oe and up to 5000 Oe for some designs. Alloys that can achieve these values exist today. Conventional alloys such as CoPtCr are extendable to > 3000 Oe with appropriate process conditions. Quaternary alloys may have higher potential. Rare earth compounds such as SmCo have great coercivity potential and have been made in thin film disks to > 3000 Oe. Barium ferrite materials also have been fabricated with coercivities in excess of 3000 Oe.

From a microstructural viewpoint, films will have to be made that eliminate the exchange coupling interactions between grains to reduce media noise. Grain sizes will have to be reduced from today's values of 20–50 nm to below 10 nm and deposited in very uniform sizes and arrangements. An intrinsic limitation occurs at these diameters when thermal energy approaches the magnetic anisotropy energy that keeps magnetic vectors aligned. The superparamagnetic limit results in spontaneous changes in magnetization, and information cannot be stored.

7.7.3 Head/Medium Interaction

As can be seen by equation (7.2), head/medium spacing d has a primary effect on PW_{50} values. Several schemes have been proposed where the head can contact the thin film disk during the recording process, theoretically giving a value of $d = 0$. Contact recording has several implications to the disk design. As mentioned in Section 7.1, the surface roughness will have to be in the 1-nm range. This level of smoothness is necessary to minimize head/disk mechanical interactions, but most importantly, to allow the head to come to zero clearance on the magnetic film without meeting surface asperities.

Several contact recording proposals require the use of a liquid bearing rather than an air bearing between the head and disk. Lubricant materials appropriate as liquid bearings will have to be engineered. Overcoat materials will be under greater stress, and new materials and processes will have to be perfected.

Even if $d = 0$ is not achieved, small d values will be in use. Surfaces will have to be smooth and kept free of contamination to achieve glide height values below 25 nm. Glide technology and calibration must be improved to handle detection of such small asperities.

REFERENCES

[1] S. M. Mirzamaani, IBM SSD, San Jose, CA, private communication.

[2] M. L. Williams and R. L. Comstock, *AIP Conf. Proc.* (1971), p. 738.

[3] R. A. Baugh, E. S. Murdock, and B. R. Natarajan, "Measurement of noise in magnetic media," *IEEE Trans. Magn.,* MAG-19 (1983), p. 1722.

[4] J. A. Thornton, "The Microstructure of sputter-deposited coatings," *J. Vac. Sci. Technol.,* A4 (1986), p. 3059.

[5] T. Yogi, T. A. Nguyen, S. E. Lambert, G. L. Gorman, and G. Castillo, "Role of atomic mobility in the transition noise of longitudinal media," *IEEE Trans. Magn.,* MAG-26 (1990), p. 1578.

[6] T. Yogi, G. L. Gorman, C. H. Hwang, M. A. Kakalec, and S. E. Lambert, "Dependence of magnetics, microstructures, and recording properties on underlayer thickness in CoNiCr/Cr media," *IEEE Trans. Magn.,* MAG-24 (1988), p. 2727.

[7] B. R. Natarajan and E. S. Murdock, "Magnetic and recording properties of sputtered Co-P/Cr thin-film media," *IEEE Trans. Magn.,* MAG-24 (1988), p. 2724.

[8] J. N. Chapman, I. R. McFadyen, and J. P. C. Bernards, "Investigation of Cr segregation within RF-sputtered CoCr films," *J. Magn. Magn. Mater.,* 62 (1986), p. 359.

[9] D. J. Rogers, J. N. Chapman, J. P. C. Bernards, and S. B. Luitjens, "Determination of local composition in CoCr films deposited at different substrate temperatures," *IEEE Trans. Magn.,* MAG-25 (1989), p. 4180.

[10] Y. Maeda and M. Asahi, "Segregated microstructure in sputtered CoCr film revealed by selective wet etching," *J. Appl. Phys.,* 61 (1987), p. 1972.

[11] M. Doerner, T. Yogi, T. Nguyen, D. Parker, B. Hermsmeier, and O. Allegranza, "Composition effects in high density CoPtCr media," *IEEE Trans. Magn.,* MAG-29 (1993), p. 3667.

[12] C. R. Paik, I. Suzuki, N. Tani, M. Ishidawa, Y. Ota, and K. Nakamura, "Magnetic properties and noise characteristics of high coercivity CoCrPtB/Cr media," *IEEE Trans. Magn.,* MAG-28 (1992), p. 3084.

[13] R. L. White, IBM SSD, San Jose, CA, private communication.

[14] A. C. Wu, IBM SSD, San Jose, CA, private communication.

[15] K. E. Johnson and M. G. Kerr, "A magnetometer for the rapid and nondestructive measurement of magnetic properties on rigid disk media," *IEEE Trans. Magn.,* MAG-26 (1990), p. 256.

[16] R. M. Josephs, 1990, Innovative Instrumentation Inc., Willow Grove, PA.

[17] R. M. Josephs, 1988, Innovative Instrumentation Inc., Willow Grove, PA.

[18] K. E. Johnson, "Thin-film recording media: challenges for physics and magnetism in the 1990s," *J. Appl. Phys.,* 69 (1991), p. 4932.

[19] E. S. Murdock, R. F. Simmons, and R. Davidson, "Roadmap for 10 Gbit/in**2 media: challenges," *IEEE Trans. Magn.,* MAG-28 (1992), p. 3078.

[20] J. Joseph, IBM SSD, unpublished results, IBM, San Jose, CA, 1996.

[21] S. Iwasaki and K. Ouchi, "CoCr recording films with perpendicular magnetic anisotropy," *IEEE Trans. Magn.,* MAG-14 (1978), p. 849.

[22] B. D. Cullity, "Introduction to magnetic materials," Addison-Wesley Publishing Company, Reading, MA, 1972, p. 67.

8

Recording Channel

8.1 INTRODUCTION

This chapter focuses on factors that affect the linear bit density of a disk drive. On-track linear density considerations are divided into three parts:

1. The channel and its modules are described in several sections (8.2–8.14). The functions of these modules and common signal-processing steps are discussed. The concepts of peak shift or bit shift, intersymbol interference, and peak detection window are introduced. A peak detection channel is assumed for general discussion while a sampling channel is described under coding. Run length codes in current use are discussed here with primary emphasis on (1, 7) peak detection coding. Partial response, maximum likelihood (PRML) and EPRML coding are reviewed and compared with the peak detection procedure.

2. This part relates to writing and reading processes and their measurements: topics of overwrite, write current optimization, roll-off curve, and resolution are explained in Sections 8.15–8.18.

3. The topics of noise in head, electronics, and medium are discussed in this group. Signal-to-noise ratio is the important *figure of merit* used in the design and performance of the drive since it is strongly tied to the error rate of the drive. These subjects are covered in Sections 8.19–8.23.

The channel is a critical part of a disk drive system. A well-designed channel can provide superior density and performance from a drive. Innovative components

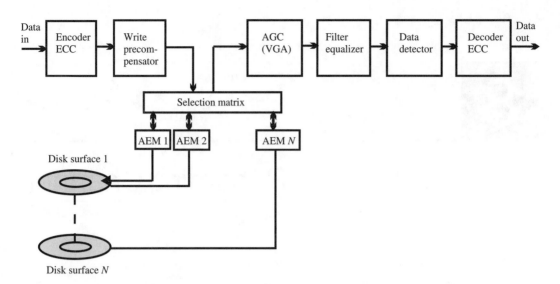

Figure 8.1 Write and read functions of a disk drive channel.

without a balanced channel can produce a substandard drive. The channel consists of several electronic circuit modules. Figure 8.1 shows a simplified flowchart of these modules. The write encoder, precompensator, read automatic gain control (AGC), equalizer, data detector, and decoder are common elements of the system. A multiplexor matrix located on the end of the arm (or stack) connects one head at a time to these modules. These electronic modules occupied a cage of printed circuit cards on the large disk drives of the 1970s. Today, all common modules are arranged on two to three semiconductor chips and efforts are under way to accommodate all the functions to one chip. The write drivers and preamplifiers are mounted in a module on the arm of a head that is often referred to as the *arm electronics module* (AEM). Every head has its own independent read/write circuits on its AEM. The wires connecting the AEM to the heads are kept as short as possible to minimize resistance and inductance in the circuit.

8.2 FUNCTIONS OF A CHANNEL

There are strong similarities between a communication channel and a recording channel. Here the word "communication" encompasses several fields, such as telephones, radio broadcasting, television, satellite transmissions, optical communication, and so on. The objectives are identical in all cases. The procedure to treat the data or information is almost equivalent. The information is coded to suit its transmission or storage in another medium, transferred, and later decoded to the original form. The common goal is to transfer the data from one medium to another and eventually retrieve it in usable form as accurately as possible with the least distortion or fewest errors.

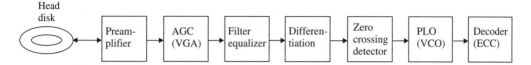

Figure 8.2 Peak detection read-process modules.

Figure 8.1 shows the writing and reading functions of a disk drive recording channel; Figure 8.2 indicates the detection process in more detail. Digital data from a computer processor or controller is first coded in a block called the *encoder*. Error correction coding is incorporated with the data at this stage. The encoded data goes through a procedure called *write precompensation*. In the next step, digital data is converted into currents by the write head drivers. This sequence of events is also depicted in a timing diagram in Figure 8.3. The head writes this sequence of pulses on disk tracks in the form of a series of transitions or magnetization changes (see Section 3.2). The rotating disk stores these transitions, and when a command to retrieve this data is received by the read head (which may be the same head that wrote the information), it transforms medium transitions into electrical voltage pulses. The information is now in analog form and includes the signal plus perturbations and noises introduced during the writing and reading processes. Detection of these signals and their conversion to digital form require several steps. Figure 8.2 and Figure 8.3 outline some of these steps.

The head output is amplified by an analog differential preamplifier. The amplification of signals is followed by automatic gain control. The automatic gain control circuit adjusts the amplitude of the signal within desirable boundaries. Next, the

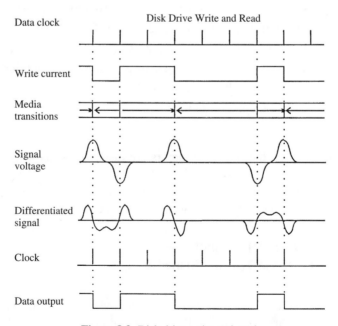

Figure 8.3 Disk drive write and read.

signal goes through low-pass filtering and/or equalization in a single module. The filtering limits the noise bandwidth, while equalization *slims* pulses so that interaction among adjacent pulses is reduced; this topic is discussed in Section 8.10. The signal is now differentiated electrically. The differentiator converts peaks of the signals into zero crossings, as shown in Figure 8.3. A comparator gate (not shown) generates pulses out of the zero-crossing-detection circuit. The leading edges of the pulses correspond to the transition locations on the medium. The series of pulses at this stage correspond to the encoded data. However, the sequence of data also contains embedded clock pulses. In the next stage, a phase-locked oscillator (PLO, also called VFO for variable frequency oscillator) monitors this embedded clock and reconstructs time intervals called *windows*. The detected zero crossings should fall within these windows. The reason for the reconstruction of clock pulses is correction of clock shifts caused by unevenness in disk rotational speed, nonlinear writing process, and noises. This topic is further discussed in Section 8.12. At the next stage, the data decoder detects the presence or absence of zero crossings within each of the windows and converts the data into its original form. This data is now in "user" bytes and the computer or controller can process it.

Figure 8.3 shows the signal processing steps described on a timing diagram. The primary function of the channel is to arrange the data for writing on the disk and retrieve it with minimum errors. The major error-causing factors in disk drive recording are as follows:

1. Intersymbol interference
2. Electronic noise from media, head, and preamplifier
3. Peak shifts generated by writing and reading processes at high bit densities
4. Overwrite loss, which relates to the effect of partially erased data
5. Effect of side writing and reading due to fringing fields at track boundaries
6. Track misregistration due to head positioning irregularities on rotating disk
7. Adjacent track interference
8. Head (magnetic) domain noises
9. Media defects.

In this chapter, the first four factors are discussed since they relate to "on-track" error-producing mechanisms. The other factors will be considered in Chapter 9 on integration. It should be noted, though, that the channel is designed to ensure error-free performance in the presence of all the factors.

8.3 PEAK SHIFT OR BIT SHIFT FROM INTERSYMBOL INTERFERENCE

When the pulse peaks deviate (shift) from the center of the expected time intervals (windows) during detection, the chances of errors increase. These peak shifts are predominantly caused by three factors:

1. Intersymbol interference or crowding of transitions
2. The addition of noises to the pulse waveforms by head, medium, and electronics
3. The writing processes.

In this section, the first cause, intersymbol interference (ISI) is discussed. Figure 8.4a shows read pulses from two isolated transitions. As these transitions are brought closer (at higher linear bit densities), the pulses due to the two transitions superimpose, as in Figure 8.4b. Note that (1) the resultant double-pulse peaks are reduced in amplitudes and (2) the location of signal peaks has been shifted outward as if the peaks have been "repelled" by each other. The reductions in amplitude of pulses cause a roll-off curve, discussed in Section 8.18. The shift in peaks is important since excessive shift tends to make the peak fall outside of its designated time interval during peak detection. In the figure, it is assumed that two pulses can be superposed linearly. As crowding becomes severe, the peak shift increases. When the peak shifts exceed 10–20% of clock window, error rates become excessive. There are several techniques that reduce the crowding and bit shifts. Equalizing or slimming the pulses is one method (Section 8.10), and an appropriate coding scheme (Section 8.5) is another. The amounts of shifts can vary depending on the sequences of 1's and 0's. However, there is some predictability of shifts in coded data, and it is used to reduce shifts by precompensated writing, as explained in Section 8.7.

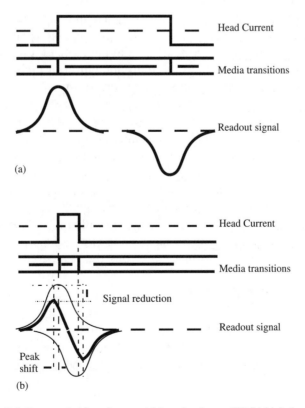

Figure 8.4 Intersymbol interference (a) low density, no ISI (b) high density, ISI and peak shift.

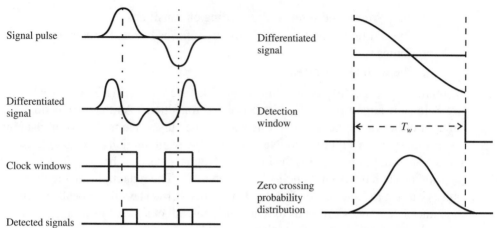

Figure 8.5 Peak detection window.

Figure 8.6 Peak detection window and peak jitter distribution.

8.4 PEAK DETECTION WINDOW

Figure 8.5 shows the signal pulses, differentiated signals, designated windows, and detected signals. The listed factors in Section 8.2 contribute to deviations in the location of a bit zero crossing in a window. Since there are several factors influencing the location of a signal peak or zero crossing, it is convenient to think of the position of peak as a statistical outcome. The position of the peak, on average, may fall at the center of the window. It may fall within or outside the window with various probabilities. The probability of the peak falling outside of a window interval denotes errors. Section 9.13 describes the translation of error probability into error rates. The following discussion addresses how the error probabilities may be calculated.

Location of the peak window has a distribution of the type shown in Figure 8.6. The mean or average location of the peak may be in the center. The distribution may be assumed to be normal or Gaussian with a mean at 0, the center of the window, and a standard deviation of σ. Normal distribution fit is an idealization that allows for analytical calculations. More critical application may need experimentally derived distribution. The probability that the bit peak falls outside of the window is given by the area of the curve outside of window boundaries. For low error rate or low probability of error, the distribution should be narrow with small σ. In this chapter, only factors causing peak jitters due to on-track variables are considered. Chapter 9 describes additional factors that cause peak jitter due to off-track variables.

8.5 CODING IN A DISK DRIVE CHANNEL

The procedure of coding for a disk drive is simply a conversion of incoming "user bits" into another bunch of bits with an objective of promoting high linear density while reducing errors. Figure 8.7 depicts the encoding process.

Figure 8.7 Customer data and coded bits.

The bits on the output side of the encoder are used by the write driving circuit to initiate and control head coil currents. Early disk drives relied on the very simple procedure of writing user data directly onto the disk. This procedure is a form of coding in which the C's are the same as the d's, or $C_i = d_i$. Figure 8.8a shows this code, known as nonreturn to zero (NRZ). The reason for the name is that the current is always in either a positive or a negative direction during writing but never at zero (the dashed baseline). The figure shows data pattern 011010 and clocking intervals. The NRZ-coded bit pattern corresponds to the direction of currents in the write head. The resultant magnetization transitions in the disk medium are also shown.

Every coding scheme has "rules" that allow construction of coded bit patterns. In the case of the code in Figure 8.8a, whenever the data bit changes from 0 to 1, the write coil current goes from negative to positive, and the magnetization reverses direction from left to right. For one or more 1's, the current continues in the same direction; hence, magnetization in the medium continues in the left-to-right direction. When incoming data bits change from 1 to 0, the current in the write coil reverses, creating the transition in the medium. For the duration of 0's, the current and magnetization

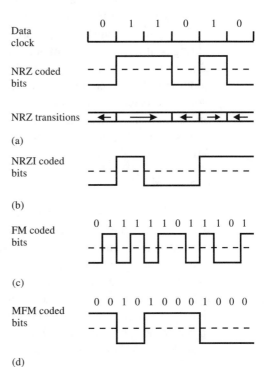

Figure 8.8 Codes and magnetic transitions.

continue to remain in the same direction. Although this is the simplest form of coding, it has several disadvantages. First, the number of transitions on the disk track are the same as the number of incoming user bits; other schemes can store more bits with fewer transitions. Second, when a long series of 0's exists in the user data, there is no clocking information in the data. Hence, the data flow cannot be used for re-creating clock pulses. Third, if there is an error in any bit of the NRZ method, the error propagates by reversing transitions erroneously.

8.6 NRZI, MFM, AND RUN LENGTH–LIMITED CODES

The procedure of coding called nonreturn to zero inverted (NRZI) is a modification of NRZ discussed earlier. It removes one of the disadvantages of the NRZ scheme. Figure 8.8b shows this method. The rule here is that, at every clock position, if the data bit is 1, the direction of the current changes, and hence the medium magnetization reverses, creating a transition at that time. Thus, transitions in the medium are synchronized with the occurrence of 1's in the data sequence. In this case, an error in any one bit can be spotted, and hence it can be corrected. The code cannot provide reliable clocking when there are many 0's in a sequence and the density of transitions is the same as the incoming data bits. These simple codes may be used as standards for comparisons with other codes used for disk drive applications.

The two methods just discussed actually involve no encoding. One major reason for encoding data prior to writing on the disk is to pack more user data on a disk. Once the maximum transition density on a disk track is determined, coding allows more user bits without exceeding allowed transition density. Another objective of coding is to rearrange the incoming data so as to reduce the possibility of errors during writing, reading, and detection. The third function of the coding procedure is to ensure that when data is read from the disk track, the sequence of coded bits should allow re-creation of timings or generation of the clock so that data detection is more accurate and self-clocking. Two codes meet this requirement. The first one is known as a frequency modulation (FM) code and is not used much for disk drives, but it is a useful stepping-stone to the understanding of the very popular MFM code.

8.6.1 FM

The objective of this code is to make itself self-clocking simply by inserting 1's between every two user bits. Figure 8.8c shows the string of user data bits converted according to this rule. The bit-reversal diagram indicates clocking bits added to the code bits. The presence of 1's at expected locations simplifies clocking. The read and write clocks have to run at twice the frequency of data bits to accommodate these additional inserted 1's. The other disadvantage of the code is that the maximum number of transitions per unit distance are twice as large as those in NRZ/NRZI coding. The window within which detection must take place is half as wide as NRZ or NRZI codes.

8.6.2 MFM

The modified frequency modulation code is also known as the Miller code. Figure 8.8c reveals that there are many more transitions than necessary to break up a string of 0's for making the code self-clocking. In other words, the FM code is "extravagant" for the objective of self-clocking. A new code was invented (Figure 8.8d) that met the following two conditions:

1. At least one 0 must exist between any two 1's so that transitions are minimized.
2. No more than three 0's must exist between any two 1's.

This latter constraint avoids a long stream of 0's, making self-clocking possible. Such a code is MFM [or (1, 3)]. The process of finding the "rules" to encode data from user bits to accomplish the foregoing objectives gets a little complex. However, the procedures for encoding data according to this and other run length–limited (RLL) codes has been well established and described in the literature [1, 2]. We shall not go into these methods. Still, it is important to understand some of the attributes of the most commonly used codes. Looking at Figure 8.8d, one can confirm that the constraints described earlier are really met in the MFM coded bits. The minimum distance between any two coded bits is two clock cycles due to the rule that there should be at least one 0 between two 1's. As a result of this condition, the intersymbol interference or crowding of the pulses is two times less than FM code and equal to NRZI code. However, the MFM code requires the same clocking frequency as the FM code or twice the frequency of user data bits or NRZI. The window within which the coded bit should be detected is half as small as in the case of NRZI. Hence the code is a hybrid of NRZI and FM codes with some advantages of both. For the analysis of attributes and comparisons among codes, a system of nomenclature has been developed. Let us define these terms with MFM code as an example. Figure 8.9 is redrawn from Ref. [2] for the comparison of codes with a 4-bit data sequence. This figure is helpful in clarifying attributes for most used codes.

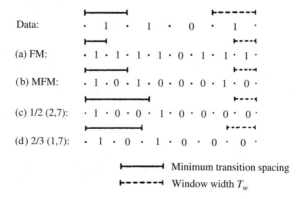

Figure 8.9 Run length–limited code patterns [2].

When x bits are encoded into y code bits, the ratio x/y is called the *code rate*. Note that y should always be larger than x if the coded data is to be constrained. This can be explained by the fact that x bits result in 2^x possible sequences and coded y bits result in 2^y sequences. The number of coded sequences should be larger than the user bit sequences so that the remaining sequences can be utilized to conform to constraints imposed by the code. In the case of MFM, the code rate is 1/2, since 4 user data bits are converted into 8 coded bits, as observed in Figure 8.9b. The minimum number of 0's required (in coded bits) between any two 1's is assigned the letter d, while the maximum number of 0's allowed between two 1's is given the letter k. For MFM, $d = 1$ and $k = 3$. The code is defined by these quantities as $x/y\,(d, k)$. So the MFM code is characterized by 1/2 (1, 3). Note that NRZI can be recognized as 1/1 $(0, \infty)$ code. The quantity d of the code relates to the minimum distance between transitions. The higher the value of d, the longer the time intervals between transitions. The parameter k relates to the allowed length of time intervals in 0's before the clocking procedure becomes ineffective.

If the clock interval T is one cycle of the data bits, the coded clock time interval is given by $(x/y)T$. This is also the time interval within which the coded bit must be detected; hence,

$$T_w = \left(\frac{x}{y}\right)T \tag{8.1}$$

For MFM code, $T_w = (1/2)T$. The minimum time intervals between transitions $T_{\min}$ for coded data can be given by referencing Figure 8.9 as

$$T_{\min} = (d + 1)T_w = (d + 1)\left(\frac{x}{y}\right)T \tag{8.2}$$

The MFM code minimum transition time $T_{\min} = 2(1/2)T = T$. One of the most useful quantities relating user bit density in bits per millimeter (b/mm) to the flux changes per millimeter (fc/mm) on the disk track is defined as a density ratio and is given by the ratio of reciprocals of time intervals as

$$\frac{\text{b/mm}}{\text{fc/mm}} = \frac{1/T}{1/T_{\min}} = (d + 1)\frac{x}{y} \tag{8.3}$$

The density ratio for the MFM code is 1; hence, fc/mm on the disk is equal to b/mm. One more quantity of interest is the ratio of the highest possible frequency content to the lowest frequency content of any specific code and is given by

$$\frac{f_h}{f_l} = \frac{k + 1}{d + 1} \tag{8.4}$$

This quantity is useful for carrying out write-over loss and resolution measurements, described later in the chapter. A method of deriving maximum frequency of a head-disk system is exemplified. Assume a disk velocity of 10 m/s and a medium density of 2000 fc/mm with a pattern of all 1's. The number of transitions traversing per second under the head is $10 \times 10^3 \times 2000$. Two transitions make one cycle. Hence the high frequency of data is 10 MHz.

8.6.3 RLL Codes

IBM introduced the run length–limited code 1/2 (2, 7) in its 3380 disk drives in 1980. This became an industry standard in all major large-size drives. As illustrated in Figure 8.9c, the clock frequency of the coded data is twice the data bit density, similar to the MFM code. The time interval window T_w is one-half of the data clock time interval. The minimum two 0's between the 1's result in T_{min} of 3/2 T. The density ratio for the code is (b/mm)/(fc/mm) = 3/2. Thus 50% more user bits are stored in a given number of flux transitions compared to MFM. The constraint of seven maximum 0's between 1's allows a sufficient rate of transitions to extract clock information from data.

Lately, a 2/3 (1, 7) code has become the standard for all sizes of disk drives. This code maps 4 bits of user data into 6 bits of coded data so the code rate is 2/3. The clock window to detect coded data is $T_w = 2/3T$, about 33% larger than that in 1/2 (2, 7) code. The code clock rate is 50% faster than the data bit clock frequency, making electronics less limiting than the 1/2 (2, 7) code where the required clock rate was twice the frequency of the data clock. The minimum time interval between transitions is $T_{min} = 4/3T$ and the density ratio bpi/fci = 4/3, about 11.3% less advantageous than the (2, 7) code. Figure 8.9d shows the attributes of the code in comparison with other codes.

We conclude this section on coding by presenting Table 8.1, which summarizes attributes of the codes discussed and includes corresponding information for PRML code as well.

TABLE 8.1 Disk Drive Recording Codes and Their Parameters

Code	Code Rate, x/y	Detection Window, T_w	Transition Time, T_{min}	(b/mm)/ (fc/mm)	bpi/ (fc/mm)	Clock Frequency Ratio	f_h/f_i
NRZI 1/1 (0, ∞)	1/1	T	T	1	25.4	1	—
MFM 1/2 (1, 3)	1/2	1/2 T	T	1	25.4	2	2
1/2 (2, 7)	1/2	1/2 T	3/2 T	3/2	38.1	2	8/3
2/3 (1, 7)	2/3	2/3 T	4/3 T	4/3	33.87	1.5	4/1
PRML 8/9 (0, 4, 4)	8/9	0.89 T	0.89 T	0.89	22.6	1.11	4/1

8.7 WRITE PRECOMPENSATION

Section 8.3 described ISI and peak shifts due to transition crowding. The last section discussed coding schemes that reduce transition crowding by inserting the number of 0's between 1's and widening the window of detection. The equalization discussed in Section 8.10 uses electronic signal processing to slim down the pulses and thus reduce ISI. This section describes another method, called *write precompensation*, to reduce intersymbol interference. Write precompensation, often referred to as *write equalization,* is a significant step practiced to reduce peak shifts in coded data. During the write process, the current pulses that write the data can be timed to compensate for peak shifts occurring during reading. The shifting of peaks depends on the coded bit patterns and density of transitions. It is desirable to have the pulse peaks fall in the center of the detection windows for minimum errors. Peak shifts with worst case data patterns at the inner diameter of the disk (where the density of transitions is highest) can cause the worst error rates.

Referring to Figure 8.4b, the current in the write coil for transition that corresponds to the positive pulse is delayed by the estimated shift interval, while the write current for the trailing, negative pulse is shifted ahead by the expected shift amount. This procedure is called *write precompensation* and is successfully applied in many drives. One would think that for different sequences of bits there would be a variety of bit shifts (the words *bit shift* and *peak shift* are used interchangeably), and it would be difficult to apply a standard compensation for possible cases. Actually, there are only a few combinations of data that require different degrees of precompensation. The estimated precompensation algorithms may be stored in look-up tables. The process of precompensation brings data pulses closer, and hence it increases the frequency content of the signal, which is also the characteristic of read equalization. For this reason, the procedure is also called *write equalization.* There is some penalty of increased noise in the channel due to widening of the frequency bandwidth.

8.8 ARM ELECTRONICS MODULE

Figure 8.1 shows the schematics of a multihead disk drive system. The arm electronics module encompasses the following functions in the read and write operations of the drive:

1. There are circuits that switch a head between the write and read operations.
2. The write drivers supply fast switching currents to the head according to the data input.
3. The preamplifier circuits amplify small readout signals.
4. The MR head requires constant-current- or constant-voltage-supply circuits to activate the sensor.

The arm electronic circuit schematic for an inductive head is shown in Figure 8.10.

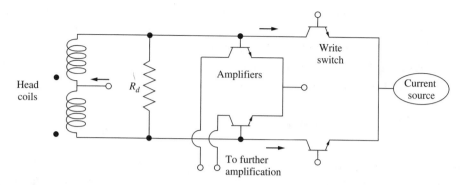

Figure 8.10 Arm electronics schematic—current driver and preamplifier.

The AEM is located on the head arm as close to the head as possible to reduce addition of inductance, resistance, and capacitance to write/read circuits. A typical write driver for a center-tapped ferrite or film head is shown in Figure 8.10. The procedure to select the optimum write current is described in Section 8.17.

For writing, signal input from the precomp circuit is applied to the base of the write drivers. For reading, the signal output is differentially applied to the bases of wide-bandwidth, low-noise transistors. This stage should amplify the signal without adding significant noise to it. Note that any noise added to the signal at this stage gets amplified along with the signal. The gain of a typical amplifier is on the order of 100. Once the signal is large enough, the later stages of amplification do not add significant noise to the detection process.

Resistor R_d has a dual function. During writing, it provides damping and reduces oscillations in the output current. During reading, it flattens the frequency-versus-output-voltage profile and reduces the effect of resonance for wide-bandwidth application. Equivalent circuits and performance of the ferrite, film, and MR heads are treated in Section 5.7.

8.9 AUTOMATIC GAIN CONTROL MODULE

The function of the AGC is to adjust the gain of read peak voltages so that the peak signal values going into detection circuits are within tolerable levels for the peak detection process. This is accomplished by means of a monitoring feedback loop before the detection stage to the AGC module. The voltage prior to the detection stage is measured and fed back to the variable gain amplifier. The gain is adjusted so as to maintain a detection voltage within a specified range. The following are some of the reasons for the variability in the magnitude of incoming voltage signals:

1. Flying height changes
2. Disk-to-disk and head-to-head variations
3. Medium coating thickness, and media remanence variations.

The AGC feedback loop is designed so that it corrects only slowly varying (low-frequency) changes but is not responsive to the high-frequency content of the signal gains. The sudden changes in signal would be undesirable since they can create distortion in signals and peak shifts.

8.10 FILTER AND EQUALIZER

The function of a low-pass filter following the AGC module is to limit high frequencies, thereby limiting noise entering the detection process. The noise is proportional to the total bandwidth of the signal, and reduction of bandwidth by high-frequency cutoff reduces noise added to the signal. The filter bandwidth should be sufficient to allow signal content. The filter cutoff frequency can be estimated from the rule that it should be equal to two times the highest frequency of recorded transitions. For example, the IBM 3380 disk drive data rate was 3 MB/s or 24 Mb/s (assuming 8 bits/byte). The drive used (2, 7) code; hence, 24 Mb/s translates into 16 Mfc/s (look at the (b/mm)/(fc/mm) ratio in Table 8.1). Two flux changes make a cycle; hence, the highest frequency of flux changes is 8 MHz, and a filter cutoff frequency of 16 MHz (at -3 dB) may be used. For (1, 7) coded data, the filter cutoff frequency (in MHz) is given by the data rate in MB/s times 6. For example, a 4.5-MB/s data rate with (1, 7) coded channel would produce a filter cutoff of 27 MHz. The fifth-order Butterworth filter is often used to provide reasonably sharp cutoff with linear phase response [3]. The filter provides a more symmetrical pulse, thereby reducing noise and, depending on the specific design, providing partial equalization.

Equalization is an electrical technique of slimming signal pulses so that intersymbol interference among adjacent pulses is significantly reduced. Chapter 5 discussed thin pole, thin film heads. Thin poles in these heads result in undershoots to the signal pulse. The undershoots tend to slim the pulses and provide built-in equalization. An interesting aspect of this type of built-in equalization is that it is "adaptive"; that is, the slimness varies according to the linear velocity as the head moves from the inner diameter to the outer diameter. Ferrite heads, MR heads, and thick pole film heads do not have significant built-in slimming or equalization. In most circumstances, these heads can benefit from electronic equalization. First, the process of shaping the pulses with equalization process is described; then the advantages and shortcomings of using equalization are discussed. Considerable work has been done and reported on the art of designing equalization for communication and magnetic recording channels. Here the principle of equalization for disk drives is explained in a simplified form. Figure 8.11a shows a pulse of voltage read from the disk transition. Figure 8.11b shows short pulses replicated from the pulse in Figure 8.11a and placed at different time locations. The summation of pulses in Figures 8.11a and 8.11b is shown in Figure 8.11c. The resultant pulse is slimmer. This and a more complex form of equalization synthesis are conveniently carried out by using a delay line with taps.

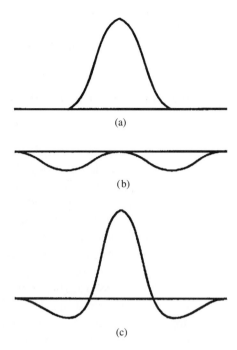

Figure 8.11 Equalization process: (a) unequalized signal, (b) fractional signals, (c) equalized (slimmer) signals.

Figure 8.12 shows a tapped delay line. The output equalized voltage pulse is given in terms of input pulse, delay times, and reduction factors of the pulse. The process indicated in Figure 8.11 is now explained in terms of input and output of the delay line, Figure 8.12. The input signal is as shown in Figure 8.11a. In the delay line A_1 represents reduction and reversal of the original signal by a factor $-a$; this represents the left-hand, short reversed signal in Figure 8.11b. For the example here A_2 is 1, that is, the unchanged magnitude of the input signal occurring at a time D after the input. Here, A_3 is again $-a$, so that the replica of the original reduced and reversed signal appears at the output after a time delay of $2D$ and represents the right-hand side of the signal in Figure 8.11b. The summation of signals occurring in these magnitudes and delays results in the output shown in Figure 8.11c. Other delay line taps are unused. This process is next indicated in analytical form:

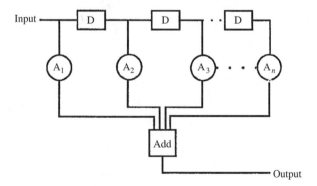

Figure 8.12 Equalization with a tapped delay line.

$$v_0(t) = -av_i(t) + v_i(t - D) - av_i(t - 2D) \tag{8.5}$$

The Fourier transform of this equation converts it into frequency domain as

$$V_0(j\omega) = (-a + e^{-j\omega D} - ae^{-j\omega 2D})V_i(j\omega) \tag{8.6}$$

For a specific case of $a = 0.5$, the equation can be rewritten as

$$\frac{V_0(j\omega)}{V_i(j\omega)} = [1 - \cos(\omega D)]e^{-j\omega D} \tag{8.7}$$

The ratio of the output voltage to the input voltage in the frequency domain is called a *transfer function of equalization*. This transfer function is referred to as a *cosine equalizer* [4]. The equalized pulse waveform for $a = 0.22$ and several values of delays D in nanoseconds are shown in Figure 8.13 [3]. The selection of specific values of a's and D's involves trade-offs between improvements in ISI and increased noise due to the increased bandwidth. The signal bandwidth and noise voltage are discussed in Section 8.19.

As indicated earlier, much work has been done on the synthesis of equalizers for optimum designs for rigid-disk drive applications. Semiconductor chips are available that allow programming of coefficients of tapped delay lines for optimizing applications. However, it should be noted that equalized signals require increased frequency bandwidth and result in the addition of noise to the signal. The transitions and pulses are most crowded at the innermost diameter. As a head reads increasing-diameter tracks, pulse crowding is reduced. For optimum results, equalization needs to be varied accordingly.

Due to the complexity of electronics and addition of noise, equalization was rarely used in large drives. Write precompensation combined with low-pass filtering has been sufficient for most applications. With thick pole, thin film heads and MR heads, equalization is routinely used. Use of PRML channel requires shaping of a signal pulse with carefully designed filtering.

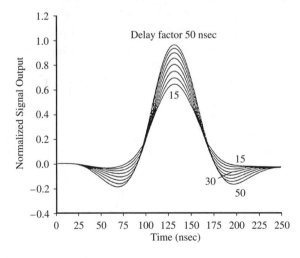

Figure 8.13 Film head equalization: $a = 0.22$; $D = 15 \cdots 50$ ns [3].

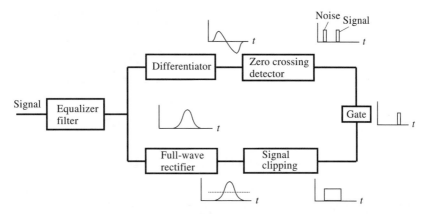

Figure 8.14 Zero crossing peak detection with clipping.

8.11 PEAK DETECTION PROCESS

In Section 8.4, on the peak detection window, the general procedure of obtaining a differentiated zero crossing signal in the window for detection was described. This section will discuss in some detail the process with a gated peak detection technique (Figure 8.14). The objective of the procedure is to detect signals accurately by eliminating the effect of low-level baseline noise and spurious noises introduced by medium surface irregularities. The coded signal passes through two parallel paths. In one path the signal goes through differentiation. Differentiation of the pulse results in the waveform with a zero crossing at the peak location. Detection of zero crossing within time window signifies a signal or "1." However, the detection process must also satisfy a second condition, discussed below.

Figure 8.14 shows the output passing through an *and* gate. The second path followed by the original signal is shown in the lower part of the figure. The isolated pulses in this path are rectified by a full-wave rectifier. As a result, all positive or negative peak waveforms are now converted into positive pulses. The rectified pulses go through a process called *clipping*, which only allows peaks larger than the designated clipping voltage. The purpose of clipping is to ensure that low-level noises are eliminated from the pulse sequence and only sufficiently large signal pulses go through. The signals from two parallel paths are logically *anded*, which means only signals that occur simultaneously in both paths are accepted as legitimate signals. Spurious noise (shown in the upper path) is not accepted as valid since the same noise signal is not present in both branches of the parallel paths after baseline noise is clipped. The procedure thus assures that only pulses larger than the designated magnitude generate output.

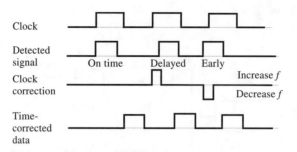

Figure 8.15 Clock correction at PLO module.

8.12 VARIABLE FREQUENCY OSCILLATOR OR PHASE-LOCKED OSCILLATOR

The function of this stage is to ensure that the read-back clock is in synchronization with the read data. Section 8.5 pointed out that the codes have embedded the clock within the data. The constraint on the code ensures that periodic pulses will appear. Digital clock pulses generated from the data are compared with the standard clock determining window timings. Any discrepancies between the two are corrected by the PLO so that data pulses are detected within corresponding detection windows.

Figure 8.15 shows a simplified process of the data timing correction. Differences between the detection window clock and data timings are registered, and a difference signal is averaged over several bits. The phase-locked loop now modifies the clock frequency according to the average effect of the required correction. The same feedback loop also modifies individual data pulse timings according to short time corrections as required. The modification of clock frequency responds only to relatively long time durations, while corrections to data intervals take place on a pulse-by-pulse basis.

8.13 PARTIAL RESPONSE MAXIMUM LIKELIHOOD CHANNEL

The acronym PRML is derived from the data communication field. The term PRML stands for two separate concepts: PR for partial response and ML for maximum likelihood. It is possible to use a non-PR code such as (1, 7) with sampling and maximum likelihood detection. The next section discusses the principle of this concept. First, we shall discuss the attributes of and motivations of using a PRML channel. Next, a simple explanation of the concept is given along with a comparison between peak detection and PRML channels. In the latter part of the section, elements of the theory are given with equations and figures for clarification.

Digital modems—long-distance communication channels—use a procedure of (1) sampling the analog input, (2) digitizing it, (3) transmitting it, and then (4) decoding it into analog output at the receiving station. Similarly, digital information is converted by the writing head to an analog input to the disk, which is later read as an analog output to the read detection channel. The PRML channel takes the analog output signal from the reading preamplifier, filters it (or equalizes it) to shape it appropriately, samples it, and then uses a procedure to detect the signal with high reliability.

The advantages of the sampled detection in a noisy environment have been well known in data communications. The applications of these procedures to the disk drive industry came into focus in the early 1970s with publication of several papers from IBM researchers. The subject took on a new importance with announcements of drives with PRML channels in 1989. Note that the first product (IBM 0681 in 1990) using PRML employed MIG heads. Application of PRML is not synonymous with the use of MR heads.

8.13.1 Motivation

The motivating factors leading to conversion of the recording channel in disk drives from peak detection to PRML are summarized as follows:

1. Researchers working on sampled detection (PRML) channels modeled and experimentally verified that a PRML channel can give 20–30% additional linear density compared to a peak detect (1, 7) channel with identical components (head, medium) and flying heights.

2. The move to PRML entails a digitization of the channel. The use of digital servo and digital controls of the spindle along with a digital channel have many advantages. Powerful digital signal processing techniques developed in other fields can be applied to disk drives. Use of digital components results in miniaturization and standardization of LSI (large-scale integration) circuitry along with a lower power requirement and lower cost.

3. The digital channel lends itself to self-diagnosis, leading to higher yields in manufacturing and potential convenience during maintenance of the device. Special test patterns are used that, when examined after sampling of data, allow medium surface monitoring and give insight into the variability of flying heights and potential for failures.

4. In the process of peak detection, the signal is differentiated for generating zero cross-over. This process amplifies higher frequencies, which in turn contributes additional noise and increased errors. The sampling process measures amplitudes at specific intervals and eliminates this step.

8.13.2 Explanation of PRML and Comparison with Peak Detection Channel

The words *pulse, signal, symbol,* and *transition* are used interchangeably in this discussion. Figure 8.16 shows the superposed data pulses as they would occur at a high linear density of flux transitions in peak detect procedure. Peaks of the pulses are detected within allocated windows. The most pulse crowding possible with peak detect is shown in this figure. Figure 8.17 indicates two consecutive pulses of a

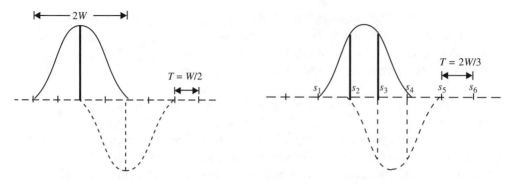

Figure 8.16 Peak detection.   **Figure 8.17** PRML sampling.

PRML channel. At every clock time T distance apart, samples of the signal voltage are taken. The W in the figure is a half pulse width. For now, let us consider a single pulse, as shown by a solid line in Figure 8.17.

At positions s_1, s_2, s_3, and s_4, the sampled outcomes are 0, 1, 1, and 0, respectively. Sampling at the two positions s_2 and s_3 for the pulse gives nonzero outcomes, while sampling at s_1 and s_4 always gives zeros. For a variety of PRML channels, this type of sampling channel, with two nonzero sampling locations per pulse, is called a *partial response channel of class IV.* Now consider both adjacent pulses (solid and dashed lines) in Figure 8.17. Two pulse waveforms are *allowed* to superpose but in prescribed positions. The second (negative) pulse is a displaced image of the first pulse. The displacement is time T. Every additional pulse (not shown) in a sequence of pulses will be similarly displaced by exactly one sample position T apart. When sampled voltages of the two pulses are measured at s_1, s_2, s_3, s_4, and s_5 and digitized, the result is the sequence 0, 1, 0, -1, and 0. Note that there are three levels to be detected for this sampling channel, compared to only two ($+1$, -1) for the peak detect channel. The pulse waveform for PRML channels should have a certain shape and frequency relationship. Special filters are developed for this purpose, and this topic is described in the next section. Higher overlap of adjacent pulses is possible with partial response channels, as seen in Figure 8.17.

The second part of PRML, that is, maximum likelihood, is also discussed in Section 8.13.4. We simply state the idea here. In the case of a peak detect procedure, every pulse is treated and detected independently without using any information from the adjacent pulses or data already read. In the maximum likelihood case, several pulses or symbols are treated as an entity and detected simultaneously. Not only is a sequence of pulses treated together, but a sliding window of a sequence of pulses is detected simultaneously in a continuous manner. For a detection of every sequence, questions are asked regarding which of the possible outcomes is most likely for the sequence being detected based on the statistical inference of the prior information. This provides a minimum error possibility or maximum likelihood detection.

One objective of the PRML channel is to increase linear bit density. A figure of merit has been devised to compare the density capabilities of a variety of channels. A magnetic transition is read as a pulse. The function of the channel and coding is to give the maximum number of customer bits per pulse width. The figure of merit is defined as the number of customer or user bits per half pulse width (P_{50}) at the preamplifier output.

To compare the figure of merits for peak detect and a PRML channel, consider an idealized Lorentzian pulse waveform and no filtering. For those unfamiliar with the concept of resolution as applied to the linear density of a disk drive, a review of Section 8.18 could be helpful here. As the density increases, interference between pulses increases and peak voltages of the pulses drop. For the (1, 7) peak detection procedure, a resolution of 50% (which means a drop in voltage to half its peak value) is considered detectable. Equation (8.16), derived for Lorentzian pulse shapes, indicates that spacing between peaks of adjacent pulses will be a certain fraction (1.39) of half-voltage pulse width (P_{50}). This also means that the highest density of 1.39 peak spacing for a given pulse width of signal pulse is allowable for reliable detection of a signal for a peak detect channel. For this example, we assume a half pulse width, W, to be the same as P_{50} where signal drops from peak to 50% signal value. To convert coded bits to customer bits, the multiplier for (1, 7) peak detect channel is $\frac{4}{3}$. So to find customer bits per half pulse width we get $\frac{4}{3} \times 1.39$, which yields 1.85. Practical numbers range between 1.5 and 1.7 bits per nonfiltered half pulse width. A PRML channel can operate at a very low resolution and still be effective in providing data extraction with an acceptably low error rate. The process of combining sampling and maximum likelihood detection provides this advantage to PRML. The total density of practical PRML channels range between 2 and 2.5 user bits per half pulse width. Table 8.2 summarizes differences between peak detection and the PRML channel.

8.13.3 Partial Response

Elements of PRML theory are addressed next. First, consider the principle of partial response (PR). Figure 8.18a shows a signal pulse resulting from reading a transition in the media.

A sampling procedure to detect the signal is to sample the amplitude of the signal at regular intervals of time T apart, as shown. When the sampling circuit shows an amplitude larger than the predefined value (threshold), existence of the '1' is realized. This procedure can be improved if the signal is equalized or filtered so that the resultant pulse to be detected is such that it has nonzero value at only one sampled time and at all other sampled times it is zero. Such an equalizer can be designed. Figure 8.18c shows a filtered output with nonzero output at a single sampled time. At all other sampling times output is ideally zero. This type of filter and channel are called "full-response" filter and "full-response" channel. The frequency boost required for such a filter is quite high and adds significant noise to the output.

A modified sampling procedure has been devised that provides a more balanced approach in the trade-off between addition of noise by high-frequency boost versus intersymbol elimination. Two sampled locations may have nonzero amplitudes corresponding to a single pulse but the response at other sampled times will be

TABLE 8.2 Comparison of Peak Detect and PRML Channels

Peak Detect Channel (1, 7)	PRML Channel
Signal peaks are detected within the time window.	Signal values are registered at sampled times.
One pulse is detected at a time to determine if the output is 1 or 0.	A series of samples are taken at regular time intervals for a set of pulses, and signal values are extracted for the sequence by using a statistical maximum likelihood process.
Signals are slimmed (equalized) to reduce ISI. Slimming adds high-frequency content and noise to the signal.	Adjacent pulses are allowed to overlap with a provision that sampling times coincide for overlapping pulses. Precise filtering is needed to shape the pulses, which add to signal noise.
Differentiation of the pulse to detect zero crossing within the window adds noise to the signal.	No signal differentiation is required.
Signal-to-noise ratio needs to be high to detect a signal from interference and noise.	The sampled signal detection process allows for a lower (1.5–3-dB) signal-to-noise ratio for the same error rates.
Two states (0, 1) are required.	Sample values have three states for the PRML channel $(+1, 0, -1)$.
The need for high signal-to-noise ratio for an acceptable error rate requires that the highest flux changes allowable are limited to about 50% resolution.	PRML sampling and detection procedures allow successful detection (acceptable error rate) at a flux change density resolution of between 10 and 30%.
The half pulse width accommodates up to 1.7 user bits.	The half pulse width of the signal may accommodate between 2 and 2.5 customer bits.
Little if any dramatic extensions of pure peak detect processes are likely in the foreseeable future.	Progress in the PRML channel depends on data communication and integrated circuit technologies, both of which are heavily explored. Chances of extending the disk drive capabilities through PRML are high as these technologies progress.

zero. Figure 8.19c shows such a modified pulse form. Such a signal is called a *partial response signal,* and a channel that uses such signals is called a *partial response channel of class IV.* The filter that results in such a signal output for an isolated transition signal is called a *class IV partial response filter,* or *PR-IV filter* (Figure 8.19b) for short. Repeating the characteristic of a partial response signal here, it has nonzero values at $t = 0$ and $t = T$ but zero at all other sampled times. It is useful to describe a PR pulse waveform mathematically that satisfies the above criteria. It turns out that there are many waveforms that can meet the criteria. Impo-

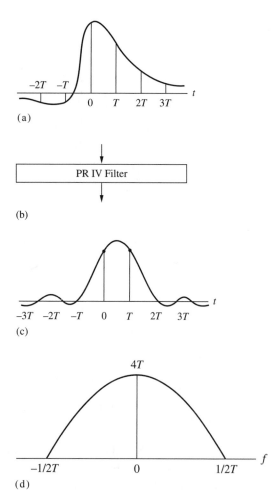

Figure 8.19 (a) Signal pulse before filtering; (b) partial response (IV) filtering; (c) ideal partial response filtered signal; and (d) frequency response of PR-IV filter.

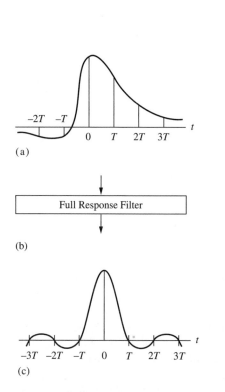

Figure 8.18 (a) Signal pulse before filtering; (b) full response filtering; and (c) full response filtered signal.

sition of an additional constraint that the waveform must have minimum frequency bandwidth results in a unique solution given by

$$V(t) = 2 \left\{ \frac{\sin(\pi t/T)}{\pi t/T} + \frac{\sin[\pi(t-T)/T]}{\pi(t-T)/T} \right\} \tag{8.8}$$

Figure 8.19c shows this time function. The frequency domain or Fourier transform magnitude of the signal is given by

$$4T \cos(\pi f T), \text{ with } |f| \langle \frac{1}{2T} \tag{8.9}$$

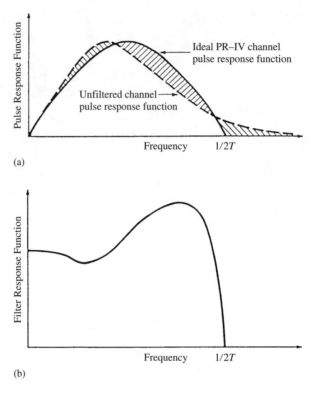

Figure 8.20 (a) Unfiltered and PR-IV filtered frequency response; (b) PR-IV frequency filter characteristic.

Figure 8.19d shows this frequency characteristic. Figure 8.20a shows an unfiltered channel pulse response function. Also shown is the ideal PR-IV response function that can result as the signal output of Figure 8.19c. It is required that the multiplication of an unfiltered channel response and the filter response function in frequency domain should result in a desired ideal PR-IV pulse response function. Figure 8.20b qualitatively indicates such a filter response function. Note the high-frequency boost and sharp cutoff frequency of the response function.

Summarizing, partial response is a sampling procedure used to detect signals after they are conditioned by a filter (or equalizer) so that intersymbol interference is less detrimental and the signal-to-noise ratio is enhanced. Digitization of the channel has several advantages in addition to the increase in linear density.

8.13.4 Maximum Likelihood

In the case of a peak detection process, every bit is individually detected. In the digital communication field, a different method became popular in which a detected sequence of bits is looked at as a unit and the question is asked, "out of a number of possible original data bit sequences, which one is most likely to result in the observed sequence?" This can most aptly be reworded as "having the highest probability." A more mathematical way to define the procedure is to reduce the

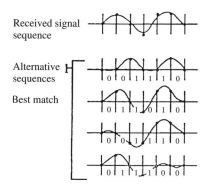

Received signal sequence

Alternative sequences

Best match

Figure 8.21 Maximum likelihood sequence detection.

Most likely information sequence:

...0 1 1 0 1 0...

mean-square error between detected data sequence and one of the several optional sequences that might cause such an output. Figure 8.21 shows a situation in which a sequence of bits is detected and compared with possible "close" sequences that could have produced the resultant sequence. The figure is an ideal representation of the output. In reality, noise and distortion will be present in the sequence. It would be laborious and impossible to compare the observed sequence of data with every conceivable input sequence within a reasonable time. However, algorithms were developed in the late 1960s for solving such error minimization problems [5]. Maximum likelihood codes for disk drive application use these algorithms.

In case of PRML, 8 user bits are converted into 9 coded bits; hence, its code rate is 8/9. Sampling is a distinctly different procedure to peak detection process. However, for comparison, peak detection terminology is often used. In Table 8.1, detection window time and other parameters are calculated as shown. No logical criterion for high- to low-frequency ratio is known, but as an analogy to (1, 7) peak detect channel, a value of 4 is customarily used. A minimum number of zeros between 1's can be 0 for PRML channel, while a maximum of 4 zeros are allowed for every odd and even sequence. This constraint comes from the use of Viterbi maximum likelihood algorithms employed for PRML detection procedure.

8.14 EXTENDED PRML AND (1, 7) MAXIMUM LIKELIHOOD CHANNELS

The PRML channel allows overlapping of the pulses, as seen in Figure 8.17. It is natural to inquire if further overlapping of pulses can be attempted. The answer is yes. Figure 8.22a shows two pulses that overlap to a larger extent than those in Figure 8.17. The sampling time interval is shortened, and more samples per pulse waveform are now taken.

Note that there are two levels of nonzero pulses compared to the PRML case. The smaller and larger amplitudes detected during sampling are designated level 1

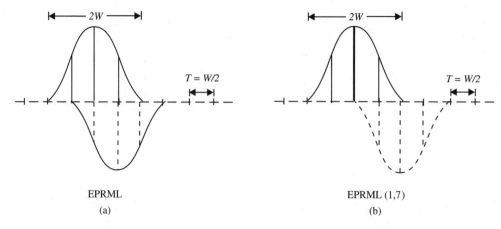

Figure 8.22 EPRML and EPRML (1, 7) signal sampling [6].

and level 2. So the sampling process here results in five levels: -2, -1, 0, $+1$, and $+2$. This type of channel is called EPRML, for extended partial response channel. There are four sampling periods within a pulse; hence, each period is one-fourth of the pulse width. The penalty in using EPRML is the increased complexity of working with five-level logic and more involved semiconductor circuits. A combination of (1, 7) coding along with EPRML-style sampling has been described [6]. The capacity of the channel for this case is the same as the PRML channel; however, the merits of the method are the constraint of a 0 between two 1's, which results in more stable sampling times; no notch filtering; and robust, less error-prone detection. Another advantage of this channel is that it avoids the severe high-frequency boost and notch of the often troublesome PRML channel filter. This channel has been used in the IBM 3390-9 drive.

8.15 MAGNETIC RECORDING MEASUREMENTS OF WRITE AND READ PARAMETERS

Often technical concepts are best realized through understanding of measurement procedures. The disk drive recording measurements most commonly carried out to characterize heads and disks are described next. Traditionally, testing and evaluation of linear density is carried out in a setup known as a *magnetic recording test,* while integration of linear density and track density parameters are done on precision test stands (PTSs). Both procedures attempt to simulate various elements of a head-disk assembly (HDA) for design and diagnostics of components. Magnetic recording testers commonly use ball-bearing spindles for disk mounting and motor-driven screw-type actuators to move the head across the disk radially. Precision testers have air-bearing spindles and laser interferometer-controlled head movement.

Another factor that separates these two test setups is the degree of stability required. The PTS is used to measure very small off-track head movements, and the results must be accurately repeatable; hence, these stands require heavy granite bases and precise environmental controls. With reduced disk sizes, reduced cost of the air-bearing spindles for small disks and modular approaches to measuring instruments, the distinction between the two types of testing becomes blurred, and a single setup is able to handle both functions at a modest cost. Here are a few of the reasons for carrying out magnetic recording measurements.

1. The process of *overwrite measurement* is to measure the remnant of the old signal after the new signal is written over it. The overwrite specification ensures that the new signal is free of old data for error-free detection during reading. This parameter is influenced by several factors:
   (a) Head writability, which depends on head current, head pole material, and head pole design
   (b) Medium coercivity, remanence magnetization, and thickness
   The disk drive writing process is highly nonlinear and complex. No simple analytical or numerical methods are satisfactory; hence, an experimental procedure is necessary. Measurement of overwrite as a function of head and medium parameters gives good insight into the design and diagnostics of read/write components and electronics. The measurement is described in Section 8.16.

2. Establishment of adequate write current. The write current must be high enough so that overwrite is sufficiently high. The current must saturate the medium for even signal magnitudes. The transition parameter a depends on the write current rise time. Too large a write current may widen written track widths and affect track density of the disk drive. Section 8.17 discusses write current measurement and its influence on these design parameters.

3. Measurements of roll-off and resolution parameters. These measurements are directly related to linear bit density; hence, they are used to establish specifications of linear bit density, select head-disk parameters, and verify design during the development cycle. The measurements also provide feedback during optimization of write electronics, filter design, and detection of circuit components.

4. Measurements of signals and noise to establish the dependence of signal-to-noise ratio for different operating conditions.

Often, additional recording measurements are tailored for specific heads and disks. For example, narrow-track thin film heads are prone to domain-related instabilities; hence, some procedure to measure this tendency is required. The MR heads are subject to uneven signal magnitudes in up-versus-down directions (asymmetry), and measurements are tailored to investigate that on a PTS.

8.16 OVERWRITE AND ITS MEASUREMENTS

The procedure of "writing" on a disk track has two functions:

1. To erase previously written information.
2. To write new data.

In principle, these functions can be performed as two separate steps. However, separate steps require twice the latency time and add to the write access time. The process of overwriting or performing these functions in one step is not new to magnetic recording. Audio recorders and digital recorders operate in a combined overwrite process. Efficacy of the write process is measured by the degree of eraseability of old data when new information is written.

From the first principles of the Fourier series, it is known that a single digital pulse consists of harmonics or a series of frequencies. Also a sequence of digital data consists of a range of frequencies. When this data is written on a magnetic track, it is equivalent to writing a band of sinusoidal frequencies. When there are many 0's compared to 1's in a stream of data, low frequencies dominate, while a large concentration of 1's in data results in more of the higher frequencies.

It is known experimentally that it is most difficult to write high-frequency data on top of prior low-frequency data. To ensure error-free data, a criterion is set for overwrite measurement that is "conservative" and simulates the condition of writing with high frequency on top of low frequency.

When a pattern of low frequency, all 1's, is written on a clean track and the track is read back displaying output on a spectrum analyzer, a line corresponding to the recorded low frequency will be seen on a frequency-versus-voltage plot. Figure 8.23 shows a plot of such responses for a range of frequencies and corresponding voltage outputs. Each of these frequencies is written with the same write current. Notice that the voltage outputs start dropping at higher frequencies. For the overwrite measurement only two of these frequencies are considered. We call these frequencies f_l for lower frequency and f_h for higher frequency. These frequencies, for different codes, are discussed in Section 8.6. The procedure for the measurement of overwrite is as follows:

1. Select a track to write on and DC erase it, which means passing a high DC current through the head coil while the disk track rotates under the head. This process removes any prior data from the track.
2. Write a low-frequency f_l, all 1's, signal on the track and measure voltage V_l (Figure 8.23).
3. Without erasing the track, superimpose writing with a high-frequency f_h pattern of 1's with the same current level as used for writing low frequency.
4. Measure leftover low-frequency V_a.

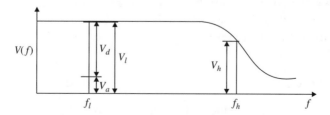

Figure 8.23 Overwrite definition and measurement.

The overwrite is now defined as

$$\text{Overwrite (dB)} = 20 \log \left(\frac{V_a}{V_l} \right) \qquad (8.10)$$

Since V_a is always smaller than V_l, the quantity is measured in negative numbers. Overwrite of -30 dB and smaller is considered good, while that of less than -25 dB will be unacceptable for a commercial drive. Sometimes the overwrite is expressed as a percentage of $100 \times (V_l - V_a)/V_l$. In this form, this quantity is referred to as *write-over loss*.

In the section on coding (Section 8.6), high and low frequencies for specific codes are described. For a $(1, 7)$ code the ratio of f_h/f_l is 4. The high-frequency f_h is half the highest flux transition rate written on the disk. Two magnetic flux transitions result in one cycle.

As an example, let us consider the linear density of flux changes or flux transitions on the disk as 2000 fc/mm at the inner diameter of the disk. Let the linear velocity of the disk at the inner diameter be 10 m/s, or 10,000 mm/s. The flux transition rate is then 20 million per second. The maximum frequency of 10 MHz and low frequency of 2.5 MHz would be applicable for the $(1, 7)$ coded data pattern.

Overwrite measurements are performed at several diameters of the disk. Generally, overwrite is weakest at the outer diameter since the head flying height is maximum there.

8.17 WRITE CURRENT OPTIMIZATION FOR RECORDING

The determination of a proper write current is an important step in the design and integration of a disk drive. The following considerations are involved in determining the appropriate value of the write current:

- The write current must be sufficiently large to saturate the medium during the writing process.
- Also, it should be large so as to achieve acceptable overwrite, as discussed in Section 8.16. Erasure of previous data on the track is necessary to reduce error rates.
- Too large a write current results in bit shifts, as discussed in Section 3.12.
- The write current also influences the erase bands at the boundaries of the track width. Large currents increase the erased track width and increase interference between adjacent tracks.

We saw in Chapter 3 that a short-transition parameter a is desirable for high peak-to-peak voltage. Detailed write analyses indicate that there is an optimum current when the slope of the H field is maximum and results in shortest a. The process of

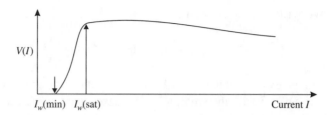

Figure 8.24 Write current optimization.

writing involves partial saturation of the head poles and a nonlinear **B–H** loop (Section 2.13) of the medium. The complexity of the processes precludes easy analytical or numerical determination of the optimum write current. Experimental procedures are heavily relied on for this purpose. Experiments are carried out by varying write currents and observing several parameters. Figure 8.24 shows a plot of peak-to-peak voltage read from a track (usually at the inner diameter of the disk) as a function of changing write currents. For small currents the medium does not saturate, and the signal output is low. As the write current increases, at some value the signal voltage is maximum, and further increase in current does not add to the voltage significantly. The current I_w (sat) or a slightly higher current is a good choice for further testing and possibly for use in the drive, provided high overwrite is also obtained at that current. Several additional tests may be carried out prior to the selection of the write current.

Figure 8.25 shows overwrite as a function of the write current. Overwrite increases with current, and after some point further increase in current does not add to the overwrite due to head saturation. These experiments are carried out at the inner and outer diameters of the disk. At the outer diameter the flying height is higher, and hence overwrite tends to be lower than that at the inner diameter of the disk. The required current to provide sufficient overwrite throughout the surface of the disk is evaluated. Since there are penalties for too large a write current, it is ensured that once the voltage signal is close to the highest level and overwrite is better than the specified value (in the range of -25 to -35 dB), the write current is restrained to the smallest possible value.

The topic of fringing fields and erase bands has been discussed in Section 3.13, and the effect of overlapping tracks is considered in Section 9.11. These fringing fields can produce crosstalk in adjacent tracks and erase part of the adjacent tracks.

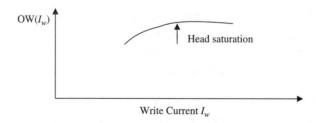

Figure 8.25 Overwrite as a function of write current.

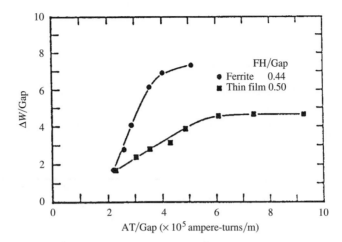

Figure 8.26 Track width widening versus ampere-turns per meter for ferrite and film heads [7].

Figure 8.26 shows the results of an experimental study to relate increased track width with increased coil ampere-turns [7]. Here it suffices to indicate that increasing the write current produces increased fringing fields at the edges of the head pole track widths, and the current is limited to avoid interference among adjacent tracks. Due to the influence of the write current on interactions among several parameters, more detailed studies of the write current versus signal, noise, peak shift, and error rates are often carried out to optimize the disk drive density.

8.18 LINEAR DENSITY ROLL-OFF CURVE AND RESOLUTION

In Section 8.3, the concept of intersymbol interference and consequent decrease in voltage as a function of increasing magnetization flux changes has been described. The graphical plot of flux change density versus signal voltage is called the *roll-off curve*. To plot the roll-off curve, a series pattern of 1111 ··· is written throughout the track of a disk at an optimized current, discussed in the last section. The sequence is now read, and the zero-to-peak voltage is measured. The process is repeated with higher density of the same pattern until a signal becomes too small. The curve is plotted with the x axis as the number of flux changes per millimeter and output voltage on the y axis. More often, though, the voltage readings are normalized by a low-frequency voltage value.

Figure 8.27 illustrates a roll-off plot. The roll-off curve is used to define the term resolution of the system. Corresponding to the low frequency (f_l) and high frequency (f_h) used for overwrite, low and high flux changes per millimeter are used to define resolution. From the plot, voltages V_l and V_h for low and high flux changes per millimeter are obtained. The "resolution" is the voltage ratio in percentage: $100 \times V_h/V_l$. For the (1, 7) peak detect channel and where resolution drops to 50%,

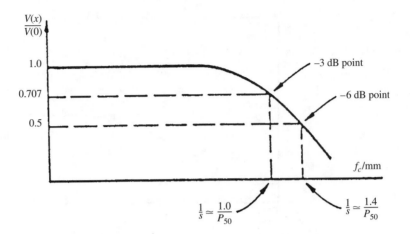

Figure 8.27 Roll-off curve of a Lorentzian pulse.

the flux change per millimeter is commonly quoted as an acceptable density. In the case of large disk drives with a (2, 7) peak detect channel and thin film and thin pole ($\approx$1 μm) heads, conservatively 70% and above resolutions were used. The required resolution defines the highest flux change per millimeter (or corresponding bits per inch) usable for the system. If the coding and detection are highly efficient, it is possible to operate the system at very low resolution along with low acceptable error rates. The PRML and EPRML are such channels and are discussed in Sections 8.13 and 8.14. The channel modeling to predict the resolution and highest density is useful in projecting future products. Usually these models are hybrids of mathematical equations and experimentally collected data. As a learning tool it is instructive to calculate resolution versus flux changes per millimeter for a simple pulse waveform. The procedure provides insight into the methods used for more complex models.

Let us assume that the voltage output of an isolated single transition is given by a pulse form known as a Lorentzian pulse (also discussed in Section 3.11):

$$V(x) = \frac{V(0)}{1 + (2x/P_{50})^2} \tag{8.11}$$

Figure 8.28 shows such a pulse. Note that at $x = 0$ the pulse has a peak value $V(0)$ and at $x = \pm P_{50}/2$, the pulse amplitude is one-half of the maximum, which is the definition of P_{50}. The question we want to answer is: "What happens to the magnitude of peak voltage when the foregoing pulse is gradually crowded by similar positive and negative pulses along the x axis from $-\infty$ to $+\infty$?" We discussed the reduction in signal due to pulse crowding in Section 8.3 on intersymbol interference. It is possible to describe this problem by an equation assuming linear superposition of pulses as

$$V(x, s) = \sum_{n=-\infty}^{\infty} (-1)^n \frac{V(0)}{1 + (2x + 2ns/P_{50})^2} \tag{8.12}$$

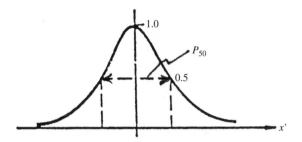

Figure 8.28 Lorentzian pulse.

where s is the spacing between peaks of consecutive pulses. Different values of n correspond to the same voltage pulse displaced by spacings given by ns. The expression (8.12) sums all these pulses for a given spacing s. This series has an explicit solution [8]:

$$V(x, s) = V(0)k\frac{\sinh(k)\ \cos(\pi x/s)}{\cosh^2 k - \cos^2(\pi x/s)} \qquad (8.13)$$

where $k = \pi P_{50}/2s$. We are only interested in the value of the signal amplitude for the pulse peak at $x = 0$; hence, substituting $x = 0$ in equation (8.13),

$$V(0, s) = V(0)\frac{k}{\sinh(k)} \qquad (8.14)$$

$V(0, s)$ is the reduced voltage due to crowding of pulses spaced s apart. At large spacings (as s approaches ∞), $V(0, s)$ approaches $V(0)$, the peak amplitude of the isolated pulse. Using this equation, the value of voltage at any spacing can be found. Asking the reverse question—"What is the spacing at which peak voltage is reduced by one-half (or -6 dB)?"—the solution is obtained from

$$\frac{V(0)}{2} = V(0)\frac{k}{\sinh k} \qquad (8.15)$$

by trial and error or plotting and gives

$$s = \frac{P_{50}}{1.39} \qquad (8.16)$$

Along the lines of the foregoing procedure, the spacing s can be determined when voltage reduces to -3 dB, or 0.707 of the original peak value, which is a criterion often used in drive design. It is simply $s = P_{50}$. If P_{50} and s are given in nanometers, the flux change that is the reciprocal of spacing is given by fc/mm $= 1/s \times 10^6$. Resolution points 0.707 and 0.5 are indicated in Figure 8.27.

If the actual pulse cannot be expressed by a Lorentzian pulse, an experimental voltage pulse can be used for higher accuracy. The procedure then would be to sum up a series of experimental pulse voltages on a computer and reduce the spacing, step by step, to calculate a series of voltage values. The spacings at which voltage reduces to a predetermined value can also be derived. Practically only a few (four to eight) pulses need to be summed for the procedure. An analytical voltage waveform or experimental pulse converted into analytical form can also be similarly used.

8.19 NOISE SOURCES IN RECORDING PROCESSES

A crucial topic in the transmission and storage of electronic information is noise. It is important in consumer electronics, the communication of data, and almost all fields of electronics where an accurate signal is to be extracted from an inevitably noisy environment. Much of the research in understanding noise sources, coding schemes to transmit data with low error rates, and error correction procedures was initiated in the telephone industry.

In the case of disk storage, the signal is relatively small, that is, less than a millivolt, while additive noises and perturbations can make detection of data difficult or result in unacceptable errors. A commonly recognized figure of merit in the industry is the signal-to-noise ratio. A higher signal-to-noise ratio results in a more robust drive. A historical fact is that the signal-to-noise ratio and the size of a signal in disk drives have remained within a short range despite dramatic changes in the technology in the last four decades. The pursuit of higher densities has resulted in increased noise. Higher linear densities require wider bandwidths, which result in increased electronic component noise. Increasing track density results in more interference from adjacent tracks and also makes the signal more susceptible to defects in medium. Major disk storage research involves the development of low-noise components and procedures to reduce interfering disturbances. The next few sections examine the sources of noise and then relate signal to noise quantitatively to the error rate performance of the disk recording system. The sources of noise affecting the performance of a disk drive are listed in Section 8.2 and categorized in Figure 8.29. There are two separate categories of noises in disk drive recording that contribute to error rates. The first—crosstalk noises—are more deterministic and can be reduced with design considerations. The other category consists of "random" noises, and the times of their occurrence are not predictable. Two discussed in this chapter, ISI (Section 8.3) and overwrite (Section 8.16), and two others discussed in Chapter 9, off-track and adjacent-track noises (Sections 9.9 and 9.10), are deterministic-type noises. Here we shall concentrate on the integration of random noises. Electronic noises in heads are quantified in the equivalent circuit in Section 5.7, while medium noise is described in Section 7.4.

An instructive and useful way of looking at the effect of noise on the detection of a recorded signal is shown in Figure 8.30. The signal from an isolated transition is differentiated prior to detection. The zero crossing is expected in the center of the window. A random noise is added to the signal, and the resultant signal now has a zero crossing shifted due to added noise. When noise sources are independent and

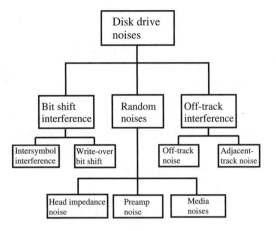

Figure 8.29 Disk drive noises.

uncorrelated, the total random noise voltage E_{nt} can be calculated by finding the square root of the sum of the squares of each random noise as

$$E_{nt} = (E_{nh}^2 + E_{np}^2 + E_{nm}^2)^{1/2} \tag{8.17}$$

where E_{nh} is the head noise voltage, E_{np} is the preamplifier noise voltage, and E_{nm} is the noise voltage due to medium. First, random noise is defined; then random noises in heads, channel preamplifiers, and media are discussed.

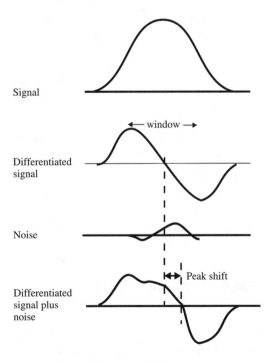

Figure 8.30 Peak shift due to noise.

8.19.1 Random Noise

The fundamental type of noise in electronics is due to the atomicity of matter and electricity. It is completely without regularity in its detailed properties; hence, it is called random noise. However, an average energy of this noise and its frequency

distribution is determinable. In 1928, J. B. Johnson showed that minute currents caused by the thermal motion of conduction electrons in a resistor can be detected as a noise source. About the same time, H. Nyquist showed that on the basis of the statistical theory of thermodynamics, thermal noise voltage in an impedance Z is given by

$$E_n = (4kTR \, \Delta f)^{1/2} \tag{8.18}$$

where E_n = rms value of thermal noise voltage
         R = resistive component of the impedance in ohms
         T = absolute temperature in Kelvin (or degrees Celsius plus 273)
         k = Boltzmann's constant = 1.37×10^{23} W-s/deg
         Δf = bandwidth of use or measuring system in cycles per second

For example, 100 Ω resistance at 27°C with a bandwidth of 10 MHz has a thermal noise voltage of approximately 4 μV RMS. It is convenient to express the noise voltage per square root of frequency. So in this case the noise voltage may be expressed as $1.27 \text{nV}/\sqrt{\text{Hz}}$. If the resistance component of a circuit is a function of frequency, as it will be for a circuit involving capacitances and inductances besides resistances, equation (8.18) is modified as

$$E_n = \left(4kT \int_0^{BW} R(f)\delta f\right)^{1/2} \tag{8.19}$$

This equation can be used to calculate head noise voltage if the resistive part of the head impedance varies significantly with the frequency.

Besides the thermal noise, there is another source of random noise called *shot noise*. This was explained by Schottky in 1918 as a variation in current from the hot cathode of a tube amplifier. The finite charge of the electron results in variation of the current and hence contributes as a noise source. The base resistance of a transistor could give rise to significant current variations, or "noise," due to this mechanism.

8.20 HEAD EQUIVALENT CIRCUIT NOISE

In Chapter 5, Section 5.7, an equivalent circuit of an inductive head was discussed. The circuit includes the front-end resistance and capacitance of the preamplifier. The impedance expression from the equivalent circuit is formulated. The real part of this impedance is the equivalent resistance of the head (including the preamplifier). This resistance is a function of frequency. The noise voltage of the head can be computed from the integration in equation (8.19). In the case of high damping resistance, the equivalent resistance R_{eq} may be approximated by an average fixed value. Also, if the variation in resistance can be approximated by a known function, say, linear, quadratic, and so on, an equivalent resistance can be derived by using a simple integration. For an average R_{eq}, head noise can be calculated from equation (8.18).

The inductive head equivalent circuit is also applicable for the MR head except the MR head is represented by a single-turn head. Its inductance is just the inductance of the leads. Typical values of parameters for MIG, two versions of thin film heads, and the MR head are shown in Table 5.1. The resistance of a 5-μm-long, 30-nm-thick, 2-μm-high MR stripe is about 20 Ω. Head noise is calculated using Equation (8.18) as 0.58 nV/$\sqrt{Hz}$.

8.21 HEAD PREAMPLIFIER NOISE

In equation (8.17), the second term is the noise due to input preamplifier. The head signal is under 1 mV, and its amplification by the front end of the read electronics requires special care. Low-noise, wide-band preamplifiers are designed as a part of an LSI circuit.

Figure 8.31 is the schematic of a differential preamplifier commonly used to amplify a head signal. Once the preamplifier amplifies the signal to between 20 and 100 times the head output, later stages of amplification and detection do not contribute significantly to the overall signal-to-noise ratio of the system and can be neglected. A differential amplifier is used as an input stage instead of a conventional single transistor in order to eliminate common mode noises, including voltage line transients and disturbances. The common mode noises and disturbances will swing (vary) both outputs of the differential amplifier; hence, the differential voltage remains unaffected by the extraneous perturbations, and the output will represent the input more accurately. The noise voltage E_{np} is a function of base resistance and gain β of the transistor. Wide-area transistors with narrow base widths are used to reduce the base resistance of the transistor with high gain. The noise voltage of the amplifier can be measured by shorting the input and observing the output, which is amplifier internal noise times the gain. There are three broad classifications of noise sources found in a transistor:

1. Flicker (or $1/f$) noise
2. Thermal noise
3. Shot noise

Flicker noise is a low-frequency phenomenon, and in wide-band applications it can be limited to very low frequencies. It is neglected for amplifiers for recording

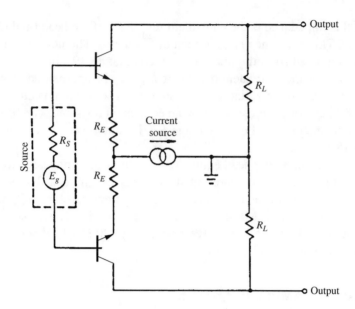

Figure 8.31 Schematic of a differential preamplifier.

applications. Thermal noise is largely due to the base resistance of a transistor and is generally quoted in amplifier specifications. Shot noise is due to current flow in the base-to-emitter diode of the transistor. Thermal noise is calculated using equation (8.18) once the resistance value is specified. The shot noise can be important for high-impedance (ferrite and MIG) heads.

Reference [9] analyzes these topics in more detail. It is a common practice to match the head and preamplifier noises for compromise between minimization of the total noise and adequate signal bandwidth. Preamplifiers are designed to provide input noise range between 0.5 and $2nV/\sqrt{Hz}$. We shall use 1.0 nV/$\sqrt{Hz}$ as an example for the discussion of signal and noise.

8.22 THIN FILM MEDIUM NOISE

Medium noise from the view of medium design is discussed in Section 7.4. Here we shall describe the characteristics of film medium noise and an experimental procedure to measure it. The noise in thin film medium originates in the transitions in which magnetizations change directions. The DC-erased noise of film medium is negligibly small. Since the noise originates in the transitions, measurement of the noise requires presence of a recorded signal. Also, because the noise source is in transitions that can be located on a disk track, it is possible to separate the thermal noise of the head and preamplifier by time averaging. Simple and practical methods for separating electronic and media noises are illustrated in Figure 8.32 [10].

The output of the head amplifier is connected to a spectrum analyzer. First, the head noise is measured when the head is lifted away from the disk. The noise spec-

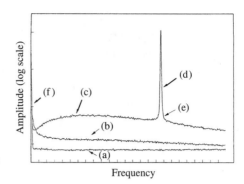

Figure 8.32 Measurement of media noise [10].

trum [curve (a)] is measured in this condition. This is only head and preamplifier electronic noise. Curve (b) is the measured noise from DC-erased media. Next a single-frequency sinusoidal signal is recorded on the disk track and a total recorded spectra is measured [curve (c)]. Curve (d) indicates the recorded single sinusoidal frequency signal. The difference between smoothed curve (c) (after eliminating single-peak frequency and DC-peak response at $f = 0$) and electronic noise spectra gives the medium noise spectrum. For most applications, a straight-line noise value is averaged for the medium, and the noise amplitude is given in nanovolts per square root of hertz. Reference [10] also discusses corrections needed in the use of the spectrum analyzer and alternative time domain measurements.

8.23 SIGNAL-TO-NOISE RATIO AND ON-TRACK ERROR RATES

A formalism to relate measurements of intersymbol interference, signal and component noise sources to error rate for a peak detection channel has been described [11]. It is desirable to have analytical equations relating these quantities in a closed form. It is difficult to obtain a single general equation to relate these parameters. In this section, several equations are discussed which give insight into the quantitative relationships among these variables. An understanding of these interactions could be helpful in formulating analytical or computer modeling of channel error rates. The track density and more generalized modeling of error rates in a system are discussed in Chapter 9.

   With noise voltages either computed or measured, total noise voltage for the three factors discussed in the last section is calculated using equation (8.17). Let the zero-to-peak voltage of the signal to be detected be E_{0p}. Then the traditional definition of the signal-to-noise ratio in recording is

$$\text{SNR} = \frac{S}{N} = \frac{E_{0p}}{E_{nt}}; \quad \left(\frac{S}{N}\right)_{dB} = 20\log_{10}\left(\frac{E_{0p}}{E_{nt}}\right) \qquad (8.20)$$

Note that the average noise voltage of random sources is zero. Here, E_{nt} is the RMS value of the combined noises and standard deviation of the error function or the Gaussian distribution. Figure 8.30 shows how the zero crossing location of the signal gets shifted by time t_n due to random noise. The following discussion considers the peak shift in signal due to only random noises. The standard deviation of distribution of variable t_n is defined as σ_n. It is assumed that σ_n is proportional to E_{nt}, that is, $\sigma_n = E_{nt}/k$; the distribution of t_n is expressed as

$$P(t_n) = \frac{1}{\sqrt{2\pi}\sigma_n} e^{-1/2(t_n/\sigma_n)^2} \tag{8.21}$$

Error occurs if t_n exceeds half the window ($T_w/2$) on either side of the window center. This is described as

$$P(E) = \int_{-\infty}^{-T_w/2} p(t_n)\,dt_n + \int_{T_w/2}^{\infty} p(t_n)\,dt_n = 2\int_{T_w/2}^{\infty} p(t_n)\,dt_n \tag{8.22}$$

The function erfc(z), which is equal to $1 - \mathrm{erf}(z)$, is defined as

$$\mathrm{erfc}(z) = \frac{2}{\sqrt{\pi}}\int_z^{\infty} e^{-u^2}\,du \tag{8.23}$$

Changing the variable $u = (t_n)/(\sqrt{2}\sigma_n)$, and substituting equation (8.22) in (8.23), the probability of error is obtained:

$$P(E) = \mathrm{erfc}\left(\frac{T_w}{2\sqrt{2}\sigma_n}\right) \tag{8.24}$$

Substituting $\sigma_n = E_{nt}/k$ and E_{nt} from equation (8.20), equation (8.24) is rewritten as

$$P(E) = \mathrm{erfc}\left(\frac{kT_w\mathrm{SNR}}{2\sqrt{2}E_{0p}}\right) \tag{8.25}$$

The equation thus gives the probability of an error, or the bit error rate, in terms of SNR, the peak voltage for a given size of time window. Assuming the Lorentzian signal pulse and other simplifications, the following equation is obtained [12]:

$$P(E) = \mathrm{erfc}\left(\frac{\sqrt{2}T_w\mathrm{SNR}}{P_{50}}\right) \tag{8.26}$$

If the error rate is specified as 10^{10}, or 1 error in 10^{10} bits read, the corresponding T_w can be obtained from the above equation using a look-up table of erfc functions. This is the minimum time window required to satisfy the error rate specification for given SNR and P_{50}. The resultant equation is [12, 13]

$$T_w \geq \frac{4.573 P_{50}}{\sqrt{2}\mathrm{SNR}} \tag{8.27}$$

The equation indicates that a large SNR and small P_{50} or slimmer pulse are desirable to keep the noise-related window narrow. Note that only random noises are included in the SNR in this equation. Figure 8.29 shows that there are other sources of (nonrandom) noises that contribute to peak shifts. The total window required to meet the bit error rate objective would be significantly wider than that indicated by the equation. In Section 9.13, following the discussion of off-track and adjacent track noises, the window margin integration procedure for the head-disk system is described.

REFERENCES

[1] A. M. Patel, "Signal and Error-Control Coding," in *Magnetic Recording Handbook,* C. Denis Mee and Eric D. Daniel, eds., McGraw-Hill, New York, 1990.

[2] P. H. Siegel, "Recording Codes for Digital Magnetic Storage," *IEEE Trans. Magn.,* MAG-21 (1985), p. 1344.

[3] R. L. Comstock and M. L. Workman, "Data Storage on Rigid Disks," in *Magnetic Recording Handbook,* C. Denis Mee and Eric D. Daniel, eds., McGraw-Hill, New York, 1990, p. 655.

[4] T. Kameyama, S. Takanami, and R. Arai, "Improvement of Recording Density by Means of Cosine Equalizer," *IEEE Trans. Magn.,* MAG-12 (1976), p. 746.

[5] J. G. Proakis, *Digital Communications,* McGraw-Hill, New York, 1983.

[6] A. M. Patel, "A New Digital Signal Processing Channel for Data Storage Products," *IEEE Trans. Magn.,* MAG-27 (1991), p. 4579.

[7] R. F. Hoyt and H. Sussner, "Precise Side Writing Measurements Using a Single Recording Head," *IEEE Trans. Magn.,* MAG-20 (1984), p. 909.

[8] R. L. Comstock and M. L. Williams, "Frequency Response in Digital Magnetic Recording," *IEEE Trans. Magn.,* MAG-9 (1973), p. 342.

[9] K. B. Klaassen, "Magnetic Recording Channel Front-Ends," *IEEE Trans. Magn.,* MAG-27 (1991), p. 4503.

[10] L. L. Nunnelley, "Practical Noise Measurements," in *Noise in Digital Magnetic Recording,* T. C. Arnoldussen and L. L. Nunnelley, eds., World Scientific, Singapore, 1992, p. 257.

[11] E. R. Katz and T. G. Campbell, "Effect of Bit Shift Distribution on Error Rate in Magnetic Recording," *IEEE Trans. Magn.,* MAG-15 (1979), p. 1050.

[12] A. S. Hoagland and J. E. Monson, *Digital Magnetic Recording,* John Wiley & Sons, New York, 1991, p. 213.

[13] E. Williams, in *Noise in Digital Magnetic Recording,* T. C. Arnoldussen and L. L. Nunnelley, eds., World Scientific, Singapore, 1992, p. 233.

9

Magnetic Disk
Recording Integration

9.1 INTRODUCTION

Integration is the process of relating component parameters to the disk drive capacity, performance, and reliability. Figure 9.1 illustrates the principles of the integration process. The user is interested in the cost of the drive, expressed in dollars per megabyte. The areal and volume densities are subsets of this requirement.

Reliability in terms of mean time to failure and error rates is another prime consideration for the user. The drive performance in terms of access time and data rate defines the application range of the drive. Earlier chapters discussed most parameters except those related to the track density (TPI, tracks per inch). This chapter describes TPI-related topics in some detail. The integration procedure may be analytical, experimental, or a hybrid of both. The design and development of a disk drive go through several stages. Mathematical simulation based on experience of the last generation of drive is useful in the design phase for defining linear and track

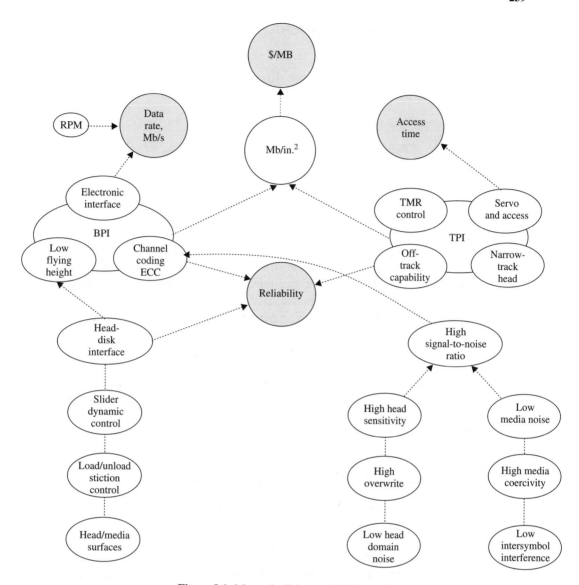

Figure 9.1 Magnetic disk recording integration.

densities. A hybrid approach is preferred for setting component specifications and their acceptable tolerances when early samples of components become available. Integration procedures discussed in this chapter are heavily used during this phase to ensure that components will meet the areal density objectives. Aggressive designs, use of new components, and diagnostic troubleshooting often require several iterations of the integration process to find a proper balance among the objectives of cost, performance, and reliability. This chapter describes experimental integration procedures.

9.2 DISK DRIVE DESIGN CONSIDERATIONS

While the specification sheet of a drive includes many parameters, the following five are the most important ones:

1. The form factor
2. Capacity and price
3. Access time
4. Data rate
5. Reliability

9.2.1 The Form Factor

The form factor refers to the volume of the drive. The size of the drive usually refers to the size of the disk, for example, 3.5 in. (90 mm). The high-capacity drives sold in large volumes have dimensions of 101.6 mm width, 146 mm depth, and 25.4 mm height. A high areal density on platters along with close placement of multiple platters in a stack results in high volumetric capacity. The smaller the form factor for a given capacity, the broader the field of application.

9.2.2 Capacity (in Megabytes or Gigabytes) and Price

With price and capacity, the dollars per megabytes can be calculated. This is often the most important factor for most users to purchase the drive. Competitive drive pricing requires that the designer pay special attention to component costs.

9.2.3 Access Time

The access time, that is, the average time required to reach random data on the disk surface, is the sum of three parameters.

1. *The average access time.* This is the average time the head actuator takes to move the head from any random track to any other random track. It is approximately one-third the maximum time required for a head to move radially from the outermost track to the innermost track of the disk.
2. *The settling time.* Once the head has approached the desired track, it takes a short time to "settle"; that is, the transients in the servo system controlling the motion of the head actuator must sufficiently diminish to start reading. Summation of these two terms is also known as seek time.
3. *Latency.* This is the average time the head has to wait for disk rotation until the data is reached. On average, half the rotation of the disk is required between one location on the circumference of a track to any other location on the same track:

    Total average access time = seek time + latency

9.2.4 Data Rate

Usually given in megabytes per second (MB/s), this is the rate at which data is available to the user. This data rate is often referred to as *user data rate*. Internal disk data rate may be different due to coding of the data, discussed in Chapter 8, Section 8.5.

9.2.5 Reliability

Disk drive reliability has two parts. One part is specified as the number of average operation hours to a failure, or mean time to failure. The second part relates to error rates when the data is read. Error correction and recovery procedures embedded in the drive eliminate most of the raw errors from the customer data. However, the drive must be designed with low error rate. The criteria vary with the manufacturer. One error in 10^{10} bits read may be considered acceptable for a small drive, while for large systems, less than one error in 10^{12} bits is required. Often the specification is written in terms of bytes, in which case, for comparison, a multiplier of 8 should be included. The assessment of error rates of a disk drive is the most important aspect of designing a drive and is discussed in Section 9.13. Another aspect of reliability has to do with a component failure or a head-disk interference or "crash." Despite ever-decreasing flying heights, head-disk crashes are rare events. The topic of head-disk interface is discussed in Chapter 10.

One should be careful about comparing mean time to failure figures quoted by different manufacturers. There are at least two ways of computing this quantity.

1. *Based on failure rates of components used in the drive.* Failure rates of all the components are added together, and the reciprocal of the combined failure rate is quoted as the mean time to failure. This is a conservative method and could result in an order-of-magnitude smaller mean time to failure compared to the method discussed next.

2. *Based on manufacturer-computed failure rates.* The ratio of failed (returned) drives to shipped drives is used, with an assumption that all drives are operational 24 hours a day. This could result in extravagant claims on reliability, with unrealistically specified long times to failure.

It is useful to understand the basis of quoted "mean time to failure" with this procedure. For simplicity of calculations, an exponentially decaying reliability curve is assumed in almost all quoted estimates. For a population of N_0 drives, the number of drives surviving after time t is given by $N = N_0 \exp(-t/M)$, where M is the mean time to failure. From this formula, the percentage of files likely to fail in the first year can be calculated. Assume that t_1 is the number of operational hours in a year. Since t_1 is usually much smaller than M, $N = N_0(1 - t_1/M)$. The number of drives failing in the first year is given by $N_0(t_1/M)$. In percentage, $100 \times (t_1/M)$ drives are likely to fail in the first year. In practice, M is calculated by counting the returned drives in the first year and using the percentage equation.

As an example, consider that 2.5% of the drives are returned in the first year. Then assuming that the drives are operating 24 hours a day, $t = 8760$, and M is calculated as 350,400 hours. One peculiarity of the exponential reliability curve is that every year the same percentage of surviving drives is likely to fail, and by the mean time to failure (M), 63% of the drives would fail. The reliability specification is just one of the factors for trouble-free operation of a drive. A drive with fewer components is likely to be more reliable, and the environment in which the drive operates has a major impact on its reliability.

9.3 TRACK DENSITY AND STORAGE CAPACITY OF A DISK

Areal density per square inch on the disk surface is given by the product of bpi (bits per inch) and tpi. Much of the discussion in previous chapters has been confined to linear bit density, bpi. Optimization of track density on the disk surface is emphasized in this and succeeding sections. The objective is to pack as many tracks as possible so as to maximize the total bit capacity of the disk. Once maximum linear bit density is specified as bpi_{max}, the theoretical maximum capacity C_{max} on the disk surface capacity can be calculated as

$$C_{max} = \text{usable disk surface area (in.}^2) \times \text{bpi}_{max} \times \text{tpi} \qquad (9.1)$$

Putting equation (9.1) in terms of outer and inner radii r_0 and r_i, respectively, the maximum disk capacity is expressed as

$$C_{max} = \pi(r_0^2 - r_i^2)\,\text{bpi}_{max} \times \text{tpi} \qquad (9.2)$$

In practice, it is difficult to realize this maximum capacity because of the following problems:

1. The length of a track at radius r is $2\pi r$. If each track has the same linear bit density, that is, bpi_{max}, each track will have a different number ($2\pi r \times \text{bpi}_{max}$) of bits. The data rate of every track will be different. The electronics to handle such a variable data rate would be complex.
2. Maintenance of the same linear density (bpi) would require the head to fly at a constant flying height over the disk surface. Generally, flying height increases with increasing radius.

One common practice followed in the industry in the past to alleviate these problems has been to use an equal number of bits for each track throughout the disk surface (fixed frequency recording). Each track now has $2\pi r_i \times \text{bpi}_{max}$ bits, and since the number of tracks on the disk surface is equal to $(r_0 - r_i) \times \text{tpi}$, the capacity of the disk surface in this case is given by

$$C = 2\pi r_i(r_0 - r_i) \times \text{bpi}_{max} \times \text{tpi} \qquad (9.3)$$

Most large disk drives (greater than 95 mm) were designed with this practice. Here the maximum bit density bpi_{max} occurs at the innermost radius and the linear bit density decreases as the radius increases. Data rate is constant for every track. Increasing head flying height at increasing radius can handle decreasing bit density more comfortably. With this strategy it is interesting to find the optimum value of the inner radius r_i that results in maximum capacity on the disk surface. This can be obtained by differentiating C in equation (9.3) with respect to r_i and equating it to zero. The result is $r_i = 1/2r_0$. Many disk drives followed this rule.

It is also interesting to work out the loss in capacity by following the second method of writing data compared to the first. For the optimized $r_i = 1/2r_0$, the ratio of capacity from equation (9.3) to that from equation (9.2) can be calculated as $\frac{2}{3}$. This means that one-third of the capacity is lost due to "single-banding practice" or single-frequency recording. With some increased complexity of electronics, the surface area can be divided in a few bands of constant areal band densities, thus recovering a good fraction of this loss in capacity. One- or two-chip channel electronics are now available incorporating built-in multiband or multizone electronics. Smaller disk drives and advanced slider designs that provide nearly constant flying heights over the disk surface make multizone recording possible.

As an example, a 1.8-in. disk with an outer diameter (O.D.) of 48 mm and inner diameter (I.D.) of 12 mm has an area of 5.25 in.^{2} (two sides), and at 1 Gb/in.^{2} density, the disk (platter) will have a maximum unformatted capacity of 655 MB. Maximum multizone banding is assumed for this example. In ideal multizoning each track is a zone. This would achieve maximum surface density for given bpi and tpi. However, after several zones, the law of diminishing returns catches up and the complexity of the drive outweighs the benefits. Eight zones may result in about 90% of the ideal capacity of a drive. Track density, or tpi (or t/mm), can be expressed as the reciprocal of *track pitch*, which is the distance between centers of adjacent tracks. Reduction and optimization of track pitch T_p is a major activity during development of a new drive. This topic is discussed next.

9.4 TRACK MISREGISTRATION

For maximum capacity it would be desirable to have head write tracks in precise circles with tracks butting against each other. This would also require that the heads be lined up precisely in the center of the designated track during reading. The servo system would be designed so that the head centers on a given track. However, several factors contribute to inaccuracies in the ability of a head to follow tracks while reading. These inaccuracies result in part of the read head crossing over into adjacent tracks, reading erroneous information or noise. This noise could result in reduction in signal-to-noise ratio, leading to increased error rates.

One solution to this problem would be to allocate wide track widths on the medium relative to the read head width. So there are guard bands or empty spaces provided on two sides of the reading track. This would reduce possibilities of the head going beyond track boundaries and reading information from adjacent tracks. However, this would result in lower track density. Hence, there is a compromise between allocation of guard band widths and track density. To study this trade-off quantitatively, make appropriate measurements, and specify track pitch, the term *track misregistration* (TMR) is now defined.

Figure 9.2 illustrates write-to-read track misregistration. The offset distance x in micrometers (or nanometers) between the center of the read head and the center of the written track is called track misregistration. This offset distance varies as the disk rotates. There are several contributing factors to these variations, discussed in the paragraphs that follow. There is also a feedback system or servo to reduce these variations, discussed in Section 9.4. The resultant variation in x is of interest.

Since the location of the center of the head varies from instant to instant, we can draw a histogram or a statistical distribution to describe the probability of x

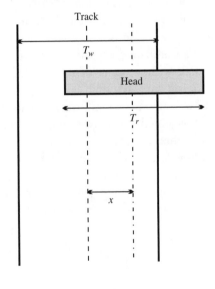

Figure 9.2 Write-to-read track misregistration.

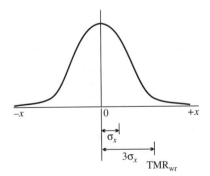

Figure 9.3 Distribution of head position while reading a written track.

being between x and Δx, as indicated in Figure 9.3. On average, the servo system keeps the head in the center, so the distribution of x has a mean of 0 and a standard deviation σ_x. If we assume a Gaussian or normal distribution for x, 99.7% of the time the head center will be offset from the written track center within the range $\pm 3\sigma_x$. The specific $3\sigma_x$ value of the track misregistration is designated as the TMR of the system. Often, the variable quantity x, discussed earlier, and the value of x at $3\sigma_x$ are interchangeably called by the same term, TMR. We shall use the term TMR to mean the $3\sigma_x$ value of x. Here, variations in the position of the head from the center of the written track is considered; hence, this TMR is called a write-to-read TMR and is defined as TMR_{wr}.

The write-to-write TMR is defined in Figure 9.4. Assume that track 1 is already written and the writing head is in the process of writing adjacent track 2. During this process it is following the servo. However, due to factors discussed shortly, its centerline of track 2 does not coincide with the intended distance, called *track pitch,* from track 1. This difference between the designed track pitch and actual spacing between two adjacent tracks is defined as TMR_{ww}. Following the definition of TMR_{wr}, TMR_{ww} is the 3σ limit of the write-to-write misregistration distribution. This quantity consists of two parts:

1. Offset of the head from the center of its own intended track centerline during writing
2. Relative wiggling or distance variations between two adjacent tracks.

One of the reasons for this wiggling is due to inaccuracy in the initial writing of reference tracks on the servo disk. Discussion of the contributing causes of both these TMRs should help to clarify these terms.

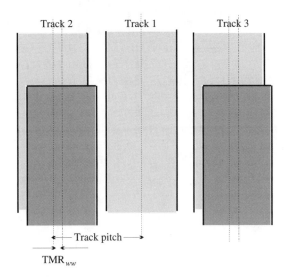

Figure 9.4 Write-to-write track misregistration.

9.4.1 Thermal Effects

In many multidisk drives one of the disk surfaces, or at least part of a disk surface, is dedicated to servo patterns. From these patterns read by the servo head, the location of the track center is determined and constantly followed. All the heads including the servo head are mounted on arms attached to the same actuator. As the servo head follows a referenced track on the servo disk, all the data heads also follow their respective tracks. Figure 9.5 shows three disks. The lower surface of disk 2 has precisely written servo tracks on it. Two heads are shown flying on this surface. The outer head reads the servo or reference tracks. These tracks have special patterns written on them. These patterns provide information about the degree to which the head is off-center. This information is decoded by modulation and control circuits, and a position error signal (PES) is generated. The size of the PES is proportional to the degree to which the head is off-center. This signal drives the coil, which controls the motion of the voice coil motor (VCM), which in turn moves all the heads mounted on the "actuator" so that all the heads approach closest to the center of their respective tracks. When the internal temperature of the disk drive changes from a cold start to some high value (10–25°C), the head arms and disks expand. The temperature coefficients of expansions of arms and disks are different. The result is relative displacement of the data heads with respect to the servo head, which depends on the temperature and location of each data head. This contributes to varying degrees of track misregistration for data heads even if the servo head is following its track perfectly. A sector servo, in place of a dedicated servo, can reduce this factor in TMRs. Servo systems are discussed in Sections 9.5 and 9.6.

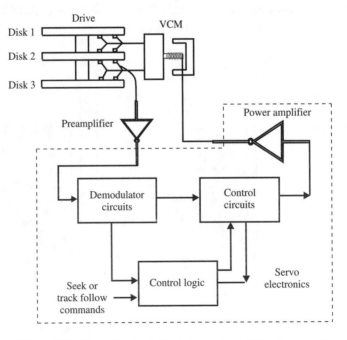

Figure 9.5 Schematic of a dedicated servo track following circuit.

9.4.2 Spindle Bearing Runouts

Ball-bearing spindles used for rotating the disks contribute to repeatable and nonrepeatable runouts of disk tracks and add to track misregistrations. Nonrepeatable runout of the spindle is a significant contributor to TMRs. Tilting the spindle and vibrations of the spindle and disk ensemble also contribute to track misregistration. Air-bearing spindles have very small runouts, and hence these are used for testing heads and media.

9.4.3 Mechanical Vibrations

While the arm and actuator are moving from one track to another, they go through cycles of accelerations and decelerations that cause them to vibrate, sometimes at a rapid rate. Track misregistrations result if the frequencies of these vibrations fall outside the range of servo electronics' ability to respond. Vibrations of the disk drive box due to its environment also get transmitted to the spindle or actuator comb and add to TMR.

9.4.4 Servo Loop Electronic Noise

Servo position detection circuits have electronic noise sources, and this noise translates into actuator motions and contributes to TMR.

Both TMRs are influenced by all these factors. The write-to-write TMR_{ww} has an additional component. Several inaccuracies are added to the servo pattern tracks when these patterns are written. Servo patterns are written in specially designed machines called servo writers to reduce inaccuracies in track following during servo pattern writing.

The TMRs between $\frac{2}{3}$ and 1 μm were state of the art in 1995, and these numbers are decreasing as track pitch is reduced. One rule of thumb used in the past has been that the track pitch should be between 5 and 8 times the TMR of the system. Before the end of this decade, multigigabit densities will require TMR reductions by a factor of 2 to 5.

9.5 DISK DRIVE SERVO

Most digital tape recorders and flexible disks for data storage do not use closed-loop (feedback) servo control for writing and reading. For relatively wide tracks, closed-loop servo systems are not essential. Rigid disk drives with narrow tracks require a servo to write radially uniform tracks and read them with a high degree of accuracy to ensure low error rates.

There are two types of servos in practice. The one described in the last section in which a disk surface and a head are dedicated solely for the servo is called a *dedicated servo* procedure. A second type of servo is called a *sector,* or *embedded, servo,* in which segments of data tracks carry servo information. First, the principles of a dedicated servo are discussed. A servo system has two major functions:

1. To ensure that data heads follow their designated tracks accurately.
2. To control and monitor smooth transitions of the data head when it moves to "seek" from one track to another track location.

Figure 9.5 shows the elements of a servo system. To perform the first function, the dedicated surface track is continuously read by the servo head. The special pattern on the servo track indicates the degree of accuracy maintained by the head over its track. The read information contains the signal proportional to the difference between ideal central line tracking and actual positions of the servo head. This signal is called the PES, as defined in the last section. Servo electronics interpret this signal and issue proportional analog output to the actuator motor drive. The motor, called the VCM, moves the actuator so as to correct the error in the servo head position. The VCM is an arrangement of permanent magnets surrounding a moving coil. This system is analogous to the speaker driver of a hi-fi, hence the name VCM. The actuator is the rigid comblike structure on which head suspensions are mounted. Since data heads are mechanically attached to the actuator, they too move accordingly to maintain their positions in the center of their respective tracks, except for the track misregistrations discussed in the last section.

The second function of servo electronics is to control and correct the motion of data heads from track to track during "seek" operations. When the control command is received to move the data head from the current track to a designated new track, the VCM starts moving the actuator. The servo head constantly reads the track patterns in the radial direction and counts the number of tracks traversed. This information, along with the position and velocity of the moving actuator, is fed into the servo system. The servo system computes the difference between the target track and the current location of the actuator and regulates the VCM motion until the target track location is achieved. The trick in the design of the servo system is to accomplish this task accurately, within the shortest possible time. Many current systems are designed with analog circuits to accomplish these servo functions. However, more and more systems are being converted to digital sampling to collect the servo information and use digital signal processing (DSP) to feed back the correction signals. A variety of servo patterns are designed and in use with the objective that the servo head can sense the position error signal accurately and provide feedback to center the head over the track. One of these patterns, called a dibit arrangement, is now considered as an example. Figure 9.6 illustrates the adjacent patterns with dibit transitions. Transitions in one track are reverses and offset with respect to the adjacent tracks. The servo head flies in the center of these two patterns. The output of the servo head is shown in the lower part of Figure 9.6. Note that the signals are generated at magnetic transitions shown in the upper part. The difference in signals between positive and negative pulses indicates the head location with respect to the center of the patterns. The center of patterns A and B

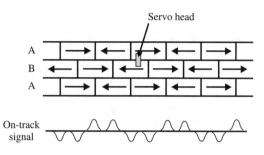

Figure 9.6 Dibit servo pattern and on-track signal.

correlates to the center of the track being followed. The difference signal is converted into VCM current by the servo electronics, and the actuator is moved until the feedback output of both polarities is equalized.

9.6 SECTOR, OR EMBEDDED, SERVO

For a disk drive with three or fewer platters (disks), it is too expensive to dedicate the full surface for a servo pattern and a servo head. An embedded,or sector, servo allows allocation of small sections of data tracks for servo patterns. These sector servo patterns are repeated several times on every track. There is no separate servo head; data heads perform the dual role of data and servo heads.

Figure 9.7 shows a segment of a sectored servo disk [1]. The head, time-multiplexes data read or write function with servo sector reading. Servo patterns are read by the head during its passage over each sector, and a position error signal is generated to correct off-track deviations. The types of patterns and process of generating a PES are conceptually similar to those used for a dedicated servo, except that they are available only while reading the servo field. In Figure 9.7, $t, t+1, t-1$, and so on, are the centerlines of data tracks. The head is centered on the track. When it is over a servo field, it reads patterns A and B. If it is perfectly in the center, the

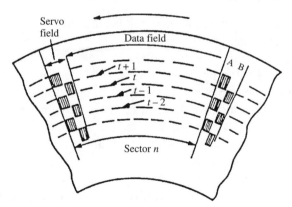

Figure 9.7 Embedded sector servo [1].

amplitudes of patterns read are equal, and a PES of zero is generated, indicating that no change in position is required. As the head center deviates from the track center, a difference signal is read, and the magnitude of the signal is proportional to the amount of head offset. This PES, after filtering and detection, is used to provide correction to the head VCM. The advantage of sector servo is that it reduces components and eliminates the thermal TMR contribution since the same head tracks the data and the servo. On the other hand, servo feedback is limited to short durations or is "sampled" (when the head is not reading the data), which reduces tracking accuracy. The servo sectors on every disk are density overhead, and each disk goes through a sector servo writing procedure. Fairly complex algorithms and procedures are required for seek operations to direct the head from one track to another. However, more and more drives are using sector servos, and semiconductor chips are available to handle these functions at reasonable costs. The sector servo significantly reduces the TMRs and is likely to be adopted for a majority of the disk drives in the future.

9.7 INTEGRATION OF HEAD, MEDIUM, AND CHANNEL

The procedures required to integrate components, heads, disks, and channel are where the "rubber meets the road" in disk drive design. The objective of integration testing is to assure that the drive operates according to the designated performance specifications during its life with negligibly small error rates. Disk drives incorporate error detection and error correction circuitry and error recovery schemes. However, the basic drive should meet specified low error rates, and there should be sufficient "margins" to ensure nominal performance under a range of environmental conditions. In the last chapter, in Section 8.2, a number of factors were given that are responsible for causing errors in the performance of a disk drive. Figure 8.26 illustrates a majority of these factors. Before discussing the remaining issues, here we review previously discussed corrective measures that reduce errors in the disk drive.

Random noises in the medium, head, and electronics add to inaccuracies in peak detection and contribute to errors. Control of bandwidth and component design optimization reduce noise and error rates. Peak shifts in data due to writing variations, high-density operations, and channel component variations contribute to error rates. Design of codes, write precompensation, equalization or filtering, regeneration of clocking while reading, automatic gain control, clamping the signals, and so on, reduce system errors. Selection of proper write current and meeting the overwrite requirement minimize errors due to unerased old information and side writing, reading, and erasing.

Component integration consists of a series of experimental procedures used to simulate critical aspects of the drive performance and reliability in the controlled environment. It is a continuous process to support various phases of drive design, development, and production. Specific experiments carried out during integration depend on prior experience on the last generation of disk drives, performance modeling, and information on components. Situations for which integration measurements are needed are summarized next.

1. The early planning stage of a next-generation drive depends on component modeling and cumulative experience with integration of the last generation of drives.

2. When new components become available, integration experiments are performed with a matrix of heads and media to arrive at optimum bit density and track densities. This procedure is used to establish acceptable component specifications.

3. During the design verification stage, the shortcomings of components and needed improvements are fed back to manufacturers after a series of integration studies. In the case of a new component technology, integration procedures provide diagnostics of persistent problems. Often, new failure modes are discovered during testing, requiring multiple cycles of design changes, diagnostics, and performance evaluations. For new component technology this phase is crucial and time-consuming. On the other hand, this is also the creative part of engineering, when new understanding is generated and new tests are designed to simplify design and production.

4. Usually integration experiments are carried out on PTSs or "spin stands." It is not uncommon to find differences between these test results and the actual performance of completed drives. Some of the tests described in this chapter are performed on fully or partly assembled drives to resolve the differences. Also, PTS tests need to be modified to improve correlation between two different environments.

The essence of integration testing is the measurement of error rates of head-disk combinations under stressed conditions on a PTS. One practical problem with the measurement of error rates is the time it takes to make repeatable measurements. For example, to observe 10 errors at the rate of 1 error in 10^{10} bits requires over an hour. It is desirable to devise experimental procedures to stress the system in a predictable way to obtain increased error rates. Once such procedures are established, tests can be performed quickly, and results could allow prediction of system error rates under low-stress, real-life environment.

Two types of stressed condition measurements are common in the industry:

1. *Observation of error rates when the head is displaced from the middle of the track to off-center positions.* This is known as off-track measurements, or sometimes as old information (OI) measurements. Another level of stress condition is added by writing adjacent tracks close together, and this is sometimes known as a "squeeze test."

2. *Measurement of accelerated error rates when the clocking interval (timing window) for peak detection is gradually reduced from the designated value.* This procedure is known as the window margin study.

The first technique partly simulates head misalignment due to track misregistrations; the second technique simulates the effect of noise and perturbation on peak detection errors.

Different drive makers often use different terminology for the same experiments. This will be clarified wherever possible. Measurements and interpretation of results get somewhat complex as applied to separate read and write elements of an MR head. Differences between inductive and MR head parameters are pointed out.

9.8 TRACK PROFILE AND MICROTRACK PROFILE

A track profile is a plot of the read head voltage as a function of the read head position on a written track. These measurements may be carried out on a precision test stand as a preliminary step prior to the error rate measurement used for the integration procedure. Alternatively, they may be used independently to observe the effect of fringing fields or to study the asymmetry in the output signal across the track. Figure 9.8 shows the reading head on a written test track. The head center

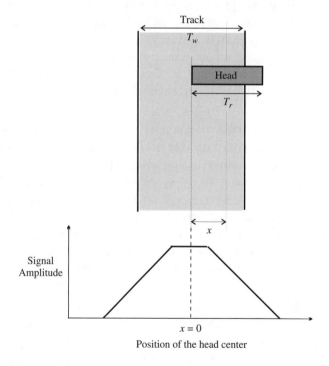

Figure 9.8 Track profile of a write wide, read narrow (MR) head.

is shown off-center from the written track by an amount x. The head track width T_r is shown shorter than the written track width T_w, representing the "write wide, read narrow" condition of separate write and read elements of an MR head. In the case of an inductive head, the same head is used for writing and reading; hence, the write track width and read width are nearly the same.

The procedure of measuring a track profile is as follows:

1. DC erase the track area and its vicinity so as to provide a noise-free medium background.
2. Write a track.
3. Read the track when the head center is located at a sufficiently long distance on the left. Progressively step the head to the right and measure output voltages.
4. Continue the procedure until a full trace of the track is obtained.

As the signal plotting is carried out for write wide, read narrow head elements, when the head is moved from a distance $x < -1/2(T_w + T_r)$ on the left to when $x > 1/2(T_w + T_r)$ on the right, a trapezoidal signal profile is obtained, as shown in Figure 9.8. This plot of the signal as a function of head displacement is called the *track profile* of the head. Note that for the write wide, read narrow MR head the output signal remains constant until the center of the read head deviates from the center by $1/2(W_w - R_w)$. Thus, separate read and write heads of an MR head provide a buffer against track misregistrations of this magnitude. In other words, guard bands of width $1/2(W_w - R_w)$ are on two sides of the track as a part of the head construction.

A triangular profile is obtained if the write and read widths of the head are equal, as is the case for an inductive head. What we have discussed so far are the expected ideal outputs of a track profile. In practice, it is the nonideal aspect of the profile that gives the most useful information. The inductive head microtrack profile ideally should have a sharp apex in the center when the head is in the center of the written track. If the apex is rounded, it indicates fringing pickup of the read function. Rounded outputs at corners where the signal should ideally become zero indicate the fringing effects of write and read processes. Similar comments apply to an MR head where the track profile has corners and where the signal approaches zero. As discussed in Section 6.21, the MR head exhibits asymmetrical signal output characteristics across the track; this could be studied with track and microtrack profiles. For the diagnostics of read and write operations, it is often useful to be able to plot the track profile measured by a very narrow read element. For example, the side writing of an inductive head can be studied accurately with such a capability. In a sense, it is the track profile discussed above, except the read element should be very narrow. If such a head was available, the read track profile would be almost rectangular; see Figure 9.9. This type of profile is called a *microtrack profile*. It is difficult to construct a very narrow track (submicrometer) read element. Side writing of the inductive heads was studied by constructing narrow strips of written

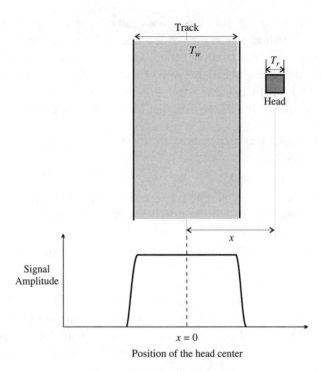

Figure 9.9 Microtrack profile.

tracks and reading the output with a conventional wide-track head [2]. This procedure is applied to construct microtrack profiles of heads. The procedure is described now:

1. A track is written with a conventional wide-track-width inductive head at a specific radius of the disk.

2. The head is shifted to another radius, toward, say, the inner diameter of the disk, such that the head track width covers part of the written track. Now, an erase current is applied so that part of the track is erased.

3. Next, the head is moved toward the outer radius of the disk so that, except for a narrow strip, it covers the remaining track. The erase current is applied. What is left is a narrow strip of the written track.

4. The same head is now shifted over the remaining narrow track for reading. The signal output is read.

Steps 1 to 4 will be repeated by creating the narrow strip at another location along the track. The signal output versus the location of narrow strips is plotted. The result is shown in Figure 9.9. Notice the difference between the track profile and the microtrack profile. To construct a microtrack profile, the test stand should be accurate enough to allow writing the track at a precise location every time and repeating the placement of the head at designated locations. The microtrack signal is small and requires careful measurements.

9.9 OFF-TRACK OR OI MEASUREMENT

The objective of this measurement is to simulate an increase in error rates when the head deviates from the center of the written track due to track misregistration (TMR_{wr}). The procedure is similar to the measurement of a track profile, except error rates are measured instead of the voltage signals, and a specific background is prepared so that the results can be closely correlated to off-track error rates of a head in a disk drive.

Figure 9.10 indicates such a procedure. First, a background noise is prepared by writing two overlapping tracks. What constitutes a correct noise environment is subject to debate. Some experimenters prefer to put random data in the background, while others may choose a sequence of frequencies in different background bands. On top of this background "noise," referred to as "old information," a test data track of a known pattern is written in the center. Generally, an entire track revolution of a "worst case" data pattern is used. Now, the read head centered on the test (data) track reads the written data and compares it with the original data sequence. The measured error rate, usually very low, is noted as the "on-track error rate." Next, the head is displaced by a short distance, and data is read again and error measurement is made. The procedure is repeated with step-by-step displacements of the read head and measurements of error rates. The amount of time each measurement takes depends on the degree of accuracy desired. It takes much longer to measure significant errors in the center of the written track, and often this measurement is even skipped. The procedure of head displacement and error rate measurement continues until a specific error rate (10^{-4} or 10^{-6}) is registered. The displacement of the head (in micrometers) that results in this error rate is registered as the OTC for off-track capability. Sometimes this quantity is referred to as OI, for old information, but this terminology is confusing. The OTC is more descriptive of the experiment, and so it is used in the text. The quantity signifies the ability of the head-disk system to handle a degree of misregistration without exceeding a specified error rate. Note that the OTC is track dependent. For specification a certain track has to be defined.

A plot of head displacement from the center versus error rate is shown in Figure 9.11. Because of its shape, the curve is referred to as a "bathtub" curve—no mystery in the name! Since there is no standardization in the names or details of the procedure, one should be careful in interpreting published results. Sometimes, an OTC in micrometers or nanometers is defined for a specific number of bytes in error.

Thus, a new parameter, OTC, is defined, and it will be used several times in the rest of the chapter. Note that the OTC is measured for a specified error rate. Since the error rate is a final indicator of the head/medium/channel capability, the OTC is used as a barometer for specifying different parameters. The following are examples of measurements commonly done during drive development:

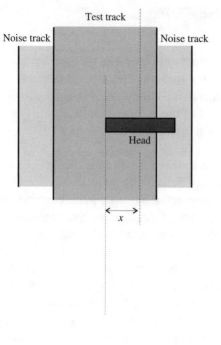

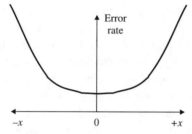

Figure 9.10 Off-track error rate (bathtub) measuring procedure.

Figure 9.11 Head off-track location versus error rates (bathtub curve).

- Write current versus OTC
- Flying height versus OTC
- For MR head use, MR bias current versus OTC
- Adjustment of channel parameters, clip level, and precomp and filter settings to maximize OTC.

However, OTC is only part of the story. This parameter by itself is insufficient for the determination of the highest possible track density and optimization between bit and track densities. What is needed is inclusion of the noise effect of adjacent tracks, and changes in error rates as tracks are brought close to each other. A discussion of the track pitch determination technique follows, but first we describe how to combine the TMR distribution curve in Figure 9.3 and the error rate distribution curve in Figure 9.11.

9.10 ESTIMATION OF THE SYSTEM ERROR RATE

Section 9.4, on TMR statistical distribution, gave the probability of the head being a distance x away from the center. The error rate curve (bathtub curve) gives the error rate of the system when the head is a distance x from the center. These two sets of information can be combined to estimate the system error rate. Figures 9.3 and 9.11 describe the TMR distribution and bathtub error rate curves. The bathtub curve is also a distribution. It is easier to understand the procedure by visualizing the distributions as histograms. The TMR distribution gives the probability of the head as a specific location x, and the bathtub curve describes the error rate if the head is at distance x. Consider a point x, and note the area of the TMR distribution within Δx (a small increment in x). Multiply this area with the error rate from the bathtub curve at distance x from the center. Do the same for every x value on the right and left and add all the error rates collected. This method is called *convolution of two distributions*. The calculated total error rate represents an estimate of the system error rate. The procedure is computerized for experimental curves or their approximations. It is common to assume Gaussian distribution for the TMR distribution. Most of the error contributions come from the sides of the bathtub, where error rates are high. An inverted parabola may be fitted to the bathtub curve to simplify the computations. In the next section, it will be seen that the measured bathtub curve for a single track is modified by the presence of adjacent tracks and erase bands. It should also be noted that a bathtub curve measured for one head-medium-channel combination is not sufficient to give aggregate information on the system error rate. Different combinations of disks, track locations, heads, sense electronics and flying heights, and so on, would have different error rate curves. It is difficult to carry out estimations of error rates that include all these variables.

A statistical procedure may be used to simplify the process of error estimation. A computer mathematical model is developed to predict error rates that correlate with specific head/medium parameters. The computer assigns random values to each of the parameters and calculates error rates. The procedure is repeated 1000 –10,000 times, and statistical distributions of error rates in an applicable specified range of component parameters are computed. The procedure is known as the *Monte Carlo method* of error projection.

The bathtub curves are not always symmetrical, and contributions to error rates from both sides must be included in computing system error rates.

9.11 TRACK PITCH DETERMINATION, "SQUEEZE," AND THE "747" CURVE

In Section 9.9 the OTC and error rate measurements were described for a single track without inclusion of adjacent tracks. In this section, the effect of adjacent tracks on error rates is included. The objective here is to specify adjacent-track spacings, or *track pitch,* which maximizes the track density (minimizes the track pitch), along with the condition that the system error rate specification is met or exceeded. The measurement procedure to accomplish this is now described. It is the process of gradually bringing an adjacent track close to the test track and studying the impact on error rates. This is done by measuring the OTC of the test track as the adjacent track is shifted toward the test track and superimposes it [3]. Figures 9.12 and 9.13 illustrate the procedure. In Figure 9.12, the test track and adjacent tracks are shown with white bands. These bands are called the *erase bands;* their origin is in the partial writing fields at the track edges and erase bands are described in Section 3.13. The procedure is now described.

1. A test track is prepared with background noise (e.g., noise tracks 1 and 2, shown lightly shaded in the figure) to represent old information. The center test track (shaded dark) is written on top with a known data sequence. The OTC is measured as described in Section 9.9.

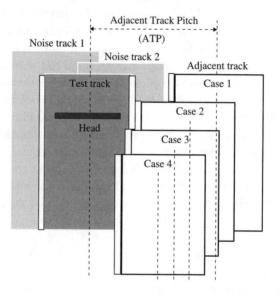

Figure 9.12 Method of measuring the effect of adjacent-track location on off-track capability.

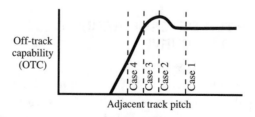

Figure 9.13 Off-track capability as a function of adjacent-track pitch, "747" curve.

2. An adjacent track is written a short distance away (case 1 in Figure 9.12), and OTC is measured. Since the adjacent track is sufficiently far, the OTC of the test track should be the same as that measured in step 1. A plot of the distance between the centers of adjacent tracks (adjacent-track pitch) and the OTC measurement on the test track is initiated (case 1 in Figure 9.13).

3. Now the adjacent track is brought closer to the test track so that erase bands butt against each other (case 2 in Figure 9.12). The OTC is measured and a corresponding point is plotted (case 2 in Figure 9.13). As shown in the figure, OTC is now somewhat larger than in the last step. This is an interesting and apparently unexpected result, and it is explained as follows. When the head is stepped to the right during OTC measurements, part of it approaches the double-erase bands. With two erase bands the head reads less noise than for case 1. This reduction in noise or improved signal-to-noise ratio as compared to case 1 results in reduced error rates. This allows the head to go farther off-track without exceeding a specified error rate and hence OTC is larger.

4. Next, the adjacent track is brought even closer to the test track, and it now partly superimposes the test track (case 3 in Figure 9.12). The erase band now erases part of the test track, which tends to lower the signal. The result of this lower signal is to decrease OTC (case 3 in Figure 9.13).

5. Further encroachment of the adjacent track reduces the read signal as the test track narrows and the adjacent-track signal (which is noise to the read head reading test track) further degrades the signal-to-noise ratio and, hence, lowers OTC, case 4. The plot in Figure 9.13 is named a *747 curve,* since it looks like the side view of a 747 airplane cockpit. The process of bringing the adjacent track close to the test track for step-by-step measurement of OTCs is called *squeeze.*

Actually, the procedure just described is carried out for both sides of the test track, particularly for an MR head that has a nonsymmetrical track profile. Designers tend to prescribe track pitch versus OTC hump as an optimized track pitch for the system. This choice of track pitch requires verification in the head-disk assembly where track misregistration influences are included. As indicated in the application example that follows, it is possible to model the system that integrates adjacent-track pitch (ATP) versus OTC error rate measurements and TMR distribution to further optimize the system.

9.12 APPLICATION OF INTEGRATION PROCEDURES

The demonstration of 500 Mb/in.^{2} density [4] is an excellent example of the integration concepts discussed. The paper refers to experimental and modeling procedures of integration. The demonstration uses an MR read and an inductive write head elements. The microtrack profile of the MR head is shown in Figure 9.14. Observe the asymmetric profile of the 3.6-μm-wide read head. The CoPtCr low-noise disk used has an H_c of 1335 Oe (107 kA/m) and an $M_r\delta$ of 0.8×10^{-3} emu/cm^2(8 mA). Figure 9.15 shows a bathtub curve (solid line) of byte error rates as a function of head center off-track positions. Actually the bathtub curve is measured with adjacent tracks at optimum track pitch. The track pitch was obtained from track pitch versus OTC shown in Figure 9.16. The squeeze or 747 curve shows maximum OTC

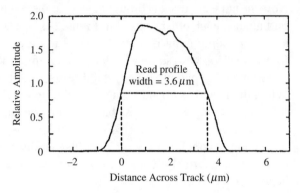

Figure 9.14 Microtrack profile of a 500-Mb/in.^{2}-density MR head [4].

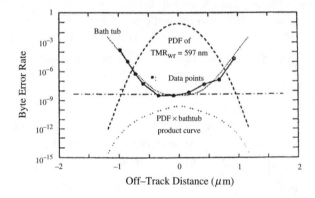

Figure 9.15 Error rate (bathtub) curve of 500 Mb/in.^{2} density [4].

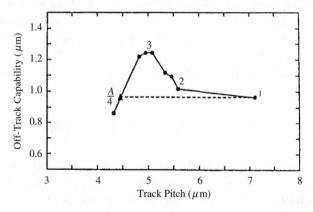

Figure 9.16 Adjacent-track squeeze and OTC peak (747 curve) [4].

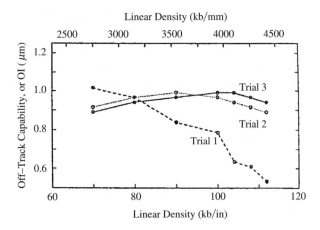

Figure 9.17 Linear bit density optimization with the 500-Mb/in.² system [4].

when the track pitch is about 5 μm, which corresponds to 5000 TPI. Further optimization of the linear density was carried out by using plots of linear density versus OTC for three different sets of equalizer and detector clip levels (Figure 9.17). A linear density of 100 Kb/in. with OTC of over 1 μm and TPI of 5000 results in 500 Mb/in.² capability of the system with achievable objectives of TMRs with reasonable error rates. Modeled integration of TMR and the error rate curve is also shown in Figure 9.15.

Integration procedures provide error rate data for head-medium-electronics under stressed and unstressed conditions and can be used as follows:

1. Linear density determination
2. Identification of critical parameters and their relative weights in the control of disk drive error rates
3. Optimization of track pitch and areal density
4. Realistic estimation of error rate for the drive
5. Specification of components and a number of design parameters
6. A diagnostic tool for weeding out problems in the early phase of a new component technology.

9.13 WINDOW MARGIN INTEGRATION PROCEDURES

The integration procedures using the direct error measurement methods just described simulate a disk drive system closely, and they are used for critical decision making and specifying components. The experiments are complex and time-consuming.

With the availability of efficient time-interval-measuring instruments, new methods of testing heads and disks on test stands and assembled disk drives are emerging. The window margin detection procedures have significant merits:

1. They can use time interval analyzers or window margin analyzers to collect statistics on bit shifts and correlate them to error rates. These tools save time and may be used on drive subassemblies, reducing the cost of testing.
2. Accelerated error rates can be measured and can be extrapolated to lower error rates.
3. They allow systematic separation of portions of the detection window attributable to error sources.
4. They allow measurement of window margins that correlate with the "ruggedness" of the drive design.

Chapter 8 discussed the peak detection process. Peak detection requires the differentiated signal to fall within the window, preferably as close to the center of the window as possible. Linear-density-related factors, intersymbol interference, head/medium/preamplifier noises and variations in data sequences, write currents, channel components, flying height, and so on, tend to shift peak position off-center. Variation in the location of the signal peak is termed *peak jitter.* In Section 8.4, the distribution of peak location within the window was described. Section 8.23 discussed how random noises of the head/medium/preamplifier relate to window detection and error rates.

Figure 9.18 shows the detection time window and distribution of peak jitter. The probability of peaks falling outside of the window is equal to the system error rate. For practical convenience it is assumed that the peak distribution is Gaussian, and it is fully described by the mean m and standard deviation σ. This distribution

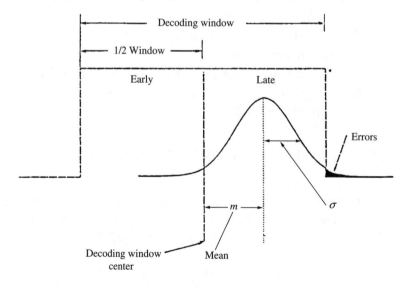

Figure 9.18 Peak detection window and distribution of peak location.

REFERENCES

[1] M. D. Sidman, "Control Systems Technology in Digital's Disk Drives," *Digit. Tech. J.*, No. 8 (February 1989), p. 61.

[2] R. F. Hoyt and H. Sussner, "Precise Side Writing Measurements Using a Single Recording Head," *IEEE Trans. Magn.*, MAG-20 (1984), p. 909.

[3] E. A. Cunningham and D. C. Palmer, "A Model for the Prediction of Disk File Performance from Basic Component Capabilities," MMM-Intermag conference presentation, Paper JE-3 (1988).

[4] R. A. Jensen, J. Mortelmans, and R. Hauswitzer, "Demonstration of 500 Megabits per Square Inch with Digital Magnetic Recording," *IEEE Trans. Magn.*, MAG-26 (1990), p. 2169.

[5] E. R. Katz and T. G. Campbell, "Effect of Bitshift Distribution on Error Rate in Magnetic Recording," *IEEE Trans. Magn.*, MAG-15 (1979), p. 1050.

[6] C. Tsang, M. Chen, T. Yogi, and K. Ju, "Performance Study and Analysis of Dual-Element Head on Thin Film Disk for Gigabit Density Recording," *IEEE Trans. Magn.*, MAG-26 (1990), p. 2948.

[7] T. Howell, D. McCown, T. Diola, Y. Tang, K. Hense, and R. Gee, "Error Rate Performance of Experimental Gigabit per Square Inch Recording Components," *IEEE Trans. Magn.*, MAG-26 (1990), p. 2298.

Head-Disk Interface

Roger F. Hoyt
IBM Corporation

10.1 INTRODUCTION

The head-disk interface is where all critical processes of magnetic recording occur. Maintaining a stable and reliable interface is required to ensure proper functioning of a disk drive. For example, if the spacing is too large, the head's fringing field will be too weak to "write" the disk properly. Also, the read-back signal is reduced, and data errors may occur. On the other hand, very low head-disk spacing may improve magnetic performance, but this can lead to mechanical wear of the head and disk, substantially reducing lifetime.

The key role of the head-disk interface in determining the achievable areal density in a disk drive is illustrated in Figure 10.1. In the figure the areal density for a number of disk drive products is plotted against the nominal flying height of the head. The logarithmic scales for both areal density and flying height reflect the fact that magnetic recording is a "near-field" process; that is, reading and writing by a head occurs in close proximity to the head's gap. This leads to the exponential dependence of the field on the spacing between head and disk and, consequently, areal density. Figure 10.1 also illustrates the important fact that as areal density increases, tolerances in the head-disk spacing must also be reduced. This places significant constraints on both head and disk parameters, as well as drive design factors such

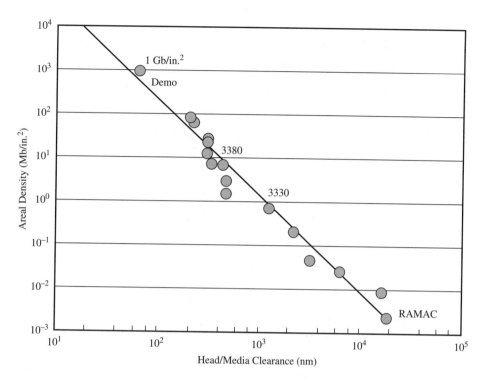

Figure 10.1 Areal density versus clearance for disk drives.

as internal air filtration, cleanliness, and mechanical excitation by spindle bearings or external shock.

The first disk drive was manufactured and shipped in 1957 by IBM. It used a head designed to operate out of contact with the disk. A spacing of 20 μm (800 microinches) between heads and disks was achieved. The head assembly incorporated three small holes through which air was pumped, creating a small pressure at the interface. A compressor built into the disk housing supplied the necessary air. The levitating force was balanced by a spring on the suspension that held the head. This was the first and last time an externally pressurized air bearing was used for maintaining head and disk separation in disk drives. All subsequent drives have used so-called self-acting or flying air-bearing designs. These heads' surfaces are shaped so that the boundary layer of air just above the disk is compressed under the head, generating the necessary pressure.

The disk's characteristics are also very critical in determining the performance and stability of the interface. For example, the roughness of the disk surface must be much smaller than the separation of the head and disk to avoid contact and wear of the surfaces. Also, the flatness of the disk must be sufficient to ensure the head is capable of tracking the disk surface to the required tolerances. It is common for current 130-mm (5.25-in.) or 95-mm (3.5-in.) rigid disks to be out of flatness by as much as 20–50 μm. This can be compared with head flying heights that are well below 0.5 μm! The compliance of the head and suspension must be sufficient to compensate for this large motion while tracking the disk surface to tolerances of a few hundredths of a micrometer during each revolution.

The environment within the disk drive must also be maintained clean and free of contaminants to ensure long life and stability of the interface. Airborne particulate contaminants must be filtered out quickly by the disk drive's air filtration system or prevented from entering entirely by proper sealing and/or filtering of the airflow. Chemical contaminants that can degrade a disk drive's performance must also be controlled. These can either enter the drive through external filters or be present from outgassing of materials used in the drive's construction (circuit boards, cables, adhesives, lubricants, etc.). Such vapor-carried chemicals can, over time, degrade performance through gradual accumulation in the interface or by chemically attaching to the head and disk. Internal air filtration designs for disk drives may incorporate elements to eliminate this problem.

10.2 AIR-BEARING SLIDERS

The "flying" air-bearing slider is a critical mechanical challenge in the design of a disk drive. However, it is important to point out that air bearings in disk drives do not "fly" in the same sense that an airplane flies. The wings of an airplane are shaped so that the difference in air speed over the upper and lower surfaces creates a pressure difference and a net upward lift. For the air bearings in a disk drive, only the slider's surface that faces the disk is important in creating the force that separates the two. The surface is shaped so that part of the boundary layer of air carried by the rotating disk is compressed and forced to flow underneath the slider. This so-called boundary layer is a thin film of air next to the surface of the disk that is moving at the same speed as the rotating disk. The thickness of this layer may be determined from fluid mechanics to be about 0.5 mm thick on the basis of the air viscosity and surface velocity gradients. It is the compression of air as it passes under the slider that creates the force (several gm-f) to lift the head from the disk. The calculation of this pressure and resultant force is a key goal of gas lubrication theory, described in Section 10.4.

For the air-bearing technology used in disk drives, there exist a large number of different designs. They were developed to satisfy somewhat different criteria, and over the years they have become more elegant, with improved performance allowing decreased head-disk spacing. Some of the requirements for specific air-bearing designs include rapid take-off, close compliance to the disk's surface, stable flying, and minimal variation of flying height of the slider at different radial positions on the disk. The last item is important since the relative velocity of the head over the disk can change by as much as a factor of 2 from the inside to the outside diameter. The different velocities alter the air pressure under the slider and result in changes in flying heights that can impact the head's ability to read and write properly. Finally, with the widespread use of rotary actuators in disk drives, the air bearing must be able to fly in a stable manner over a range of azimuthal orientations (20–25 degrees) of the head with the disk.

10.3 SELF-ACTING AIR BEARINGS

10.3.1 Cylindrical Crown Bearings

The earliest type of self-acting air bearing used in disk drives was a *cylindrically crowned* bearing (Figure 10.2). The bottom surface was in the shape of a circular cylinder, with its axis parallel to the disk surface. The large radius of curvature of the air bearing's crowned surface allowed for easy compression of the incoming air under the slider and a reduction of the channel between head and disk to create the necessary pressure to support the slider. The read/write head was a separate magnetic assembly mounted in the air bearing. The head was located so that the gap for reading and writing was positioned at the point on the slider closest to the disk. This allowed the highest fields and gradients from the head while writing and the highest resolution on readback. The slider itself was constructed of nonmagnetic stainless steel for robust mechanical performance. The entire slider and head assembly was mounted in a spring-loaded gimbal assembly, so that the head would be able to comply properly with the mechanical vibrations and the out of flatness of the rotating disk.

10.3.2 Winchester Slider

Probably the most famous air-bearing slider design used in disk drives is the so-called *Winchester* design (Figure 10.3). This slider was introduced with the IBM 3340 and 3350 disk drive family and continues to be used in many products today, although it has been superseded by smaller sliders more suited for MIG and thin film heads. A key feature of the Winchester slider was that it was fabricated entirely

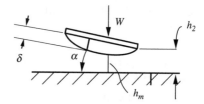

Figure 10.2 Self-acting hydrodynamic crowned bearing slider.

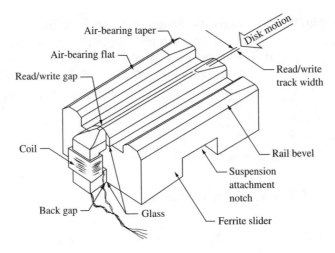

Figure 10.3 Trirail Winchester slider.

of ferrite. This slider body satisfied both mechanical and magnetic requirements, removing the need to attach a separate magnetic read/write head to a mechanical air-bearing design. The strong mechanical properties of ferrite ceramics were well-suited to the requirements, while being fit for the lapping and polishing needed for the air bearing's surface during fabrication. The air-bearing surface consisted of two parallel rails adjusted for a specific design to give the needed head flying height and pitch angle.

10.3.3 Taper Flat Slider

The development of the thin film head, introduced in 1979, brought requirements for a new type of air-bearing design. The so-called *taper flat* slider is the logical descendant of the Winchester design, modified for thin film heads (Figure 10.4). With the magnetic element and coils fabricated with semiconductor-like lithographic and deposition processes, the material for the slider itself had to be different from the Permalloy and copper materials used for the head. The material chosen was a hard ceramic made of titanium nitride and aluminum oxide. The air-bearing geometry for the taper flat slider is similar to that of the Winchester slider, without the small center rail, which provided the ferrite head's pole pieces and gap. The front taper provided compression of the incoming air, with the two straight rails on either side of the slider developing the lift. The mechanical suspension for the taper flat slider was a simplified gimbal design. The three-piece load beam, attach, and gimbal provided for sufficient downward "loading" forces on the slider to be applied, while allowing rotational freedom and stiffness in the "pitch" and "roll" directions to permit the slider to comply with the disk's surface while flying. In summary, the taper flat slider is a reduced version of the Winchester slider fabricated of ceramic material with a smaller simplified suspension.

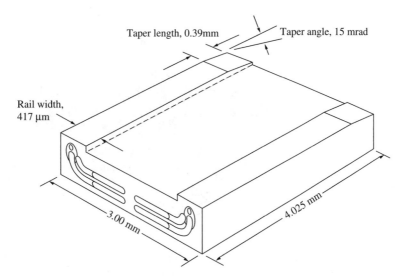

Figure 10.4 Taper flat slider for thin film heads.

10.3.4 "Self-Loading" Slider

Invented in 1976, the self-loading slider is a novel variation on the Winchester/taper flat design. It provides some interesting enhancements in stiffness and disk compliance. The air-bearing surface design is practically identical to the taper flat head with the critical difference that the front taper region extends completely across the slider body, and a small "crossbar" region directly behind connects the two rails on each side (Figure 10.5). Directly behind this area, a recessed region of the slider forms a "pocket." While the front taper provides compression, as in the taper flat slider, the flat region connecting the two rails results in a subambient pressure region created in the pocket of the slider. This has the effect of sucking

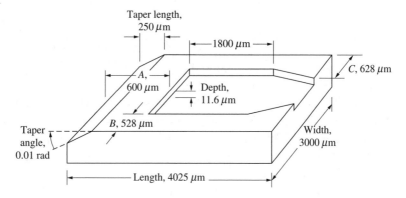

Figure 10.5 Self-loading slider.

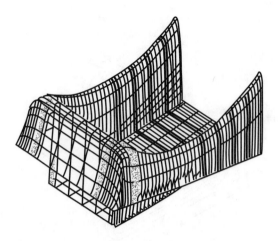

Figure 10.6 Pressure profile of a self-loading slider.

the slider toward the disk at the same time the air compression on the two rails provides the upward lift seen in Figure 10.6. With proper design, a net upward force is generated. The downward force in the pocket region results in an air bearing that is stiffer with somewhat less velocity dependence on the flying height. The self-loading slider concept has received a great deal of attention and study and can offer some performance advantages. Up to the present time, however, it has not found major product application, primarily because more recent designs that have evolved from the taper flat slider have been able to satisfy product specification requirements. After the first invention of the self-loading slider, manufacturing issues associated with it were also a concern.

10.3.5 Miniaturized Designs

The introduction of disk drives of ever-shrinking form factors, particularly since 1980, has increased the need for air-bearing sliders of reduced dimensions. The evolution of sliders of reduced dimensions is illustrated in Figure 10.7 [1]. From the "full sizes" (dimensions $5.6 \times 4 \times 1.93$ mm) associated with the Winchester ferrite sliders, the thin film taper flat "minislider," also known as the 100% slider, had dimensions of $4 \times 3 \times 0.8$ mm. This was the size of the air-bearing slider that was commonly used in large disk drives and the first 135-mm (5.25-in.) disks, with thin film heads as well as its competing ferrite MIG heads. The next reduced-size slider commonly used in 95-mm (3.5-in.) and smaller form factor disk drives was the "microslider," often named the 70% slider, with dimensions of $2.84 \times 2.23 \times 0.61$ mm. The reduced dimensions of the microslider only allowed for a single read/write element on the rear, which was placed at the center of the slider. This dictated a further alteration of the air-bearing designs, with a larger central rail, which provided the required lift and stability. A further miniaturized version of the microslider has been introduced, the "nano," or 50% type, with dimensions of $2.05 \times 1.6 \times 0.43$ mm. The nanoslider is mainly a scaled microdesign and is suitable for 65-mm (2.5-in.) and

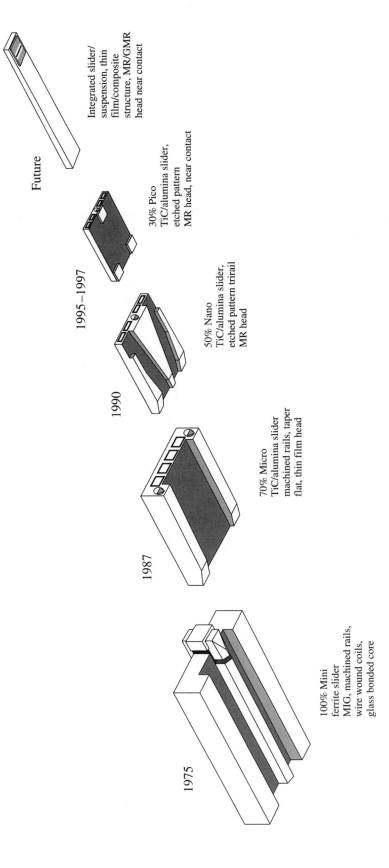

Future

Integrated slider/
suspension, thin
film/composite
structure, MR/GMR
head near contact

1995–1997

30% Pico
TiC/alumina slider,
etched pattern
MR head, near contact

1990

50% Nano
TiC/alumina slider,
etched pattern trirail
MR head

1987

70% Micro
TiC/alumina slider
machined rails, taper
flat, thin film head

1975

100% Mini
ferrite slider
MIG, machined rails,
wire wound coils,
glass bonded core

Figure 10.7 Evolution of the slider/air-bearing surface showing the miniaturization of slider dimensions.

smaller disk drives. The "pico," or 30%, slider is considered for future drives, with dimensions standardized at $1.25 \times 1 \times 0.3$ mm.

10.4 GAS LUBRICATION FOR AIR BEARINGS

As applied to air-bearing slider designs for disk drives, the goal of gas lubrication theory is to calculate the head's flying characteristics given the slider geometry, disk surface, and gas type (generally air). This includes the so-called steady-state parameters of trailing-edge flying height and the slider's pitch and roll (Figure 10.8). The dynamic characteristics of the slider are also of interest, in order to know the stiffness and resonances of the air bearing.

The pressure distribution along a slider's rails can be calculated from the Reynolds equation for a wedge-shaped slider's flying attitude in viscous fluid (air), carried by the moving disk boundary layer. Typical assumptions in the calculations are as follows:

1. The spacing between the head and disk is thin enough so that the head flies in the boundary layer of the disk (within about 0.3 mm of the surface).
2. The air behaves as a Newtonian fluid.
3. The inertia of the fluid is neglected.
4. The air flow is isothermal.
5. The air pressure is constant across the thickness of the film.

Using these assumptions and considering the balance of forces on a fluid element, a compressible one-dimensional Reynolds equation can be derived [2]:

$$\frac{\partial}{\partial x}\left(h^3 p \frac{\partial p}{\partial x}\right) = 6vU \frac{\partial(hp)}{\partial x} + 12v \frac{\partial(hp)}{\partial t} \tag{10.1}$$

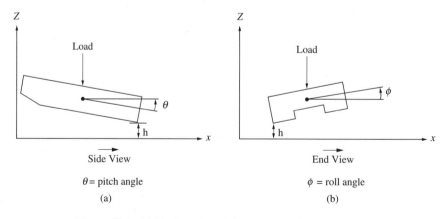

θ = pitch angle ϕ = roll angle

(a)   (b)

Figure 10.8 (a) Pitch angle and (b) roll angle of a flying slider.

where h = slider/disk spacing
p = pressure
v = viscosity
U = disk velocity

This equation can be generalized to two dimensions, and correction for the first-order air slip can be included, to write the two-dimensional Reynolds equation as

$$\frac{\partial}{\partial x}\left(h^3 p \frac{\partial p}{\partial x}\left(1 + \frac{6K}{hp}\right)\right) + \frac{\partial}{\partial y}\left(h^3 p \frac{\partial p}{\partial y}\left(1 + \frac{6K}{hp}\right)\right) = 6vU\frac{\partial(hp)}{\partial x} + 12v\frac{\partial(hp)}{\partial t}$$

(10.2)

where $K = [\lambda p(2 - f)/f]$
λ = ambient mean free path of air (about 66 nm at room temperature and pressure)
f = air reflection coefficient from the slider's rails (0.7–0.9)

For most applications, this equation may be used to determine a slider's flying characteristics. However, second-order slip corrections may also be included, and for those cases where the mean free path of the air becomes large relative to the minimum head-disk spacing, Boltzmann's equation has been used [3].

For flying heights that are on the order of the air molecules' mean free path, one might expect large deviations from the behavior predicted by the Reynolds equation (above). However, studies have shown that the deviations in steady-state air-bearing performances from that predicted by the Reynolds equation are not large [4]. The width of the air-bearing rails is large enough that the collisions of the air molecules with the slider's rails are averaged, and the Reynolds equation provides a useful tool to calculate the slider's flying height. However, for flow approaching the molecular regime (high Knudsen number), a full Boltzmann equation must be used.

Using the above Reynolds equation and including first-order slip and the finite difference method, the pressure and velocity distribution along the slider's rails may be determined. The results for the 3380-style taper flat slider designs are shown schematically in Figures 10.9 and 10.10. Similarly, the pressure profile of a

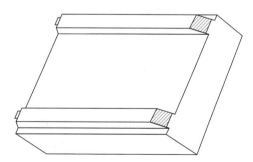

Figure 10.9 Schematic of taper flat slider.

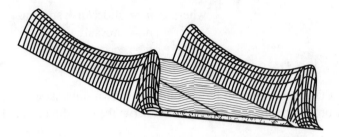

Figure 10.10 Air-bearing pressure profile of the taper flat slider.

self-loading slider is shown in Figure 10.6. Using this pressure distribution with the suspension stiffness, the steady-state head flying characteristics as well as the resonances may be determined. From the calculations, a summary of typical air-bearing steady-state flying characteristics is shown in Table 10.1.

TABLE 10.1 Trailing-Edge Flying Characteristics of 3380-Like Air-Bearing Slider

	Velocity (m/s)	Fly Height (nm)	Pitch Angle (μrad)
I.D.	40	250	83
O.D.	65	360	97

10.5 CHARACTERIZATION AND TEST MEASUREMENTS OF THE AIR-BEARING INTERFACE

As discussed in Sections 3.10 and 10.1, flying height is the key parameter determining the achievable areal density of a disk drive. The smallest possible magnetic spacing is the physical "air-bearing" spacing plus thicknesses of nonmagnetic coatings of the head and media. However, low-flying sliders could result in more frequent contacts between head and disk surfaces and cause data loss and other reliability problems. Optimum design of the drive requires accurate measurements and understanding of the several parameters related to the head-disk interface:

1. The mean value of the flying height or physical spacing between a slider and the disk. This strongly influences head and disk design parameters.
2. The variations in the slider-to-disk air-bearing spacing due to the changes in disk surface flatness, disk rotational variations, slider suspension variations, influence of external vibrations, and so on.
3. The head location on the slider may vary with respect to the disk surface due to the pitch and roll motions of the slider. These motions also influence the air flow between the slider and disk surface and modify the slider flying conditions.

The last two items are generally considered together, under the label "dynamics of slider-disk spacing." We shall review the most commonly used methods of measuring these quantities and summarize the most practical techniques developed for disk drive applications. It is also useful to obtain information related to any slider-disk contacts. The modeling described in Section 10.4 provides a theoretical background and preliminary data regarding the behavior of the head-disk interface under consideration.

10.5.1 Capacitance Measurement Technique for Air-Bearing Separation

This method was first used for disk drives developed in the 1950s and 1960s, when the spacing between head sliders and disks was several micrometers. Conducting surfaces on the slider and disk provided the parallel plates of a capacitor (Figure 10.11). The sliders were specially prepared for this measurement by applying conductive layer material to the surface area used as one plate of the capacitor. This modification of the slider may influence its flying property. The parallel-plate capacitance between two surfaces is given (in picofarads) by $C = 0.0885\epsilon A/d$, where ϵ is the dielectric constant of air (approximately 1), A is the area of the conductive plates, and d is the slider-disk spacing. All linear dimensions are in centimeters. Taking into account a combined capacitance of air-bearing spacing and insulating coating on the disk medium surface [5], the measured capacitance could be expressed as

$$C = \frac{0.0885A}{\dfrac{d_2}{\epsilon_2} + \dfrac{d_1}{\epsilon_1}} \tag{10.3}$$

where subscripts 1 and 2 refer to spacing and coating, respectively. The capacitance can be measured by making it a component of the detection circuitry.

Application of the capacitance method to measure the flying height of ceramic sliders over an aluminum disk in the range of 1–5 μm has been reported [6]. The procedure also describes three capacitance probes to study the pitch and roll angle variations of the slider. The multiprobe capacitances on a tapered two-rail slider

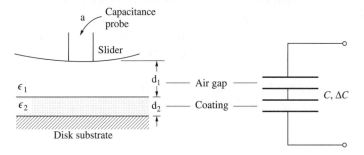

Figure 10.11 Capacitive arrangement of measuring air-bearing spacing for a metal-coated disk.

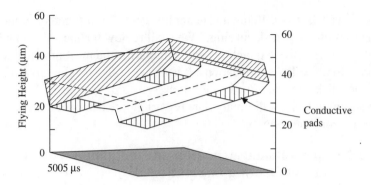

Figure 10.12 Multiple-probe capacitive arrangement for evaluating slider
flying dynamics [7].

(Figure 10.12) have been used to study submicrometer flying heights and pitch and
roll angles of a slider relative to a disk [7]. The following capacitance equation
encompassing effective flying height h', pitch, and roll angles allows computations
of these variables:

$$C = \epsilon_0 \int_0^{x_l} \int_0^{y_l} \frac{dx\,dy}{[h' + x\tan\theta - y\tan\phi]} \tag{10.4}$$

where x_l, y_l = length and width of the rail, respectively
θ = pitch angle
ϕ = roll angle
h' = effective flying height

The flying height (spacing) h is related to the effective flying height by the relation $h' = h + (t_l/\epsilon_l + t_c/\epsilon_c)$. The subscripts l and c refer to lubricant and coating
thicknesses and corresponding dielectric constants. The above equation can be expressed in a closed form [7]. The three variables h, θ, and ϕ can be evaluated from
measurement of three capacitance values at three of the conductive pads. Ref. [7]
describes how these measurements were used to produce frame-by-frame movie
depiction of slider dynamics.

The capacitance measurement techniques for flying height evaluation and
slider dynamics study require special preparation of the slider and electronics.
These techniques have the advantage of using standard production-level disks. We
shall compare different methods at the end of this section.

10.5.2 Optical Interference Method
to Evaluate Slider Flying Characteristics

Optical interferometry has long been used for the accurate measurements of
thin films. The principle of the method and its application for measuring spacing
between slider and disk surface will now be described. The basic concept is shown

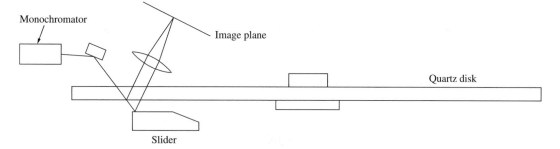

Figure 10.13 Optical method for measuring disk-slider air-bearing spacing.

in Figure 10.13. A monochromatic light beam is directed to pass through a transparent flat glass disk. Some light is reflected from the lower surface of the disk, and the rest passes into the air-bearing film. This part of the light reflects from the slider and is imaged into a detector that could be a photodetector or the human eye. Figure 10.14a shows the two optical paths merging at the detector P. Our interest is in knowing the intensity of resultant light detected at the detector P as the distance h between the disk surface and the slider surface varies from low to high values.

The intensity detected at P is due to the interference of two optical waves, one along the path ADP and another along path BCEP, given by

$$I_T = I_1 + I_2 - 2\sqrt{I_1 I_2}\cos\delta \qquad (10.5)$$

where I_1 and I_2 are intensities of two optical waves. The phase angle difference δ between two paths is proportional to the difference in path lengths between ADP and BCEP. The value of δ can be derived simply from the geometry shown in Figure 10.14a and using Snell's law of refraction for angles $\sin\theta$ and $\sin\theta'$. Ref. [8] shows this derivation with an assumption that the slider material is a dielectric and light reflects from it with a phase change π. This assumption requires modification for small flying heights, as discussed later in this section. The result is $\delta = (4\pi/\lambda)h + \pi$. Assuming $I_1 = I_2$, the plot of intensity at the detector as a function of head disk spacing is as shown in Figure 10.14b. As the value of h approaches $\frac{1}{4}\lambda$ (called first order) or $\frac{3}{4}\lambda$ (second order), the intensity is maximum, while at 0, $\frac{1}{2}\lambda$, and λ the detected intensity is zero. These intensities can be shown as fringes on a plot or by video imaging. The slope of the periodic curve in Figure 10.14b shows that the sensitivity of the measurements will be very small at maximum and minimum intensities, that is, at peaks and valleys of the curve, while it will be highest at locations of highest slope, $h = \frac{1}{8}\lambda, \frac{3}{8}\lambda, \ldots$. In the past, the wavelength of light was sometimes selected to optimize measurement sensitivity for a given flying height [8]. A standard source for these experiments is a mercury arc monochromator with a wavelength (λ) of 545 nm. The first-order optimized point for maximum sensitivity in this case is ($\frac{1}{8}\lambda$) or 68 nm. Measurements of air-bearing spacing can be made at several points along a slider's rails. The accurate flying height at the head's location can be computed based on the slider's geometry and the calculated pitch and roll angles.

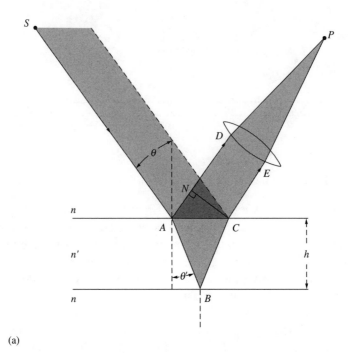

(a)

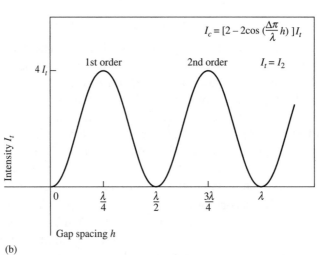

$$I_c = [2 - 2\cos(\frac{\Delta\pi}{\lambda} h)]I_t$$

(b)

Figure 10.14 (a) Parallel-plate interferometry for flying height measurements; (b) intensity variation (fringes) as a function of head-disk separation [8].

One interesting technique to study the dynamic characteristics of the air-bearing slider is shown in Figure 10.15 [9]. The objective is to measure head flying height variations caused by disk surface fluctuations and head arm vibrations. Head arm vibrations are generated by a voice coil type shaker and monitored with a piezoelectric accelerometer. Disk surface variations are also separately monitored by a capacitive probe. The flying height is measured by optical interferometry,

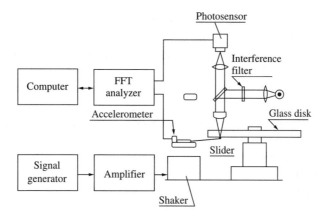

Figure 10.15 Measurement system for the study of the dynamic characteristics of the head-disk interface [9].

described above, using a monochromator light source of 527 nm. The head flying height of 320 nm was observed with a resolution of 1 nm. Spacing fluctuations of 20 nm (p-p) were measured. A frequency spectral content of 0.1–12 kHz was observed with several resonance peaks. Low-frequency peaks were attributed to fluctuations in the suspension spring. Good correlation between calculations using the Reynolds equation and experimental data was obtained.

Improved detection electronics and instrumentation have allowed more precise measurements of slider dynamics [10]. The experiments are carried out with the apparatus shown in Figure 10.16. A mercury arc lamp source output is tuned at the wavelength of 545 nm. The slider is not excited by external means. Variations in slider flying height are the result of normal excitation sources such as disk runout, suspension resonance, and air-bearing resonance modes. The two-beam interferometric procedure discussed above can be used for directly measuring the flying height and dynamic vibrations of the slider from DC to 100 kHz. The signal-to-noise ratio of the detection electronics was sufficiently large to allow

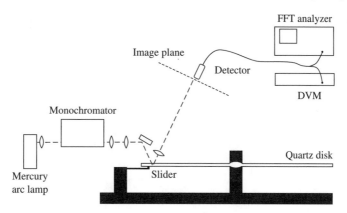

Figure 10.16 Experimental setup for measuring slider dynamics on a quartz disk [10].

measurement of air-bearing thickness variations of less than 0.5 nm in the full range of frequencies. Suspension mode resonances were below 10 kHz and all significant resonances were below 30 kHz. These suspension resonances are distinguished from the air-bearing mode peaks since they do not change frequency with increased velocity of the disk. Figures 10.17a and 10.17b show amplitude-versus-frequency plots for leading-edge and trailing-edge flying heights of the slider. Note that the amplitudes of slider dynamics are higher at the leading edge than those at the trailing edge. Amplitudes under 10 kHz are due to suspension resonances and show no change in frequencies with flying heights between leading and trailing edges. On the other hand, the air-bearing resonance mode shifts from 15 to 25 kHz, with decreased flying height at the trailing edge.

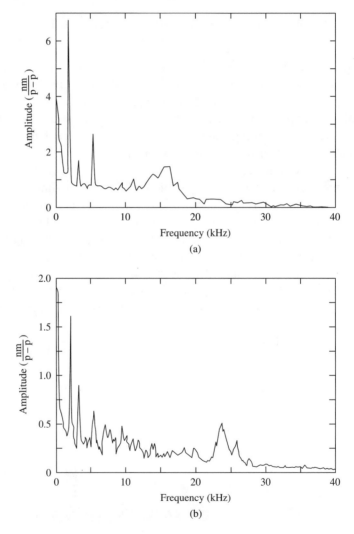

Figure 10.17 Plots of amplitude versus frequency of (a) the leading edge of a slider and (b) the trailing edge of a slider.

A comparative study of average flying height and its dynamic variations has been carried out using both capacitive and optical measurement methods on the same slider and glass disk [11]. A 100-nm transparent coating of tin oxide sputtered on the quartz disk was used. The coating allows transparency for optical measurements and provides a conductive probe for the capacitive procedure. The multiple-probe technique described previously was used for the capacitive measurements of flying height and slider roll and pitch angles. The same locations were used for optical interferometric measurements. Absolute flying heights in the range of 200–450 nm agreed within 7 nm for the two methods used. Vibration amplitudes agreed within 0.2 nm in the range of 0–100 kHz.

As flying heights are reduced to less than 100 nm, more precision is required. Optical interference methods require correction to achieve this. It has been pointed out [12] that correct phase shift at the reflection of a light beam from sliders is required for sliders that are not dielectrics. The general form of phase shift between interfering light beams is given by $\delta = 4\pi h/\lambda + 2\pi - \Phi_s$. For a dielectric slider, the shift $\Phi_s = \pi$, and the formula becomes the one given earlier. The error in flying height (the difference between one measured with a dielectric assumption and one measured with a more accurate reflectance coefficient) due to phase shift Φ_s is defined by

$$\Delta h = \frac{\lambda}{4}\left[\frac{1 - \varphi_s}{\pi}\right] \tag{10.6}$$

For $\Phi_s = \pi$, the measurement error vanishes. The appropriate Φ_s for a given slider material can be calculated from its complex refraction coefficient $(n - ik)$. Values of n and k are obtained by using an ellipsometric measurement on the slider. Errors in flying heights for important slider materials have been measured [12]. It has been shown that, for a wavelength of 633 nm, the error for a ferrite slider would be 5–7 nm, and for a calcium titanate slider the error can range 2–3 nm. The error could be as large as 12–13 nm for most commonly used sliders of alumina-titanium carbide.

10.5.3 Piezoelectric Technique to Measure Head-Disk Interactions

Piezoelectricity can be defined as electricity generated through contort of a body. When crystals of some dielectric materials such as quartz, Rochelle salt, and some ceramics are mechanically stressed, net charges of opposite polarity are induced on opposite crystal faces. Thus an electric field and an electromotive force (emf) is produced between diametrically opposite faces of the crystal. Thin film plastics such as PVDF (polyvinylidine difluoride) also exhibit piezoelectricity when electrodes are placed on two sides of the thin sheet of material. Figure 10.18 [13] shows piezoelectric sensors mounted on a slider (a) and suspension (b) for the experiments.

Studies can be conducted with a sensor attached directly to the slider. This sensor has two separate modes of operation. The first is the detection of slider

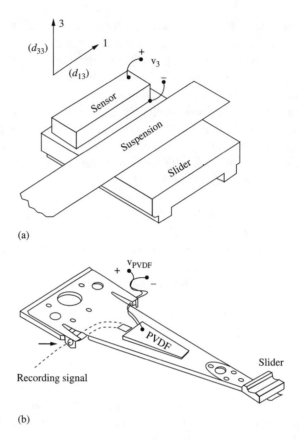

(a)

(b)

Figure 10.18 (a) Piezoelectric transducer mounted on a slider; (b) a plastic
piezoelectric transducer bonded to the slider suspension [13].

accelerations. The slider accelerates up and down over a rotating disk to accommodate vertical runout of the disk and its waviness. The slider movements also reflect
mechanical transients due to air-bearing resonance effects. Both these slider movements result in compressions or expansions of sensor in direction d_{33} (indicated in
Figure 10.18a). Electrical signals measured by the sensor also show high-frequency
perturbations beyond 100 kHz. These are considered to be due to the plate mode
or the sensor bending modes of vibrations in direction d_{13} and are the result of
actual slider-disk impacts. These concepts are easier to understand by comparing
the signal outputs of capacitive measurements and piezoelectric measurements
of head-disk interactions. Figure 10.19a shows the capacitive signal of the slider
movements over a disk, and Figure 10.19b shows the signal of a piezoelectric sensor over precisely the same track. The second signal has low-frequency variations
similar to the capacitive signal output, but it also has an additional structure indicating a high-frequency content. When these signals are filtered to allow outputs in
the range of 100–400 kHz frequency, the piezoelectric signal shows a distinct structure (pings) (Figure 10.19c). The capacitance output is simply the noise within the
frequency band. Hence, the piezoelectric signal in the high-frequency range allows

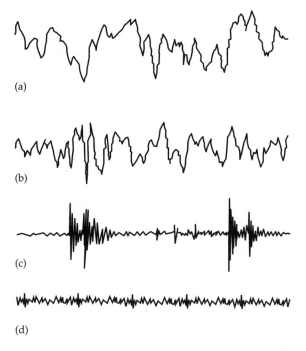

Figure 10.19 (a) Unfiltered capacitance measurement signal; (b) unfiltered piezoelectric signal acquired simultaneously; (c) 100–400 kHz filtered output of capacitance; (d) piezoelectric signals [13].

observations of slider movements, including microhead-disk contacts, not readily observable with conventional methods. Additional details of the theory and experiments can be seen in the reference. This concept, also known as AE (acoustic emission), is often used in the assessment of glide height and contact start-stop (CSS) experiments.

There is an inverse phenomenon of the PZT (piezoelectric) effect called electrostriction. A high-frequency electrical voltage applied across a PZT crystal produces mechanical vibrations; hence, a crystal can be used to generate ultrasonic waves. This concept is used to study mechanical resonance modes in the slider and simulation of slider-disk contacts [14]. Two long PZT crystals are mounted near the trailing and leading edges of the slider, and the following experiments are carried out:

1. By flying the slider over a disk at low flying heights, asperity contacts were registered in a manner similar to the discussion described above. The FFT (fast Fourier transform) analysis indicated resonance modes of the slider at 330, 550, and 634 kHz.

2. A second set of experiments was carried out on a stationary slider. By applying an electrical signal to the leading-edge PZT, forced mechanical vibrations are generated in the stationary slider, and these vibrations are monitored by the trailing-edge PZT. The resonance modes detected in this

experiment were identical to the ones observed for the flying slider described in experiment 1. Both sinusoidal voltage and an applied step function electrical voltage gave similar results.

Thus, the study of a stationary slider with forced vibrations simulated the plate resonance modes of the flying slider due to contacts with disk asperities.

10.6 HEAD-DISK TRIBOLOGY

The dictionary definition of *tribology* is "the science of the mechanisms of friction, lubrication, and wear of interacting surfaces that are in relative motion." Sections 7.5 and 7.6 in Chapter 7 describe several aspects of thin film media tribology. Here we extend the discussion to head media interactions. The design and production of disk drives involve numerous compromises of storage density, cost, and reliability of head-disk assemblies. The most challenging aspect includes factors related to head-disk tribology. In this section, we survey a number of these issues as well as introduce terminology and techniques used to evaluate the "flyability" of air-bearing sliders over disks.

10.6.1 Flying Height and Glide Height

Figure 10.20 shows a schematic of the head-disk interface depicting disk roughness, asperities, and waviness. The average distance between the disk surface and the trailing edge of the slider where the head is located is called the *nominal flying height, h.* As the head-to-disk separation is reduced by reducing the disk velocity, at some separation, the head will come into contact with some asperities. This spacing, which is smaller than the nominal flying height, is called the *glide height.* It defines the shortest possible flying height between a specified standard head and the disk. The range of flying heights in the production of disk drives must include the variabilities of disks and heads plus environmental factors. There are several methods of testing for glide height, one of which is the acoustic emission

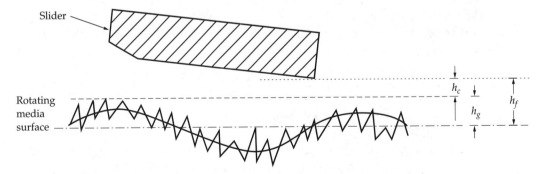

Figure 10.20 Glide height and flying height at head-disk interface.

or piezoelectric measurement method described in the last section. For a 100-nm product flying height, disk glide height may range between 60 and 80 nm. For gigabit-per-square-inch density, less than 50-nm flying height and 25 nm of glide height are needed (Figure 10.1).

Factors that influence magnetic flying height are as follows:

1. Magnetic film thickness, carbon coating, and lubrication. Chapter 7 describes these factors in detail.

2. Disk surface roughness and asperities. Burnishing is commonly used to reduce them, and surface roughness under 10 nm is achievable. In principle, a very smooth surface is desirable for low flying heights. However, a very smooth surface can lead to stiction! (See the next section.)

3. Disk radial curvature and radial slope contribute to increases in the flying height. These factors become more important as the thickness of the substrate is reduced to accommodate more disks within the head-disk assembly. This is one reason why glass substrates are considered in place of Al-Mg substrates. Glass substrates provide rigidity and surface flatness, and both factors reduce flying height.

4. Clamping of an Al-Mg disk during HDA manufacturing can result in distortion of the disk, which needs to be considered in determining the final flying height for the drive.

5. Design of the air bearing. As the head traverses from the inner diameter to the outer diameter, the flying height can increase with increased linear velocity. Thus, disk drive design must include extra flying height variation. Slider ABS (air-bearing surface) can be designed to reduce this variation, as discussed in Section 10.9.

10.6.2 Friction, Stiction, and Contact Start-Stops

During disk drive power-on and power-off cycles the air-bearing slides in contact with the disk. The disk surface consists of a thin magnetic film with a hard carbon coating and lubrication. The stability of this surface-to-surface contact with the chosen design materials is a major activity during development. One critical objective of the study is to select materials such that the sliding is as wear-free as possible. Significant friction at the interface could result in creation of particles that interfere with the head flying environment and may result in unstable flying or crashes. Friction varies as the head-disk goes through starts and stops. A friction coefficient of less than 1 after 20,000 cycles of start-stops is required in high-reliability drives.

Stiction is defined as the static friction between the head and disk and is the amount of force required to allow the disk to start spinning from a full stop. For a short period, the slider remains in sliding contact with the disk. During this period the slider-disk interface experiences dynamic friction. At a certain velocity (typically a few meters per second), the slider starts flying due to air-bearing pressure buildup under its rails. The velocity at which the slider leaves the disk is called the *take-off velocity*, or TOV. This is an important parameter since it is an indicator of sliding distance and is proportional to the resultant wear volume. It is desirable to minimize this wear volume to improve long-term reliability. The TOV depends on the slider geometry parameters—crown, camber, rail widths, gram load, taper angle, and so on [15]—and is a strong function of disk surface properties, skew angle, disk clamping, disk-head surface materials, and so on.

If the stiction exceeds the spindle motor torque, the system cannot function. As noted before, a very smooth disk surface is desirable for low flying heights. However, this increases stiction force. A rougher disk surface fills lubrication and contamination in the surface valleys and also reduces the contact area between the slider and the disk surfaces. These factors are beneficial for lowering the stiction force. Thus, there is a trade-off between disk surface roughness and tolerable stiction force. The strategy commonly used is to produce the smoothest possible surface and then use controlled roughness by texturing. Disk texturing is discussed in Sections 7.5 and 7.7. For less than 50-nm flying heights, several concepts are advanced to resolve this conflict between the requirements of smooth disk surface and low stiction:

1. *Zone texturing.* As described in Section 7.7 and illustrated in Figure 7.22, a special textured zone near the disk I.D. can be provided for starting and stopping, while the rest of the disk surface is smooth, which is essential for low flying heights.

2. *Textured heads.* The air-bearing surfaces can be textured to provide low stiction between the smooth disk surface and the head. This concept has resulted in collection of debris on the head surface, altering the flying characteristics of the head with time.

3. *Dynamic loading.* The head normally flies at high flying height and is controllably lowered soon before the read/write operations.

Stiction force is specified with consideration of the expected number of CSS cycles during the disk drive's life. These tests and resultant measurements of stiction force ensure compatibility of selected materials for the head and disk surfaces, lubrication, design of the slider, suspension, gram load, arm assembly, and so on. The CSS is a procedure to test head-disk contact dynamics during take-off and landing. A spin stand is instrumented to measure forces on the slider at the start of and during sliding prior to TOV. A piezoelectric transducer on the slider or suspension base is used.

A noninvasive electrical method of measuring touch-down velocity (TDV) has been proposed [16]. The procedure involves writing a fixed frequency signal at the inner disk diameter. The signal read from this written track goes through electronic processing and results are obtained as two variables. One is a voltage proportional to the average velocity of the head, and the other is a voltage proportional to the jitter in velocity. The velocity jitter is measured with a sensitivity of

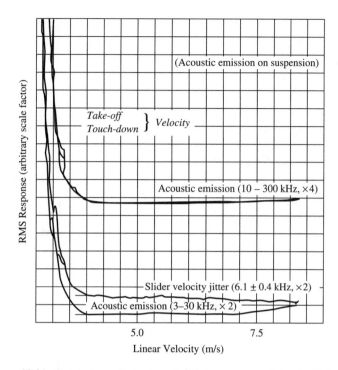

Figure 10.21 Comparison of spin-up and spin-down curves obtained with the velocity jitter method and the (suspension-mounted) acoustic emission sensor method (multiple traces) [16].

displacement as small as 0.08 nm (RMS). This is an indicator of the onset of the slider in contact with the disk. Figure 10.21 depicts the onset of slider-disk contact by a sharp change in the curve of velocity versus velocity jitter. The figure also shows the comparison between an acoustic emission sensor and velocity jitter, both of which are nearly identical.

10.7 NOVEL SLIDER DESIGNS

As disk drive technology advances to achieve flying heights under 50 nm and near-contact recording, slider air-bearing design must evolve as well. In this section, after describing the desirable attributes of a slider for high-density and reliable operations, recent approaches and activities in the recording industry to achieve these objectives are summarized:

1. *Constant flying height over the recording surface.* The flying height of a conventional machine tapered flat (MTF) slider used with a linear actuator increases when the slider is moved from I.D. to O.D. This was acceptable since linear density increased from I.D. to O.D. for these drives. Moreover, flying height tolerances are larger at the O.D. compared to the I.D., primarily due to higher disk surface variations; hence a higher O.D. flying

height was tolerable. With the advent of zone recording (Section 9.3) and nearly uniform linear densities from I.D. to O.D., constant flying height throughout the disk surface is necessary. To some extent, as disk diameters have been reduced from 355 to 65 mm and smaller, it has become easier to design ABSs for uniform flying heights.

2. *Low gram loads and low TOV during CSSs.* Low gram loads reduce stiction and improve surface durability. Low TOVs result in short sliding distance and allow many more CSSs without excessive wear on disk surface and improvements in drive reliability. Both factors are important for long-term reliability, especially for small drives in mobile applications with many more start-stops to conserve battery power. Miniaturization of the slider accomplished the following:

   (a) It reduced the slider-disk surface area, which in turn reduced ABS wear during start-stops.

   (b) It required reduced gram load as the slider volume decreased.

3. *Other factors considered in ABS design.* Stiffness should be high to reduce flying height variations and maintenance of the flying height during accessing. Current manufacturing processes for an air bearing employ ion milling and photolithography in the construction and shaping of rails. Tolerances on these processes could vary depending on the ABS design. In addition, slider surface crown/camber, the skew angles of the slider due to rotary arm movement from I.D. to O.D., and slider pitch angle should be considered. A higher pitch angle increases average flying height while maintaining the required spacing at the trailing edge where the head is located. The trailing edge of the slider surface must provide wide enough space to accommodate the multiconductor head. The magnetoresistive head has different constraints in this regard in comparison with the thin film head.

As discussed in Section 10.4, an MIF profile results in positive pressure under the slider to lift it off the disk. The suspension load counterbalances this force. As discussed above, for a self-loading slider, a negative pressure is generated under the slider that tends to reduce the flying height. As discussed below, the construction of rails, a cavity at the ABS, and suspension loading provide flexibility in achieving appropriate slider flying characteristics.

In the literature, the loading force is either given in newtons (SI) or grams (cgs). The conversion factor of 1 N is equal to approximately 102 g; thus, 5 g of load equals 0.049 N.

10.7.1 Simulated Comparison of Various ABS Designs [17]

Figure 10.22 depicts five ABS designs. An MTF profile is given for comparison with two positive pressure designs, one negative pressure type, and one transverse pressure contour (TPC) design [17]. Simulations were performed with the following design parameters: 50% nanoslider, I.D. flying height of 76 nm,

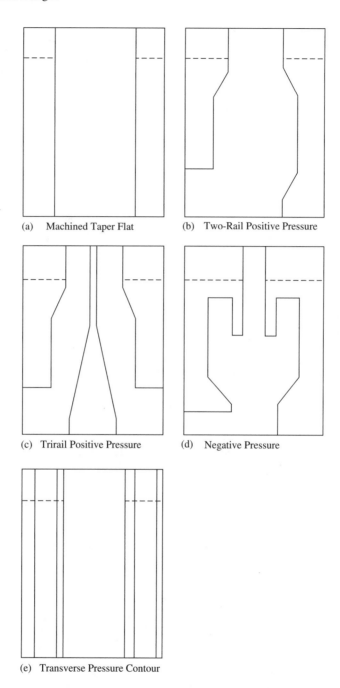

(a)   Machined Taper Flat   (b)   Two-Rail Positive Pressure

(c)   Trirail Positive Pressure   (d)   Negative Pressure

(e)   Transverse Pressure Contour

Figure 10.22 Air-bearing designs [17].

a 95-mm disk drive, 5400 RPM, and a skew angle range of −2 degrees at I.D. to 18 degrees at O.D. Results from trilayer and two-rail designs were similar. The TPC design consists of relatively thin rails tapering down to wider dimensions at the bottom of the rails. Figure 10.23a shows changes in flying height as a

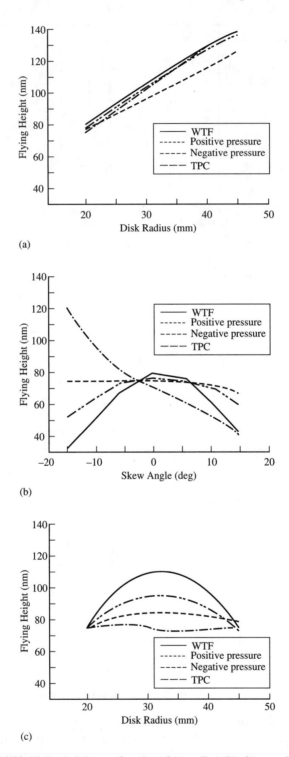

Figure 10.23 Flying height as a function of (a) radius, (b) skew angle, and (c) combined influence of radius and skew angle [17].

function of radius or velocity from I.D. to O.D., assuming zero skew angle. The MTF shows the largest change in flying height and positive pressure and TPC show significant changes, while the negative pressure slider shows a minimum difference in the flying heights. Figure 10.23b shows flying height as a function of skew angle for the four designs. Within the range of interest skew angle varies from −2 to 18 degrees. The combined effect of velocity and skew variations in the I.D.-to-O.D. range on the flying heights of four designs is plotted in Figure 10.23c. The negative pressure case shows 9-nm total variation, the TPC design can be minimized to about 4 nm by the compensation of opposite factors, whereas the MTF and positive pressure sliders have ranges of 17 and 36 nm, respectively. The shaped-rail positive pressure rails reduce the flying height variations compared to the MTF but still have a hump in the intermediate radii that is considered unacceptable for the low-flying-height environment. The TPC design can be tailored for minimum change in flying heights. However, this design is shown [17] as having wide manufacturing parameter sensitivity. Simulations indicate that the negative pressure design is the preferred path to constant flying heights.

10.7.2 Novel Slider Designs

The use of ion milling and photolithographic processing has provided a high degree of flexibility in slider footprint layouts. With these processes the slider's surface and the cavity space between rails can be shaped to tailor positive and negative pressure contours for fine adjustments of slider performance. Miniaturized sliders with low load requirements at short flying heights can be designed with relatively shallow negative pressure cavities. Figure 10.24 [18] shows the variation of two parameters of a slider, loading force and rail width, as its dimensions are reduced and flying heights are decreased from 100 to 50 nm. Loading force decreases as a cubic function of slider volume for a given flying height. Higher fly heights require increased loading, as shown in Figure 10.24a. Figure 10.24b indicates the required decrease in rail width if conventional parallel rails are used.

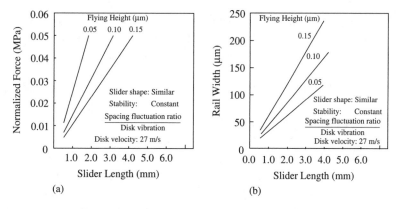

Figure 10.24 Loading force and rail widths as functions of slider dimensions [18].

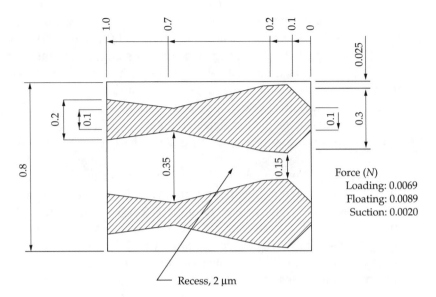

Figure 10.25 Shaped-rail negative pressure slider [18].

Reference [18] describes a 50-nm-flying-height negative pressure slider design miniaturized to one-fourth the size of an MTF minidesign. The footprint of the subpicoslider is shown in Figure 10.25. The rails are not tapered but are shaped to provide varying amounts of pressure profile along the length of the slider. The mean width of the rails is 0.195 mm, compared to the much thinner rails (of the order of 0.050 mm) required if straight rails were used. The cavity between rails is recessed and is shaped to provide negative pressure and adjustment of the loading center for optimum performance. Flying height as a function of velocity for three different depths of cavity depths is shown in Figure 10.26. The slider was nicknamed "guppy" by the authors due to the resemblance of its shaped rail to a fish. A similar type of rail design is often called an "hourglass" rail.

An *advanced air bearing* (AAB) has been described [19] that features hourglass-shaped rails, partially stepped edges along the rails, a negative pressure cavity created by the shaped rails, and a relieved leading edge (Figure 10.27). Due to the suction of the negative pressure cavity, flying height as a function of disk velocity has a gentle slope (Figure 10.28), compared to the straight rail design of an MTF (also called a catamaran). The slider appears to be tailored for under 100-nm flying height at the outer rail near the disk I.D. The large leading edge provides a high pitch angle, which reduces slider-disk interactions. Use of partially stepped edges for the shaped rails provides better control over the flying profile of this slider. Increased bearing stiffness, pitch stiffness, and improved TOV are other advantages of this design compared to the MTF minislider.

The concept of a negative pressure slider has been known for many years. When used with disks with particulate coatings, it was observed that the suction

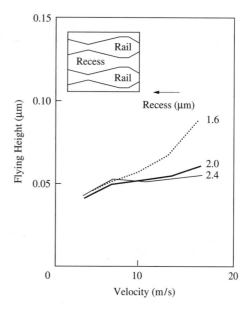

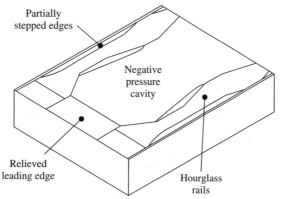

Figure 10.26 Flying height versus velocity of the shaped-rail slider [18].

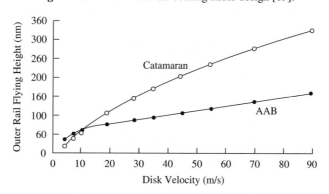

Figure 10.27 Advanced air-bearing slider design [19].

Figure 10.28 The AAB flying height versus disk velocity [19].

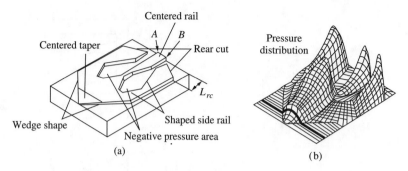

Figure 10.29 Shape and pressure distribution of "parasol" slider [20].

cavity at the ABS resulted in collection of disk particles and organic debris at the slider corners, gradually altering the flying characteristics of the slider. With a relatively smooth metallic disk surface and better understanding and control of lubricants, this issue has significantly diminished in importance. A recent slider design [20] addresses this concern along with the provision of smaller flying height for an MR head. Figure 10.29a shows the slider ABS features and Figure 10.29b its computed pressure distribution. Two shaped side rails and the central rail provide flying height insensitivity during the tendency to roll while accessing. The two cavities between the three rails result in negative pressure and contribute to constancy of flying height during change in linear velocity from inner to outer radii write/read operations. The novel feature of the slider, the central wedge-shaped taper at the leading edge, is meant to plow away debris and to reduce the probability of its being caught in the taper. Figure 10.30 shows flying height as a function of disk radius for a 65-mm disk drive. Nearly constant flying height is achieved as a result of the balance between flying height variations due to linear velocity and skew angle. The hump in the center is small, less than 6% attributed to the negative pressure cavities. The roll stiffness at the trailing-edge short rail is high. The worst-case drop of 4.5 nm was computed, due to the combined effect of 50 g seek acceleration and 1.5 m/s seek velocity during accessing. Experiments with a disk partially contaminated with cellulose showed no debris accumulation on the centered taper region of the slider.

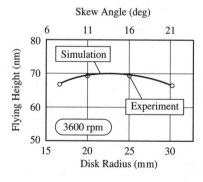

Figure 10.30 Flying height versus disk radius of parasol slider [20].

10.7.3 Tripad Slider Design [21]

This slider consists of two parallel rails with a short third rail or a pad at the trailing edge to accommodate a thin film head. Figure 10.31 shows the air-bearing surface footprint. The design has some similarities to the positive trirail design and shaped-rail concept discussed above. Two rails have no taper and do not extend to the trailing edge. They provide aerodynamic lift at the leading edge but avoid positive pressure areas at the trailing edge. A short pad at the trailing edge has high rolling stiffness and has minimum exposure to slider-disk interactions due to the small pad area. Because of the small pad area and roll tolerance, the flying height of the head can be designed significantly lower than conventional two-rail sliders. Figure 10.32 shows the flying height distribution of several sliders for 95-mm disk drives. In the figure, ABC refers to the air-bearing clearance and the y-axis scale is in microinches (1 microinch = 25.4 nm). The small pad area is also advantageous in reducing the "velocity to take off" parameter.

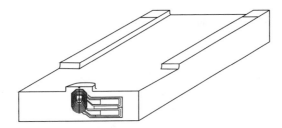

Figure 10.31 Tripad slider design [21].

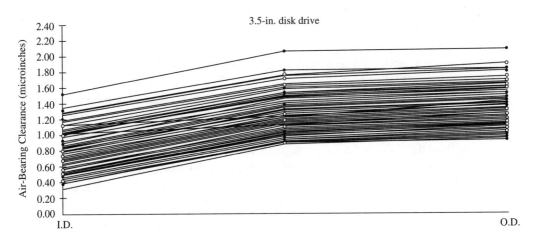

Figure 10.32 Radius versus flying heights of a batch of sliders [21].

10.8 ENVIRONMENT, PARTICLES, AND CHEMICAL CONTAMINATION

The close head-disk spacing required by current rigid-disk recording (less than 100 nm) demands the internal environment be free of contaminants. These can be in the form of loose debris from components, external contaminants, particles generated during operation, or magnetic particulate debris (flaking from actuator or motor magnets) that can be carried by the air during operation and land on the disk, erasing data. The effect of loose debris on air bearings has also been considered [22]. To protect against these types of problems during operation, disk drives are designed with internal filters to remove particulate debris. In addition, some components may be sealed with coatings to prevent flaking of material. This is to ensure that the interior of the disk drive is maintained at Class 1 (< 1 particle/ft^3) for the life of the product. This ensures data reliability and long product life (currently 500,000 to 1 million hours mean time before failure).

10.9 CONTACT RECORDING APPROACHES

The goal of recording "in contact" is to operate the head and disk as close as possible. This will achieve the maximum performance with the available head, media, and signal processing. Although one might note that physical contact recording regularly occurs in tape storage systems, the constraints of media roughness, lubricant thickness, and air-bearing formation at the interface may mean the magnetic separation is greater than the physical "contact" spacing. For disk drive technology, the goal is more challenging, with additional factors of air-bearing design, higher velocities, lubricant, and head and media tribology complicating the problem further. Presently, achieving the reliable design of a contact recording system for disk drive technology remains an area of active research and development. Recent progress in lubricant and head and media design indicates that reliable in-contact recording may soon be realized.

The fundamental reasons underlying contact recording are the rapid drop of the writing head field from the gap during writing and the Wallace spacing *loss factor* $\exp(-2\pi d/\lambda)$ affecting the read back signal. Lambda (λ) is the written wavelength on the disk, and d is the magnetic head-disk *clearance*. Refer to Section 3.14 for additional discussion of this topic. In contact, d is made as close to zero as possible, making the Wallace spacing factor near its maximum value, 1. It is convenient to express the spacing loss factor in decibels (see Section 3.14):

$$Spacing\ loss\ (dB)\ =\ 54.6\left(\frac{d}{\lambda}\right) \tag{10.7}$$

A simple rule to remember from this is that at a magnetic head-disk spacing of 0.1, the recorded wavelength on the disk will result in about a 5-dB signal reduction on readback. For current high-density recording on rigid disks, the effective recorded wavelength is 0.5 μm, meaning that maintaining a head-disk magnetic clearance of 50 nm is critical to avoid significant signal loss! For future technologies in which the recorded wavelengths are less than 100 nm, the maintenance of head-disk clearance in the contact regime of 10 nm and below will be critical.

10.9.1 Head Spacing Controller

A demonstration of the advantages of contact recording for a rigid-disk system has been made [23]. A specially designed *head spacing controller* was built to allow recording at arbitrary (and continuously variable) spacing. The head-and-disk spacing was measured by a capacitance bridge. This electronic measurement was then fed into a servo amplifier with *feed forward* runout compensation. This allows the head spacing to be accurately controlled, in spite of the "runout," or nonflatness of the disk. The servo system drives a stack of piezoelectric transducers on which the head is mounted.

Using this system, the advantages of recording at closer head-disk spacing were clearly demonstrated (Figure 10.33). For example, at a recorded wavelength of 1 μm (2000 fc/mm), the amplitude improvements from the Wallace spacing factor were clearly seen. In addition, the finer features in the spectral amplitude roll-off curve, such as the effects of the finite pole tip thicknesses and the "gap null" at 3100 fc/mm, were easily visible. Although not intended for product-level implementation, the head spacing controller allowed recording toward the contact regime to be well quantified.

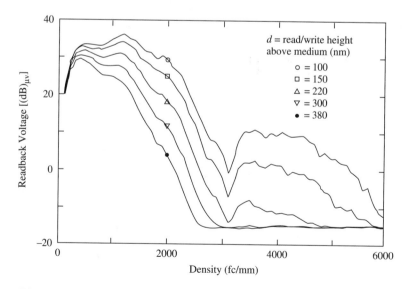

Figure 10.33 Spectral amplitude roll-off curves made using the head spacing controller [23].

10.9.2 Taildragger Head

An example of a head designed for operational contact recording is the hybrid *taildragger* head (Figure 10.34) [24]. This head can have a standard air-bearing design that incorporates a piezoelectric bending or flexure beam (Figure 10.35). The magnetic head element attached to the end of the flexing beam can be moved into contact with the disk by a voltage applied to the beam. The standard air bearing can be designed to fly over the disk at a spacing much higher than would normally be the case, reducing the likelihood of wear or damage. The air bearing also easily compensates for the disk runout, or nonflatness. The taildragger design also takes advantage of the fact that the time spent reading and writing on a rigid disk

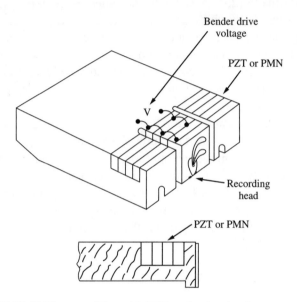

Figure 10.34 Taildragger slider with PZT active bender for contact recording [24].

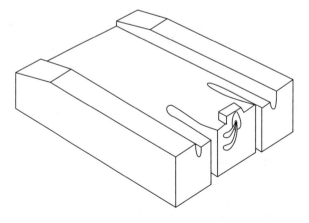

Figure 10.35 Air-bearing surface or a taildragger slider [24].

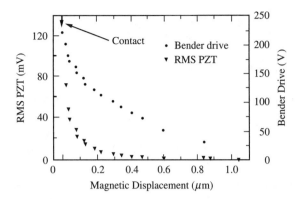

Figure 10.36 Bender displacement versus PZT drive voltage and contact signal [24].

is a small fraction of the time the disk drive is in operation. The lift provided by the air under the slider's rails is balanced by the spring force of the suspension. This reduces to a very low value the contact force on the disk when the head flexure beam is lowered.

Recording studies carried out using prototype taildragger heads showed clearly that the spacing between the head and disk could be continuously varied and recording in contact could be achieved. To further develop the design, a few challenges remain to be addressed. These include the relatively high driving voltage (30–50 V) (Figure 10.36) needed by the piezo flexure element, the additional electrical leads required, and the processing and assembly issues for a slider of two very dissimilar materials. A taildragger-like slider design that meets these challenges could provide a path practical for contact recording on a hard disk drive.

10.9.3 Continuous Contact

Two more recent approaches to contact for rigid disk drive recording utilize concepts that are close to current disk drive design. Both dispense with a self-acting air bearing using a combination of liquid lubrication with a lightly loaded head-slider assembly.

The continuously lubricated interface for contact recording has been described in a U.S. patent [25]. In this design, the disk drive is saturated with a proprietary lightweight lubricant. During operation, the spinning disks act as a pump to circulate the lubricant. The head used in this "Visqus" design is a relatively standard slider with a spring suspension. The air-bearing rail surface of the slider is replaced with a simple arrangement of pads at each corner. The lubricating fluid flows under the pads on the slider element, providing a stable, wear-free interface.

Head-disk spacings to 25 nm and below have been reported using this continuously lubricated interface. Prototype-level implementations of the scheme have featured wick designs with a filter for continuous reflow of the lubricant during operation. In addition, long-term operation will require compatibility of the lubricant with other materials within the drive housing.

10.9.4 Integrated Head Suspension Design

The design for a contact recording head suspension element, called Flexhead, suitable for perpendicular recording on rigid disk drives has been proposed [26] (see Section 11.6). In this design, the magnetic head element is contained in a small pad geometry integrated into a long, thin flexurelike suspension (Figure 11.15). The loading force of the head is very small ($\ll$ 1 g), leading to little head wear. It has been reported that wear of 4–5 μm of the head over a seven-year lifetime may be expected. This amount of wear may have a negligible effect on the performance of the perpendicular pole-type recording head. Recording performance studies at the Censtor company have shown that head/media spacing of 25 nm and below may be achieved.

REFERENCES

[1] R. A. Scranton, "The Era of Magnetoresistive Heads," paper presented at the IDEMA Symposium, Santa Clara, CA, February 1994. (Figure 10.7 Courtesy of E. Grochowski).

[2] W. A. Gross, *Gas Film Lubrication*, John Wiley & Sons, New York, 1980.

[3] S. Fukui and R. Kaneko, "Analysis of Ultra-Thin Gas Film Lubrication Based on Linearized Boltzmann Equation: First Report—Derivation of the Generalized Lubrication Equation Including Thermal Creep Flow," *ASME J. Trib.*, 110 (1988), pp. 253–262.

[4] Y. Mitsuya, "Molecular Mean Free Path Effects in Gas Lubricated Slider Bearings," *Bull. JSME*, 22:167 (1979), pp. 863–670.

[5] C. Lin, "Techniques for the Measurements of Air-Bearing Separation—A Review," *IEEE Trans. Magn.*, MAG-9, (1973), p. 673.

[6] G. R. Briggs and P. G. Herkart, "Determining Disk Memory Ceramic Slider Flying Characteristics," *IEEE Trans. Magn.*, MAG-7 (1971), p. 418.

[7] S. E. Millman, R. F. Hoyt, D. E. Horne, and B. Beye, "Motion Pictures of In-situ Air Bearing Dynamics," *IEEE Trans. Magn.*, MAG-22 (1986), p. 1031.

[8] J. M. Fleischer and C. Lin, "Infrared Laser Interferometer for Measuring Air-Bearing Separation," *IBM J. Res. Devel.*, MAG-18 (1974), pp. 529–533.

[9] Y. Mizoshita, K. Aruga, and T. Yamada, "Dynamic Characteristics of a Magnetic Head Slider," *IEEE Trans. Magn.*, MAG-21 (1985), p. 1509.

[10] G. L. Best, D. E. Horne, A. Chiou, and H. Sussner, "Precise Optical Measurement of Slider Dynamics," *IEEE Trans. Magn.*, MAG-22 (1986), p. 1017.

[11] G. L. Best, "Comparison of Optical and Capacitive Measurements of Slider Dynamics," *IEEE Trans. Magn.*, MAG-23 (1987), p. 3453.

[12] C. Lacey, R. Shelor, A. J. Cormier, and F. E. Talke, "Interferometric Measurement of Disk/Slider Spacing: The Effect of Phase Shift on Reflection," *IEEE Trans. Magn.,* MAG-29 (1993), p. 3906.

[13] C. E. Yeack-Scranton, "Novel Piezoelectric Transducers to Monitor Head-Disk Interactions," *IEEE Trans. Magn.,* MAG-22 (1986), p. 1011.

[14] A. Wallash, "Reproduction of Slider Vibrations During Head/Disk Interactions Using PZT Sensors," *IEEE Trans. Magn.,* MAG-24 (1988), p. 2763.

[15] J. K. Lee, J. Enguero, M. Smallen, and A. Chao, "The Influence of Head Parameters on Take-Off Velocity," *IEEE Trans. Magn.,* MAG-29 (1993), p. 3915.

[16] K. B. Klaassen, J. C. L. van Peppen, and R. E. Eaton, "Non-Invasive Take-Off/Touch-Down Velocity Measurements," *IEEE Trans. Magn.,* MAG-30 (1994), p. 4164.

[17] D. S. Chhabra, S. A. Bolasna, K. D. Lee, and L. S. Samuelson, "Air Bearing Design Considerations for Constant Flying Height Applications," *IEEE Trans. Magn.,* MAG-30 (1994), p. 477.

[18] S. Yoneoka, M. Katayama, T. Ohwe, Y. Mizoshita, and T. Yamada, "A Negative Pressure Microhead Slider for Ultraslow Spacing with Uniform Flying Height," *IEEE Trans. Magn.,* MAG-27 (1991), p. 5085.

[19] C. Hardie, A. Menon, P. Crane, and D. Egbert, "Analysis and Performance Characteristics of the Seagate Advanced Air Bearing Slider," *IEEE Trans. Magn.,* MAG-30 (1994), p. 424.

[20] M. Matsumoto, Y. Takeuchi, H. Agari, and H. Takahashi, "Design and Performance of Novel Air Bearing Slider," *IEEE Trans. Magn.,* MAG-30 (1994), p. 4158.

[21] C. Leung, "Tri Pad Technology," paper presented at DISKCON, September 28, 1994.

[22] M. Tokuyama and S. Hirose, "Dynamic Flying Characteristics of Magnetic Head Slider with Dust," *J. Tribol.,* 116 (1994), p. 95.

[23] M. Jefferson, "A Variable Head to Disk Spacing Controller for Magnetic Recording on Rigid Disks," *IEEE Trans. Magn.,* MAG-24 (1988), p. 2736.

[24] C. E. Yeack-Scranton, V. D. Khanna, K. F. Etzold, and A. P. Praino, "An Active Slider for Practical Contact Recording," *IEEE Trans. Magn.,* MAG-26 (1990), p. 2478.

[25] W. W. French and J. U. Lemke, "Information Recording Apparatus with a Liquid Bearing," U. S. Patent 5,193,046, September 25, 1990.

[26] H. J. Hamilton, "Integrated Magnetic Read/Write Head/Flexure/Conductor Structure," U.S. Patent 5,111,351, June 5, 1991.

11

Future Trends in
Technology

11.1 INTRODUCTION

This chapter reviews the state of the art in disk drive technology and projects expected advances. It summarizes information presented in other chapters through discussion of critical disk drive parameters and their advances for future disk drives. New concepts likely to play an important role in advancing the technology are discussed. The next section describes the historical progress in disk drives and projects areal density increases to the end of this decade. Three important parameters influencing areal density are flying height, linear bit density, and track density. The progress in these three parameters is examined with graphical representation of the past record and extrapolation of the trends to the year 2000.

It is a common practice in the storage industry to make projections about short- and long-term developments in components and drive technology. Historical trends provide a meaningful basis for these predictions. Other ingredients for the predictions are demonstrated progress in research and development (R&D) and possibilities of technical breakthroughs. Short-term projections contribute to the judgment about one to two generations of components and products in the market. Long-term predictions are used for estimating resource allocations, product planning, profitability, and so on; looking into the future trends may also help professionals to plan their careers. Hence, there is more to the examination of these predictions than curiosity. It is believed that the industry is poised for more rapid progress for the next decade than projected by the historical measure. The following factors are cited for the change from the past:

- Current and potential markets for the technology products
- Highly competitive industry infrastructure
- Demonstrated and projected progress in key components of the technology
- Availability of trained and talented scientists and engineers.

These are powerful reasons for the expected progress. However, there are many serious challenges ahead, and there are alternative paths to meet these challenges. Section 11.3 describes the technical issues, conflicting requirements of the components, and compromises faced by drive designers.

The same section also discusses scaling of components for achieving high densities. Multigigabit demonstrations in the last five years are analyzed to exemplify scaling procedures and to give a feel of the technical challenges. Another objective of the section is to consolidate information presented in various chapters in this book by connecting this knowledge to multigigabit recording density demonstrations and other high-density projections. The progress in future disk drive technology will come from several directions. Different topics, with a variety of information on giant magnetoresistance, spin valve head, optical servo, perpendicular recording, and application-oriented issues such as small drives and arrays, are covered later in this chapter. The last section summarizes long-term prospects for the technology.

11.2 PROJECTIONS AND PREDICTIONS OF TECHNOLOGY PARAMETERS

Figure 11.1 shows areal density increases in the disk drive industry since 1970. The data is basically the same as that described in Table 1.2 of Chapter 1. The trend depicts IBM products, as IBM has been the trendsetter in density advances over the last three decades. The density increases from 1970 through 1990 can be approximately described by a straight line on a logarithmic plot. This line is shown in the figure and is represented by the following equation:

$$\text{Density (Mb/in.}^2) = 10^{0.1(\text{year}-1970)} \tag{11.1}$$

Through this equation one can see that (1) density doubled every three years; (2) density increased tenfold every decade; and (3) yearly density increase is about 26%. The yearly increase in density is called *compound growth rate,* or CGR. Based on the extrapolation of this trend, a gigabit-per-square-inch density is predicted for the year 2000. However, with introduction of the MR head in 1991, the trend in density increase has accelerated. A near gigabit (0.923 Gb)-per-square-inch density product already was introduced in 1995. The changed direction in areal density trend is represented by the dashed line in Figure 11.1. An equation to represent this line is given by

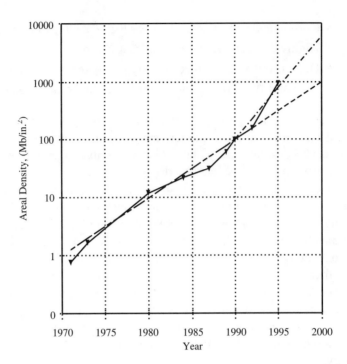

Figure 11.1 Areal density versus years.

$$\text{Density} = 100 \times 10^{0.178(\text{year}-1990)} \qquad (11.2)$$

According to this equation, CGR during the years 1990 to 2000 is almost doubled, to 51% from the earlier CGR of 26%. According to this equation, the density should increase 60 times in the decade from the year 1990 to the year 2000. This CGR puts the areal density of 6 Gb/in.^{2} in the year 2000. A linear density of 250 Kb/in. and track density of 25 Kt/in. is one plausible combination to achieve 6 Gb/in.^{2} Limitations of linear and track densities are discussed later in the section. More optimistic predictions have put the CGR of 60% for the decade, and it projects relatively higher density (about 8 Gb/in.^{2}) by the year 2000 [1]. Analytical and trend lines are revealing; however, a better perspective is offered by demonstrated results and an understanding of factors affecting hardware development.

IBM scientists presented the results of 1 Gb/in.^{2} density demonstration through a series of papers at the 1990 Intermag[2–5]. In a similar test-stand demonstration, Hitachi scientists presented results of 2 Gb/in.^{2} in 1991[6–8]. In 1995, an IBM group demonstrated 3 Gb/in.^{2} density on a test stand [9]. These experimental evidences, with an announced 65-mm drive with 10-GB capacity and areal density as high as 923 Mb/in.^{2} in 1995, give assurance that the projected progress in disk drives for the decade is reasonable. Rapid advances in MR-head technology, low-noise thin film media, and PRML sampling channels are the major reasons for this progress.

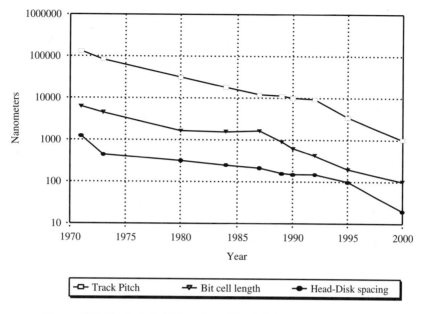

Figure 11.2 Track pitch, bit length, and head-disk spacing versus years.

Figure 11.2 shows the evolution of bit length, track pitch, and head-disk spacings in the last three decades. The y axis dimension is in nanometers. Head-disk spacing data points for the Nineties are not related to specific products but are indicators of the state of the art in respective years. The points at the year 2000 for track pitch and bit-cell size are based on assumed 250 Kb/in. and 25 Kt/in. densities. One gigabit density demonstration [2] had about 76 nm head-media spacing, the projected spacing of 20 nm for the year 2000 correspond to near contact recording. For dimensional comparison the thickness of one human hair is about 80,000 nm, and the wavelength of visible light is 550 nm. At 20 nm spacing, the head and medium are considered in virtual contact. Contact recording is discussed in Chapter 10 and partly in Section 11.7. Several combinations of bit and track densities can result in a density of 6 Gb/in.^{2} The next section discusses multigigabit density demonstrations and challenges of high density recording.

11.3 MULTIGIGABIT DENSITY DEMONSTRATIONS

With the introduction of the MR head to disk drive recording, there has been much discussion on the potential and limits of this technology. This has led to the building of prototypes or engineering demonstrations that may pave the way to future products as well as establish benchmarks for further exploration of the technology. In the last five years, three such efforts have been presented. Table 11.1 provides the summary of data generated out of these activities. The first such experiments in

TABLE 11.1 Density Demonstration Parameters (1, 2, and 3 Gb/in.^{2})^a

Parameter	1 Gb/in.^{2}, (1990, IBM)	2 Gb/in.^{2}, (1991, Hitachi)	3 Gb/in.^{2}, (1995, IBM)
Linear density, Kb/in. ($\times$39.4 b/mm)	158	120	185
Flux change density (fc/mm)	7000	5315	8194
50% density (fc/mm)	4190	3150	5000
Track density, t/mm (t/in.)	250 (6350)	670 (17,000)	665 (16,900)
Track pitch (μm)	4	1.5	1.5
Write width (μm)	3.5	1.2	1.4
MR read width (μm)	2.0	1	1.1
$M_r\delta$, in 10^{-3} emu/cm^2 ($\times$10 mA in SI)	0.73	1.5	0.53
H_c in Oe ($\times$80 A/m in SI)	1800	2120	1900
PW$_{50}$ (nm)	344	NA	NA
Head/media spacing (nm)	76	>50	<80
Signal sensitivity, μV/μm (p-p)	300	420	400
MR gap shield to shield (μm)	0.25	0.3	0.2
MR thickness (nm)	15	15	12

^{a}Times 1.55 Mb/mm^2.

1990 (IBM) demonstrated 1 Gb/in.^{2} density with a dual-element MR head [2–5]. In 1991 all the components for 2 Gb/in.^{2} density were demonstrated (Hitachi) [6–8]. In 1995, an MR head, thin film medium, electronic channel were realized that shows the capability of 3 Gb/in.^{2} areal density on test-stand experiments (IBM) [9]. Some additional comments are given here to help in understanding the issues involved in each case.

1. One gigabit per square inch density [2–5]. For this experiment, the MR read element and inductive write element were constructed in a PMR (piggyback MR, Section 6.4) structure. Soft adjacent layer (SAL) biasing was used for transverse bias, and pattern exchange biasing was employed to eliminate domain noise in the MR sensor. The MR sensor was shielded with a shield-to-shield gap of 250 nm. The write element had Permalloy poles, eight turns, and provided 3.5 μm track width, making a track pitch of 4 μm and track density of 6350 t/in. Relatively low $M_r\delta$ of 0.73×10^{-3} emu/cm^2 is used in this design. A smaller $M_r\delta$ results in shorter PW$_{50}$ (see Figure 6.33), leading to a higher linear density, but it reduces pulse sensitivity. In comparison, 2-Gb experiments used $M_r\delta$ of 1.5×10^{-3} emu/cm^2. A 2-Gb head had a comparatively large (300-nm) gap between shields. Both these factors possibly contributed to the relatively low linear density of 120 Kb/in.

The choice of $M_r\delta$ plays an important role in a compromise between signal sensitivity and pulse width. Development of media for gigabit density was a major effort. This group developed a fine-grain CoPtCr magnetic layer with a grain isolation approach to achieve low-noise, high-coercivity media for this study.

The 158 Kb/in. linear density was obtained with optimization in $M_r\delta$ and use of a PRML channel. It is instructive to calculate the advantage gained from the PRML channel compared to the peak detection (1, 7) code in this case. It is assumed that use of peak detection requires 50% resolution. According to Table 11.1, 4190 fc/mm corresponds to 50% density. Referring to Table 8.1, the ratio bpi/(fc/mm) for (1, 7) code is given as 33.87; hence, bpi with (1, 7) code is obtained as 4190 × 33.87 = 142 Kb/in. The PRML provided 158 Kb/in., or 11.26%, extra linear bit density over the peak detection channel. Section 8.14 discussed a figure of merit of user bits per PW_{50} (or P_{50}) of the pulse. In Table 11.1, PW_{50} is given as 344 nm. Using Table 8.1 for the PRML of 7000 fc/mm, bits per millimeter is calculated as 6225. Taking the reciprocal of bits per millimeter and converting it to nanometers results in 161 nm per user bit. The ratio 344/161 = 2.11 is the number of user bits accommodated within a half-pulse width (P_{50}). A similar procedure for (1, 7) code results in a figure-of-merit ratio of 1.93. Note that the real performance assessments of different coding channels are complex. The preceding analysis is intended only to show the use of code formulas with practical numbers. In Section 8.18, the ratio P_{50}/s at 50% resolution for a Lorentzian pulse was obtained as 1.39. For the gigabit experiments, P_{50} is 344 nm, and spacing s can be obtained from flux changes per millimeter of 4190 as $s = 239$ nm. To check how close this demonstration pulse compares with the Lorentzian pulse, the ratio $P_{50}/s = 344/239 = 1.44$, which is fairly close.

2. Two gigabit per square inch density [6–8]. This demonstration emphasized a high track density of 17,000 t/in. Write-head width of 1.2 μm and MR read width of 1 μm resulted in a track pitch of 1.5 μm. Optical servos with dual-stage actuators for magnetic recording were separately demonstrated to validate such a high track density potential. Section 11.5 discusses this servo arrangement. Figure 6.15 describes the structure of the PMR head. The MR shields were made of CoTaZr amorphous material to provide a smooth surface for MR layer deposition. The MR sensor was shunt biased with an Nb conductor and used a high current density of 3×10^7 A/cm^2. For domain stability, longitudinal bias was provided by exchange material across the full length of the sensor. Write head poles were made of Fe-based multilayers that provided a high B_s of 20 kG (2 T). High-coercivity medium was made of a double layer to optimize separate parameters. The head-disk clearance of > 50 nm was used for the experiments. An advanced PRML channel was used to get a linear density of

120 Kb/in. This group developed a two-layered medium (CoCrPt on top of CoCrPtSi) where the top layer was responsible for high coercivity and the lower layer was optimized for low noise.

3. Three gigabit per square inch density. This demonstration extends the high linear density exhibited in the 1-Gb study from 158 Kb/in. to 185 Kb/in. A new head is developed with small track width, comparable to that developed for the 2-Gb study. The $M_r\delta$ is further reduced to 0.53×10^{-3} emu/cm^2, possibly to reduce P_{50}. Reduction in signal sensitivity (see Figure 6.33) due to smaller $M_r\delta$ is possibly compensated by the reduction of sensor thickness to 12 nm and sensor height to about $\frac{1}{2}$ μm.

There may be several combinations of track and bit densities for achieving high densities. We consider two options to achieve 6 Gb/in.^{2} density. One is contact recording, which emphasizes linear density as high as 600 Kb/in. along with track density of 10 Kt/in. However, such a high linear density has not yet been demonstrated with longitudinal recording. With perpendicular recording, up to 650 Kfc/in. has been shown to exist [10]. Perpendicular recording is discussed in Section 11.5. With this option, the track pitch is 2.5 μm, and an advanced form of conventional servo technique may be usable. Another problem with this option is the high data rate along with high rotational speed (10,000 RPM) of the drive. For example, a 2.5-in. drive with an inner diameter of 40 mm at 10,000 RPM would result in a 60-MB/s data rate. Write and read electronics to handle such data rates would pose a serious challenge. A second alternative to achieve 6 Gb/in.^{2} appears more plausible and is assumed in Figures 11.1 and 11.2. The optical servo technique of the 2 Gb/in.^{2} can possibly be extended to 25 Kt/in. from the demonstrated 17 Kt/in. The required linear density of 250 Kb/in. then results in a data rate of 25 MB/s, which may be more feasible with advances in semiconductor technology. Validation of 185 Kb/in. in 3-Gb demonstrations further supports the possibility of achieving 250 Kb/in. by the year 2000.

Following is a list of areas currently pursued from which the path for high-density recording will emerge, depending on the successes in one or several of these areas:

- Optical servo for magnetic drives (Section 11.5)
- Dual-slider approach to follow the magnetic track (see Section 10.9, on the taildragger, the main slider to provide aerodynamic floating, a miniature part of which includes the head for close-to-contact recording)
- Forms of giant magnetoresistance effects (Section 11.4)
- Perpendicular recording (Section 11.7)
- Contact recording and low-mass flexible head for writing and reading on magnetic media (Sections 11.7 and 10.9)
- Noncontact pressure bearings for disk drive motors to reduce nonrepeatable runouts and TMR

- High-density circuit chips for handling enhanced data rates and further integration of drive functions in smaller packages
- Advanced sampling channels and DSP for servo, data, and head motion control
- Glass and ceramic substrates to provide smooth magnetic media surfaces that promote smaller head/media spacing
- Multilayered media
- Emergence of new materials and ideas from consumer electronics.

A crucial research activity is the development of more sensitive magnetic sensors. The next section describes the principles of giant magnetoresistance (GMR) and implementation of one form of GMR in a disk drive head.

11.4 GIANT MAGNETORESISTANCE AND SPIN-VALVE MAGNETIC HEAD

11.4.1 GMR

The MR head discussed in Chapter 6 and currently used in disk drives depends on the phenomenon called *anisotropic magnetoresistance* (AMR). Operation of the AMR sensor [made of a stripe of Permalloy (NiFe)] is described in Section 6.2. The maximum increase in resistivity with the field for NiFe is about 2.5% at room temperature. Certain alloys of cobalt show higher magnetoresistivity, but they have higher intrinsic anisotropy H_k. High magnetic anisotropy causes less change in magnetic rotation with the small magnetic fields associated with magnetic disk recording, and hence the overall sensitivity ($\Delta R/H_{app}$) of the sensor does not improve significantly. It is imperative that submicrometer track widths and high linear densities require an advanced form of MR head.

A 1988 publication [11] reported the observation of large magnetoresistance in multilayered structures composed of alternating magnetic and nonmagnetic films (Figure 11.3). The MR effect approaching 80% at 4.2°K temperature with 20 kG (2 T) has been noted. This high-MR phenomenon was termed giant magnetoresistance (GMR). In this section we shall first describe elements of GMR, then depict the concept of "spin valve," which is a practical embodiment of GMR for application to recording head, and then summarize spin-valve head characteristics. With the advent of molecular beam epitaxy (MBE) developed for semiconductor technology, it became possible to create magnetic multilayered structures composed of alternating layers of ferromagnetic materials such as Fe, Ni, Co, or NiFe and non-magnetic metallic layers of Cr, Ag, Au, and so on. Highly crystalline multilayered structures thus deposited exhibited novel physical properties not realized in bulk ferromagnetic materials. Between 30 and 60 bilayers of alternating Fe and Cr films of 0.9–9 nm thickness were employed in the first reported GMR studies [11].

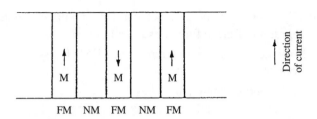

Figure 11.3 Giant magnetoresistance, multilayered structure.

Figure 11.3 shows a segment of the multilayered structure of this type. For the GMR it is necessary that the adjacent ferromagnetic layers be magnetized in reverse directions. The magnetic coupling between adjacent ferromagnetic layers and appropriate thicknesses of the nonmagnetic layers results in reverse magnetization between these layers. The resistance of the structure is highest in the absence of an external magnetic field. As the magnetic field is applied to reverse magnetization in intermediate layers, the resistance of the structure drops. The resultant curves of magnetic field versus resistance are similar to the MR sensor characterization curve in Section 6.2, Figure 6.4a.

Figure 11.4 indicates GMRs in three such cases. Notice that the material layers are an order of magnitude thinner than those used for AMR head films. Following are other interesting points relevant to the GMR effect.

1. As the nonmagnetic layer increases in thickness, the GMR effect diminishes. The magnetic exchange between alternate layers that gives rise to magnetization reversals in adjacent layers diminishes exponentially as the interlayer (Cr in this case) thickness is increased. For GMR, the interlayer thickness must be of the order of the electron mean free path in the nonmagnetic layer so that electrons can freely migrate between magnetic layers.

2. Low temperature of 4.2 K (near liquid helium) is required to observe large GMR. The GMR decreases linearly with temperature in the range of 4.2 K (liquid helium temperature) to 300 K (27°C).

3. Very large external magnetic fields are required to see large GMR. The exchange coupling between adjacent magnetic layers through a thin nonmagnetic layer is very strong, and a large external field is required to reverse magnetization direction in antiferromagnetic films. Notice in the figure that the fields required to saturate the structure from a high-resistance (0 field) to a low-resistance state diminish as the thickness of the Cr layer increases. However, GMR sensitivity also diminishes at the same time.

The principles of GMR are described in several papers. A good source of information and bibliography is given in [12] (Chap. 2.4). A simple and easy-to-understand explanation of GMR is found in [13]. In spite of the appealing potential of this type of GMR, difficulties in processing the structure, its insensitivity to small fields

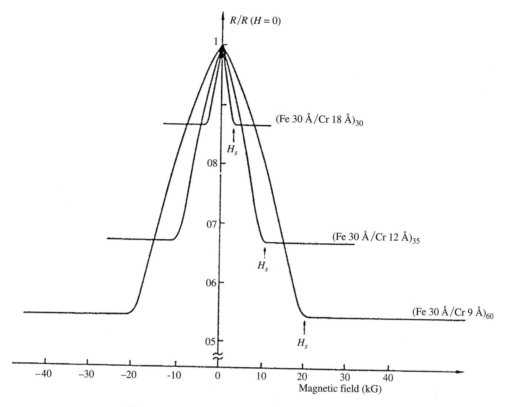

Figure 11.4 GMR properties of FeCr sandwich layers [11].

(available from recorded media), and the requirement of a low temperature make it difficult to implement as a head sensor. Hence, numerous research laboratories and academic institutions around the world have been engaged in finding new structures that would be more suitable for disk drive application. The result of one such effort is the discovery of the "spin valve."

11.4.2 Spin Valve

Experiments on sandwich structures consisting of two uncoupled ferromagnetic films separated by a nonmagnetic film were demonstrated to exhibit a relatively large MR effect at low fields and room temperature [14]. The reason this structure was named "spin valve" will become clear with the discussion of its operation. The term spin valve refers to the sandwich structure shown in Figure 11.5a. The preferred ferromagnetic layers M_1 and M_2 are usually NiFe or Co. The nonmagnetic metal layer of Cu, Ag, or Au is thin (about 2 nm) to provide free passage of electrons from one ferromagnetic layer to the other. The property of a spin-valve trilayer structure is that its resistance is proportional to the magnetization angle between two magnetic layers. For operational convenience, the magnetization in layer M_2 is pinned in a specific direction. An antiferromagnetic layer of FeMn is

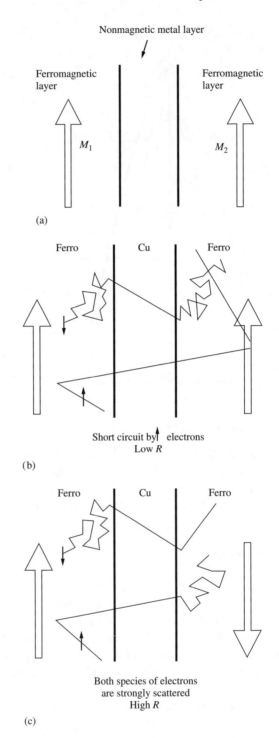

Figure 11.5 (a) Spin-valve trilayer structure; (b) electron trajectories in the spin-valve sandwich for parallel alignment of magnetizations; (c) electron trajectories in the spin-valve sandwich for antiparallel alignment of magnetizations [14].

used to pin the magnetization in M_2. The pinning property of FeMn is discussed in Section 2.16, and its utilization in the reduction of Barkhausen noise in an MR head is described in Section 6.13.

A simplified explanation of the operation of a spin-valve trilayer follows. It has been known that, in ferromagnetic materials, scattering of electrons depends on the spin on the carriers. Resistivity is proportional to the scattering of electrons. In NiFe, for example, the resistivity for electrons with spin in a parallel direction to the magnetization can be 20 times the resistivity of electrons with antiparallel direction. This difference arises out of the existence of available states or lack of them in the ferromagnetic crystal for the two different types of electrons. Figure 11.5b shows the basic spin-valve trilayer, with magnetization directions indicated by large arrows and electrons of parallel and antiparallel spins designated by small arrows. The current through the trilayer is contributed by electrons zigzagging between two ferromagnetic layers via a thin nonmagnetic low-resistivity layer.

In Figure 11.5b, the electrons with spins parallel to the magnetization direction experience very little scattering and hence provide a low-resistance path. The electrons with antiparallel spins are highly scattered, and their resistance is shunted by the low resistance of up-spin electrons. The trilayer experiences relatively low resistance. The magnetization in the M_2 layer is now reversed, as seen in Figure 11.5c. Electrons of both spins now suffer scattering in one or the other layer, and the total resistance of the structure is thus increased. If magnetization of one side of the trilayer (M_2) is pinned and M_1 is gradually rotated from a parallel to an antiparallel direction, the resistance of the structure increases in proportion to the cosine of the angle of magnetizations of the two layers M_1 and M_2. This is the characteristic of spin-valve operation. Notice that the spin valve is sensitive at low fields because the ferromagnetic layers are uncoupled; hence a small magnetic field from the magnetic media can rotate the magnetization in one layer relative to the other.

11.4.3 Spin-Valve Read Head

Figure 11.6 [15] shows the schematic of a spin-valve read sensor for disk drive application. The trilayer consists of 100 Å NiFe/25 Å Cu/22 Å Co. The magnetization in M_2 (the cobalt layer) is pinned in a direction that is 90° to the current flow by depositing a layer of 110 Å of FeMn exchange layer on top. The sensor was constructed using a DC magnetron sputtering, in contrast to the early GMR multilayers, which required MBE. The magnetoresistance observed in the "as-deposited" sensor is shown in Figure 11.7. The MR effect ΔR is proportional to the cosine of an angle $(\theta_1 - \theta_2)$ of magnetizations between ferromagnetic layers. The sensor for Gb/in.^{2} density had a track width of 2 μm and stripe height of 1 μm and was centered in a shielded gap of 0.25 μm. It had a net spin-valve MR coefficient of 3.5% and a resultant signal sensitivity of between 750 and 1000 μV/μm of track width when flown at a head-disk clearance of 37.5 nm.

The demonstration of a 1-Gb-density spin-valve was done with the read head structure. The writing in a test stand was done with a separate write head.

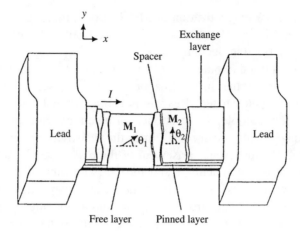

Figure 11.6 Spin-valve sensor as a recording head [15].

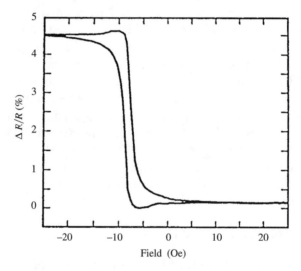

Figure 11.7 MR response of the NiFe-Cu-Co-FeMn spin-valve sensor in as-deposited film [15].

Because of the linearity of the spin-valve sensor coefficient, higher medium magnetization thickness product ($M_r\delta = 1.25 \times 10^{-3}$ emu/cm^2) was usable, compared to that (0.73×10^{-3} emu/cm^2) for the AMR head discussed in Section 11.2. A 1-Gb-density demonstration goal was realized with the spin-valve sensor, with the potential for further extension and optimization of the technology in the future.

With numerous materials and processing techniques being explored, the chances of discovering appropriate structures for magnetic disk recording are high. The availability of highly sensitive GMR sensors may open up avenues for numerous applications beyond their use in disk drives. Larger and lower cost nonvolatile magnetoresistive memories can become possible with GMR. The position sensitivity of the GMR sensor may open up its use for machine tools, automobile brakes, and safety systems.

11.5 OPTICAL SERVO FOR MAGNETIC RECORDING

One of the advantages of optical disk recording is its high track density, made possible with its embedded optical servo. It is natural that a scheme of combining the optical servo to maximize track density with magnetic recording to maximize linear density can provide very high areal densities. This idea has been implemented for a floppy disk called a "floptical drive," which uses a closed-loop optical servo to increase floppy disk track density from 135 to 1250 t/in. The servo pattern of pits is optically inscribed on the floppy disk at a track pitch distance of 20 μm. Figure 11.8 [16] shows the arrangement of a light-emitting diode (LED), reflecting a groove in the media and reflected beam sensing (after passing through the hole in the slider) by a photo detector. The head slider with a hole is shown separately. A more complex scheme with a basically similar concept has been developed for rigid-disk drives.

The Hitachi group [7, 17] developed an optical servo procedure with a dual-stage actuator to achieve 17,000 t/in. for the 2-Gb/in.^2-density demonstration. These concepts are now summarized.

Figure 11.9 shows the optical servo arrangement. The slider with the dual inductive-write, MR-read head is shown on a magnetic track. A laser diode is mounted on the side of the slider. A beam from the laser diode is reflected from the disk surface. The disk surface has a series of pits. The reflected light beam from the disk surface goes through the laser cavity and registers on the photo sensor. The photo sensor provides optical position detection.

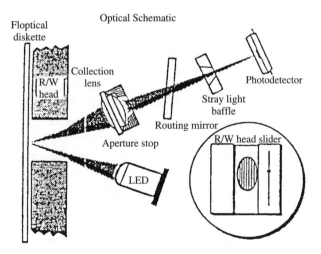

Figure 11.8 Principle of a floptical disk drive [16].

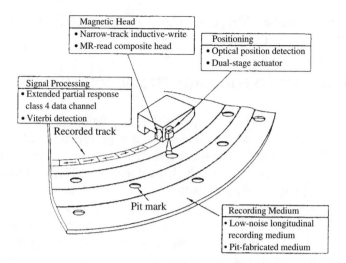

Figure 11.9 Optical servo for 17-Kt/in. magnetic recording [17].

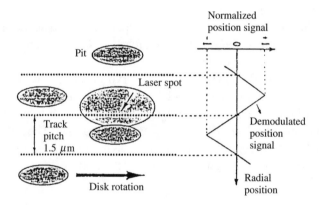

Figure 11.10 Position error signal by laser beam feedback [17].

Figure 11.10 illustrates how the reflected light from the disk surface produces track-following servo information. The laser spot detects the pit positions on either side of the magnetic track and produces a position signal through the photo detector output. The VCM of a conventional slider cannot respond fast enough to the optical position error signal since it does not have wide enough response bandwidth. A dual-stage actuator was designed to resolve this problem.

Figure 11.11 shows the arrangement. The coarse rotary motion of the head gimbal assembly is controlled by the VCM coil. The fine motion of the slider is actuated by a piezoelectric device as shown. Piezoelectricity produces a precise motion by the expansion of a crystal when a voltage is applied to the crystal terminals. A maximum fine stroke of 4.6 μm is produced when voltage changes from 0 to 100 V across the device electrodes. Since the track pitch is 1.5 μm, it is a

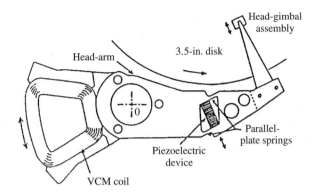

Figure 11.11 Dual-stage actuator for 2-Gb/in.^{2} magnetic recording [17].

sufficiently large stroke to correct fine position errors. These ideas of optical servo and fine track error controls provide impetus for further research for higher track densities.

11.6 APPLICATION OF DISCRETE TRACKS
FOR SERVO AND RECORDING

An experimental procedure to enhance track density by discrete tracks has been explored [18]. Discrete tracks 0.5–10 μm wide were produced by etching grooves, separating magnetic recording tracks. The objective of these discrete tracks was to study amplitude and noise variations as functions of track widths without the influence of side writing and side reading. The grooves between tracks were formed using electron beam etching through a photomask procedure.

The Sony group has developed an optical disklike technology called preembossed rigid magnetic (PERM) disk technology for magnetic recording. It uses the principle of discrete tracks for servo and magnetic recording. Figure 11.12

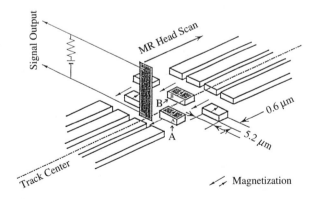

Figure 11.12 Discrete track servo following (PERM) with MR sensor [19].

shows the operational principle. Discrete tracks of 5.2 μm, embossed servo patterns (A, B), and the vertical MR head (discussed in Section 6.17) for reading are shown. Reference [19] describes the details of embossed patterns and successful track following on discrete-track recording with this method. The tracks and servo marks were made by etching the glass substrate. The head positioning accuracy of 0.09 μm (rms) was achieved. The demonstrated version has 3.6 μm track width and 1.2-μm grooves, resulting in 5.2 μm track pitch. This resulted in 5000 t/in. density. The idea of creating preembossed tracks and servo patterns by precise laser mastering and then stamping, similar to the way it is done for CDs and optical disks, has a potential for realizing high track density at low cost.

11.7 PERPENDICULAR RECORDING AND CONTACT RECORDING

Theoretically perpendicular recording should result in higher linear density than longitudinal recording. Figure 11.13 shows magnetic bits and transitions in longitudinal and perpendicular recording.

In Chapter 3 we discussed demagnetizing fields between two magnetic bits for longitudinal recording. These demagnetization fields tend to separate bits, making transition space between bits, that is, transition parameter a, large. At very high bit densities, the limiting parameter may be the length of the transition region. Perpendicular recording bits do not face each other, and hence they can be written at closer distances. Because of this reasoning, perpendicular recording has been pursued intermittently at various laboratories throughout the last three decades. One of the problems in the past was availability of a medium with perpendicular anisotropy.

In 1974, it was discovered that CoCr can support close to ideal perpendicular recording [20]. Use of a probe head on one side and an auxiliary head on the other

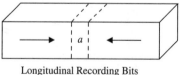

Longitudinal Recording Bits

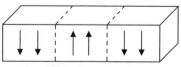

Perpendicular Recording Bits

Figure 11.13 Longitudinal and perpendicular recording bits.

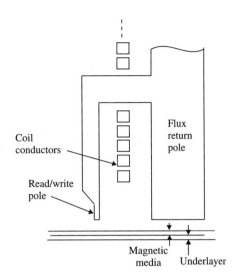

Figure 11.14 Perpendicular pole head and
dual-layer media.

side of the flexible media disk was demonstrated to exhibit high perpendicularly
recorded linear densities. The next step in the evolution of this recording was the
single-pole head and double-layer media, shown in Figure 11.14. The lower layer of
NiFe provides a return path for the flux during writing and reading. The pole head is
constructed in a manner similar to thin film heads for longitudinal recording, but it
has significantly fewer process steps. During the period 1982 through 1988, there
were intense activities in major research organizations, particularly in Japan, pur-
suing perpendicular recording for flexible and rigid media. Thin film single-pole
heads were explored with CoCr/NiFe double-layer media on rigid disks. Ferrite
and film ring heads were combined with barium ferrite for use in flexible and rigid
drive applications. Specially prepared high-resolution pole heads were studied for
in-contact study on dual-layer flexible media. Hundreds of papers were written every year dedicated to perpendicular recording.

Linear density in excess of 200 kiloflux reversals per inch (kfr/in.) have been
demonstrated with perpendicular recording. The team at Tohoku University demonstrated fifth-lobe flux reversal density as high as 650 kfr/in. [10]. This demonstration used a CoCr/NiFe double-layer medium and single-pole head that was specially
constructed with a return path structure to increase the head efficiency. No production hard disk drive has been made with perpendicular recording. Enthusiasts of the
technology believe that perpendicular recording and near-contact recording would
produce the ultimate high linear densities.

Techniques of contact recording have been discussed in Chapter 10, Section
10.9. In one of the schemes, a low-mass head called a *flexhead* is used with a
perpendicular recording pole (Figure 11.15) [21]. The flexhead performs the functions of a head, suspension, and flexure all in one structure. In contact recording, a
substantial head erosion is likely during the life of the disk drive. Experimental results have indicated that due to the low mass, head wear of no more than 12.5 nm per

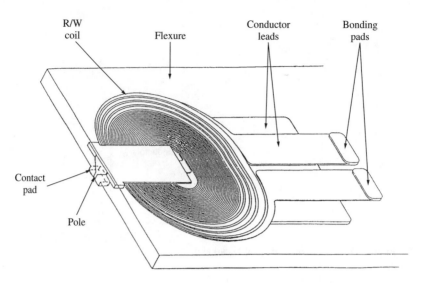

Figure 11.15 Flexhead for contact recording [21].

week results in rigid-disk application. The pole head is constructed such that the head performs to the total erosion of 5 μm. This gives 7 years of life for the head. So the flexhead with a perpendicular pole structure has been considered to deliver long life with high linear density. With surface protection and planar head construction, it may be possible to use the flexhead with longitudinal recording as well.

11.8 APPLICATIONS OF DISK DRIVES

With the availability of low-cost massive storage in small packages, the computer industry, telecommunications, consumer appliances, office products, and portable information devices appear to have an almost insatiable demand for disk drives. The parameters of storage that are most important for these applications are cost (in dollars per megabyte), rapid access to the data, and reliability of the storage devices. While disk drives themselves are tending to be standardized at sizes of 2.5 in. (65 mm) and 3.5 in. (95 mm), the range of applications is broadening. This phenomenon produces challenges and opportunities for the drive makers and system integrators. Here we examine concepts and issues involved for the two ends of the application spectrum. Section 11.9 describes the basics of arrays, and Section 11.10 addresses small-form-factor drives.

Arrays provide a system solution of utilizing low-cost small disk drives in a range of applications, including storage for mid-sized and large computers. This application is likely to impact disk drive technology in several ways: high reliability, rapid access to data, parallel pathing of data input/output to disk drives, and special control electronics, some of which may be embedded inside the drives.

11.9 MULTISPINDLE ARRAYS OR RAIDS (REDUNDANT ARRAYS OF INDEPENDENT DRIVES)

The basic concept of a multispindle array is the replacement of a single-spindle large drive with several low-cost small drives. Arrays of disk drives have been employed for increasing throughput and reliability for use with supercomputers and high-speed processors since the 1960s. However, now the arrays of small drives are designed and used for multiuser workstations, minicomputers, and single-computer-user systems. Consider a number of small drives, say, N, whose total capacity is comparable to that of a large drive. These drives have N spindles and N actuators. Independent drives can serve separate tasks in parallel or one big task through paralleling inputs and outputs. The important issue is the reliability of an array of drives compared to a single drive of the same capacity. It is known that the reliabilities (and mean times to failure) of large and small drives are comparable. When an array of N small drives replaces one large drive, the MTBF of the array is reduced by a factor N. So methods must be devised to enhance reliability of the array system. Some form of redundancy is used in the design of an array to increase reliability of the storage system. An array can be used to increase the system performance by paralleling the input and outputs of several drives. The design of an array thus includes compromises among three variables:

1. Reliability
2. Accessing or throughput of the data during read and write cycles
3. Cost

We describe here three approaches that are in use and are likely to be most applicable in the systems. Several publications from researchers at the University of California, Berkeley [22] popularized the concepts and terminology of RAID systems.

11.9.1 Mirroring, or RAID-1

Mirroring has been in use for applications requiring high reliability. Typical uses include airline reservation systems, defense establishments, and air-control databases. Two disk drives are used in place of every single drive so as to duplicate the data on both drives. Figure 11.16 illustrates the principle. If the capacity requirement for an installation is 5 drives, 10 drives will be used instead, and every 2 drives contain the same data. The reliability and availability of such a system can be very high, but the cost is high also. During writing, it is possible to synchronize data input to two duplicating drives by synchronizing spindles and actuators

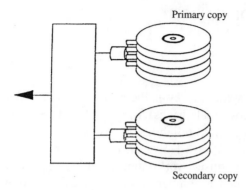

Primary copy

Secondary copy

Figure 11.16 Mirroring "RAID-1" config-uration of disk drives [24].

for the data flow; however, in practice, this is generally not done. Each data set is independently written. The writing time is almost doubled. However, randomized locations of the same data in two independent disks can allow accessing of data at a higher speed, since the disk surface location closest to the data responds when the controller gives the read command. Thus this scheme is good for applications requiring fewer writes and many reads. Installations requiring reading of long records at very high speeds along with high reliability can benefit the most from this type of a system. When a drive fails, the system can continue operation without interruption. The failed unit is replaced or repaired as soon as is practical. Assuming that times to failures are exponentially distributed with a mean M and repair times are exponentially distributed with mean time to repair R, the mean time to failure for the mirrored two drives can be computed [23] as $2M + M^2/R$.

11.9.2 RAID-3

One solution to the high cost of mirroring is the use of a parity system. For the N-drive array, a single extra drive called a parity drive is added. The system thus has $N + 1$ drives, as shown in Figure 11.17. For those unfamiliar with the concept of parity, it is a scheme of looking at N bits of N drives at a time and computing an additional control bit called a parity bit, which is stored in the redundant disk drive. If a single drive has an error, examination of parallel bits of remaining N drives (which includes a parity bit on the parity drive) is sufficient to compute the value (0 or 1) of the failed unit. The system can continue working while the failed unit is repaired or replaced unless another failure occurs before the repair is complete. The user can decide the degree of data integrity required and trade off reliability versus cost by appropriate value of N. Writing is done in parallel on all $N + 1$ disk drives. The inputs to all the drives are synchronized by "locking" spindles and actuators. The parity bits of the incoming data are computed "on the fly" and are written on the parity disk drive. The system has relatively low redundancy, that is, one extra parity drive per N data drives, but provides high reliability, high availability, and good performance. It is most suited for high-performance applications such as

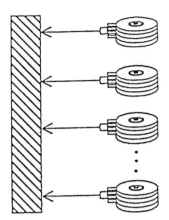

Figure 11.17 High data rate, RAID-3 configuration of disk drives [24].

multimedia, video, and intensive graphics. It is not well suited for short records and multitasking database applications.

11.9.3 RAID-5

This is also a configuration of $N + 1$ drives for N-drive capacity data. The system of data writing also uses parity as utilized in the case of RAID-3. However, there are several differences between the two schemes. The parity is not stored in a separate disk but is distributed, or "striped," systematically on all $N + 1$ drives. Striping of parity reduces the data flow congestion of a single-parity drive. Each disk drive can be independently accessed by separate tasks. Figure 11.18 illustrates the concept. It is also possible to use all the drives in parallel to accomplish a large job. Thus this scheme is more adaptable to different tasks. Because of this, the scheme is likely to gain in popularity for use with time-sharing networks and multiple-user applications. One drawback of the system is the time for writing and generating parity information. Every write requires four disk accesses:

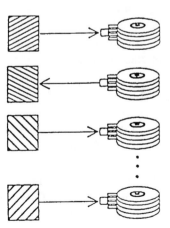

Figure 11.18 RAID-5, adaptive, multiple-task application of disk drive arrays [24].

1. Read old data
2. Read old parity
3. Write the new data
4. Generate and write new parity.

Thus redundant drive arrays provide the means of using several disks in place of a large one with comparable or higher reliability, better availability, and wide-band access to data. The array control electronics can be quite complex, and more creative solutions are expected to emerge as the number and variety of applications increase.

11.10 SMALL-FORM-FACTOR DRIVES

Drives smaller than 3.5 in. are becoming the center of interest in newer applications of disk drive storage. The types of applications responsible for this trend are laptop computers, notebooks and sub-notebooks, and as integral parts of fax machines, copiers, printers, scanners, and so on. There are special requirements for this market. The units must have adequate storage capacity, small size, and light weight, be able to withstand high levels of shock and consume low power for running on batteries, and meet the Personal Computer Memory Card International Association (PCMCIA) standard. The PCMCIA standard refers to a semiconductor or disk drive card that is interchangeable or replaceable.

New operating systems and application programs require much larger disk drive capacities in notebooks and smaller computers. The industry is gearing up to this demand. Capacities as high as 1 GB per 2.5-in. platter have been announced for 1995, while a gigabyte capacity for a single 1.8-in.-diameter disk has been aggressively projected for the year 2000. Gigabyte capacities and higher areal densities use increasing linear densities. Conservation of power demands low-disk velocity.

The MR head provides an adequate signal at low velocity along with high linear density. Currently, 12.5–17 mm drive heights are most common. The PCMCIA type II standard for the card height is 5 mm, and more and more 1.8-in. drives will be made to this standard. Decreasing the drive height requires thinner disk substrates, smaller head sliders, and more integrated flat suspensions. The 30% Picosliders, possibly integrated slider/suspensions, thinner glass substrates approaching 380 μm (15 mils), and other innovations are under development to reach the short height requirements.

For battery-operated applications, the power required for disk drive operations is a major concern. Smaller drives need less power. A 1.3-in. drive needs one-eighth as much power as a 2.5-in. unit. So, to conserve power, the drives are designed to revert to a sleep mode after the initial operation. Also, the drive is in an inactive mode when data is not transferred. It is desirable to have semiconductor circuits and drives operate at 3 V instead of at 5 V, so that battery voltage can be utilized directly without the need for a voltage regulator.

Currently, attempts to improve the ability of drives to absorb shock in the operating and idle modes are under way. Drives are being built to withstand nonoperating shocks of 500 G and operating shocks of 100 G so as to conform to PCMCIA standards.

11.11 SUMMARY: DISK DRIVE R&D DIRECTIONS

The following is an overview of the technical progress that is likely to result in new disk drives for the expanding markets and applications described earlier. Here, we consider what we can expect from the technology. Some concepts have already been implemented, some are being explored for use in three to five years, some may require a decade for fruition, while a number of them may be considered speculative. The objective is to point out possibilities and likely research directions. The topics are divided into heads, media, signal processing electronics, and servo mechanics.

11.11.1 Heads

The MR head sensitivity may be enhanced by using more efficient biasing techniques, changing from NiFe to NiCo or other high-magnetoresistive alloys, and use of high current density with improved thermal paths to the sensor. Concepts of GMR may be perfected for sensor use. This requires gaining experience with thin thin (a fraction of a nanometer) film geometries, the use of these devices in a realistic environment, and improvements in the permeability of materials. Writing at high data rates is likely to require laminated nitride or amorphous poles and circuits to provide current rise times in the low-nanosecond range. Control of sensor instabilities at narrow track widths would require continuous progress in understanding of materials and processes. Processing and alignments of submicrometer write and read head elements are significant challenges for the next several years. Protection of sensitive sensors from chemical, electrical, thermal, and mechanical damage from head-disk surface contacts becomes even more critical at submicrometer dimensions.

11.11.2 Media

The development of low noise media will probably be one of the most critical issues to achieve multigigabit-per-square inch densities. Approaches like (a) isolated grain low-noise media and (b) laminated media initiated in one- and two-gigabit density demonstrations will likely extend to 10 Gb/in.^{2} density. Glass and/or ceramic substrates will become standard for 20–50-nm flying heights. The merits of these substrates are surface smoothness and flatness at thinner dimensions plus higher ability to withstand shocks. In addition to glass and ceramics, plastic, carbon, and silicon carbide substrates are being investigated. Texturing methods will have to be modified for low flying heights. Chemically etched glass substrates might be pursued for controlled texturing. Perpendicular recording may become a strong contender for ultrahigh densities and in contact recording.

11.11.3 Signal Processing Electronics

The sampling detection schemes for increasing density and reducing errors will be extended with long-sequence data detection algorithms and further sophistication in filtering and precompensation procedures. Increased densities will decrease signal-to-noise ratios and require extensive error correction and coding for decreasing raw bit error rates from 10^{-4} to greater than 10^{-12}. Also, capabilities of digital channels will be increasingly utilized for diagnostics and detection of drive operations and reliability improvements. The write, sense, and channel electronics will be further integrated into a few and possibly a single semiconductor chip. Electronics on modules or small PC cards within a drive will occupy less and less space as a part of improving volumetric efficiencies. High-data-rate electronics pose special problems of fast rise times and relatively large current requirements. By the end of the decade higher than 20 MB/s data rate channels for performance devices will be common. The supply voltage reductions along with increased performance would challenge semiconductor technology to employ the latest tools for disk drive electronics. Adaptive and fuzzy logic applications are considered for disk drives for putting more intelligence into small and integrated storage packages.

11.11.4 Servo and Track-Following Mechanics

Track following by read/write heads requires highly sensitive position error signals and low-mass actuators to be able to follow these signals accurately. Methods used for optical servo in optical disk drives may be used for magnetic recording, as indicated in the 2-Gb-density demonstration. There are several issues of substrate and media design, formation of pits and mass of optical components on magnetic head, and so on, that need to be examined. It is likely that optical servo methods will predominate in the research for the application to magnetic disk drives. For the high-bandwidth track, miniaturization of the head is a necessity. Flexhead is an attractive approach, while dual sliders with micro controls by piezoelectric elements are being developed at various laboratories. Possibilities of using silicon micromechanisms for low-mass actuators are being considered for further explorations. Piezoelectric methods require close to a 100-V supply, and integration of silicon with magnetic elements is still under development. Reduction of spindle nonrepeatable runout has been a major factor in advancing track densities to 7000 t/in., and it could possibly be extended beyond 10,000 t/in. Fully digital servos combined with digitally controlled spindle drive electronics along with channel digital signal processing techniques are being explored for the development of high density drives. Figure 11.19 [1] summarizes the progress in disk drive technology and projects future directions.

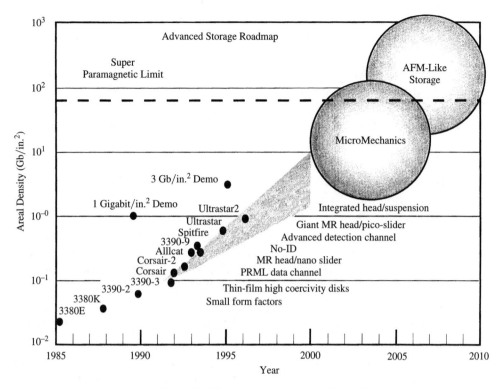

Figure 11.19 Advanced storage road map [1].

The lower part of the figure describes current technology advances. The super-paramagnetic limit refers to a longitudinal magnetic recording limit, but it does not rule out some form of perpendicular recording. Micromechanics refers to work done on forming miniaturized tools, gears, motors, and so on, on silicon surfaces using photolithography and vacuum deposition processes. Atomic force microscopy is an outgrowth of STM, used for analyzing material surfaces at the atomic level. Atomic force microscopy uses a similar atomic scale tip, but it uses magnetic, capacitive, or other force mechanisms to record and interrogate high-density impressions on a material surface.

REFERENCES

[1] R. A. Scranton, "Progress in the MR head industry," presented at IDEMA Symposium, Santa Clara, CA, February 1995. (Figure 11.19 courtesy of E. Grochowski)

[2] C. Tsang, M. Chen, T. Yogi, and K. Ju, "Gigabit density recording using dual-element MR/inductive heads on thin-film disks," *IEEE Trans. Magn.,* MAG-26 (1990), p. 1689.

[3] T. Yogi, C. Tsang, T. Nguyen, K. Ju, G. Gorman, and G. Castillo, "Longitudi-nal media for 1 Gb/in.^{2} areal density," *IEEE Trans. Magn.*, MAG-26 (1990), p. 2271.

[4] T. Howell, D. McCowan, T. Diola, Y. Tang, K. Hense, and R. Gee, "Error rate performance of experimental gigabit per square inch recording components," *IEEE Trans. Magn.*, MAG-26 (1990), p. 2298.

[5] C. Tsang, M. Chen, T. Yogi, and K. Ju, "Performance study and analysis of dual-element head on thin film disk for gigabit-density recording," *IEEE Trans. Magn.*, MAG-26 (1990), p. 2948.

[6] H. Takano, H. Fukuoka, M. Suzuki, K. Shiiki, and M. Kitada, "Submicrometer-track width inductive/MR composite head," *IEEE Trans. Magn.*, MAG-27 (1991), p. 4678.

[7] M. Futamoto, F. Kugiya, M. Suzuki, H. Takano, Y. Matsuda, N. Inaba, Y. Miyamura, K. Akagi, T. Nakao, H. Sawaguchi, H. Fukuoka, T. Munemoto, and T. Takagaki, "Investigation of 2 Gb/in.^{2} magnetic recording at a track density of 17 kTPI," *IEEE Trans. Magn.*, MAG-27 (1991), p. 5280.

[8] K. Akagi, T. Nako, and Y. Miyamura, "High-density magnetic recording tracking method using a laser diode," *IEEE Trans. Magn.*, MAG-27 (1991), p. 5301.

[9] C. Tsang, D. McCowan, H. A. Santini, J. Lo, and R. E. Lee, "3 Gb/in.^{2} Record-ing demonstration with dual element heads and thin film disks," *IEEE Trans. Magn.*, MAG-32 (1996), p. 7.

[10] S. Yamamoto, Y. Nakamura, and S. Iwasaki, "Extremely high bit density recording with single-pole perpendicular head," *IEEE Trans. Magn.*, MAG-23 (1987), p. 2070.

[11] M. Baibich, J. Broto, A. Fert, F. Nguyen Van Dau, and F. Petrof, "Giant mag-netoresistance of (001)Fe/(001)Cr magnetic superlattices," *Phys. Rev. Lett.*, 61, 21 (1988), pp. 2472–2475.

[12] S. S. P. Parkin, in *Ultra-Thin Magnetic Structures,* B. Heinrich and J. A. C. Bland, eds., Springer-Verlag, Berlin, 1994, p. 148.

[13] R. White, "Giant magnetoresistance: a premier," *IEEE Trans. Magn.*, MAG-28 (1992), p. 2482.

[14] B. Dieny, V. Speriosu, S. Parkin, B. Gurney, D. Wilhoit, and D. Mauri, "Giant magnetoresistance in soft ferromagnetic multilayers," *Phys. Rev. B,* 43, 1 (1991), pp. 1297–1300. (Figure from IBM magazine ACCESS, (1990).)

[15] C. Tsang, R. Fontana, T. Lin, D. Heim, V. Speriosu, B. Gurney, and M. Williams, "Design, fabrication and testing of spin-valve read heads for high density recording," *IEEE Trans. Magn.*, MAG-30 (1994), p. 3801.

[16] R. Williams and J. Adkisson, "Increasing diskette capacity with floptical tech-nology," *IEEE Trans. Magn.*, MAG-25 (1989), p. 4.

[17] K. Mori, T. Munemoto, H. Otsuki, Y. Yamaguchi, and K. Akagi, "A dual-stage magnetic disk drive actuator using a piezoelectric device for a high track density," *IEEE Trans. Magn.,* MAG-27 (1991), p. 5298.

[18] S. E. Lambert, I. L. Sanders, A. M. Patlach, and M. T. Krounbi, "Recording characteristics of submicron discrete magnetic tracks," *IEEE Trans. Magn.,* MAG-23 (1987), p. 3690.

[19] T. Ishida, O. Morita, M. Noda, S. Seko, S. Tanaka, and H. Ishioka, " Discrete-track magnetic disk using embossed substrate," *IEICE Trans. Fund.*(Japan), E76-A, 7 (1993), p. 1161.

[20] S. Iwasaki, "Perpendicular magnetic recording—evolution and future," *IEEE Trans. Magn.,* MAG-20 (1984), p. 657.

[21] H. Hamilton, R. Anderson, and K. Goodson, "Contact perpendicular recording on rigid media," *IEEE Trans. Magn.,* MAG-27 (1991), p. 5301.

[22] D. A. Patterson, P. Chen, G. Gibson, and R. H. Katz, "Introduction to redundant arrays of inexpensive disks (RAID)," *IEEE Trans. Magn.,* MAG-25 (1989), p. 112.

[23] K. G. Ashar, "Probabilistic model of system operation with a varying degree of spares and service facilities," *J. Oper. Res.,* 8 (September 1960), p. 707.

[24] J. Menon, private communication.

Index

BIOGRAPHY OF DR. KANU G. ASHAR

Kanu G. Ashar was manager and technical leader at IBM for 34 years, and in 1992 he retired from his position as senior technical staff member. He is currently consultant and adjunct professor at Santa Clara University, California.

Dr. Ashar received a B.E. in electrical engineering (EE) from the University of Baroda, India, an M.S. (EE) from the University of Michigan, and a Ph.D. (EE) from Syracuse University in 1954, 1958, and 1966, respectively. Early in his career at IBM, he managed a group of engineers involved in the development of emitter-coupled logic (ECL) bipolar circuits for a high-speed computer system. In 1964, he was awarded IBM's resident Ph.D. fellowship. From 1966 to 1973, he established and managed the Semiconductor Device Technology departments at IBM, East Fishkill, New York. Under his leadership, submicrometer, high-speed transistors and LSI circuits were developed that included innovations such as an arsenic emitter for bipolar transistors, isoplanar technology, and BI-CMOS (bipolar and complementary MOS transistors on one chip) circuitry. He received nine patents relevant to some of this activity and achieved three invention plateau awards.

After coming to San Jose in 1974, Dr. Ashar managed a group working on magnetic bubble devices. In 1978, he was invited as a visiting professor at the Indian Institute of Science, Bangalore, India, where he taught microprocessors and their applications for one year. On his return to the United States, he managed a department in San Jose involved in the design and development of advanced thin film and MR heads. In 1986, he accepted an assignment to establish a magnetic and optical storage research organization at IBM's Tokyo Research Lab. In 1987, he received IBM Japan's Management Excellence Award. He returned to the United States and worked on theoretical and experimental limits of thin film heads, MR heads, and head/media integration issues. He was promoted to the position of senior technical staff member in 1990.

Dr. Ashar is author and coauthor of several publications involving reliability applications, semiconductor technology, and magnetic recording technologies. In 1990, he was publicity chairman of the first TMRC Conference on Heads, San Diego. He is senior member of IEEE.

CONTRIBUTING AUTHORS

Dr. Roger F. Hoyt is program director for Storage Manufacturing Research at IBM's Almaden Research Lab.

Dr. Kenneth E. Johnson is manager of Disk Media Development at Storage Systems Division, IBM, San Jose.

Dr. James C. Suits is a technical consultant. He retired in 1992 from the position of research staff member at IBM's Almaden Research Lab.